Mastering pandas
Second Edition

A complete guide to pandas, from installation to advanced
data analysis techniques

Ashish Kumar

BIRMINGHAM - MUMBAI

Mastering pandas
Second Edition

Commissioning Editor: Sunith Shetty
Acquisition Editor: Amey Varangaonkar
Content Development Editor: Roshan Kumar
Senior Editor: Ayaan Hoda
Technical Editor: Utkarsha S. Kadam
Copy Editor: Safis Editing
Project Coordinator: Kirti Pisat
Proofreader: Safis Editing
Indexer: Tejal Daruwale Soni
Production Designer: Deepika Naik

First published: June 2015
Second edition: October 2019

Production reference: 1251019

Published by Packt Publishing Ltd.
Livery Place
35 Livery Street
Birmingham
B3 2PB, UK.

ISBN 978-1-78934-323-6

www.packt.com

Packt>

Contributors

About the author

Ashish Kumar is a seasoned data science professional, a publisher author and a thought leader in the field of data science and machine learning. An IIT Madras graduate and a Young India Fellow, he has around 7 years of experience in implementing and deploying data science and machine learning solutions for challenging industry problems in both hands-on and leadership roles. Natural Language Procession, IoT Analytics, R Shiny product development, Ensemble ML methods etc. are his core areas of expertise. He is fluent in Python and R and teaches a popular ML course at Simplilearn. When not crunching data, Ashish sneaks pff to the next hip beach around and enjoys the company of his Kindle. He also trains and mentors data science aspirants and fledling start-ups.

I owe all of my career accomplishments to my beloved grandfather. I thank my mom, my siblings Sanjeev, Ritesh, Rahul, Sandeep, Ritesh, and my sister-in-law Anamika for all they have done for me.

My long-term friends Pranav, Ajit, Vidya, Adarsh, Ashweetha, and Simer have been my support system.

I am indebted to Ram Sukumar and Zeena Johar for their guidance. I want to thank Ramya S, S Abdullah, Sandhya S, and Kirthi T for their help on this book.

About the reviewer

Jamshaid Sohail is a data scientist who is highly passionate about data science, machine learning, deep learning, big data, and other related fields. He spends his free time learning more about the data science field and learning how to use its emerging tools and technologies. He is always looking for new ways to share his knowledge with other people and add value to other people's lives. He has also attended Cambridge University for a summer course in computer science, where he studied under great professors; he would like to impart this knowledge to others. He has extensive experience as a data scientist in a US-based company. In short, he would be extremely delighted to educate and share knowledge with other people.

Packt is searching for authors like you

If you're interested in becoming an author for Packt, please visit authors.packtpub.com and apply today. We have worked with thousands of developers and tech professionals, just like you, to help them share their insight with the global tech community. You can make a general application, apply for a specific hot topic that we are recruiting an author for, or submit your own idea.

Table of Contents

Section 4: Going a Step Beyond with pandas

Preface

pandas is a popular Python library used by data scientists and analysts worldwide to manipulate and analyze their data. This book presents useful data manipulation techniques in pandas for performing complex data analysis in various domains. It provides features and capabilities that make data analysis much easier and faster than with many other popular languages, such as Java, C, C++, and Ruby.

Who this book is for

This book is for data scientists, analysts, and Python developers who wish to explore advanced data analysis and scientific computing techniques using pandas. Some fundamental understanding of Python programming and familiarity with basic data analysis concepts is all you need to get started with this book.

What this book covers

Chapter 1, *Introduction to pandas and Data Analysis*, will introduce pandas and explain where it fits in the data analysis pipeline. We will also look into some of the popular applications of pandas and how Python and pandas can be used for data analysis.

Chapter 2, *Installation of pandas and Supporting Software*, will deal with the installation of Python (if necessary), the pandas library, and all necessary dependencies for the Windows, macOS X, and Linux platforms. We will also look into the command-line tricks and options and settings for pandas as well.

Chapter 3, *Using NumPy and Data Structures with pandas*, will give a quick tour of the power of NumPy and provide a glimpse of how it makes life easier when working with pandas. We will also be implementing a neural network with NumPy and exploring some of the practical applications of multi-dimensional arrays.

Chapter 4, *I/O of Different Data Formats with pandas*, will teach you how to read and write commonplace formats, such as **comma-separated value (CSV)**, with all the options, as well as more exotic file formats, such as URL, JSON, and XML. We will also create files in those formats from data objects and create niche plots from within pandas.

Chapter 5, *Indexing and Selecting in pandas,* will show you how to access and select data from pandas data structures. We will look in detail at basic indexing, label indexing, integer indexing, mixed indexing, and the operation of indexes.

Chapter 6, *Grouping, Merging, and Reshaping Data in pandas,* will examine the various functions that enable us to rearrange data, by having you utilize such functions on real-world datasets. We will also learn about grouping, merging, and reshaping data.

Chapter 7, *Special Data Operations in pandas,* will discuss and elaborate on the methods, syntax, and usage of some of the special data operations in pandas.

Chapter 8, *Time Series and Plotting Using Matplotlib,* will look at how to handle time series and dates. We will also take a tour of some topics that are necessary for you to know about in order to develop your expertise in using pandas.

Chapter 9, *Making Powerful Reports Using pandas in Jupyter,* will look into the application of a range of styling, as well as the formatting options that pandas has. We will also learn how to create dashboards and reports in the Jupyter Notebook.

Chapter 10, *A Tour of Statistics with pandas and NumPy,* will delve into how pandas can be used to perform statistical calculations using packages and calculations.

Chapter 11, *A Brief Tour of Bayesian Statistics and Maximum Likelihood Estimates,* will examine an alternative approach to statistics, which is the Bayesian approach. We will also look into the key statistical distributions and see how we can use various statistical packages to generate and plot distributions in `matplotlib`.

Chapter 12, *Data Case Studies Using pandas,* will discuss how we can solve real-life data case studies using pandas. We will look into web scraping with Python and data validation as well.

Chapter 13, *The pandas Library Architecture,* will discuss the architecture and code structure of the pandas library. This chapter will also briefly demonstrate how you can improve performance using Python extensions.

Chapter 14, *pandas Compared with Other Tools,* will focus on comparing pandas, with R and other tools such as SQL and SAS. We will also look into slicing and selection as well.

Chapter 15, *Brief Tour of Machine Learning,* will conclude the book by giving a brief introduction to the `scikit-learn` library for doing machine learning and show how pandas fits within that framework.

To get the most out of this book

The following software will be used while we execute the code:

- Windows/macOS/Linux
- Python 3.6
- pandas
- IPython
- R
- scikit-learn

For hardware, there are no specific requirements. Python and pandas can run on a Mac, Linux, or Windows machine.

Download the example code files

You can download the example code files for this book from your account at `www.packt.com`. If you purchased this book elsewhere, you can visit `www.packt.com/support` and register to have the files emailed directly to you.

You can download the code files by following these steps:

1. Log in or register at `www.packt.com`.
2. Select the **SUPPORT** tab.
3. Click on **Code Downloads & Errata**.
4. Enter the name of the book in the **Search** box and follow the onscreen instructions.

Once the file is downloaded, please make sure that you unzip or extract the folder using the latest version of:

- WinRAR/7-Zip for Windows
- Zipeg/iZip/UnRarX for Mac
- 7-Zip/PeaZip for Linux

The code bundle for the book is also hosted on GitHub at `https://github.com/PacktPublishing/Mastering-Pandas-Second-Edition`. In case there's an update to the code, it will be updated on the existing GitHub repository.

We also have other code bundles from our rich catalog of books and videos available at `https://github.com/PacktPublishing/`. Check them out!

Download the color images

We also provide a PDF file that has color images of the screenshots/diagrams used in this book. You can download it here: https://static.packt-cdn.com/downloads/9781789343236_ColorImages.pdf.

Conventions used

There are a number of text conventions used throughout this book.

CodeInText: Indicates code words in text, database table names, folder names, filenames, file extensions, pathnames, dummy URLs, user input, and Twitter handles. Here is an example: "Python has an built-in array module to create arrays."

A block of code is set as follows:

```
source_python("titanic.py")
titanic_in_r <- get_data_head("titanic.csv")
```

Any command-line input or output is written as follows:

```
python --version
```

Bold: Indicates a new term, an important word, or words that you see onscreen. For example, words in menus or dialog boxes appear in the text like this. Here is an example: "Any notebooks in other directories could be transferred to the current working directory of the Jupyter Notebook through the **Upload** option."

 Warnings or important notes appear like this.

 Tips and tricks appear like this.

Get in touch

Feedback from our readers is always welcome.

General feedback: If you have questions about any aspect of this book, mention the book title in the subject of your message and email us at customercare@packtpub.com.

Errata: Although we have taken every care to ensure the accuracy of our content, mistakes do happen. If you have found a mistake in this book, we would be grateful if you would report this to us. Please visit www.packt.com/submit-errata, selecting your book, clicking on the Errata Submission Form link, and entering the details.

Piracy: If you come across any illegal copies of our works in any form on the Internet, we would be grateful if you would provide us with the location address or website name. Please contact us at copyright@packt.com with a link to the material.

If you are interested in becoming an author: If there is a topic that you have expertise in and you are interested in either writing or contributing to a book, please visit authors.packtpub.com.

Reviews

Please leave a review. Once you have read and used this book, why not leave a review on the site that you purchased it from? Potential readers can then see and use your unbiased opinion to make purchase decisions, we at Packt can understand what you think about our products, and our authors can see your feedback on their book. Thank you!

For more information about Packt, please visit packt.com.

Section 1: Overview of Data Analysis and pandas

In this section, we give you a quick overview of the concepts of the data analysis process and where pandas fits into that picture. You will also learn how to install and set up the pandas library, along with the other supporting libraries and environments required to build an enterprise-grade data analysis pipeline.

This section is comprised of the following chapters:

- `Chapter 1`, *Introduction to pandas and Data Analysis*
- `Chapter 2`, *Installation of pandas and Supporting Software*

Introduction to pandas and Data Analysis 1

We start the book and this chapter by discussing the contemporary data analytics landscape and how pandas fits into that landscape. pandas is the go-to tool for data scientists for data pre-processing tasks. We will learn about the technicalities of pandas in the later chapters. This chapter covers the context, origin, history, market share, and current standing of pandas.

The chapter has been divided into the following headers:

- Motivation for data analysis
- How Python and pandas can be used for data analysis
- Description of the pandas library
- Benefits of using pandas

Motivation for data analysis

In this section, we discuss the trends that are making data analysis an increasingly important field in today's fast-moving technological landscape.

We live in a big data world

The term **big data** has become one of the hottest technology buzzwords in the past two years. We now increasingly hear about big data in various media outlets, and big data start-ups have increasingly been attracting venture capital. A good example in the area of retail is Target Corporation, which has invested substantially in big data and is now able to identify potential customers by using big data to analyze people's shopping habits online; refer to a related article at `http://nyti.ms/19LT8ic`.

Loosely speaking, big data refers to the phenomenon wherein the amount of data exceeds the capability of the recipients of the data to process it. Here is an article on big data that sums it up nicely: `https://www.oracle.com/in/big-data/guide/what-is-big-data.html`.

The four V's of big data

A good way to start thinking about the complexities of big data is called the four dimensions, or **Four V's of big data**. This model was first introduced as the three V's by Gartner analyst Doug Laney in 2001. The three V's stood for Volume, Velocity, and Variety, and the fourth V, Veracity, was added later by IBM. Gartner's official definition states the following:

> *"Big data is high volume, high velocity, and/or high variety information assets that require new forms of processing to enable enhanced decision making, insight discovery and process optimization."*
>
> *Laney, Douglas. "The Importance of 'Big Data': A Definition", Gartner*

Volume of big data

The **volume** of data in the big data age is simply mind-boggling. According to IBM, by 2020, the total amount of data on the planet will have ballooned to 40 zettabytes. You heard that right! 40 zettabytes is 43 trillion gigabytes. For more information on this, refer to the Wikipedia page on the zettabyte: `http://en.wikipedia.org/wiki/Zettabyte`.

To get a handle on how much data this is, let me refer to an EMC press release published in 2010, which stated what 1 zettabyte was approximately equal to:

> *"The digital information created by every man, woman and child on Earth 'Tweeting' continuously for 100 years " or "75 billion fully-loaded 16 GB Apple iPads, which would fill the entire area of Wembley Stadium to the brim 41 times, the Mont Blanc Tunnel 84 times, CERN's Large Hadron Collider tunnel 151 times, Beijing National Stadium 15.5 times or the Taipei 101 Tower 23 times..."*
>
> *EMC study projects 45× data growth by 2020*

The growth rate of data has been fuelled largely by a few factors, such as the following:

- The rapid growth of the internet.
- The conversion from analog to digital media, coupled with an increased ability to capture and store data, which in turn has been made possible with cheaper and better storage technology. There has been a proliferation of digital data input devices, such as cameras and wearables, and the cost of huge data storage has fallen rapidly. Amazon Web Services is a prime example of the trend toward much cheaper storage.

The *internetification* of devices, or rather the *Internet of Things*, is the phenomenon wherein common household devices, such as our refrigerators and cars, will be connected to the internet. This phenomenon will only accelerate the above trend.

Velocity of big data

From a purely technological point of view, **velocity** refers to the throughput of big data, or how fast the data is coming in and is being processed. This has ramifications on how fast the recipient of the data needs to process it to keep up. Real-time analytics is one attempt to handle this characteristic. Tools that can enable this include Amazon Web Services Elastic MapReduce.

At a more macro level, the velocity of data can also be regarded as the increased speed at which data and information can now be transferred and processed faster and at greater distances than ever before.

The proliferation of high-speed data and communication networks coupled with the advent of cell phones, tablets, and other connected devices are primary factors driving information velocity. Some measures of velocity include the number of tweets per second and the number of emails per minute.

Variety of big data

The **variety** of big data comes from having a multiplicity of data sources that generate data and the different formats of data that are produced.

This results in a technological challenge for the recipients of the data who have to process it. Digital cameras, sensors, the web, cell phones, and so on are some of the data generators that produce data in differing formats, and the challenge is being able to handle all these formats and extract meaningful information from the data. The ever-changing nature of data formats with the dawn of the big data era has led to a revolution in the database technology industry with the rise of NoSQL databases, which handle what is known as *unstructured* data or rather data whose format is fungible or constantly changing.

Veracity of big data

The fourth characteristic of big data—**veracity**, which was added later—refers to the need to validate or confirm the *correctness* of the data or the fact that the data represents the truth. The sources of data must be verified and errors kept to a minimum. According to an estimate by IBM, poor data quality costs the US economy about $3.1 trillion dollars a year. For example, medical errors cost the United States $19.5 billion in 2008; you can refer to a related article at
`http://www.wolterskluwerlb.com/health/resource-center/articles/2012/10/economic` `s-health-care-quality-and-medical-errors` for more information.

The following link provides an infographic by IBM that summarizes the four V's of big data: `https://www.ibmbigdatahub.com/infographic/four-vs-big-data`.

So much data, so little time for analysis

Data analytics has been described by Eric Schmidt, the former CEO of Google, as the *Future of Everything*. For more information, check out a YouTube video called *Why Data Analytics is the Future of Everything* at `https://www.youtube.com/watch?v=9hDnO_ykC7Y`.

The volume and velocity of data will continue to increase in the big data age. Companies that can efficiently collect, filter, and analyze data that results in information that allows them to better meet the needs of their customers in a much quicker timeframe will gain a significant advantage over their competitors. For example, data analytics (the *Culture of Metrics*) plays a very key role in the business strategy of Amazon. For more information, refer to the *Amazon.com case study* by Smart Insights at `http://bit.ly/1glnA1u`.

The move towards real-time analytics

As technologies and tools have evolved to meet the ever-increasing demands of business, there has been a move towards what is known as real-time analytics. More information on this is available from Intel in their *Insight Everywhere* whitepaper at `http://intel.ly/1899xqo`.

In the big data internet era, here are some examples of real-time analytics on big data:

- Online businesses demand instantaneous insights into how the new products/features they have introduced online are doing and can adjust their online product mix accordingly. Amazon is a prime example of this with their *Customers Who Viewed This Item Also Viewed* feature.
- In finance, risk management and trading systems demand almost instantaneous analysis in order to make effective decisions based on data-driven insights.

Data analytics pipeline

Data modeling is the process of using data to build predictive models. Data can also be used for descriptive and prescriptive analysis. But before we make use of data, it has to be fetched from several sources, stored, assimilated, cleaned, and engineered to suit our goal. The sequential operations that need to be performed on data are akin to a manufacturing pipeline, where each subsequent step adds value to the potential end product and each progression requires a new person or skill set.

The various steps in a data analytics pipeline are shown in the following diagram:

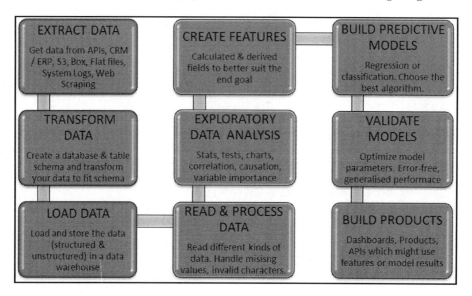

Steps in data analytics pipeline

1. Extract Data
2. Transform Data
3. Load Data
4. Read & Process Data
5. Exploratory Data Analysis
6. Create Features
7. Build Predictive Models
8. Validate Models
9. Build Products

These steps can be combined into three high-level categories: data engineering, data science, and product development.

- **Data Engineering**: *Step 1* to *Step 3* in the preceding diagram fall into this category. It deals with sourcing data from a variety of sources, creating a suitable database and table schema, and loading the data in a suitable database. There can be many approaches to this step depending on the following:
    - **Type of data**: Structured (tabular data) versus unstructured (such as images and text) versus semi-structured (such as JSON and XML)
    - **Velocity of data upgrade**: Batch processing versus real-time data streaming
    - **Volume of data**: Distributed (or cluster-based) storage versus single instance databases
    - **Variety of data**: Document storage, blob storage, or data lake
- **Data Science**: *Step 4* to *Step 8* in figure 1.2 fall into the category of data science. This is the phase where the data is made usable and used to predict the future, learn patterns, and extrapolate these patterns. Data science can further be sub-divided into two phases.

Step 4 to *Step 6* comprise the first phase, wherein the goal is to understand the data better and make it usable. Making the data usable requires considerable effort to clean it by removing invalid characters and missing values. It also involves understanding the nitty-gritty of the data at hand—what is the distribution of data, what is the relationship between different data variables, is there a causatory relationship between the input and outcome variable, and so on. It also involves exploring numerical transformations (features) that might explain this causation (between input and outcome variables) better. This phase entails the real forensic effort that goes into the ultimate use of data. To use an analogy, bamboo seeds remain buried in the soil for years with no signs of a sapling growing, and suddenly a sapling grows, and within months a full bamboo tree is ready. This phase of data science is akin to the underground preparation the bamboo seeds undergo before the rapid growth. This is like the stealth mode of a start up wherein a lot of time and effort is committed. And this is where the `pandas` library, protagonist of this book, finds it raison d'etre and sweet spot.

Step 7 to *Step 8* constitute the part where patterns (the parameters of a mathematical expression) are learned from historic data and extrapolated to future data. It involves a lot of experimentation and iterations to get to the optimal results. But if *Step 4* to *Step 6* have been done with the utmost care, this phase can be implemented pretty quickly thanks to the number of packages in Python, R, and many other data science tools. Of course, it requires a sound understanding of the math and algorithms behind the applied model in order to tweak its parameters to perfection.

- **Product Development**: This is the phase where all the hard work bears fruit and all the insights, results, and patterns are served to the users in a way that they can consume, understand, and act upon. It might range from building a dashboard on data with additional derived fields to an API that calls a trained model and returns an output on incoming data. A product can also be built to encompass all the stages of the data pipeline, from extracting the data to building a predictive model or creating an interactive dashboard.

Apart from these steps in the pipeline, there are some additional steps that might come into the picture. This is due to the highly evolving nature of the data landscape. For example, deep learning, which is used extensively to build intelligent products around image, text, and audio data, often requires the training data to be labeled into a category or augmented if the quantity is too small to create an accurate model.

For example, an object detection task on video data might require the creation of training data for object boundaries and object classes using some tools, or even manually. Data augmentation helps with image data by creating slightly perturbed data (rotated or grained images, for example) and adding it to training data. For a supervised learning task, labels are mandatory. This label is generally generated together with the data. For example, to train a churn model, a dataset with customer descriptions and when they churned out is required. This information is generally available in the company's CRM tool.

How Python and pandas fit into the data analytics pipeline

The **Python** programming language is one of the fastest-growing languages today in the emerging field of data science and analytics. Python was created by Guido van Rossum in 1991, and its key features include the following:

- Interpreted rather than compiled
- Dynamic type system
- Pass by value with object references
- Modular capability
- Comprehensive libraries
- Extensibility with respect to other languages
- Object orientation
- Most of the major programming paradigms: procedural, object-oriented, and, to a lesser extent, functional

For more information, refer to the following article on Python at `https://www.python.org/about/`.

Among the characteristics that make Python popular for data science are its very user-friendly (human-readable) syntax, the fact that it is interpreted rather than compiled (leading to faster development time), and it has very comprehensive libraries for parsing and analyzing data, as well as its capacity for numerical and statistical computations. Python has libraries that provide a complete toolkit for data science and analysis. The major ones are as follows:

- **NumPy**: The general-purpose array functionality with an emphasis on numeric computation
- **SciPy**: Numerical computing
- **Matplotlib**: Graphics
- **pandas**: Series and data frames (1D and 2D array-like types)
- **Scikit-learn**: Machine learning
- **NLTK**: Natural language processing
- **Statstool**: Statistical analysis

For this book, we will be focusing on the fourth library in the preceding list, pandas.

What is pandas?

The pandas we are going to obsess over in this book are not the cute and lazy animals that also do kung fu when needed.

pandas is a high-performance open source library for data analysis in Python developed by Wes McKinney in 2008. pandas stands for **panel data**, a reference to the tabular format in which it processes the data. It is available for free and is distributed with a 3-Clause BSD License under the open source initiative.

Over the years, it has become the de-facto standard library for data analysis using Python. There's been great adoption of the tool, and there's a large community behind it, (1,200+ contributors, 17,000+ commits, 23 versions, and 15,000+ stars) rapid iteration, features, and enhancements are continuously made.

Some key features of pandas include the following:

- It can process a variety of datasets in different formats: time series, tabular heterogeneous, and matrix data.
- It facilitates loading/importing data from varied sources, such as CSV and databases such as SQL.
- It can handle myriad operations on datasets: subsetting, slicing, filtering, merging, groupBy, re-ordering, and re-shaping.
- It can deal with missing data according to rules defined by the user/developer, such as ignore, convert to 0, and so on.
- It can be used for parsing and munging (conversion) of data as well as modeling and statistical analysis.
- It integrates well with other Python libraries such as statsmodels, SciPy, and scikit-learn.
- It delivers fast performance and can be sped up even more by making use of **Cython** (C extensions to Python).

For more information, go through the official pandas documentation at `http://pandas.pydata.org/pandas-docs/stable/`.

Where does pandas fit in the pipeline?

As discussed in the previous section, pandas can be used to perform *Step 4* to *Step 6* in the pipeline. And *Step 4* to *Step 6* are the backbone of any data science process, application, or product:

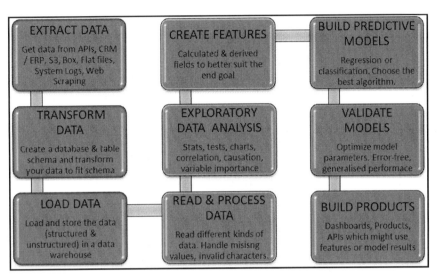

Where does pandas fit in the data analytics pipeline?

The *Step 1* to *Step 6* can be performed in pandas by some methods. Those in the *Step 4* to *Step 6* are the primary tasks while the *Step 1* to *Step 3* can also be done in some way or other in pandas.

pandas is an indispensable library if you're working with data, and it would be near impossible to find code for data modeling that doesn't import pandas into the working environment. Easy-to-use syntax in Python and the availability of a spreadsheet-like data structure called a dataframe make it amenable even to users who are too comfortable and too unwilling to move away from Excel. At the same time, it is loved by scientists and researchers to handle exotic file formats such as parquet, feather file, and many more. It can read data in batch mode without clogging all the machine's memory. No wonder the famous news aggregator Quartz called it *the* **most important tool in data science**.

pandas is suited well for the following types of dataset:

- Tabular with heterogeneous type columns
- Ordered and unordered time series
- Matrix/array data with labeled or unlabeled rows and columns

pandas can perform the following operations on data with finesse:

- Easy handling of missing and NaN data
- Addition and deletion of columns
- Automatic and explicit data alignment with labels
- GroupBy for aggregating and transforming data using split-apply-combine
- Converting differently indexed Python or NumPy data to DataFrame
- Slicing, indexing, hierarchical indexing, and subsetting of data
- Merging, joining, and concatenating data
- I/O methods for flat files, HDF5, feather, and parquet formats
- Time series functionality

Benefits of using pandas

pandas forms a core component of the Python data analysis corpus. The distinguishing feature of pandas is that the suite of data structures that it provides is naturally suited to data analysis, primarily the DataFrame and, to a lesser extent, series (1-D vectors) and panel (3D tables).

Simply put, pandas and statstools can be described as Python's answer to R, the data analysis and statistical programming language that provides both data structures, such as R-dataframes, and a rich statistical library for data analysis.

The benefits of pandas compared to using a language such as Java, C, or C++ for data analysis are manifold:

- **Data representation**: It can easily represent data in a form that's naturally suited for data analysis via its DataFrame and series data structures in a concise manner. Doing the equivalent in Java/C/C++ requires many lines of custom code as these languages were not built for data analysis but rather networking and kernel development.
- **Data subsetting and filtering**: It permits easy subsetting and filtering of data, procedures that are a staple of doing data analysis.

- **Concise and clear code**: Its concise and clear API allows the user to focus more on their core goal, rather than having to write a lot of scaffolding code in order to perform routine tasks. For example, reading a CSV file into a DataFrame data structure in memory takes two lines of code, while doing the same task in Java/C/C++ requires many more lines of code or calls to non-standard libraries, as illustrated below. Let's suppose that we had the following data to read:

Country	Year	CO2Emissions	PowerConsumption	FertilityRate	InternetUsagePer1000People	LifeExpectancy	Population
Belarus	2000	5.91	2988.71	1.29	18.69	68.01	1.00E+07
Belarus	2001	5.87	2996.81		43.15		9970260
Belarus	2002	6.03	2982.77	1.25	89.8	68.21	9925000
Belarus	2003	6.33	3039.1	1.25	162.76		9873968
Belarus	2004		3143.58	1.24	250.51	68.39	9824469
Belarus	2005			1.24	347.23	68.48	9775591

In a CSV file, this data that we wish to read would look like the following:

```
Country,Year,CO2Emissions,PowerConsumption,FertilityRate,
 InternetUsagePer1000, LifeExpectancy, Population
 Belarus,2000,5.91,2988.71,1.29,18.69,68.01,1.00E+07
 Belarus,2001,5.87,2996.81,,43.15,,9970260
 Belarus,2002,6.03,2982.77,1.25,89.8,68.21,9925000
 . . .
 Philippines,2000,1.03,514.02,,20.33,69.53,7.58E+07
 Philippines,2001,0.99,535.18,,25.89,,7.72E+07
 Philippines,2002,0.99,539.74,3.5,44.47,70.19,7.87E+07
 . . .
 Morocco,2000,1.2,489.04,2.62,7.03,68.81,2.85E+07
 Morocco,2001,1.32,508.1,2.5,13.87,,2.88E+07
 Morocco,2002,1.32,526.4,2.5,23.99,69.48,2.92E+07
 . .
```

The data here is taken from World Bank Economic data, available at http://data.worldbank.org.

In Java, we would have to write the following code:

```
public class CSVReader {
public static void main(String[] args) {
        String[] csvFile=args[1];
        CSVReader csvReader = new csvReader();
        List<Map>dataTable=csvReader.readCSV(csvFile);
    }
 public void readCSV(String[] csvFile)
 {
   BufferedReader bReader=null;
   String line="";
   String delim=",";
   //Initialize List of maps, each representing a line of the csv file
```

```
    List&lt;Map&gt; data=new ArrayList&lt;Map&gt;();
  try {
        bufferedReader = new BufferedReader(new    FileReader(csvFile));
        // Read the csv file, line by line
          while ((line = br.readLine()) != null){
            String[] row = line.split(delim);
            Map&lt;String,String&gt; csvRow=new
HashMap&lt;String,String&gt;();
            csvRow.put('Country')=row[0];
            csvRow.put('Year')=row[1];
        csvRow.put('CO2Emissions')=row[2];
csvRow.put('PowerConsumption')=row[3];
                csvRow.put('FertilityRate')=row[4];
                csvRow.put('InternetUsage')=row[1];
                csvRow.put('LifeExpectancy')=row[6];
                csvRow.put('Population')=row[7];
                data.add(csvRow);
        }
    } catch (FileNotFoundException e) {
   e.printStackTrace();
    } catch (IOException e) {
   e.printStackTrace();
    }
  return data;
  }
```

But, using pandas, it would take just two lines of code:

```
import pandas as pd
 worldBankDF=pd.read_csv('worldbank.csv')
```

In addition, pandas is built upon the NumPy library and hence inherits many of the performance benefits of this package, especially when it comes to numerical and scientific computing. One oft-touted drawback of using Python is that as a scripting language, its performance relative to languages such as Java/C/C++ has been rather slow. However, this is not really the case for pandas.

History of pandas

The basic version of pandas was built in 2008 by Wes McKinney, an MIT grad with heavy quantitative finance experience. Now a celebrity in his own right, thanks to his open source contributions and the wildly popular book called **Data Analysis with Python**, he was reportedly frustrated with the time he had to waste doing simple data manipulation tasks at his job, such as reading a CSV file, with the popular tools at that time. He said he quickly fell in love with Python for its intuitive and accessible nature after not finding Excel and R suitable for his needs. But he found that it was missing key features that would make it the go-to tool for data analysis—for example, an intuitive format to deal with spreadsheet data or to create new calculated columns from existing columns.

According to an interview he gave to Quartz, the design considerations and vision that he had in mind while creating the tool were the following:

- Quality of data is far more important than any fancy analysis
- Treating in-memory data like a SQL table or an Excel spreadsheet
- Intuitive analysis and exploration with minimal and elegant code
- Easier compatibility with other libraries used for the same or different steps in the data pipeline

After building the basic version, he went on to pursue a PhD at Duke University but dropped out in a quest to make the tool he had created a cornerstone for data science and Python. With his dedicated contribution, together with the release of popular Python visualization libraries such as Matplotlib, followed by machine learning libraries such as Scikit-Learn and interactive user interfaces such as Jupyter and Spyder, pandas and eventually Python became the hottest tool in the armory of any data scientist.

Wes is heavily invested in the constant improvement of the tool he created from scratch. He coordinates the development of new features and the improvement of existing ones. The data science community owes him big time.

Usage pattern and adoption of pandas

The popularity of Python has skyrocketed over the years, especially after 2012; a lot of this can be attributed to the popularity of pandas. Python-related questions make up around 12% of the total questions asked from high-income countries on Stack Overflow, a popular platform for developers to ask questions and get answers from other people in the community about how to get things done and fix bugs in different programming languages. Given that there are hundreds of programming languages, one language occupying 12% of market share is an extraordinary achievement:

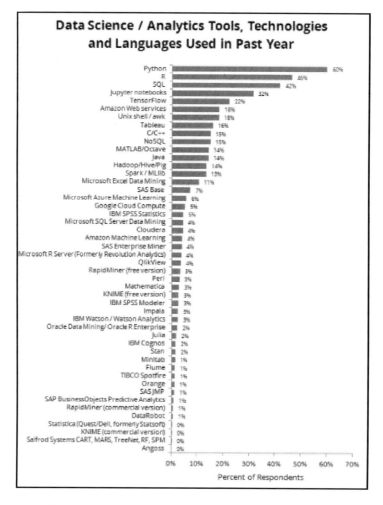

The most popular data analytics tools based on a survey of Kaggle users conducted in 2017-18

According to this survey conducted by Kaggle, 60% of the respondents said that they were aware of or have used Python for their data science jobs.

According to the data recorded by Stack Overflow about the types of question asked on their platform, Python and pandas have registered steady growth year on year, while some of the other programming languages, such as Java and C, have declined in popularity and are playing catch-up. Python has almost caught up with the number of questions asked about Java on the platform, while the number for Java has shown a negative trend. pandas has been showing constant growth in numbers.

The following chart is based on data gathered from the SQL API exposed by Stack Overflow. The *y* axis represents the number of questions asked about that topic on Stack Overflow in a particular year:

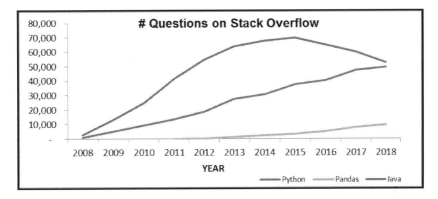

Popularity of tools across years based on the # questions asked on Stack Overflow

Google Trend also shows a surge in popularity for pandas, as demonstrated in the following chart. Numbers represent surge in interest for pandas relative to the highest point (historically) on the chart for the given region and time.

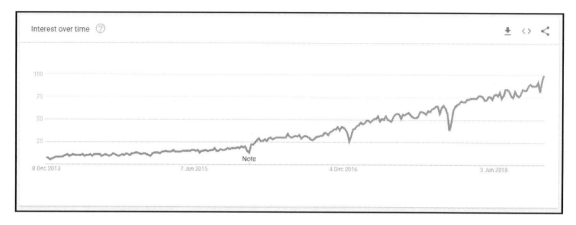

Popularity of pandas based on data from Google Trends

The geographical split of the popularity of pandas is even more interesting. The highest interest has come from China, which might be an indicator of the high adoption of open source tools and/or a very high inclination towards building powerful tech for data science:

Popularity of pandas across geographies based on Google Trends data

Apart from the popularity with its users, pandas (owing to its open source origins) also has a thriving community that is committed to constantly improving it and making it easier for the users to get answers about the issues. The following chart shows the weekly modifications (additions/deletions) to the pandas source code by the contributors:

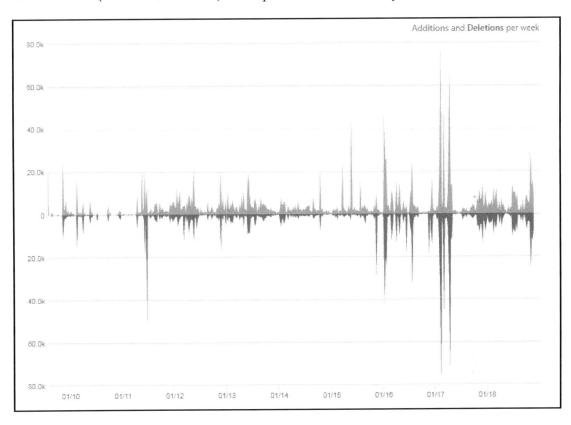

Number of additions/deletions done to the pandas source code by contributors

pandas on the technology adoption curve

According to a popular framework called **Gartner Hype Cycle**, there are five phases in the process of the proliferation and adoption of technologies:

- Technology trigger
- Peak of inflated expectations
- Trough of disillusionment
- Slope of enlightenment
- Plateau of productivity

The following link contains a chart that shows different technologies and the stage they are at on the technology adoption curve `https://blogs-images.forbes.com/gartnergroup/files/2012/09/2012Emerging-Technologies-Graphic4.gif`.

As can be seen, Predictive Analytics has already reached the steady plateau of productivity, which is where the optimum and stable return on investment can be extracted from a technology. Since pandas is an essential component of most predictive analytics initiatives, it is safe to say that pandas has reached the plateau of productivity.

Popular applications of pandas

pandas is built on top of NumPy. Some of the noteworthy uses of the pandas, apart from every other data science project of course, are the following:

- pandas is a dependency of statsmodels (`http://www.statsmodels.org/stable/index.html`), making it a significant part of Python's numerical computing ecosystem.
- pandas has been used extensively in the production of many financial applications.

Summary

We live in a big data era characterized by the four V's- volume, velocity, variety, and veracity. The volume and velocity of data are set to increase for the foreseeable future. Companies that can harness and analyze big data to extract information and take actionable decisions based on this information will be the winners in the marketplace. Python is a fast-growing, user-friendly, extensible language that is very popular for data analysis.

pandas is a core library of the Python toolkit for data analysis. It provides features and capabilities that make it much easier and faster than many other popular languages, such as Java, C, C++, and Ruby.

Thus, given the strengths of Python outlined in this chapter as a choice for the analysis of data and the popularity it has gained from users, contributors, and industry leaders, data analysis practitioners utilizing Python should become adept at pandas in order to become more effective. This book aims to help you achieve this goal.

In the next chapter, we proceed towards this goal by first setting up the infrastructure required to run pandas on your computer. We will also see different ways and scenarios in which pandas can be used and run.

References

- https://activewizards.com/blog/top-20-python-libraries-for-data-science-in-2018/
- https://qz.com/1126615/the-story-of-the-most-important-tool-in-data-science/

2
Installation of pandas and Supporting Software

Before we can start work on pandas for doing data analysis, we need to make sure that the software is installed and the environment is in proper working order. This chapter deals with the installation of Python (if necessary), the pandas library, and all necessary dependencies for the Windows, macOS/X, and Linux platforms. The topics we address include, among other things, selecting a version of Python, installing Python, and installing pandas.

The steps outlined in the following section should work for the most part, but your mileage may vary depending upon the setup. On different operating system versions, the scripts may not always work perfectly, and the third-party software packages already in the system may sometimes conflict with the instructions provided.

The following topics will be covered in this chapter:

- Selecting a version of Python to use
- Installation of Python and pandas using Anaconda
- Dependency packages for pandas
- Review of items installed with Anaconda
- Cross tooling—combining the pandas awesomeness with R, Julia, H20.ai, and Azure ML Studio command line tricks for pandas
- Options and settings for Pandas

Selecting a version of Python to use

This is a classic battle among Python developers—Python 2.7.x or Python 3.x—which is better? Until a year back, it was Python 2.7.x that topped the charts; the reason being it was a stable version. More than 70% of projects used Python 2.7, in the year 2016. This number began to fall and by 2017 it was 63%. This shift in trends was due to the announcement that Python 2.7 would not be maintained from January 1, 2018, meaning that there would be no more bug fixes or new releases. Some libraries released after this announcement are only compatible with Python 3.x. Several businesses have started migrating towards Python 3.x. Hence, as of 2018, Python 3.x is the preferred version.

 For further information, please see `https://wiki.python.org/moin/Python2orPython3`.

The main differences between Python 2.x and 3 include better Unicode support in Python 3, `print` and `exec` changed to functions, and integer division. For more details, see *What's New in Python 3.0* at `http://docs.python.org/3/whatsnew/3.0.html`.

However, for scientific, numeric, or data analysis work, Python 2.7 is recommended over Python 3 for the following reason: Python 2.7 is the preferred version for most current distributions, and the support for Python 3.x is not as strong for some libraries, although that is increasingly becoming less of an issue.

For reference, have a look at the documentation titled *Will Scientists Ever Move to Python 3?* at `http://bit.ly/1DOgNuX`. Hence, this book will use a mix of Python 2.7 and 3.x as and when required. Translating Python code from 2.7 to 3.x or vice versa is not difficult, and the following documentation can be used as a reference *Porting Python 2 Code to Python 3* at `http://docs.python.org/2/howto/pyporting.html`.

However, there is a middle ground and a way to get the best of the both worlds. One can use the `virtualenv` package in Python that allows you to create separate light virtual environments from within the installed Python environment. This makes it possible to have, for example, the 2.7 version installed on your machine and to access and run the 3.x version code by launching a virtual environment in your computer using `virtualenv`. This virtual environment is just a separate installation/instance of Python at a separate location. One can install the packages compatible with that version and do all the computations citing that version/installation while running. You can create as many virtual environments as you wish. This package comes pre-installed with the Anaconda distribution. You can visit the following website for more details on using `virtualenv`: `https://docs.python-guide.org/dev/virtualenvs/`.

The latest major release of pandas—pandas 0.23.4—was in August, 2018. The following are some of the interesting feature upgrades that were made:

- Reading and writing JSON I pandas has been made more elegant as metadata will be preserved with the `orient = True` option set.
- For Python 3.6 and above, the dictionary will be assigned an order based on the order in which the entities were inserted. This order will be carried over to DataFrames or a series created from the dict.
- Merging and sorting could now make use of a combination of index names and column names.
- Earlier, the `DataFrame.apply()` function with `axis = 1` returned a list-like object. The latest improvements to pandas have modified the output to be of a consistent shape—either a series or a DataFrame.
- Categories without any observations can now be controlled in the `groupby` function through the `observed = True` setting.
- `DataFrame.all()` and `DataFrame.any()` now accept `axis=None` to reduce across all axes to a scalar.

But before we start using pandas, let's spend some time installing Python on our computers.

Standalone Python installation

Here, we detail the standalone installation of Python on multiple platforms—Linux, Windows, and macOS/X. Standalone means just the IDLE IDE, interpreter, and some basic packages. Another option is to download from a distribution, which is a richer version and comes pre-installed with many utilities.

Linux

If you're using Linux, Python will most probably come pre-installed. If you're not sure, type the following at Command Prompt:

```
which python
```

Python is likely to be found in one of the following folders on Linux, depending on your distribution and particular installation:

- `/usr/bin/python`
- `/bin/python`
- `/usr/local/bin/python`
- `/opt/local/bin/python`

You can determine which particular version of Python is installed by typing the following at Command Prompt:

```
python --version
```

In the rare event that Python isn't already installed, you need to figure out which flavor of Linux you're using and download and install it. Here are the install commands as well as links to the various Linux Python distributions:

- Debian/Ubuntu (14.04):

  ```
  sudo apt-get install python2.7
  sudo apt-get install python2.7-devel
  ```

  For more information, see the Debian Python page at `https://wiki.debian.org/Python`.

- Redhat Fedora/Centos/RHEL:

  ```
  sudo yum install python
  sudo yum install python-devel
  ```

  To install Fedora software, visit `http://docs.fedoraproject.org/en-US/Fedora/13/html/User_Guide/chap-User_Guide-Managing_software.html`.

- openSUSE:

  ```
  sudo zypper install python
  sudo zypper install python-devel
  ```

  More information on installing software can be found at `http://en.opensuse.org/YaST_Software_Management`.

- **Slackware**: For this distribution of Linux, it may be best to download a compressed tarball and install it from the source, as described in the following section.

Installing Python from a compressed tarball

If none of the preceding methods works for you, you can also download a compressed tarball (XZ or Gzip) and get it installed. Here is a brief synopsis of the steps:

```
#Install dependencies
sudo apt-get install build-essential
sudo apt-get install libreadline-gplv2-dev libncursesw5-dev libssl-dev
libsqlite3-dev tk-dev libgdbm-dev libc6-dev libbz2-dev

#Download the tarball
mkdir /tmp/downloads
cd /tmp/downloads
wget http://python.org/ftp/python/2.7.5/Python-2.7.5.tgz
tar xvfz Python-2.7.5.tgz
cd Python-2.7.5

# Configure, build and install
./configure --prefix=/opt/python2.7 --enable-shared
make
make test
sudo make install
echo "/opt/python2.7/lib" >> /etc/ld.so.conf.d/opt-python2.7.conf
ldconfig
cd ..
rm -rf /tmp/downloads
```

Information on this can be found on the Python download page at
`http://www.python.org/download/`.

Windows

Unlike Linux and Mac distributions, Python does not come pre-installed on Windows.

Core Python installation

The standard method is to use the Windows installers from the CPython team, which are MSI packages. The MSI packages can be downloaded here:
`http://www.python.org/download/releases/2.7.6/`.

Select the appropriate Windows package depending on whether your Windows is the 32-bit or 64-bit version. Python by default gets installed to a folder containing the version number, so, in this case, it will be installed to the following location: `C:\Python27`.

This enables you to have multiple versions of Python running without problems. Upon installation, the following folders should be added to the `PATH` environment variable: `C:\Python27\` and `C:\Python27\Tools\Scripts`.

Installing third-party Python and packages

There are a couple of Python tools that need to be installed in order to make the installation of other packages such as pandas easier. Install `Setuptools` and `pip`. Setuptools is very useful for installing other Python packages such as pandas. It adds to the packaging and installation functionality that is provided by the `distutils` tool in the standard Python distribution.

To install Setuptools, download the `ez_setup.py` script from the following link: `https://bitbucket.org/pypa/setuptools/raw/bootstrap`.

Then, save it to `C:\Python27\Tools\Scripts`.

Then, run `ez_setup.py`: `C:\Python27\Tools\Scripts\ez_setup.py`.

The `pip` associated command provides the developer with an easy-to-use command that enables a quick and easy installation of Python modules. Download the `get-pip` script from the following link: `http://www.pip-installer.org/en/latest/`.

Then, run it from the following location: `C:\Python27\Tools\Scripts\get-pip.py`.

For reference, you can also go through the documentation titled *Installing Python on Windows* at `http://docs.python-guide.org/en/latest/starting/install/win/`.

There are also third-party providers of Python on Windows that make the task of installation even easier. They are listed as follows:

- **Enthought**: `https://enthought.com/`
- **Continuum Analytics**: `http://www.continuum.io/`
- **Active State Python**: `http://www.activestate.com/activepython`

macOS/X

Python 2.7 comes pre-installed on the current and recent releases (for the past five years) of macOS X. The pre-installed Apple-provided build can be found in the following folders on the Mac:

- `/System/Library/Frameworks/Python.framework`
- `/usr/bin/python`

However, you can install your own version from `http://www.python.org/download/`. The one caveat to this is that you will now have two installations of Python, and you have to be careful to make sure the paths and environments are cleanly separated.

Installation using a package manager

Python can also be installed using a package manager on the Mac, such as Macports or Homebrew. I will discuss installation using Homebrew here as it seems to be the most user-friendly. For reference, you can go through the documentation titled *Installing Python on macOS X* at `http://docs.python-guide.org/en/latest/starting/install/osx/`. Here is a summary of the steps:

1. Install Homebrew and run the following command:

   ```
   ruby -e "$(curl -fsSL https://raw.github.com/mxcl/homebrew/go)"
   ```

2. You then need to add the Homebrew folder at the top of your `PATH` environment variable.
3. Install Python 2.7 at the Unix prompt:

   ```
   brew install python
   ```

4. Install third-party software – distribute and pip. Installation of Homebrew automatically installs these packages. Distribute and pip enable you to easily download and install/uninstall Python packages.

Installation of Python and pandas using Anaconda

After a standalone installation of Python, each library will have to be separately installed. It is a bit of a hassle to ensure version compatibility between newly installed libraries and the associated dependencies. This is where a third-party distribution like Anaconda comes in handy. Anaconda is the most widely used distribution for Python/R, designed for developing scalable data science solutions.

What is Anaconda?

Anaconda is an open source Python/R distribution, developed to seamlessly manage packages, dependencies and environments. It is compatible with Windows, Linux and macOS and requires 3 GB of disk space. It needs this memory to download and install quite a collection of IDEs and more than 720 packages. For instance, NumPy and pandas are two of the packages that come pre-installed with Anaconda.

The following image shows a summary of the constituents of the Anaconda distribution. Each component has been summarized in the list:

1. **ANACONDA NAVIGATOR**: A portal to access all the IDEs and tools
2. **ANACONDA PROJECT**: Reproducible experiments saved as a file using notebooks with text guidelines, code snippets, and their output
3. **DATA SCIENCE LIBRARIES**: Includes pre-installed packages for IDEs, scientific computing, visualization, and machine learning
4. **CONDA**: A command line-based package manager to install, uninstall, and upgrade packages/libraries:

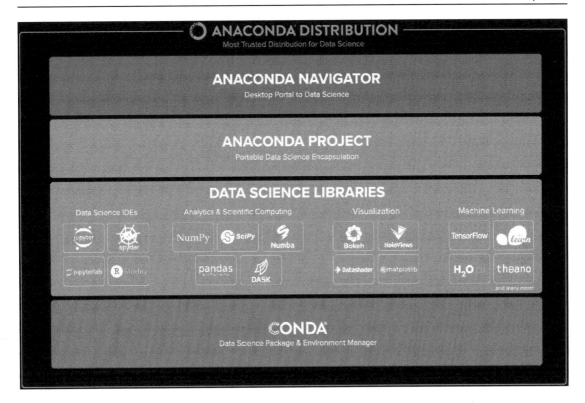

Utilities under Anaconda

Why Anaconda?

Anaconda makes program development easier, and it is a tool of choice for beginners. Anaconda provides a simple system to set up and handle separate programming environments where packages can be maintained consistently to remain compatible with an application. This facilitates smooth collaboration and deployment. When a package is being installed or updated, Anaconda ensures that the dependencies are compatible and performs an auto-update for the dependencies if needed.

Installing Anaconda

Separate Anaconda installers are available for 32-bit OS and 64-bit OSes. Also, there are different installers for Python 2.7 and Python 3.7. The installer can be downloaded from `https://www.anaconda.com/download/`. The website would have the following options shown in the screenshot:

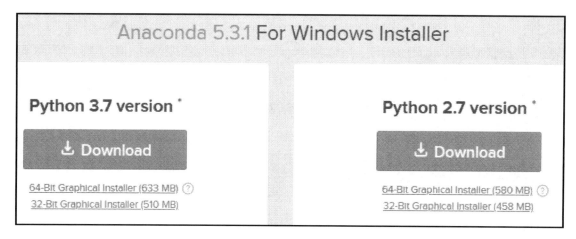

Anaconda installers for different platforms

Observe the following steps to install Anaconda on a Windows machine once the download is done.

Windows Installation

Download the Windows installer (the 32-bit/64-bit version).

- Launch the `.exe` file after the download completes.
- Follow the instructions and accept the license terms.
- Specify the destination for the installation.

Dialogue boxes like these should guide you through the next steps. Go with the default options unless you want to customize the destination folders or don't want to install certain features:

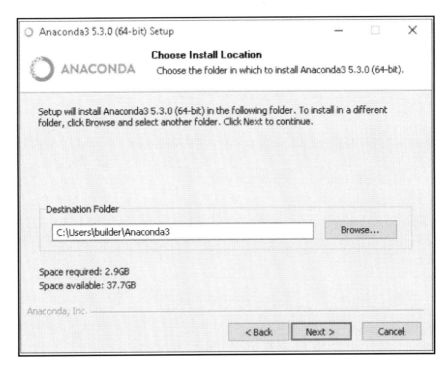

Setup dialog:

Anaconda3 5.3.0 (64-bit) Setup

Choose Install Location
Choose the folder in which to install Anaconda3 5.3.0 (64-bit).

Setup will install Anaconda3 5.3.0 (64-bit) in the following folder. To install in a different folder, click Browse and select another folder. Click Next to continue.

Destination Folder
C:\Users\builder\Anaconda3   Browse...

Space required: 2.9GB
Space available: 37.7GB

Anaconda, Inc.

< Back   Next >   Cancel

Windows installation of Anaconda

If you are a Mac user instead, follow the following steps for installing Anaconda on a windows machine once the download is done.

macOS Installation

Download the macOS installer (the 32-bit/64-bit version):

- Launch the .pkg file after the download completes by double-clicking it.
- Follow the instructions and accept the license terms.
- It is recommended to install Anaconda in the home user directory.

Dialogue boxes like these should appear once you start installing. Just follow the instructions:

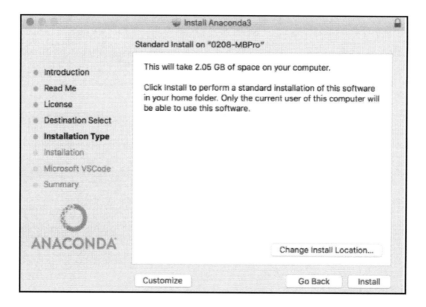

macOS installation of Anaconda

Follow the following steps for a Linux installation.

Linux Installation

Download the macOS installer (the 32-bit/64-bit version):

- Enter the following commands in the shell to start installation.

  For Python 3.7 installer, enter the following:

  ```
  bash ~/Downloads/Anaconda3-5.3.0-Linux-x86_64.sh
  ```

  For Python 2.7 installer, enter the following:

  ```
  bash ~/Downloads/Anaconda2-5.3.0-Linux-x86_64.sh
  ```

- Enter Yes to accept the license agreement.
- Accept the default installation location or choose a new location to complete the installation.

Cloud installation

Anaconda can also be installed on a cloud machine provided by popular cloud infrastructure providers like AWS and Azure. Depending on which kind of instance (Linux or Windows) you choose on your cloud account, similar steps as described previously can be followed to install Anaconda on your cloud machine.

There are two ways you can get Anaconda running on your cloud machine:

- Choose a machine with Anaconda pre-installed on it—AWS and Azure provide machines with many software packages pre-installed on them. You can choose one of the machines that has Anaconda. The following link has more details: `https://aws.amazon.com/marketplace/seller-profile?id=29f81979-a535-4f44-9e9f-6800807ad996`
- Choose a Linux/Windows machine and install Anaconda on it. This is a better and cheaper option giving you more flexibility for the cost of a little installation effort. Once you launch your cloud machine, it involves similar steps as the previous installation steps. The following link has the end-to-end steps for installation using a cloud, `https://chrisalbon.com/aws/basics/run_project_jupyter_on_amazon_ec2/`.

Other numeric and analytics-focused Python distributions

The following outlines various third-party data analysis-related Python distributions, apart from Anaconda. All of the following distributions include pandas:

- **Enthought Canopy**: This is a comprehensive Python data analysis environment. For more information, refer to `https://www.enthought.com/products/canopy/`.
- **Python(x,y)**: This is a free scientific and engineering-oriented Python distribution for numerical computing, data analysis, and visualization. It is based on the Qt GUI package and Spyder interactive scientific development environment. For more information, refer to `http://python-xy.github.io/`.
- **WinPython**: This is a free open source distribution of Python for the Windows platform focused on scientific computing. For more information, refer to `http://winpython.sourceforge.net/`.

For more information on Python distributions, go to `http://bit.ly/1yOzB7o`.

Dependency packages for pandas

 Please note that if you are using Anaconda distribution, you don't need to install pandas separately and hence don't need to worry about installing the dependencies. It is still good to know the dependency packages that are being used behind the hood in pandas to better understand the functioning.

At the time of writing, the latest stable version of pandas is the 0.23.4 version. The various dependencies along with the associated download locations are as follows:

Package	Required	Description	Download location
NumPy : 1.9.0 or higher	Required	NumPy library for numerical operations	http://www.numpy.org/
python-dateutil 2.5.0	Required	Date manipulation and utility library	http://labix.org/
Pytz	Required	Time zone support	http://sourceforge.net/
Setuptools 24.2.0	Required	Packaging Python projects	https://setuptools.readthedocs.io/en/latest/
Numexpr	Optional, recommended	Speeding up of numerical operations	https://code.google.com/
bottleneck	Optional, recommended	Performance related	http://berkeleyanalytics.com/
Cython	Optional, recommended	C-extensions for Python used for optimization	http://cython.org/
SciPy	Optional, recommended	Scientific toolset for Python	http://scipy.org/
PyTables	Optional	Library for HDF5-based storage	http://pytables.github.io/

matplotlib	Optional, recommended	Matlab-like Python plotting library	http://sourceforge.net/
statsmodels	Optional	Statistics module for Python	http://sourceforge.net/
Openpyxl	Optional	Library to read/write Excel files	https://www.python.org/
xlrd/xlwt	Optional	Libraries to read/write Excel files	http://python-excel.org/
Boto	Optional	Library to access Amazon S3	https://www.python.org/
BeautifulSoup and one of html5lib, lxml	Optional	Libraries needed for the read_html() function to work	http://www.crummy.com/
html5lib	Optional	Library for parsing HTML	https://pypi.python.org/pypi/html5lib
Lmxl	Optional	Python library for processing XML and HTML	http://lxml.de/

Review of items installed with Anaconda

Anaconda installs more than 200 packages and several IDEs. Some of the widely used packages that get installed are: NumPy, pandas, scipy, scikit-learn, matplotlib, seaborn, beautifulsoup4, nltk, and dask.

Packages, which are not installed along with Anaconda, could be installed manually through Conda, Anaconda's package manager. Any package upgradation can also be done through Conda. Conda will fetch the packages from the Anaconda repository, which is huge and has more than 1400 packages. The following commands will install and update packages through `conda`:

- To install, use `conda install pandas`
- To update, use `conda update pandas`

The following IDEs are installed with Anaconda:

- JupyterLab
- Jupyter Notebook
- QTConsole
- Spyder

The IDEs could be launched either through Conda or Anaconda Navigator.

Anaconda Navigator is a GUI that lets you manage environments and packages and launch applications like Jupyter Notebook and Spyder. In essence, the Navigator provides an easy interface without the problems of command-line coding, and it is available for Windows, Linux, and macOS.

As the following screenshot of the Anaconda Navigator shows, Anaconda provides a one-stop place to access Jupyter/Spyder/IPython IDEs for Python as well as RStudio IDE for R:

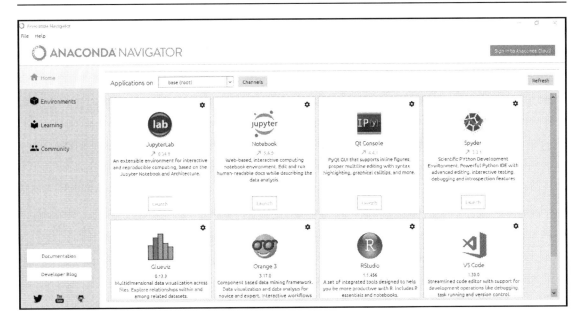

The Anaconda Navigator

JupyterLab

JupyterLab is a tool used to integrate notebooks, documents, and activities. Some of its salient features are as follows:

- It has a drag and drop facility to rearrange, move, and copy notebook cells between notebooks

- It can run code blocks interactively from text files (.py, .R, .md, .tex, and so on) from within Jupyter Notebook

- It can link a code console to a notebook kernel to explore code interactively without cluttering up the notebook with temporary scratch work

- It can facilitate live previews and edit popular file formats, such as Markdown, JSON, CSV, Vega, VegaLite, and more

GlueViz

Glue is a useful Python library to explore relationships within and among related datasets. Its main features include the following:

- **Linked Statistical Graphics**: Glue helps users create scatter plots, histograms, and images (two- and three-dimensional) from their data.
- **Flexible linking across data**: Glue uses the logical links to overlay different data visualizations existing between different datasets and to relay choices across datasets. These links need to be specified by the user, and are arbitrarily flexible.
- **Full scripting capability**: Glue is written in Python, and built on top of its standard scientific libraries (that is, NumPy, Matplotlib, and Scipy). For data input, cleaning, and analysis, users can easily incorporate their own Python code.
- **Orange**: Orange provides open source machine learning, data visualization, and interactive data analysis workflow. Its USPs are interactive data visualization and visual programming using a GUI-based environment.
- **Visual Studio Code**: VS Code or Visual Studio Code is a lightweight but powerful source code editor that runs on your desktop and is available for Windows, macOS, and Linux. It comes with built-in support for JavaScript, TypeScript, and Node.js, and it has a rich ecosystem of extensions for other languages (such as C++, C#, Java, Python, PHP, and Go) and runtimes (such as .NET and Unity)

Walk-through of Jupyter Notebook and Spyder

Let's catch a glimpse of working with two of the widely used Python IDEs – Jupyter Notebook and Spyder.

Jupyter Notebook

Jupyter gets installed during Anaconda installation. To install Jupyter without Anaconda, you can execute the following command in the terminal:

```
pip install jupyter
```

Jupyter Notebook can be opened through Anaconda Navigator or by clicking on the icon in the start menu, or by entering the following command in Conda:

```
jupyter notebook
```

Jupyter Notebook opens in the browser. All folders within the startup directory are accessible from Jupyter. However, the main directory cannot be changed after opening Jupyter. A local Python server is created for Jupyter to get launched:

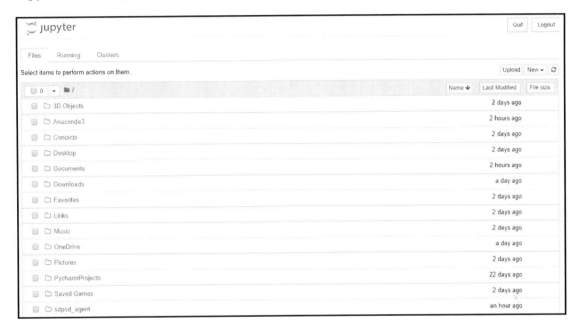

Jupyter home page

A new notebook can be opened by clicking on the **New** button. The new notebook will be created as `Untitled.ipynb`, unlike any other Python IDE, where the script is stored with `.py` extension. Here, **ipynb** stands for **IPython Notebook**. An `.ipynb` file is just a text file that converts all the content—the code, markdown text, and any image or plot—to metadata in a JSON format:

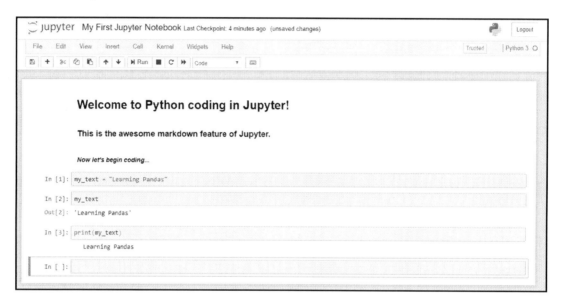

Jupyter Notebook

A Jupyter notebook is comprised of cells; a cell is where your code goes in. The cells can be used to display Markdown code or to execute the code. In the preceding screenshot, the first three cells have been converted to Markdown cells, while the next three are code cells. A code in a cell can be run by clicking the **Run** button in the notebook or by hitting *Ctrl + Enter*.

Jupyter Notebook features the **Save and Checkpoint** option (keyboard shortcut: *Ctrl + S*). Jupyter automatically saves and creates a checkpoint every 120 seconds. This checkpoint helps to recover any unsaved work, and it also helps to revert to a previous checkpoint.

Spyder

Spyder can be installed with pip or through Anaconda, just like Jupyter. However, the developers of Spyder recommend installation through Anaconda.

Spyder can also be launched using methods similar to those for Jupyter Notebook or by typing `spyder` in the terminal:

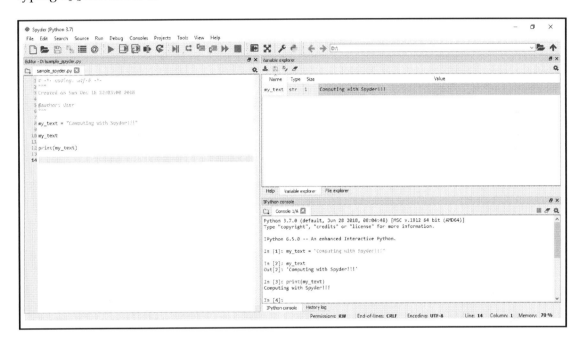

Spyder

Spyder features a script editor and an IPython console. The upper-right pane can shift between a help browser, variable explorer, and file explorer. The editor can be split into a number of cells for a more systematic programming. The IPython console comes in handy when using small snippets of code. The variable explorer provides a summary of all the global objects in the Python session.

Cross tooling – combining pandas awesomeness with R, Julia, H20.ai, and Azure ML Studio

Pandas can be regarded as a "wonder tool" when it comes to applications like data manipulation, data cleaning, or handling time series data. It is extremely fast and efficient, and it is powerful enough to handle small to intermediate datasets. The best part is that the use of pandas is not restricted just to Python. There are methods enabling the supremacy of pandas to be utilized in other frameworks, like R, Julia, Azure ML Studio and H20.ai. These methods of using the benefits of a superior framework from another tool is called cross-tooling and is frequently applied. One of the main reasons for this to exist is that it is almost impossible for one tool to have all the functionalities. Suppose one task has two sub-tasks: sub-task 1 can be done well in R while the sub-task 2 in Python. One can handle this by doing sub-task 1 in R and sub-task 2 by calling Python code from R or doing sub-task 2 in Python and sub-task 1 by calling R code from Python.

This option makes pandas even more powerful. Let's see how pandas methods and /or Python code in general can be used with other tools.

Pandas with R

R has a class of objects called **DataFrame**, which is the same as a pandas DataFrame. The R DataFrame is several times slower than pandas. Hence, learning pandas will also help tackle data manipulation problems in R. However, using the `data.table` data type to handle huge DataFrames in R is the best solution.

The `reticulate` package helps to access and use Python packages in R. For example, you can run these Python snippets in R:

```
library(reticulate)

# Installing a python package from R
py_install("pandas")

# Importing pandas
pd <- import("pandas", convert = FALSE)

# Some basic pandas operations in R
pd_df <- pd$read_csv("train.csv")
pd_head <- pd_df$head()
pd_dtypes <- pd_df$dtypes
```

The same can be done on any other package such as NumPy as well:

```
numpy <- import("numpy")

y <- array(1:4, c(2, 2))
x <- numpy$array(y)
```

If you already have a concrete pandas function written in Python, you can make use of it in R through the reticulate package.

Consider the following Python code snippet:

```
import pandas
def get_data_head(file):
    data = pandas.read_csv(file)
    data_head = data.head()
    return(data_head)
```

Now, the preceding script is saved as `titanic.py`. This script could be used in R as shown:

```
source_python("titanic.py")
titanic_in_r <- get_data_head("titanic.csv")
```

An interactive Python session from R can be created using `repl_python()`.

For example, you can write something like the following:

```
library(reticulate)
repl_python()
import pandas as pd
[i*i for i in range(10)]
```

And it returns the results in the R shell itself as though it was a Python IDE.

Python objects (lists, dictionaries, DataFrames, and arrays) created in a Python session can be accessed via R. Suppose `df` is a Python DataFrame whose summary needs to be found using R. It can be done as follows:

```
summary(py$df)
```

pandas with Azure ML Studio

Azure ML Studio offers predictive analytics solutions through a drag and drop interface. It features the capability to add a Python script that would read a dataset, perform data manipulation, and then deliver the output dataset. pandas could play a crucial role in this data processing module of the Azure ML Studio:

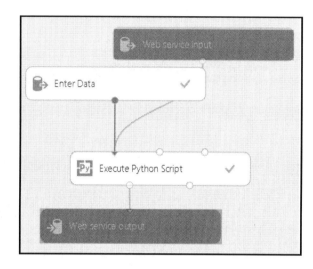

Azure ML Studio – Flowchart

From the flow diagram, you can see that data is fed to the **Execute Python Script** module. This module can receive datasets in two of the three input ports and gives a DataFrame as output in one of the two output ports.

The following diagram shows the **Execute Python Script** module. This module accepts only DataFrames at the input ports. It allows for further data processing steps to take place before a single DataFrame is produced as the result at the output port. This is where pandas and its numerous wonderful functions play a role:

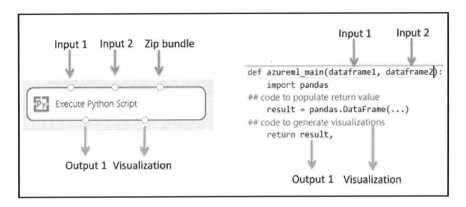

Python execution module of Azure ML Studio

pandas with Julia

Julia has a DataFrame package to handle operations on DataFrames. Benchmarking results has shown that pandas is the clear winner when it comes to speed and computational efficiency. Just like R, Julia allows us to integrate pandas in the script.

After installation, pandas can be loaded into the Julia environment directly, as shown:

```
Pkg.add("Pandas")
using Pandas
# Creating a dataframe object
df = DataFrame(Dict(:score=>[67, 89, 32], :name=>["A", "B", "C"]))

# Any Pandas function or method could be applied on the created dataframe.
head(df)
describe(df)
```

pandas with H2O

H2O is the super-powerful big data analysis product of H2O.ai, encapsulating separate modules within it to handle several aspects of a data science model, including data manipulation and model training.

H2O deals with data as H2O frames, and this data is entirely located within a designated H2O cluster. Hence, the data is not found in the memory, unlike a pandas dataframe.

H2O has a `as_data_frame()` method, which allows conversion from a H2O frame to a pandas dataframe. Following this conversion, all pandas operations could be performed on the converted dataframe.

Command line tricks for pandas

The command line is an important arsenal for pandas users. The command line can be used as an efficient and faster but tedious-to-use complement/supplement to pandas. Many of the data operations, like breaking a huge file into multiple chunks, cleaning a data file of unsupported characters, and so on, can be performed in the command line before feeding the data to pandas.

The head function of pandas is extremely useful to quickly assess the data. A command line function for head makes this option even more useful:

```
# Get the first 10 rows
$ head myData.csv

# Get the first 5 rows
$ head -n 5 myData.csv

# Get 100 bytes of data
$ head -c 100 myData.csv
```

The translate (`tr`) function packs within it the ability to replace characters. The following command converts all uppercase characters in a text file to lowercase characters:

```
$ cat upper.txt | tr "[:upper:]" "[:lower:]" >lower.txt
```

It is tedious and sometimes infeasible to read huge data files. In such cases, it becomes necessary to systematically break the huge file into smaller files. The split function at the command line does exactly this. It splits a file into several files, based on the number of lines that can be present in each file:

```
$ split -l 100 huge_file.csv small_filename_
```

Use `split -b` to perform a split at a certain byte size instead of the number of lines.

Sort is yet another useful pandas-like command line function. It can be used to sort alphabetically, by numerical value, or in reverse order with respect to any column. The preferred sorting order and the column key can be specified in the command line function. Let's look at the following examples:

```
# Sort the 5th column alphabetically
    $ sort -t, -k5 orderfile.csv

# Sort the 3rd column in reverse numerical order
    $ sort -t,  -k3nr orederfile.csv
```

The -t indicates that the file is comma delimited.

The current working directory should be changed to the directory where your data file in question is stored before any of these methods is applied.

Options and settings for pandas

pandas allows the users to modify some display and formatting options.

The get_option() and set_option() commands let the user view the current setting and change it:

```
pd.get_option("display.max_rows")
Output: 60

pd.set_option("display.max_rows", 120)
pd.get_option("display.max_rows")
Output: 120

pd.reset_option("display.max_rows")
pd.get_option("display.max_rows")
Output: 60
```

The preceding options discussed set and reset the number of rows that are displayed when a dataframe is printed. Some of the other useful display options are the following:

- max_columns: Set the number of columns to be displayed.
- chop_threshold: Float values below the limit set here will be displayed as zeros.
- colheader_justify: Set the justification for the column header.

- `date_dayfirst`: Setting to `'True'` prints day first when displaying a datetime value.
- `date_yearfirst`: Setting to True prints year first when displaying a datetime value.
- `precision`: Setting the precision for the float values displayed.

The following is an example of a number formatting option, which sets the accuracy and determines the use of any prefix:

```
s = pd.Series(np.random.randn(5))

pd.set_eng_float_format(accuracy=3, use_eng_prefix=False)

s
0   -114.938E-03
1   -928.960E-03
2   -745.716E-03
3      1.261E+00
4    115.968E-03
dtype: float64

pd.set_eng_float_format(accuracy=3, use_eng_prefix=True)

s
0   -114.938m
1   -928.960m
2   -745.716m
3      1.261
4    115.968m
dtype: float64
```

Numeric formatting in Pandas

We will discuss this in further detail in later chapters.

Summary

Before we delve into the awesomeness of pandas, it is mission critical that we install Python and pandas correctly, choose the right IDEs, and set the right options. In this chapter, we discussed these and more. Here is a summary of key takeaways from the chapter:

- Python 3.x is available, but many users still prefer to use version 2.7 as it is more stable and scientific-computation friendly.
- The support and bug fixing for version 2.7 has now been stopped.
- Translating code from one version to other is a breeze. One can also use both versions together using the `virtualenv` package, which comes pre-installed with Anaconda.
- Anaconda is a popular Python distribution that comes with 700+ libraries/packages and several popular IDEs, such as Jupyter and Spyder.
- Python codes are callable from, and usable in, other tools, like R, Azure ML Studio, H20.ai, and Julia.
- Some of the day-to-day data operations, like breaking a large file into smaller chunks, `reading` a few lines of data, and so on, can be performed in the command line/shell as well.
- The default setting options for pandas can be seen and changed via the `get_option()` and `set_option()` commands. Some of the options that can be changed are the maximum number of rows and columns displayed, the number of decimal points for float variables, and so on.

In the next chapter, we will expand our scope a little bit from pandas and explore tools such as NumPy that enrich the capabilities of pandas in the Python ecosystem. It will be an exhaustive NumPy tutorial with real-life case studies.

Further reading

- https://www.r-bloggers.com/run-python-from-r/
- https://pandas.pydata.org/pandas-docs/stable/index.html
- http://docs.glueviz.org/en/stable/
- https://blog.jupyter.org/jupyterlab-is-ready-for-users-5a6f039b8906
- https://orange.biolab.si/

Section 2: Data Structures and I/O in pandas

The key feature of pandas is its ability to give you all the flexibility and ease of use to work with different data structures, such as 1D, 2D, or even 3D arrays, as well as different types of file formats—ranging from text files to CSV files. In this section, we see how to work with these different file types, and also the different operations you can perform on that data, using pandas.

This section is comprised of the following chapters:

- Chapter 3, *Using NumPy and Data Structures with pandas*
- Chapter 4, *I/O of Different Data Formats with pandas*

3
Using NumPy and Data Structures with pandas

This chapter is one of the most important ones in this book. We will now begin to dive into the nitty-gritty of pandas. We start by taking a tour of NumPy `ndarrays`, a data structure not in pandas but NumPy. Knowledge of NumPy `ndarrays` is useful as they are the building blocks on which pandas DataFrames have been built. One key benefit of NumPy arrays is that they execute what is known as *vectorized* operations, which are operations that require traversing/looping on a Python array and are much faster.

In this chapter, I will present the material via numerous examples using Jupyter.

The topics we will cover in this chapter include a tour of the `numpy.ndarray` data structure, the `pandas.Series` **one-dimensional (1D)** pandas data structure, the `pandas.DataFrame` **two-dimensional (2D)** pandas tabular data structure, and the `pandas.Panel` **three-dimensional (3D)** pandas data structure.

The following topics will be covered in this chapter:

- NumPy `ndarrays`
- Implementing neural networks with NumPy
- Practical applications of multidimensional arrays
- Data structures in pandas

NumPy ndarrays

Arrays are vital objects in the data analysis scenario. Arrays allow for structured handling of elements that are stacked across rows and columns. The elements of an array are bound by the rule that they should all be of the same data type. For example, the medical records of five patients have been presented as an array as follows:

	Blood glucose level	Heart rate	Cholesterol level
Peter Parker	100	65	160
Bruce Wayne	150	82	200
Tony Stark	90	55	80
Barry Allen	130	73	220
Steve Rogers	190	80	150

It is seen that all 15 elements are of data type `int`. Arrays could also be composed of `strings`, `floats`, or complex numbers. Arrays could be constructed from lists—a widely used and versatile data structure in Python:

```
array_list = [[100, 65, 160],
[150, 82, 200],
[90, 55, 80],
[130, 73, 220],
[190, 80, 150]]
```

An element in the ith row and j^{th} column (for example, first row and second column in the first example) of an array or matrix can be accessed as shown in the following code. Note that indexing in Python starts from 0:

```
In [2]: array_list[1][2]
Out[2]: 200

In [3]: array_list[3][0]
Out[3]: 130
```

Python has an built-in `array` module to create arrays. However, this array module is more like a glorified list where all elements are required to have the same data type. An array can be created using the `array` module by providing two arguments—the type code of the data type, and the elements in a list, string, or any iterable object. Let's create an array of floats. Here, d is the type code for a double-floating point value:

```
import array as arr
arr_x = arr.array("d", [98.6, 22.35, 72.1])
```

It is not possible to create a two-dimensional entity with rows and columns using the `array` module. This can be achieved through a nested list of such arrays. Special functions implicit with matrices or arrays, such as matrix multiplication, determinants, and eigenvalues, are not defined in this module.

NumPy is the preferred package to create and work on array-type objects. NumPy allows multidimensional arrays to be created. Multidimensional arrays provide a systematic and efficient framework for storing data. Complex computations, which are built-in vectorized operations in the NumPy package, can be done quickly on these multidimensional arrays without the need for loops. Consider the earlier example where we created a two-dimensional array to store the medical records of five patients. The patients' names and the clinical indicators were the two dimensions in this case. Now, if the clinical parameters of the same patients were recorded for three years, from 2016 to 2018, then all this information could be conveniently represented in a three-dimensional array. The year in which the records were fetched will get in as the third dimension. The resultant array will be of dimension 3 x 5 x 3, and entirely composed of integers:

2016			2017			2018		
100	65	160	95	68	140	110	72	160
150	82	200	145	80	222	160	95	185
90	55	80	90	62	100	100	80	110
130	73	220	150	92	200	140	92	120
190	80	150	140	60	90	100	55	100

In NumPy, these multidimensional arrays are referred to as `ndarrays` (*n*-dimensional arrays). All NumPy array objects are of the type `numpy.ndarray`.

Let's view the preceding data as an `ndarray`:

```
In [4]: ndarray_1

Out[4]:
array([[[100, 65, 160],
[150, 82, 200],
[ 90, 55, 80],
[130, 73, 220],
[190, 80, 150]],
[[ 95, 68, 140],
[145, 80, 222],
[ 90, 62, 100],
[150, 92, 200],
[140, 60, 90]],
[[110, 72, 160],
[160, 95, 185],
```

```
    [100, 80, 110],
    [140, 92, 120],
    [100, 55, 100]]])
```

Attributes of an ndarray such as the data type, shape, number of dimensions, and size can be accessed by different attributes of the array. Some attributes for the ndarray ndarray_1 have been explored in the following code:

```
# Data type of the array
In [5]: ndarray_1.dtype
Out[5]: dtype('int32')

# Shape of the array
In [6]: ndarray_1.shape
Out[6]: (3, 5, 3)

# Number of dimensions in the array
In [7]: ndarray_1.ndim
Out[7]: 3

# Size of the array (number of elements in the array)
In [8]: ndarray_1.size
Out[8]: 45
```

NumPy's ndarray makes use of a strided indexing scheme for its internal memory layout. A memory segment by itself can accommodate only one-dimensional structures. Hence, a specific memory allocation scheme such as the strided indexing scheme is needed to facilitate easy indexing and slicing of ndarrays. A stride indicates the number of bytes to jump to traverse to the subsequent element. The number of bytes for each stride is determined by the data type of the array. Let's understand strides through the array explored earlier. The number of bytes occupied by each element can be determined as shown in the following code:

```
In [9]: ndarray_1.itemsize
Out[9]: 4
In [10]: ndarray_1.nbytes
Out[10]: 180
```

It is seen that each element occupies 4 bytes, and the entire array occupies 180 bytes. The strides for the array are represented as follows:

```
In [11]: ndarray_1.strides
Out[11]: (60, 12, 4)
```

The shape of the array is given by the tuple (3, 5, 3). The values in the tuple represent the number of years for which there is data, the number of patients, and the number of clinical parameters, respectively. For each year or first dimension, there are 15 records, and hence to move from one year to another in the array, 60 bytes should be jumped across. On a similar note, each distinct patient has 3 records for a given year, and 12 bytes of memory should be moved past to get to the next patient.

NumPy array creation

NumPy arrays can be created in several ways via calls to various NumPy methods. The arrays can be created using the data in lists or any other data structures, by specifying numerical ranges to obtain uniformly spaced values or by generating random samples.

The simplest routine to create an array is through the `array` function. This function accepts any sequential object, such as a list or tuple, and converts it to an array. The following code snippet shows how a 1D array can be created through the `array` function:

```
In [12]: array1d = np.array([1, 2, 3, 4])
In [13]: array1d
Out [13]: array([1, 2, 3, 4])
```

Similarly, a multidimensional array can be created by passing a list of lists to the array function:

```
In [14]: array2d = np.array([[0, 1, 2],[2, 3, 4]])
In [15]: array2d
Out [15]:
array([[0, 1, 2],
[2, 3, 4]])
```

Instead of lists, the same result can be achieved with tuples, a list of tuples, or a tuple of tuples as well.

Array of ones and zeros

Several operations on arrays call for the creation of arrays or matrices with ones and zeros. Some special functions in NumPy provide for easy creation of such arrays. Usually, these functions take in the shape of the resultant array as an input argument in the form of a tuple:

```
# Creating an array of ones with shape (2, 3, 4)
In [27]: np.ones((2, 3, 4))
Out [27]:
array([[[1., 1., 1., 1.],
[1., 1., 1., 1.],
[1., 1., 1., 1.]],
[[1., 1., 1., 1.],
[1., 1., 1., 1.],
[1., 1., 1., 1.]]])

# Creating an array of zeros with shape (2, 1, 3)
In [28]: np.zeros((2, 1, 3))
Out [28]:
array([[[0., 0., 0.]],
[[0., 0., 0.]]])
```

The identity function returns a 2D *n x n* square matrix, where *n* is the order of the matrix passed as an input argument:

```
In [29]: np.identity(3)
Out [29]:
array([[1., 0., 0.],
[0., 1., 0.],
[0., 0., 1.]])
```

The eye function can also be used to create an identity matrix. It differs from the identity matrix in two main aspects:

- The eye function returns a 2D rectangular matrix and accepts both the number of rows and number of columns (optional argument) as the input. If the number of columns is not specified, a square matrix is returned using just the number of rows passed in.
- The diagonal can be offset to any position in the upper triangle or lower triangle.

Take a look at the following code:

```
# Creating an identity matrix of order 3 with the eye function
In [39]: np.eye(N = 3)
Out [39]:
array([[1., 0., 0.],
[0., 1., 0.],[0., 0., 1.]])

# Creating a rectangular equivalent of identity matrix with 2 rows and 3
columns
In [40]: np.eye(N = 2, M = 3)
Out [40]:
array([[1., 0., 0.],
[0., 1., 0.]])

# Offsetting the diagonal of ones by one position in the upper triangle
In [41]: np.eye(N = 4, M = 3, k = 1)
Out [41]:
array([[0., 1., 0.],
[0., 0., 1.],
[0., 0., 0.],
[0., 0., 0.]])

# Offsetting the diagonal of ones by two positions in the lower triangle
In [42]: np.eye(N = 4, M = 3, k = -2)
Out [42]:
array([[0., 0., 0.],
[0., 0., 0.],
[1., 0., 0.],
[0., 1., 0.]])
```

By default, k holds the value 0 in the eye function.

Array based on a numerical range

The `arange` function of NumPy functionally resembles Python's range function. Based on a start value, stop value, and step value to increment or decrement subsequent values, the `arange` function generates a set of numbers. Just like the range function, the start and step arguments are optional here. But unlike range, which generates a list, `arange` generates an array:

```
# Creating an array with continuous values from 0 to 5
In [44]: np.arange(6)
Out [44]: array([0, 1, 2, 3, 4, 5])

# Creating an array with numbers from 2 to 12 spaced out at intervals of 3
In [45]: np.arange(2, 13, 3)
Out [45]: array([ 2, 5, 8, 11])
```

The `linspace` function generates an array of linearly spaced samples for a given start point and end point. Unlike the arrange function, which specifies the incremental/decremental interval, the `linspace` function accepts the number of samples to be generated as an optional argument. By default, 50 samples are generated for a given start point and end point:

```
# Creating a linearly spaced array of 20 samples between 5 and 10
In [47]: np.linspace(start = 5, stop = 10, num = 20)
Out [47]:
array([ 5. , 5.26315789, 5.52631579, 5.78947368, 6.05263158,
6.31578947, 6.57894737, 6.84210526, 7.10526316, 7.36842105,
7.63157895, 7.89473684, 8.15789474, 8.42105263, 8.68421053,
8.94736842, 9.21052632, 9.47368421, 9.73684211, 10. ])
```

Similarly, the `logspace` and `geomspace` functions create an array of numbers following logarithmic and geometric sequences to be created.

The `arange` function and `linspace` function do not allow for any shape specification by themselves and produce 1D arrays with the given sequence of numbers. We can very well use some shape manipulation methods to mold these arrays to the desired shape. These methods will be discussed in the last part of this chapter.

Random and empty arrays

The `random` module of the NumPy package packs within it a whole range of functions for random sampling that perform operations right from creating a simple array of random numbers to drawing random samples from distribution functions.

The `random.rand` function generates random values from 0 to 1 (uniform distribution) to create an array of given shape:

```
# Creating a random array with 2 rows and 4 columns, from a uniform
distribution
In [49]: np.random.rand(2, 4)
Out [49]:
array([[0.06573958, 0.32399347, 0.60926818, 0.99319404],
[0.46371691, 0.49197909, 0.93103333, 0.06937098]])
```

The `random.randn` function samples values from a standard normal distribution to build an array of given shape. If the shape parameter is not specified, a single value is returned as output:

```
# Creating a 2X4 array from a standard normal distribution
In [50]: np.random.randn(2, 4)
Out [50]:
array([[ 1.29319502, 0.55161748, 0.4660141 , -0.72012401],
[-0.64549002, 0.01922198, 0.04187487, 1.35950566]])

# Creating a 2X4 array from a normal distribution with mean 10 and standard
deviation 5
In [51]: 5 * np.random.randn(2, 4) + 10
Out [51]:
array([[ 6.08538069, 12.10958845, 15.27372945, 15.9252008 ],
[13.34173712, 18.49388151, 10.19195856, 11.63874627]])
```

The `random.randint` function generates an array of integers between the specified lower and upper bounds, with the given shape. The limit excludes the upper bound. If the upper bound is not mentioned, it is considered to be 1 more than the lower bound defined:

```
# Creating an array of shape (2, 3) with random integers chosen from the
interval [2, 5)
In [52]: np.random.randint(2, 5, (2, 3))
Out [52]:
array([[2, 4, 3],
[3, 4, 4]])
```

The `empty` function returns an array with arbitrary values for the given shape. This array requires no initialization and would perform faster than functions such as zeros and ones where the values have to be initialized. Caution is needed when using this function, and it is to be used only when it is certain that all the values in the array would be filled:

```
# Creating an uninitialized empty array of 4X3 dimensions
In [58]: np.empty([4,3])
Out [58]:
array([[0., 0., 0.],
```

```
[0., 0., 0.],
[1., 0., 0.],
[0., 1., 0.]])
```

Arrays based on existing arrays

Some of the NumPy array-creation routines are extremely useful to perform matrix operations such as constructing the **diagonal matrix (diag)**, the **upper triangular matrix (triu)**, and the **lower triangular matrix (tril)**.

The `diag` function works only on 1D and 2D arrays. If the input array is 2D, the output is a 1D array with the diagonal elements of the input array. If the input is a 1D array, the output is a matrix with the input array along its diagonal. Here, a parameter k helps to offset the position from the main diagonal and can be positive or negative:

```
# The 2D input matrix for diag function
In [68]: arr_a = np.array([[1, 2, 3], [4, 5, 6], [7, 8, 9]])
In [69]: arr_a
Out [69]:
array([[1, 2, 3],
[4, 5, 6],
[7, 8, 9]])

# Getting the diagonal of the array
In [70]: np.diag(arr_a)
Out [70]: array([1, 5, 9])

# Constructing the diagonal matrix from a 1D array
# diag returns a 1D array of diagonals for a 2D input matrix. This 1D array
of diagonals can be used here.
In [71]: np.diag(np.diag(arr_a))
Out [71]:
array([[1, 0, 0],
[0, 5, 0],
[0, 0, 9]])

# Creating the diagonal matrix with diagonals other than main diagonal
In [72]: np.diag(np.diag(arr_a, k = 1))
Out [72]:
array([[2, 0],
[0, 6]])
```

The `triu` and `tril` functions have a similar parameter k, which helps offset the diagonal. These functions work with any `ndarray`.

Given an array of *n* dimensions, a new array can be created by repeating this array multiple times along each axis. This can be done with the `tile` function. This function accepts two input arguments—the input array and the number of repetitions:

```
# Repeating a 1D array 2 times
In [76]: np.tile(np.array([1, 2, 3]), 2)
Out [76]: array([1, 2, 3, 1, 2, 3])

# Repeating a 2D array 4 times
In [77]: np.tile(np.array([[1, 2, 3], [4, 5, 6]]), 4)
Out [77]:
array([[1, 2, 3, 1, 2, 3, 1, 2, 3, 1, 2, 3],
[4, 5, 6, 4, 5, 6, 4, 5, 6, 4, 5, 6]])

# Repeating a 2D array 4 times along axis 0 and 1 time along axis 1
In [78]: np.tile(np.array([[1, 2, 3], [4, 5, 6]]), (4,1))
Out [78]:
array([[1, 2, 3],
[4, 5, 6],
[1, 2, 3],
[4, 5, 6],
[1, 2, 3],
[4, 5, 6],
[1, 2, 3],
[4, 5, 6]])
```

NumPy data types

All the array-creation functions described earlier (except the functions for arrays based on existing arrays—`diag`, `triu`, `tril`, and `tile`) have an argument `dtype` to define the data type of the array.

Let's create an array without predefining the data type, and then check for its data type:

```
In [80]: np.array([-2, -1, 0, 1, 2]).dtype
Out [80]: dtype('int32')
```

Now, let's define the same array by also setting its data type to `float`:

```
In [81]: np.array([-2, -1, 0, 1, 2], dtype = "float")
Out [81]: array([-2., -1., 0., 1., 2.])
```

It is seen that the elements of the array are all casted as floating points. It is also possible to cast this array as a string:

```
In [83]: np.array([-2, -1, 0, 1, 2], dtype = "str")
Out[83]: array(['-2', '-1', '0', '1', '2'], dtype='<U2'
```

In this case, the elements are cast as strings. The output also specifies the data type as <U2. It indicates that the elements of the array are Unicode strings and the maximum accepted length of string for this array is 2. This threshold on length is decided based on the length of the longest string in the array. Let's understand this with another example:

```
In [87]: np.array(["a", "bb", "ccc", "dddd", "eeeee"])
Out[87]: array(['a', 'bb', 'ccc', 'dddd', 'eeeee'], dtype='<U5')
```

Such typecasting is observed in arrays with strings, as optimal memory has to be allocated for the array. A single character occupies four bytes. Based on the maximum string length, each element will be allotted a memory block of size equal to four times the maximum string length.

NumPy arrays also support data types such as boolean and complex:

```
# Boolean array
In [89]: np.array([True, False, True, True]).dtype
Out[89]: dtype('bool')
In [90]: np.array([0, 1, 1, 0, 0], dtype = "bool")
Out[90]: array([False, True, True, False, False])
In [91]: np.array([0, 1, 2, 3, -4], dtype = "bool")
Out[91]: array([False, True, True, True, True])

# Complex array
In [92]: np.array([[1 + 1j, 2 + 2j], [3 + 3j, 4 + 4j]])
Out[92]:
array([[1.+1.j, 2.+2.j],
[3.+3.j, 4.+4.j]])
In [93]: np.array([[1 + 1j, 2 + 2j], [3 + 3j, 4 + 4j]]).dtype
Out[93]: dtype('complex128')
```

The data type of ndarray can be changed in much the same way as we cast in other languages such as Java or C/C++. The ndarray.astype method helps in type conversion:

```
# Int to float conversion
In [94]: int_array = np.array([0, 1, 2, 3])
In [95]: int_array.astype("float")
Out[95]: array([0., 1., 2., 3.])

# Float to int conversion
In [97]: float_array = np.array([1.56, 2.95, 3.12, 4.65])
```

```
In [98]: float_array.astype("int")
Out[98]: array([1, 2, 3, 4])
```

 More information on casting can be found in the official documentation at
`http://docs.scipy.org/doc/numpy/reference/generated/numpy.ndarra`
`y.astype.html`.

NumPy indexing and slicing

Array indices in NumPy start at 0 as in languages such as Python, Java, and C++ and unlike
in Fortran, Matlab, and Octave, which start at 1. Arrays can be indexed in the standard way
as we would index into any other Python sequences:

```
# print entire array, element 0, element 1, last element.
In [36]: ar = np.arange(5); print ar; ar[0], ar[1], ar[-1]
[0 1 2 3 4]
Out[36]: (0, 1, 4)
# 2nd, last and 1st elements
In [65]: ar=np.arange(5); ar[1], ar[-1], ar[0]
Out[65]: (1, 4, 0)
```

Arrays can be reversed using the : : -1 idiom as follows:

```
In [24]: ar=np.arange(5); ar[::-1]
Out[24]: array([4, 3, 2, 1, 0])
```

Multidimensional arrays are indexed using tuples of integers:

```
In [71]: ar = np.array([[2,3,4],[9,8,7],[11,12,13]]); ar
Out[71]: array([[ 2,  3,  4],
                [ 9,  8,  7],
                [11, 12, 13]])
In [72]: ar[1,1]
Out[72]: 8
```

Here, we set the entry at row1 and column1 to 5:

```
In [75]: ar[1,1]=5; ar
Out[75]: array([[ 2,  3,  4],
                [ 9,  5,  7],
                [11, 12, 13]])
```

Retrieve row 2:

```
In [76]:  ar[2]
Out[76]: array([11, 12, 13])
In [77]: ar[2,:]
Out[77]: array([11, 12, 13])
```

Retrieve column 1:

```
In [78]: ar[:,1]
Out[78]: array([ 3,  5, 12])
```

If an index is specified that is out of bounds of the range of an array, `IndexError` will be raised:

```
In [6]: ar = np.array([0,1,2])
In [7]: ar[5]
---------------------------------------------------------------------
-------
    IndexError                      Traceback (most recent call last)
    <ipython-input-7-8ef7e0800b7a> in <module>()
    ----> 1 ar[5]
        IndexError: index 5 is out of bounds for axis 0 with size 3
```

Thus, for 2D arrays, the first dimension denotes rows and the second dimension, the columns. The colon (`:`) denotes selection across all elements of the dimension.

Array slicing

Arrays can be sliced using the syntax `ar[startIndex: endIndex: stepValue]`:

```
In [82]: ar=2*np.arange(6); ar
Out[82]: array([ 0,  2,  4,  6,  8, 10])
In [85]: ar[1:5:2]
Out[85]: array([2, 6])
```

Note that if we wish to include the `endIndex` value, we need to go above it, as follows:

```
In [86]: ar[1:6:2]
Out[86]: array([ 2,  6, 10])
```

Obtain the first `n elements` using `ar[:n]`:

```
In [91]: ar[:4]
Out[91]: array([0, 2, 4, 6])
```

The implicit assumption here is that `startIndex=0, step=1`.

Start at element 4 and select all the elements till the end:

```
In [92]: ar[4:]
Out[92]: array([ 8, 10])
```

Slice array with `stepValue=3`:

```
In [94]: ar[::3]
Out[94]: array([0, 6])
```

To illustrate the scope of indexing in NumPy, let's refer to the following diagram, which is taken from a NumPy lecture given at SciPy 2013 and can be found at `http://scipy-lectures.github.io/_images/numpy_indexing.png`:

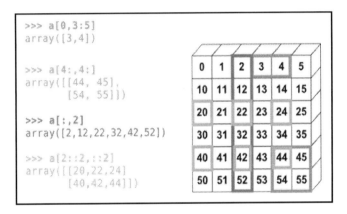

Pictorial illustration of NumPy indexing

Let's now examine the meanings of the expressions in the preceding diagram:

- The expression `a[0,3:5]` indicates the start at row 0, columns 3-5, column 5 not included.
- In the expression `a[4:,4:]`, the first 4 indicates the start at row 4 and will give all columns, that is, the array [[40, 41,42,43,44,45] [50,51,52,53,54,55]]. The second 4 shows the cutoff at the start of column 4 to produce the array [[44, 45], [54, 55]].
- The expression `a[:,2]` gives all rows from column 2.
- Now, in the last expression, `a[2::2,::2]`, 2::2 indicates that the start is at row 2 and the step value here is also 2. This would give us the array [[20, 21, 22, 23, 24, 25], [40, 41, 42, 43, 44, 45]]. Further, ::2 specifies that we retrieve columns in steps of 2, producing the end result array ([[20, 22, 24], [40, 42, 44]]).

Assignment and slicing can be combined as shown in the following code snippet:

```
In [96]: ar
Out[96]: array([ 0,  2,  4,  6,  8, 10])
In [100]: ar[:3]=1; ar
Out[100]: array([ 1,  1,  1,  6,  8, 10])
In [110]: ar[2:]=np.ones(4);ar
Out[110]: array([1, 1, 1, 1, 1, 1])
```

Array masking

NumPy arrays can be used as filters on the larger original array. This process of using arrays as filters is called **array masking**. For example, see the following snippet:

```
In [146]: np.random.seed(10)
          ar=np.random.random_integers(0,25,10); ar
Out[146]: array([ 9,  4, 15,  0, 17, 25, 16, 17,  8,  9])
In [147]: evenMask=(ar % 2==0); evenMask
Out[147]: array([False,  True, False,  True, False, False,  True,
False,  True, False], dtype=bool)
In [148]: evenNums=ar[evenMask]; evenNums
Out[148]: array([ 4,  0, 16,  8])
```

In the following example, we randomly generate an array of 10 integers between 0 and 25. Then, we create a boolean mask array that is used to filter out only the even numbers. This masking feature can be very useful, say, for example, if we wished to eliminate missing values by replacing them with a default value. Here, the missing value ' ' is replaced by 'USA' as the default country. Note that ' ' is also an empty string:

```
In [149]: ar=np.array(['Hungary','Nigeria',
                       'Guatemala','','Poland',
                       '','Japan']); ar
Out[149]: array(['Hungary', 'Nigeria', 'Guatemala',
                 '', 'Poland', '', 'Japan'],
                dtype='|S9')
In [150]: ar[ar=='']='USA'; ar
Out[150]: array(['Hungary', 'Nigeria', 'Guatemala',
   'USA', 'Poland', 'USA', 'Japan'], dtype='|S9')
```

Arrays of integers can also be used to index an array to produce another array. Note that this produces multiple values; hence, the output must be an array of type `ndarray`. This is illustrated in the following snippet:

```
In [173]: ar=11*np.arange(0,10); ar
Out[173]: array([ 0, 11, 22, 33, 44, 55, 66, 77, 88, 99])
In [174]: ar[[1,3,4,2,7]]
Out[174]: array([11, 33, 44, 22, 77])
```

In the preceding code, the selection object is a list, and elements at indices 1, 3, 4, 2, and 7 are selected. Now, assume that we change it to the following:

```
In [175]: ar[1,3,4,2,7]
```

We get an `IndexError` error since the array is 1D and we're specifying too many indices to access it:

```
IndexError              Traceback (most recent call last)
<ipython-input-175-adbcbe3b3cdc> in <module>()
----> 1 ar[1,3,4,2,7]
IndexError: too many indices
```

This assignment is also possible with array indexing, as follows:

```
In [176]: ar[[1,3]]=50; ar
Out[176]: array([ 0, 50, 22, 50, 44, 55, 66, 77, 88, 99])
```

When a new array is created from another array by using a list of array indices, the new array has the same shape.

Complex indexing

Here, we illustrate the use of complex indexing to assign values from a smaller array into a larger one:

```
In [188]: ar=np.arange(15); ar
Out[188]: array([ 0,  1,  2,  3,  4,  5,  6,  7,  8,  9, 10, 11, 12,
13, 14])
In [193]: ar2=np.arange(0,-10,-1)[::-1]; ar2
Out[193]: array([-9, -8, -7, -6, -5, -4, -3, -2, -1,  0])
```

Slice out the first 10 elements of `ar`, and replace them with elements from `ar2`, as follows:

```
In [194]: ar[:10]=ar2; ar
Out[194]: array([-9, -8, -7, -6, -5, -4, -3, -2, -1,  0, 10, 11, 12,
13, 14])
```

Copies and views

A view on a NumPy array is just a particular way of portraying the data it contains. Creating a view does not result in a new copy of the array, rather the data it contains may be arranged in a specific order, or only certain data rows may be shown. Thus, if data is replaced on the underlying array's data, this will be reflected in the view whenever the data is accessed via indexing.

The initial array is not copied into the memory during slicing and is thus more efficient. The np.may_share_memory method can be used to see whether two arrays share the same memory block. However, it should be used with caution as it may produce false positives. Modifying a view modifies the original array:

```
In [118]:ar1=np.arange(12); ar1
Out[118]:array([ 0,  1,  2,  3,  4,  5,  6,  7,  8,  9, 10, 11])
In [119]:ar2=ar1[::2]; ar2
Out[119]: array([ 0,  2,  4,  6,  8, 10])
In [120]: ar2[1]=-1; ar1
Out[120]: array([ 0,  1, -1,  3,  4,  5,  6,  7,  8,  9, 10, 11])
```

To force NumPy to copy an array, we use the np.copy function. As we can see in the following array, the original array remains unaffected when the copied array is modified:

```
In [124]: ar=np.arange(8);ar
Out[124]: array([0, 1, 2, 3, 4, 5, 6, 7])
In [126]: arc=ar[:3].copy(); arc
Out[126]: array([0, 1, 2])
In [127]: arc[0]=-1; arc
Out[127]: array([-1,  1,  2])
In [128]: ar
Out[128]: array([0, 1, 2, 3, 4, 5, 6, 7])
```

Operations

Many methods on NumPy arrays require running mathematical operators such as addition, subtraction, multiplication, division, and so on, on the arrays. The following section deals with explaining how these operators are applied on the arrays.

Basic operators

NumPy is highly efficient in performance as it works based on vectorized operations, where the need for loops is avoided and the process becomes several times faster. All basic arithmetic operations involving +, -, *, and / take place elementwise and are vectorized:

```
# Arithmetic operation on arrays with scalars
In [71]: array_1 = np.array([[1, 2, 3], [4, 5, 6]])
In [72]: array_1
Out[72]:
array([[1, 2, 3],
[4, 5, 6]])
In [73]: array_1 + 5
Out[73]:
array([[ 6, 7, 8],
[ 9, 10, 11]])
In [74]: array_1 * 5
Out[74]:
array([[ 5, 10, 15],
[20, 25, 30]])
In [75]: array_1 ** 2
Out[75]:
array([[ 1, 4, 9],
[16, 25, 36]], dtype=int32)
```

Operations involving two arrays, such as adding or multiplying two arrays, also takes place in a vectorized manner:

```
# Element-wise addition of two arrays
In [76]: array_1 + array_1
Out[76]:
array([[ 2, 4, 6],
[ 8, 10, 12]])

# Element-wise multiplication of two arrays
In [77]: array_1 * array_1
Out[77]:
array([[ 1, 4, 9],
[16, 25, 36]])

# Matrix multiplication of an array and its transpose
In [78]: array_1 @ array_1.T
Out[78]:
array([[14, 32],
[32, 77]])
```

Python's `timeit` function will give us a sense of how efficient vectorized operations are compared to looping over items:

```
# Computing the cube of each element in an array, for an array with 1000
elements
In [79]: %timeit np.arange(1000) ** 3
5.05 µs ± 195 ns per loop (mean ± std. dev. of 7 runs, 100000 loops each)

# Computing the cube of each number from 0 to 1000, using a for loop
In [80]: array_list = range(1000)
...: %timeit [array_list[i]**3 for i in array_list]
533 µs ± 8.06 µs per loop (mean ± std. dev. of 7 runs, 1000 loops each)
```

This shows that numpy operations are about 100 times faster than for loops.

Mathematical operators

The mathematical operators of NumPy can mainly support trigonometric operations, arithmetic operations, and exponential and logarithmic operations.

A class of these operators, such as `prod`, `sum`, and so on, perform computations within the array and serve to reduce the matrix. For example, the `sum` function calculates the sum along a given axis. The output will be the sum of elements along the axis. These functions can be called as a `numpy.function` or as an `ndarray.method`:

```
# Sum of all elements in an array
In [62]: np.array([[1, 2, 3], [4, 5, 6]]).sum()
Out[62]: 21

# Column sum of elements
In [63]: np.array([[1, 2, 3], [4, 5, 6]]).sum(axis = 0)
Out[63]: array([5, 7, 9])

# Cumulative sum of elements along axis 0
In [64]: np.array([[1, 2, 3], [4, 5, 6]]).cumsum(axis = 0)
Out[64]:
array([[1, 2, 3],
[5, 7, 9]], dtype=int32)

# Cumulative sum of all elements in the array
In [65]: np.array([[1, 2, 3], [4, 5, 6]]).cumsum()
Out[65]: array([ 1, 3, 6, 10, 15, 21], dtype=int32)
```

Statistical operators

A wide range of statistical operations, such as computing mean, median, variance, and standard deviation, can be calculated for NumPy arrays using the available statistical operators. The aggregates, such as mean, median, variance, and standard deviation, for an entire array can be calculated as shown in the following code:

```
In [16]: array_x = np.array([[0, 1, 2], [3, 4, 5]])
In [17]: np.mean(array_x)
Out[17]: 2.5
In [18]: np.median(array_x)
Out[18]: 2.5
In [19]: np.var(array_x)
Out[19]: 2.9166666666666665
In [20]: np.std(array_x)
Out[20]: 1.707825127659933
```

By default, these statistical parameters are computed by flattening out the array. To compute the statistical parameters along any of the axes, the axis argument can be defined when calling these functions. Let's look at this behavior with the mean function as an example:

```
In [27]: np.mean(array_x, axis = 0)
Out[27]: array([1.5, 2.5, 3.5])
In [28]: np.mean(array_x, axis = 1)
Out[28]: array([1., 4.])
```

There are special implementations of these functions to handle arrays with missing values or NAs. These functions are nanmean, nanmedian, nanstd, nanvar:

```
In [30]: nan_array = np.array([[5, 6, np.nan], [19, 3, 2]])

# The regular function returns only nan with a warning
In [31]: np.median(nan_array)
C:\Users \Anaconda3\lib\site-packages\numpy\lib\function_base.py:3250:
RuntimeWarning: Invalid value encountered in median
r = func(a, **kwargs)
Out[31]: nan
In [32]: np.nanmedian(nan_array)
Out[32]: 5.0
```

The corrcoeff and cov functions help compute the Pearson's correlation coefficients and the covariance matrix for a given array or two given arrays:

```
In [35]: array_corr = np.random.randn(3,4)
In [36]: array_corr
Out[36]:
```

```
array([[-2.36657958, -0.43193796, 0.4761051 , -0.11778897],
[ 0.52101041, 1.11562216, 0.61953044, 0.07586606],
[-0.17068701, -0.84382552, 0.86449631, 0.77080463]])
In [37]: np.corrcoef(array_corr)
Out[37]:
array([[ 1. , -0.00394547, 0.48887013],
[-0.00394547, 1. , -0.76641267],
[ 0.48887013, -0.76641267, 1. ]])
In [38]: np.cov(array_corr)
Out[38]:
array([[ 1.51305796, -0.00207053, 0.48931189],
[-0.00207053, 0.18201613, -0.26606154],
[ 0.48931189, -0.26606154, 0.66210821]])
```

Logical operators

The logical operators help compare arrays, check the type and contents of an array, and perform logical comparison between arrays.

The `all` and `any` functions help to evaluate whether all or any values along the specified axis evaluate to `True`. Based on the evaluation result, it returns `True` or `False`:

```
In [39]: array_logical = np.random.randn(3, 4)
In [40]: array_logical
Out[40]:
array([[ 0.79560751, 1.11526762, 1.21139114, -0.36566102],
[ 0.561285 , -1.27640005, 0.28338879, 0.13984101],
[-0.304546 , 1.58540957, 0.1415475 , 1.53267898]])

# Check if any value is negative along each dimension in axis 0
In [42]: np.any(array_logical < 0, axis = 0)
Out[42]: array([ True, True, False, True])

# Check if all the values are negative in the array
In [43]: np.all(array_logical < 0)
Out[43]: False
```

For both the `all` and `any` methods described previously, `axis` is an optional parameter. When it is not provided, the array is flattened and considered for computation.

Some functions test for the presence of NAs or infinite values in the array. Such functionalities are an essential part of data processing and data cleaning. These functions take in an array or array-like object as input and return the truth value as output:

```
In [44]: np.isfinite(np.array([12, np.inf, 3, np.nan]))
Out[44]: array([ True, False, True, False])
```

```
In [45]: np.isnan((np.array([12, np.inf, 3, np.nan])))
Out[45]: array([False, False, False, True])
In [46]: np.isinf((np.array([12, np.inf, 3, np.nan])))
Out[46]: array([False, True, False, False])
```

Operators such as greater, less, and equal help to perform element-to-element comparison between two arrays of identical shape:

```
# Creating two random arrays for comparison
In [50]: array1 = np.random.randn(3,4)
In [51]: array2 = np.random.randn(3, 4)
In [52]: array1
Out[52]:
array([[ 0.80394696, 0.67956857, 0.32560135, 0.64933303],
[-1.78808905, 0.73432929, 0.26363089, -1.47596536],
[ 0.00214663, 1.30853759, -0.11930249, 1.41442395]])
In [54]: array2
Out[54]:
array([[ 0.59876194, -0.33230015, -1.68219462, -1.27662143],
[-0.49655572, 0.43650693, -0.34648415, 0.67175793],
[ 0.1837518 , -0.15162542, 0.04520202, 0.58648728]])

# Checking for the truth of array1 greater than array2
In [55]: np.greater(array1, array2)
Out[55]:
array([[ True, True, True, True],
[False, True, True, False],
[False, True, False, True]])

# Checking for the truth of array1 less than array2
In [56]: np.less(array1, array2)
Out[56]:
array([[False, False, False, False],
[ True, False, False, True],
[ True, False, True, False]])
```

Broadcasting

Using broadcasting, we can work with arrays that don't have exactly the same shape. Here is an example:

```
In [357]: ar=np.ones([3,2]); ar
Out[357]: array([[ 1.,   1.],
                 [ 1.,   1.],
                 [ 1.,   1.]])
In [358]: ar2=np.array([2,3]); ar2
```

```
Out[358]: array([2, 3])
In [359]: ar+ar2
Out[359]: array([[ 3.,   4.],
                 [ 3.,   4.],
                 [ 3.,   4.]])
```

Thus, we can see that `ar2` is broadcast across the rows of `ar` by adding it to each row of `ar`, producing the preceding result. Here is another example, showing that broadcasting works across dimensions:

```
In [369]: ar=np.array([[23,24,25]]); ar
Out[369]: array([[23, 24, 25]])
In [368]: ar.T
Out[368]: array([[23],
                 [24],
                 [25]])
In [370]: ar.T+ar
Out[370]: array([[46, 47, 48],
                 [47, 48, 49],
                 [48, 49, 50]])
```

Here, both row and column arrays were broadcast and we ended up with a 3 × 3 array.

Array shape manipulation

More often than not, data needs to be transformed before it becomes usable in analysis. The same is true for arrays. NumPy has some special sets of functions that help in reshaping and transforming arrays.

Reshaping

The `reshape` function helps to modify the shape of the array. It accepts two main input arguments—the array to be processed and the expected shape as an integer or tuple of integers.

Previously in this chapter, we saw that `np.arange` should rely upon an external function to transform the data from being 1D:

```
In [78]: reshape_array = np.arange(0,15)
In [79]: np.reshape(reshape_array, (5, 3))
Out[79]:
array([[ 0, 1, 2],
 [ 3, 4, 5],
 [ 6, 7, 8],
```

```
[ 9, 10, 11],
[12, 13, 14]]
```

The np.reshape function returns a view of the data, meaning the underlying array remains unchanged. In special cases, however, the shape cannot be changed without the data being copied. For more details on this, see the documentation at http://docs.scipy.org/doc/numpy/reference/generated/numpy.reshape.html.

Transposing

The transpose function reverses the dimensions of an array:

```
In [80]: trans_array = np.arange(0,24).reshape(4, 6)
In [82]: trans_array
Out[82]:
array([[ 0, 1, 2, 3, 4, 5],
[ 6, 7, 8, 9, 10, 11],
[12, 13, 14, 15, 16, 17],
[18, 19, 20, 21, 22, 23]])
In [83]: trans_array.T
Out[83]:
array([[ 0, 6, 12, 18],
[ 1, 7, 13, 19],
[ 2, 8, 14, 20],
[ 3, 9, 15, 21],
[ 4, 10, 16, 22],
[ 5, 11, 17, 23]])
```

The following result is obtained on applying transpose on a multidimensional array:

```
In [84]: trans_array = np.arange(0,24).reshape(2, 3, 4)
In [85]: trans_array.T.shape
Out[85]: (4, 3, 2)
```

Ravel

Ravel helps to flatten the data from multidimensional to 1D:

```
In [86]: ravel_array = np.arange(0,12).reshape(4, 3)
In [87]: ravel_array.ravel()
Out[87]: array([ 0, 1, 2, 3, 4, 5, 6, 7, 8, 9, 10, 11])
```

The order in which the array is raveled can be set. The order can be "C", "F", "A", or "K". "C" is the default order, where the array gets flattened along the row major, while with "F", flattening occurs along the column major. "A" reads the array elements in a Fortran-like index-based order and "K" reads the elements in the order in which they are stored in memory:

```
In [88]: ravel_array.ravel(order = "F")
Out[88]: array([ 0, 3, 6, 9, 1, 4, 7, 10, 2, 5, 8, 11])
```

Adding a new axis

NumPy has the newaxis method to add additional axes to the existing array:

```
# Creating a 1D array with 7 elements
In [98]: array_x = np.array([0, 1, 2, 3, 4, 5, 6])
In [99]: array_x.shape
Out[99]: (7,)

# Adding a new axis changes the 1D array to 2D
In [100]: array_x[:, np.newaxis]
Out[100]:
array([[0],
[1],
[2],
[3],
[4],
[5],
[6]])
In [101]: array_x[:, np.newaxis].shape
Out[101]: (7, 1)

# Adding 2 new axis to the 1D array to make it 3D
In [102]: array_x[:, np.newaxis, np.newaxis]
Out[102]:
array([[[0]],
[[1]],
[[2]],
[[3]],
[[4]],
[[5]],
[[6]]])
In [103]: array_x[:, np.newaxis, np.newaxis].shape
Out[103]: (7, 1, 1)
```

Basic linear algebra operations

Linear algebra constitutes a set of vital operations for matrices and arrays. The NumPy package is built with a special module called `linalg` to deal with all linear algebra requirements. The following segment discusses some frequently used functions of the `linalg` module in detail.

The dot function of the `linalg` module helps in matrix multiplication. For 2D arrays, it behaves exactly like matrix multiplication. It requires the last dimension of the first array to be equal to the last dimension of the second array. The arrays need not have equal numbers of dimensions. For an N-dimensional array, the output will have 2N-2 dimensions:

```
# For 2D arrays
In [23]: array_1 = np.random.randn(2, 4)
In [24]: array_2 = np.random.randn(4, 2)
In [25]: np.dot(array_1, array_2)
Out[25]:
array([[-2.89783151, 5.34861977],
[-0.98078998, -3.47603638]])

# For N dimensional arrays
In [37]: array_1 = np.random.randn(2, 4, 2)
In [38]: array_2 = np.random.randn(1, 1, 2, 1)
In [39]: np.dot(array_1, array_2).shape
Out[39]: (2, 4, 1, 1, 1)
```

The `linalg.multidot` function can help in computing the product of several arrays at once, instead of using a nested sequence of dot functions. This function automatically finds the most efficient order for evaluating the sequence of products.

The `linalg.svd` function helps in singular value decomposition and returns three arrays as the result of decomposition. It accepts an array with two or more dimensions as the input:

```
In [42]: array_svd = np.random.randn(4, 3)
In [43]: np.linalg.svd(array_svd)
Out[43]:
(array([[-0.31366226, 0.27266983, 0.17962633, -0.89162858],
[ 0.72860587, 0.51810374, 0.44793275, -0.00763141],
[-0.59309456, 0.61499855, 0.26103908, 0.44930416],
[-0.13779807, -0.52820115, 0.83603183, 0.05537156]]),
array([1.68668514, 0.91044852, 0.65293131]),
array([[ 0.43322222, 0.10710679, 0.89490035],
[-0.73052453, 0.62326903, 0.27905131],
[-0.52787538, -0.77463789, 0.34825813]]))
```

Eigenvalues and eigenvectors of an array can be calculated with the `linalg.eig` function. The `eig` function requires the last two dimensions of the input array to be a square. The same function returns both the eigenvalues and the eigenvectors:

```
In [50]: np.linalg.eig(np.random.randn(5, 5))
Out[50]:
(array([ 2.52146488+0.j , -2.80191144+0.j ,
0.57756977+0.j , -0.65032217+1.22149327j,
-0.65032217-1.22149327j]),
array([[-0.85628289+0.j , -0.04688595+0.j ,
-0.71887813+0.j , -0.51046122-0.03158232j,
-0.51046122+0.03158232j],
[ 0.15793025+0.j , 0.7517844 +0.j ,
0.45393309+0.j , 0.52887467+0.j ,
0.52887467-0.j ],
[-0.35226803+0.j , 0.33640372+0.j ,
0.51482125+0.j , 0.40554944-0.02802925j,
0.40554944+0.02802925j],
[ 0.08722806+0.j , -0.07904384+0.j ,
-0.03872718+0.j , -0.41252898+0.16212983j,
-0.41252898-0.16212983j],
[ 0.33186767+0.j , 0.55964858+0.j ,
0.10304501+0.j , 0.14346541-0.27643973j,
0.14346541+0.27643973j]]))
```

The `linalg` module also has functions to solve linear equations. The `linalg.solve` function takes in a coefficient matrix and the dependent variable, and solves for the exact solution. It requires that all rows of the coefficient matrix must be linearly independent:

```
In [51]: a = np.array([[1, 2, 3], [5, 4, 2], [8, 9, 7]])
In [52]: b = np.array([6, 19, 47])
In [53]: np.linalg.solve(a, b)
Out[53]: array([-6.27272727, 15.81818182, -6.45454545])
```

If the best possible solution is needed instead of the exact solution, the least-squares solution could be obtained from the `linalg.lstsq` function.

The `linalg.det` function computes the determinant of a square array. If there are more than two dimensions in the input array, it is treated as a stack of matrices and the determinant is computed for each stack. The last two dimensions must, however, correspond to a square matrix:

```
In [55]: np.linalg.det(np.random.randn(3,3))
Out[55]: -0.08292700167707867
In [56]: np.linalg.det(np.random.randn(2,3,3))
Out[56]: array([-0.22575897, 1.47647984])
```

Array sorting

Arrays can be sorted in various ways:

1. Sorting the array along an axis; first, let's discuss this along the *y* axis:

```
In [43]: ar=np.array([[3,2],[10,-1]])
         ar
Out[43]: array([[ 3,  2],
                [10, -1]])
In [44]: ar.sort(axis=1)
         ar
Out[44]: array([[ 2,  3],
                [-1, 10]])
```

2. Here, we will explain the sorting along the *x* axis:

```
In [45]: ar=np.array([[3,2],[10,-1]])
         ar
Out[45]: array([[ 3,  2],
                [10, -1]])
In [46]: ar.sort(axis=0)
         ar
Out[46]: array([[ 3, -1],
                [10,  2]])
```

3. Sorting by in-place (`np.array.sort`) and out-of-place (`np.sort`) functions.
4. Other operations that are available for array sorting include the following:

- `np.min()`: This returns the minimum element in the array
- `np.max()`: This returns the maximum element in the array
- `np.std()`: This returns the standard deviation of the elements in the array
- `np.var()`: This returns the variance of elements in the array
- `np.argmin()`: This returns indices of minimum value in the array
- `np.argmax()`: This returns indices of maximum value in the array
- `np.all()`: This returns elementwise logical 'and' of all the elements
- `np.any()`: This returns elementwise logical 'or' of all the elements

Up to now, we have been getting acquainted with the functionalities of NumPy. In the coming sections, we will look at two practical examples where NumPy arrays are widely used for performing complex computations. After that, we will move on to delving deeper into the core data structures of pandas, such as DataFrames, Series, and Panels—how they are created, modified, and used.

Implementing neural networks with NumPy

While NumPy is definitely not the go-to package for training a neural network in real-time scenarios, learning to implement it in NumPy brings out the flexibility and might of NumPy for doing complex matrix computations and also provides a better understanding of neural networks.

First, let's synthetically generate a dataset for a binary classification problem that will be used for training the neural network. The data will be from two different Gaussian distributions, and the model will be trained to classify this data into either of the two categories. Let's generate the data with 1,000 samples in each category:

```
N = 1000
X1 = np.random.randn(N, 2) + np.array([0.9, 0.9])
X2 = np.random.randn(N, 2) + np.array([-0.9, -0.9])
```

Now we have two 1000 x 2 arrays. For the predictor variable, we can use the `zeros` and `ones` functions to create two different 1D arrays:

```
Y1 = np.zeros((N, 1))
Y2 = np.ones((N, 1))
```

The four arrays—X1, X2, Y1, and Y2—must be stacked together to create the complete training set with dimensions 2000 x 3:

```
X = np.vstack((X1, X2))
Y = np.vstack((Y1, Y2))
train = np.hstack((X, Y))
```

Our aim is to build a simple neural network with one hidden layer and three neurons. For a moment, let's move away from NumPy to understand the architecture of the neural network we will be building from scratch.

The following is a schematic diagram of a simple neural network architecture:

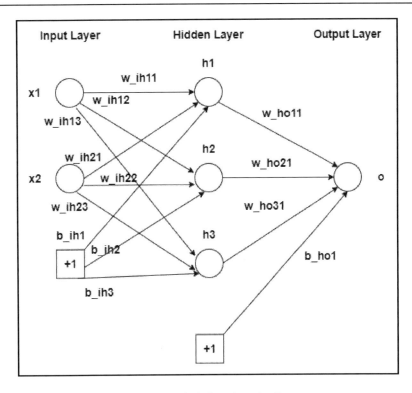

Schematic diagram of a simple neural network architecture

There are two neurons in the input layer, three neurons in the hidden layer, and a single output neuron. The squares represent the bias. To implement the neural network, the independent variables and predictor have been stored in x and t:

```
x = train[:, 0:2]
t = train[:, 2].reshape(2000, 1)
```

As this is a binary classification problem, a sigmoid function would be an ideal choice for the activation function:

```
def sigmoid(x, derive = False):
if (derive == True):
    return x * (1 - x)
    return 1 / (1 + np.exp(-x))
```

The preceding function does the sigmoid transformation and also derivative computation (for backpropagation). The process of training consists of two modes of propagation—feedforward and backpropagation.

The first stage of feedforward is from the input layer to the hidden layer. This stage can be summarized with the following set of equations:

$$ah1 = sigmoid(x1*w\_ih11 + x2*w\_ih21 + 1* b\_ih1)$$

$$ah2 = sigmoid(x1*w\_ih12 + x2*w\_ih22 + 1*b\_ih2)$$

$$ah3 = sigmoid(x1*w\_ih13 + x2*w\_ih23 + 1*b\_ih3)$$

Here, `ah1`, `ah2`, and `ah3` are inputs to the next stage of the feedforward network, from the hidden layer to the output. This involves multiplying the input matrix of dimensions 2000 x 2 and weight matrix `w_ih` of dimensions 2 x 3 (three hidden neurons, hence 3), and then adding the bias. Instead of handling the bias components separately, they could be handled as part of the weight matrix. This can be done by adding a unit column vector to the input matrix and inserting the bias values as the last row of the weight matrix. Hence, the new dimensions of the input matrix and weight matrix would be 2000 x 3 and 3 x 3:

```
x_in = np.concatenate([x, np.repeat([[1]], 2000, axis = 0)], axis = 1)
w_ih = np.random.normal(size = (3, 3))
```

The weight matrix is initialized with random values:

```
y_h = np.dot(x_in, w_ih)
a_h = sigmoid(y_h)
```

Here, a_h is the input matrix for the second stage of feedforward. Just as in the case of input matrix *x*, a_h should be appended with unit column vectors for the bias and the second weight matrix should be initialized:

```
a_hin = np.concatenate([a_h, np.repeat([[1]], 2000, axis = 0)], axis = 1)
w_ho = np.random.normal(size = (4, 1))
```

Now the matrix multiplication and sigmoid transformation can be done for this stage:

```
y_o = np.dot(a_hin, w_ho)
a_o = sigmoid(y_o)
```

For simplicity's sake, let's use mean squared error as the loss function, though it would be more appropriate to use a log loss function for a classification problem:

$$E = ((1 / 2) * (np.power((a\_o - t), 2)))$$

This marks the end of feedforward and the beginning of backpropagation. Backpropagation aims to find the delta or difference to be made to the weights and biases for the error E to reduce. The entire process of backpropagation can be summarized in the following two equations.

The first one calculates the change in loss function E w.r.t w_ho and the second one calculates the change in loss function E w.r.t w_ih:

$$\frac{\partial E}{\partial w\_ho} = \frac{\partial E}{\partial a\_o} * \frac{\partial a\_o}{\partial y\_o} * \frac{\partial y\_o}{\partial w\_ho}$$

$$\frac{\partial E}{\partial w\_ih} = \frac{\partial E}{\partial a\_h} * \frac{\partial a\_h}{\partial y\_h} * \frac{\partial y\_h}{\partial w\_ih}$$

Now, the implementation of these equations in NumPy is as simple as computing all the derivatives necessary and finding the corresponding products:

```
# Output layer
delta_a_o_error = a_o - t
delta_y_o = sigmoid(a_o, derive=True)
delta_w_ho = a_hin
delta_output_layer = np.dot(delta_w_ho.T,(delta_a_o_error * delta_y_o))

# Hidden layer
delta_a_h = np.dot(delta_a_o_error * delta_y_o, w_ho[0:3,:].T)
delta_y_h = sigmoid(a_h, derive=True)
delta_w_ih = x_in
delta_hidden_layer = np.dot(delta_w_ih.T, delta_a_h * delta_y_h)
```

The change to be made to the weight has been computed. Let's use these delta values to update the weights:

```
eta = 0.1
w_ih = w_ih - eta * delta_hidden_layer
w_ho = w_ho - eta * delta_output_layer
```

Here, `eta` is the learning rate of the model. Feedforward will take place again using the updated weights. Backpropagation will again follow to reduce the error. Hence, feedforward and backpropagation should take place iteratively for a set number of epochs. The complete code is as follows:

```
### Neural Network with one hidden layer with feedforward and
backpropagation
x = train[:,0:2]
t = train[:,2].reshape(2000,1)
x_in = np.concatenate([x, np.repeat([[1]], 2000, axis = 0)], axis = 1)
w_ih = np.random.normal(size = (3, 3))
w_ho = np.random.normal(size = (4, 1))
def sigmoid(x, derive = False):
if (derive == True):
return x * (1 - x)
return 1 / (1 + np.exp(-x))
epochs = 5000
eta = 0.1

for epoch in range(epochs):
# Feed forward
    y_h = np.dot(x_in, w_ih)
    a_h = sigmoid(y_h)
    a_hin = np.concatenate([a_h, np.repeat([[1]], 2000, axis = 0)],
axis = 1)
    y_o = np.dot(a_hin, w_ho)
    a_o = sigmoid(y_o)

    # Calculate the error
    a_o_error = ((1 / 2) * (np.power((a_o - t), 2)))

    # Backpropagation
    ## Output layer
    delta_a_o_error = a_o - t
    delta_y_o = sigmoid(a_o, derive=True)
    delta_w_ho = a_hin
    delta_output_layer = np.dot(delta_w_ho.T, (delta_a_o_error * delta_y_o))

    ## Hidden layer
    delta_a_h = np.dot(delta_a_o_error * delta_y_o, w_ho[0:3,:].T)
    delta_y_h = sigmoid(a_h, derive=True)
    delta_w_ih = x_in
    delta_hidden_layer = np.dot(delta_w_ih.T, delta_a_h * delta_y_h)
    w_ih = w_ih - eta * delta_hidden_layer
    w_ho = w_ho - eta * delta_output_layer
    print(a_o_error.mean())
```

The neural network has been implemented for 5,000 epochs. This is a simple yet efficient model quite suitable for a range of problems. Good accuracy can be obtained by choosing the right epoch, learning rate, loss function, and activation function. To test and validate, make use of just the feedforward module.

Practical applications of multidimensional arrays

Panel data (spreadsheet-like data with several distinguishable rows and columns; the kind of data we generally encounter) is best handled by the DataFrame data structure available in pandas and R. Arrays can be used too but it would be tedious.

So what is a good example of data in real life that can be best represented by an array? Images, which are generally represented as multidimensional arrays of pixels, are a good example. In this section, we will see examples of multidimensional representation of an image and why it makes sense.

Any object detection or image-processing algorithm performed on an image requires it to be represented in a numerical array format. For text data, term-document matrix and **term frequency-inverse document frequency (TF-IDF)** are used to vectorize (create numerical arrays) the data. In the case of an image, pixel values are used to represent an image.

For a 100 x 50 pixel RGB image, there would be the following:

- 5,000 pixel values in one channel
- Three channels each for red, blue, and green

Hence, if you flatten the image pixels as one single vector, its length would be 15,000 (5,000 for each of the three channels). A grayscale image would contain a single channel. Each pixel value represents the degree of brightness for each channel.

A dataset of multiple images then becomes four-dimensional data representing the following:

- Width of the image in pixels
- Height of the image in pixels
- Number of channels
- Serial number of the image

Let's verify the shape of the resultant image pixel arrays by reading an image. To work with images, a Python package called **opencv** (cv2) is quite helpful:

```
# reading images using opencv package
import cv2
import matplotlib.pyplot as plt
import os
os.chdir('')
img=cv2.imread('view.jpg')
img2=cv2.imread('rose.jpg')
```

The imread method returns an array of pixels. Let's check the object type of the returned object img:

```
print(type(img))
```

This returns <class 'numpy.ndarray'>, which confirms that it returns a numpy array.

Next, let's have a look at the shape of the array. It should return us the pixel width, pixel height, and number of channels:

```
img.shape
```

This returns (183, 275, 3).

It is a tuple of three numbers representing image height in pixels, image width in pixels, and number of channels. Hence, this image has a height of 183 pixels, a width of 275 pixels, and three channels of the dimension 183 x 275 representing red, blue, and green.

The img object looks as follows on printing:

```
array([[[110,   65,    0],
        [111,   66,    0],
        [111,   66,    0],
        ...,
        [ 64,   27,    1],
        [ 64,   27,    1],
        [ 64,   27,    1]],

       [[111,   66,    0],
        [111,   66,    0],
        [111,   66,    0],
        ...,
        [ 65,   28,    0],
        [ 65,   28,    0],
        [ 65,   28,    0]],

       [[111,   66,    0],
        [111,   66,    0],
        [111,   66,    0],
        ...,
        [ 67,   28,    0],
        [ 67,   28,    0],
        [ 67,   28,    0]],

       ...,

       [[  0,   11,    0],
        [  0,   15,    0],
        [  0,   28,    0],
        ...,
```

Image pixels as a multidimensional array

Now the question arises, why would someone want to subset an array of image pixels? There can be multiple reasons for that:

- Selecting and/or manipulating a region of interest in the image. This can be a small block of the image representing an object.
- Selecting only one color channel from the image.

The array of pixels can be seen as a plot/image with pixel height and pixel width as the axes labels as shown in the following code:

```
plt.imshow(img)
```

Take a look at the following output:

Image pixel arrays plotted as an image

Selecting only one channel

As we saw earlier, the third dimension denotes the RGB channel. Hence, to filter all the pixels in one channel, we should select all the pixels in the first two dimensions and only the channel of interest. Also, the indexing in Python starts from 0, thus 0 represents red, 1 represents green, and 2 represents blue. Keeping these in mind, let's have a look at the snippets to select the red, green, and blue channels of an image.

The snippet to select the red is as follows:

```
img_r=img[:,:,0]
plt.imshow(img_r)
```

The following is the output:

Image pixel array made of selecting only pixels in the red channel visualized as an image

The snippet to select the green is as follows:

```
img_g=img[:,:,1]
plt.imshow(img_g)
```

The following is the output:

Image pixel array made of selecting only pixels in the green channel visualized as an image

The snippet to select the blue is as follows:

```
img_b=img[:,:,2]
plt.imshow(img_b)
```

The following is the output:

Image pixel array made of selecting only pixels in the blue channel visualized as an image

Selecting the region of interest of an image

Let's try to select the tree in the preceding screenshot. Looking at the image with axis labels, it is evident that vertical bounds of the tree are within 50 to 155 pixels while horizontal bounds are within 95 to 190 pixels. Let's try to subset this region with all the channels:

```
img_tree=img[50:155,95:190,:]
plt.imshow(img_tree)
```

The following image shows us the **region of interest (ROI)** that is selected therein:

Selecting an ROI in an image

This operation is akin to cropping an image.

The pixel values of a certain ROI or a channel can be assigned some different values. This can be used to do the following:

- Remove certain channels (if we replace the values in that channel with 0)
- Copy and paste a certain ROI to another part of the image

The following code shows an example of the latter case:

```
img3=img
img3[50:155,1:96,:]=img_tree
plt.imshow(img3)
```

The following image shows the selected ROI that is being pasted to another image area:

Pasting a selected ROI to another image area

In this example, we have copied the tree ROI and pasted it to an area to the left of the selected ROI. This has been obtained by assigning the pixels of the pasting destination values equal to the pixel value of the copy source.

Multiple channel selection and suppressing other channels

To show pixels of only a certain color, the pixels of other colors need to be suppressed or assigned a value of 0. The channel selection can happen via indexing or by passing a list:

- **Indexing**: Keep in mind that, while indexing, the value to the right of the colon represents the higher limit of the channel. It also counts up to *n*-1. For example, `img[:,:,1:3]` will select channels up to channel 2, namely blue, starting from channel 1, namely green, but not channel 0, namely red. The snippet `img[:,:,0:2]` will select channel 0 (red channel) and channel 1 (green) but not channel 2 (blue).
- **List**: A list such as [0,2] would mean selecting channels 0 and 2, namely red and blue.

In the following example, we suppress the non-red, non-green, and non-blue pixels so that the resultant pixels appear red, green, and blue respectively:

```
fig, axes = plt.subplots(1, 3)

# Red Channel
imgR = img.copy()
imgR[:, :, 1:3] = 0 # Assigning Green and Blue channel pixels to 0
axes[0].imshow(imgR)

# Green Channel
imgG = img.copy()
imgG[:, :, [0,2]] = 0 # Assigning Red and Blue channel pixels to 0
axes[1].imshow(imgG)

# Blue Channel
imgB = img.copy()
imgB[:, :, 0:2] = 0 0 # Assigning Red and Green channel pixels to 0
axes[2].imshow(imgB)
```

The following is the output:

Panel showing image obtained by suppressing the two channels so that it shows only the third color (green and blue, red and blue, and red and green respectively are suppressed in the three images from left to right)

Audio data can also be represented as arrays of pressure readings across a horizontal distance. Similar array manipulation techniques can be used there.

Data structures in pandas

The pandas package was created by Wes McKinney in 2008 as a result of frustrations he encountered while working on time series data in R. It is built on top of NumPy and provides features not available in it. It provides fast, easy-to-understand data structures and helps fill the gap between Python and a language like R. NumPy deals with homogeneous blocks of data. Using pandas helps to deal with data in a tabular structure composed of different data types.

The official documentation for pandas can be found at `http://pandas.pydata.org/` `pandas-docs/stable/dsintro.html`.

There are three main data structures in pandas:

- Series—1D
- DataFrame—2D
- Panel—3D

Series

A Series is really a 1D NumPy array under the hood. It consists of a NumPy array coupled with an array of labels. Just like a NumPy array, a series can be wholly composed of any data type. The labels are together called the index of the series. A series consists of two components—1D data and the index.

Series creation

The general construct for creating a series data structure is as follows:

```
import pandas as pd
ser = pd.Series(data, index = idx)
```

Here, data can be one of the following:

- An `ndarray`
- A Python dictionary
- A scalar value

If an index is not specified, the following default index [0,... n-1] will be created, where n is the length of the data.

A series can be created from a variety of sources as shown in the following subsections.

Using an ndarray

In this case, the index must be the same length as the data. The following example creates a Series structure of seven random numbers between 0 and 1; the index is not specified:

```
In [4]: ser = pd.Series(np.random.randn(7))
In [5]: ser
```

```
Out[5]:
0 3.063921
1 0.097450
2 -1.660367
3 -1.221308
4 -0.948873
5 0.454462
6 0.586824
dtype: float64
```

An index can also be string objects. The following example creates a Series structure of the first five months of the year with a specified index of month names:

```
In [6]: import calendar as cal
In [7]: monthNames=[cal.month_name[i] for i in np.arange(1,6)]
In [8]: months = pd.Series(np.arange(1,6), index = monthNames)
In [10]: months
Out[10]:
January 1
February 2
March 3
April 4
May 5
dtype: int32
In [11]: months.index
Out[11]: Index(['January', 'February', 'March', 'April', 'May'],
dtype='object')
```

Using a Python dictionary

A dictionary consists of key-value pairs. When a dictionary is used to create a Series, the keys form the index, and the values form the 1D data of the Series:

```
In [12]: currDict={'US' : 'dollar', 'UK' : 'pound', 'Germany': 'euro',
'Mexico':'peso', 'Nigeria':'naira', 'China':'yuan', 'Japan':'yen'}
In [13]: currSeries = pd.Series(currDict)
In [14]: currSeries
Out[14]:
US dollar
UK pound
Germany euro
Mexico peso
Nigeria naira
China yuan
Japan yen
dtype: object
```

The index of a pandas Series structure is of type `pandas.core.index.Index` and can be viewed as an ordered multiset.

If an index is also specified when creating the Series, then this specified index setting overrides the dictionary keys. If the specified index contains values that are not keys in the original dictionary, NaN is appended against that index in the Series:

```
In [18]: stockPrices = {'GOOG':1180.97, 'FB':62.57, 'TWTR': 64.50,
'AMZN':358.69, 'AAPL':500.6}
# "YHOO" is not a key in the above dictionary
In [19]: stockPriceSeries = pd.Series(stockPrices,
index=['GOOG','FB','YHOO','TWTR','AMZN','AAPL'], name='stockPrices')
In [20]: stockPriceSeries
Out[20]:
GOOG 1180.97
FB 62.57
YHOO NaN
TWTR 64.50
AMZN 358.69
AAPL 500.60
Name: stockPrices, dtype: float64
```

Note that a Series also has a name attribute that can be set as shown in the preceding snippet. The name attribute is useful in tasks such as combining Series objects into a DataFrame structure.

Using a scalar value

A Series can also be initialized with just a scalar value. For scalar data, an index must be provided. The value will be repeated for as many index values as possible. One possible use of this method is to provide a quick and dirty method of initialization, with the Series structure to be filled in later. Let's see how to create a Series using scalar values:

```
In [21]: dogSeries=pd.Series('chihuahua', index=['breed',
'countryOfOrigin', 'name', 'gender'])
In [22]: dogSeries = pd.Series('chihuahua', index=['breed',
'countryOfOrigin', 'name', 'gender'])
In [23]: dogSeries
Out[23]:
breed chihuahua
countryOfOrigin chihuahua
name chihuahua
gender chihuahua
dtype: object
```

Operations on Series

The behavior of a Series is very similar to that of NumPy arrays, discussed previously in this chapter, with one caveat being that an operation such as slicing also slices the index of the series.

Assignment

Values can be set and accessed using the index label in a dictionary-like manner:

```
# Accessing value from series using index label
In [26]: currDict['China']
Out[26]: 'yuan'

# Assigning value to series through a new index label
In [27]: stockPriceSeries['GOOG'] = 1200.0
In [28]: stockPriceSeries
Out[28]:
GOOG 1200.00
FB 62.57
YHOO NaN
TWTR 64.50
AMZN 358.69
AAPL 500.60
Name: stockPrices, dtype: float64
```

Just as in the case of `dict`, `KeyError` is raised if you try to retrieve a missing label:

```
In [29]: stockPriceSeries['MSFT']
KeyError: 'MSFT'
```

This error can be avoided by explicitly using `get` as follows:

```
In [30]: stockPriceSeries.get('MSFT, np.NaN)
Out[30]: nan
```

In this case, the default value of `np.NaN` is specified as the value to return when the key does not exist in the Series structure.

Slicing

The slice operation behaves the same way as a NumPy array. Slicing can be done using the index numbers as shown in the following code:

```
# Slice till the 4th index (0 to 3)
In [31]: stockPriceSeries[:4]
```

```
Out[31]:
GOOG 1200.00
FB 62.57
YHOO NaN
TWTR 64.50
Name: stockPrices, dtype: float64
Logical slicing also works as follows:
In [32]: stockPriceSeries[stockPriceSeries > 100]
Out[32]:
GOOG 1200.00
AMZN 358.69
AAPL 500.60
Name: stockPrices, dtype: float64
```

Other operations

Arithmetic and statistical operations can be applied, just like for a NumPy array. Such operations take place in a vectorized mode in a Series, just as in NumPy arrays, and do not require to be looped through:

```
# Mean of entire series
In [34]: np.mean(stockPriceSeries)
Out[34]: 437.27200000000005

# Standard deviation of entire series
In [35]: np.std(stockPriceSeries)
Out[35]: 417.4446361087899
```

Elementwise operations can also be performed on a Series:

```
In [36]: ser
Out[36]:
0 3.063921
1 0.097450
2 -1.660367
3 -1.221308
4 -0.948873
5 0.454462
6 0.586824
dtype: float64

In [37]: ser * ser
Out[37]:
0 9.387611
1 0.009496
2 2.756819
3 1.491593
```

```
4 0.900359
5 0.206535
6 0.344362
dtype: float64
```

An important feature of a Series is that data is automatically aligned based on the label:

```
In [40]: ser[1:]
Out[40]:
1 0.097450
2 -1.660367
3 -1.221308
4 -0.948873
5 0.454462
6 0.586824
dtype: float64
In [41]: ser[1:] + ser[:-2]
Out[41]:
0 NaN
1 0.194899
2 -3.320734
3 -2.442616
4 -1.897745
5 NaN
6 NaN
dtype: float64
```

Thus, we can see that for non-matching labels, NaN is inserted. The default behavior is that the union of the indexes is produced for unaligned Series structures. This is preferable as information is preserved rather than lost. We will handle missing values in pandas in a later chapter of the book.

DataFrames

A DataFrame is a two-dimensional data structure composed of rows and columns—exactly like a simple spreadsheet or a SQL table. Each column of a DataFrame is a pandas Series. These columns should be of the same length, but they can be of different data types—float, int, bool, and so on. DataFrames are both value-mutable and size-mutable. This lets us perform operations that would alter values held within the DataFrame or add/delete columns to/from the DataFrame.

Similar to a Series, which has a name and index as attributes, a DataFrame has column names and a row index. The row index can be made of either numerical values or strings such as month names. Indexes are needed for fast lookups as well as proper aligning and joining of data in pandas multilevel indexing is also possible in DataFrames. The following is a simple view of a DataFrame with five rows and three columns. In general, the index is not counted as a column:

Index	Event type	Total attendees	Percentage of student participants
Monday	C	42	23.56%
Tuesday	B	58	12.89%
Wednesday	A	27	45.90%
Thursday	A	78	47.89%
Friday	B	92	63.25%

DataFrame creation

A DataFrame is the most commonly used data structure in pandas. The constructor accepts many different types of arguments:

- Dictionary of 1D ndarrays, lists, dictionaries, or Series structures
- 2D NumPy array
- Structured or record ndarray
- Series
- Another DataFrame

Row label indexes and column labels can be specified along with the data. If they're not specified, they will be generated from the input data in an intuitive fashion, for example, from the keys of `dict` (in the case of column labels) or by using `np.range(n)` in the case of row labels, where n corresponds to the number of rows.

A DataFrame can be created from a variety of sources as discussed in the following subsections.

Using a dictionary of Series

Each individual entity of a dictionary is a key-value pair. A DataFrame is, in essence, a dictionary of several Series put together. The name of the Series corresponds to the key, and the contents of the Series correspond to the value.

As the first step, the dictionary with all the Series should be defined:

```
stockSummaries = {
'AMZN': pd.Series([346.15,0.59,459,0.52,589.8,158.88],
```

```
index=['Closing price','EPS',
'Shares Outstanding(M)',
'Beta', 'P/E','Market Cap(B)']),
'GOOG': pd.Series([1133.43,36.05,335.83,0.87,31.44,380.64],
index=['Closing price','EPS','Shares Outstanding(M)',
'Beta','P/E','Market Cap(B)']),
'FB': pd.Series([61.48,0.59,2450,104.93,150.92],
index=['Closing price','EPS','Shares Outstanding(M)',
'P/E', 'Market Cap(B)']),
'YHOO': pd.Series([34.90,1.27,1010,27.48,0.66,35.36],
index=['Closing price','EPS','Shares Outstanding(M)',
'P/E','Beta', 'Market Cap(B)']),
'TWTR':pd.Series([65.25,-0.3,555.2,36.23],
index=['Closing price','EPS','Shares Outstanding(M)',
'Market Cap(B)']),
'AAPL':pd.Series([501.53,40.32,892.45,12.44,447.59,0.84],
index=['Closing price','EPS','Shares Outstanding(M)','P/E',
'Market Cap(B)','Beta'])}
```

The preceding dictionary summarizes the performance of six different stocks and indicates that the DataFrame will have six columns. Observe that each series has a different set of indices and is of different length. The final DataFrame will contain a unique set of the values in each of the indices. If a certain column has no value at a row index, NA is appended to that cell automatically. Now, the following step wraps up this dictionary into a DataFrame:

```
stockDF = pd.DataFrame(stockSummaries)
```

Let's print the DataFrame created in the preceding step:

	AMZN	GOOG	FB	YHOO	TWTR	AAPL
Beta	0.52	0.87	NaN	0.66	NaN	0.84
Closing price	346.15	1133.43	61.48	34.90	65.25	501.53
EPS	0.59	36.05	0.59	1.27	-0.30	40.32
Market Cap(B)	158.88	380.64	150.92	35.36	36.23	447.59
P/E	589.80	31.44	104.93	27.48	NaN	12.44
Shares Outstanding(M)	NaN	335.83	NaN	NaN	NaN	NaN
Shares Outstanding(M)	459.00	NaN	2450.00	1010.00	555.20	892.45

The DataFrame need not necessarily have all the row and column labels from the original dictionary. At times, only a subset of these rows and columns may be needed. In such cases, the row and column indices can be restricted as shown in the following code:

```
stockDF = pd.DataFrame(stockSummaries,
index=['Closing price','EPS',
'Shares Outstanding(M)',
'P/E', 'Market Cap(B)','Beta'],
columns=['FB','TWTR','SCNW'])
```

Here, a new column name, SCNW, which is not found in the original dictionary, has been added. This will result in a column named SCNW with NAs throughout. Similarly, manually passing an index name that is absent in the original data structure will result in a row with NAs throughout.

Let's print the preceding DataFrame:

	FB	TWTR	SCNW
Closing price	61.48	65.25	NaN
EPS	0.59	-0.30	NaN
Shares Outstanding(M)	2450.00	555.20	NaN
P/E	104.93	NaN	NaN
Market Cap(B)	150.92	36.23	NaN
Beta	NaN	NaN	NaN

The row index and column names can be accessed as attributes of the DataFrame:

```
In [47]: stockDF.index
Out[47]:
Index(['Closing price', 'EPS', 'Shares Outstanding(M)', 'P/E', 'Market
Cap(B)',
'Beta'],
dtype='object')
In [48]: stockDF.columns
Out[48]: Index(['FB', 'TWTR', 'SCNW'], dtype='object')
```

Using a dictionary of ndarrays/lists

In the preceding example, the dictionary consisted of Series as the values in the key-value pair. It is possible to construct a DataFrame with a dictionary of lists instead of a dictionary of Series. Unlike the previous case, the row index will not be defined anywhere in the dictionary. Hence, the row label indices are generated using `np.range(n)`. Therefore, it is crucial in this case for all lists or arrays in the dictionary to be of equal length. If this condition is not met, an error occurs.

The dictionary of lists is defined in the following code:

```
algos = {'search': ['DFS','BFS','Binary Search',
'Linear','ShortestPath (Djikstra)'],
'sorting': ['Quicksort','Mergesort', 'Heapsort',
'Bubble Sort', 'Insertion Sort'],
'machine learning': ['RandomForest', 'K Nearest Neighbor',
'Logistic Regression', ''K-Means Clustering', 'Linear Regression']}
```

Now, let's convert this dictionary to a DataFrame and print it:

```
algoDF = pd.DataFrame(algos)
```

Take a look at the following output:

	search	sorting	machine learning
0	DFS	Quicksort	RandomForest
1	BFS	Mergesort	K Nearest Neighbor
2	Binary Search	Heapsort	Logistic Regression
3	Linear	Bubble Sort	K-Means Clustering
4	ShortestPath (Djikstra)	Insertion Sort	Linear Regression

Here, the row indices are assigned continuous values from 0 to 4. The row indices can also be given custom values as shown in the following code:

```
pd.DataFrame(algos,index=['algo_1','algo_2','algo_3','algo_4','algo_5'])
```

Take a look at the following output:

	search	sorting	machine learning
algo_1	DFS	Quicksort	RandomForest
algo_2	BFS	Mergesort	K Nearest Neighbor
algo_3	Binary Search	Heapsort	Logistic Regression
algo_4	Linear	Bubble Sort	K-Means Clustering
algo_5	ShortestPath (Djikstra)	Insertion Sort	Linear Regression

Using a structured array

Structured arrays are slightly different from `ndarrays`. Each field in a structured array can be of a different data type. For more information on structured arrays, refer to the following: `http://docs.scipy.org/doc/numpy/user/basics.rec.html`.

The following is an example of a structured array:

```
memberData = np.array([('Sanjeev',37,162.4),
('Yingluck',45,137.8),
('Emeka',28,153.2),
('Amy',67,101.3)],
dtype = [('Name','a15'),
('Age','i4'),
('Weight','f4')])
```

This structured array has three fields for which the data types have been defined in a list of tuples along with the field names. The same `DataFrame` function can be used to construct a `DataFrame` function from a structured array:

```
memberDF = pd.DataFrame(memberData)
```

Take a look at the following output:

	Name	Age	Weight
0	b'Sanjeev'	37	162.399994
1	b'Yingluck'	45	137.800003
2	b'Emeka'	28	153.199997
3	b'Amy'	67	101.300003

By default, continuous range of integral values have been assigned to the index. It is possible to replace the indices:

```
pd.DataFrame(memberData, index=['a','b','c','d'])
```

Take a look at the following output:

	Name	Age	Weight
a	b'Sanjeev'	37	162.399994
b	b'Yingluck'	45	137.800003
c	b'Emeka'	28	153.199997
d	b'Amy'	67	101.300003

The columns can be reordered through the `columns` argument of the `DataFrame` function:

```
pd.DataFrame(memberData, columns = ["Weight", "Name", "Age"])
```

Take a look at the following output:

	Weight	Name	Age
0	162.399994	b'Sanjeev'	37
1	137.800003	b'Yingluck'	45
2	153.199997	b'Emeka'	28
3	101.300003	b'Amy'	67

Using a list of dictionaries

When a list of dictionaries is converted to a DataFrame, each dictionary in the list corresponds to a row in the DataFrame and each key in each dictionary represents a column label.

Let's define a list of dictionaries:

```
demographicData = [{"Age": 32, "Gender": "Male"}, {"Race": "Hispanic",
"Gender": "Female", "Age": 26}]
```

Now the list of dictionaries can be converted to a DataFrame as shown in the following code:

```
demographicDF = pd.DataFrame(demographicData)
```

The following is the output:

	Age	Gender	Race
0	32	Male	NaN
1	26	Female	Hispanic

Using a dictionary of tuples for multilevel indexing

A dictionary of tuples can create a structured DataFrame with hierarchically indexed rows and columns. The following is a dictionary of tuples:

```
salesData = {("2012", "Q1"): {("North", "Brand A"): 100, ("North", "Brand
B"): 80, ("South", "Brand A"): 25, ("South", "Brand B"): 40},
("2012", "Q2"): {("North", "Brand A"): 30, ("South", "Brand B"): 50},
("2013", "Q1"): {("North", "Brand A"): 80, ("North", "Brand B"): 10,
("South", "Brand B"): 25},
("2013", "Q2"): {("North", "Brand A"): 70, ("North", "Brand B"): 50,
("South", "Brand A"): 35, ("South", "Brand B"): 40}}
```

Instead of a regular key-value pair, the key is a tuple with two values denoting two levels in the row index, and the value is a dictionary in which each key-value pair represents a column. Here, again, the key is a tuple and denotes two column indices.

Now this dictionary of tuples can be converted to a DataFrame and printed:

```
salesDF = pd.DataFrame(salesData)
```

The following is the output:

		2012		2013	
		Q1	Q2	Q1	Q2
North	Brand A	100	30.0	80.0	70
	Brand B	80	NaN	10.0	50
South	Brand A	25	NaN	NaN	35
	Brand B	40	50.0	25.0	40

Using a Series

Consider the following series:

```
In [12]: currDict={'US' : 'dollar', 'UK' : 'pound', 'Germany': 'euro',
'Mexico':'peso', 'Nigeria':'naira', 'China':'yuan', 'Japan':'yen'}
In [13]: currSeries = pd.Series(currDict)
Out[13]:
US dollar
UK pound
Germany euro
Mexico peso
Nigeria naira
China yuan
Japan yen
Name: Currency, dtype: object
```

Here, the series has a defined index and name. When being converted to a DataFrame, this index is retained and the name of the Series gets assigned as a column name:

```
currDF = pd.DataFrame(currSeries)
```

The following is the output:

	Currency
US	dollar
UK	pound
Germany	euro
Mexico	peso
Nigeria	naira
China	yuan
Japan	yen

There are also alternative constructors for DataFrames; they can be summarized as follows:

- `DataFrame.from_dict`: It takes a dictionary of dictionaries or sequences and returns a DataFrame. It slightly differs from the method discussed earlier due to an argument to specify order. While the other method always converts keys of dictionaries to columns, this constructor provides an option to convert the keys to row labels:

```
# Default setting
pd.DataFrame.from_dict(algos, orient = "columns")
```

The following is the output:

	search	sorting	machine learning
0	DFS	Quicksort	RandomForest
1	BFS	Mergesort	K Nearest Neighbor
2	Binary Search	Heapsort	Logistic Regression
3	Linear	Bubble Sort	K-Means Clustering
4	ShortestPath (Djikstra)	Insertion Sort	Linear Regression

Another method to do this is as follows:

```
pd.DataFrame.from_dict(algos, orient = "index", columns = ["A",
"B", "C", "D", "E"])
```

The following is the output:

	A	B	C	D	E
search	DFS	BFS	Binary Search	Linear	ShortestPath (Djikstra)
sorting	Quicksort	Mergesort	Heapsort	Bubble Sort	Insertion Sort
machine learning	RandomForest	K Nearest Neighbor	Logistic Regression	K-Means Clustering	Linear Regression

- `DataFrame.from_records`: It takes a list of tuples or structured `ndarray` to construct a DataFrame. Unlike the method mentioned earlier for structured arrays, this function allows you to set one of the fields of the array as an index:

```
pd.DataFrame.from_records(memberData, index="Name")
```

The following is the output:

Name	Age	Weight
b'Sanjeev'	37	162.399994
b'Yingluck'	45	137.800003
b'Emeka'	28	153.199997
b'Amy'	67	101.300003

Operations on pandas DataFrames

Many operations, such as column/row indexing, assignment, concatenation, deletion, and so on, can be performed on DataFrames. Let's have a look at them in the following subsections.

Column selection

A specific column can be selected out from the DataFrame, as a Series, using the column name:

```
In [60]: memberDF["Name"]
Out[60]:
0 b'Sanjeev'
1 b'Yingluck'
2 b'Emeka'
3 b'Amy'
Name: Name, dtype: object
```

Adding a new column

A new column can be added to a DataFrame by inserting a scalar value into it. Inserting a scalar value into any column of a DataFrame will cause the entire column to be filled with that scalar value:

```
In [61]: memberDF['Height'] = 60
In [62]: memberDF
```

The following is the output:

	Name	Age	Weight	Height
0	b'Sanjeev'	37	162.399994	60
1	b'Yingluck'	45	137.800003	60
2	b'Emeka'	28	153.199997	60
3	b'Amy'	67	101.300003	60

Instead of a scalar value, a list of values can also be assigned:

```
In [63]: memberDF['Height2'] = [57, 62, 65, 59]
In [64]: memberDF
```

The following is the output:

	Name	Age	Weight	Height	Height2
0	b'Sanjeev'	37	162.399994	60	57
1	b'Yingluck'	45	137.800003	60	62
2	b'Emeka'	28	153.199997	60	65
3	b'Amy'	67	101.300003	60	59

A column can also be inserted at the desired position using the `insert` method. This needs three arguments: the position in which the column is to be inserted, the new column name, and the values to be passed:

```
In [65]: memberDF.insert(1, "ID", ["S01", "S02", "S03", "S04"])
In [66]: memberDF
```

The following is the output:

	Name	ID	Age	Weight	Height	Height2
0	b'Sanjeev'	S01	37	162.399994	60	57
1	b'Yingluck'	S02	45	137.800003	60	62
2	b'Emeka'	S03	28	153.199997	60	65
3	b'Amy'	S04	67	101.300003	60	59

Deleting columns

The `del` command can be used to delete a single column as shown in the following code:

```
In [67]: del memberDF["Height"]
In [68]: memberDF
```

The following is the output:

	Name	ID	Age	Weight	Height2
0	b'Sanjeev'	S01	37	162.399994	57
1	b'Yingluck'	S02	45	137.800003	62
2	b'Emeka'	S03	28	153.199997	65
3	b'Amy'	S04	67	101.300003	59

Instead of `del`, the `pop` method can be used, just like in dictionaries:

```
In [65]: height2 = memberDF.pop("Height2")
In [66]: memberDF
```

The following is the output:

	Name	ID	Age	Weight
0	b'Sanjeev'	S01	37	162.399994
1	b'Yingluck'	S02	45	137.800003
2	b'Emeka'	S03	28	153.199997
3	b'Amy'	S04	67	101.300003

Alignment of DataFrames

The union of two DataFrames occurs based on row and column indices. Let's understand this through an example. Consider two DataFrames:

```
ore1DF=pd.DataFrame(np.array([[20,35,25,20],
[11,28,32,29]]),
```

```
columns=['iron','magnesium',
'copper','silver'])
ore2DF=pd.DataFrame(np.array([[14,34,26,26],
[33,19,25,23]]),
columns=['iron','magnesium',
'gold','silver'])
```

The + operator will add values in columns with the same labels in both DataFrames:

```
ore1DF + ore2DF
```

The following is the output:

	copper	gold	iron	magnesium	silver
0	NaN	NaN	34	69	46
1	NaN	NaN	44	47	52

The columns—copper and gold—were not found in both the DataFrames. Hence, NA has been appended in these columns.

If you combine a DataFrame object and a Series object, the default behavior is to broadcast the Series object across the rows:

```
ore1DF + pd.Series([25,25,25,25], index=['iron', 'magnesium', 'copper',
'silver'])
```

The following is the output:

	iron	magnesium	copper	silver
0	45	60	50	45
1	36	53	57	54

Other mathematical operations

The basic mathematical operators work on DataFrames. For example, a new column can be obtained as a result of adding, multiplying, subtracting, or dividing two columns:

```
In [67]: ore1DF["add_iron_copper"] = ore1DF["iron"] + ore1DF["copper"]
```

The following is the output:

	iron	magnesium	copper	silver	add_iron_copper
0	20	35	25	20	45
1	11	28	32	29	43

Logical operators such as | (or), & (and), and ^ (not) work on DataFrames. Consider the following two DataFrames:

```
logical_df1 = pd.DataFrame({'Col1' : [1, 0, 1], 'Col2' : [0, 1, 1] },
dtype=bool)
logical_df2 = pd.DataFrame({'Col1' : [1, 0, 0], 'Col2' : [0, 0, 1] },
dtype=bool)
```

Now, performing the logical or between these two columns yields the following result:

```
logical_df1 | logical_df2
```

The following is the output:

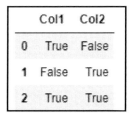

	Col1	Col2
0	True	False
1	False	True
2	True	True

Operations can also be performed on DataFrames using the NumPy functions:

```
np.sqrt(ore1DF)
```

The following is the output:

	iron	magnesium	copper	silver
0	4.472136	5.916080	5.000000	4.472136
1	3.316625	5.291503	5.656854	5.385165

Panels

A Panel is a 3D array. It is not as widely used as Series or DataFrames. It is not as easily displayed on screen or visualized as the other two because of its 3D nature. The Panel data structure is the final piece of the data structure puzzle in pandas. It is less widely used. It is generally used for 3D time-series data. The three axis names are as follows:

- `items`: This is axis 0. Each item corresponds to a DataFrame structure.
- `major_axis`: This is axis 1. Each item corresponds to the rows of the DataFrame structure.
- `minor_axis`: This is axis 2. Each item corresponds to the columns of each DataFrame structure.

Panels are deprecated and will not be available in future versions. Hence, it's advisable to use multi-indexing in DataFrames instead of Panels.

As with Series and DataFrames, there are different ways to create Panel objects. They are explained in the upcoming sections.

Using a 3D NumPy array with axis labels

Here, we show how to construct a Panel object from a 3D NumPy array. After defining the 3D array, a panel could be created by defining each of the three axes:

```
In [68]: stockData = np.array([[[63.03,61.48,75],
[62.05,62.75,46],
[62.74,62.19,53]],
[[411.90, 404.38, 2.9],
[405.45, 405.91, 2.6],
[403.15, 404.42, 2.4]]])
In [69]: stockHistoricalPrices = pd.Panel(stockData,
items=['FB', 'NFLX'], major_axis=pd.date_range('2/3/2014', periods=3),
minor_axis=['open price', 'closing price', 'volume'])
In [70]: stockHistoricalPrices
Out[70]:
<class 'pandas.core.panel.Panel'>
Dimensions: 2 (items) x 3 (major_axis) x 3 (minor_axis)
Items axis: FB to NFLX
Major_axis axis: 2014-02-03 00:00:00 to 2014-02-05 00:00:00
Minor_axis axis: open price to volume
```

Using a Python dictionary of DataFrame objects

A panel consists of several DataFrames. To create a panel, let's define two DataFrames:

```
USData = pd.DataFrame(np.array([[249.62 , 8900],
[ 282.16,12680],
[309.35,14940]]),
columns=['Population(M)','GDP($B)'],
index=[1990,2000,2010])
ChinaData = pd.DataFrame(np.array([[1133.68, 390.28],
[ 1266.83,1198.48],
[1339.72, 6988.47]]),
columns=['Population(M)','GDP($B)'],
index=[1990,2000,2010])
```

Now, a dictionary of these DataFrames can be created:

```
In [73]: US_ChinaData={'US' : USData, 'China': ChinaData}
In [74]: pd.Panel(US_ChinaData)
Out[74]:
<class 'pandas.core.panel.Panel'>
Dimensions: 2 (items) x 3 (major_axis) x 2 (minor_axis)
Items axis: US to China
Major_axis axis: 1990 to 2010
Minor_axis axis: Population(M) to GDP($B)
```

Using the DataFrame.to_panel method

A multi-indexed DataFrame is comparable to a Panel. Hence, a multi-indexed DataFrame can be directly converted to a Panel:

```
In [75]: mIdx = pd.MultiIndex(levels = [['US', 'China'], [1990,2000,
2010]], labels=[[1,1,1,0,0,0],[0,1,2,0,1,2]])
In [76]: ChinaUSDF = pd.DataFrame({'Population(M)' : [1133.68, 1266.83,
1339.72, 249.62, 282.16, 309.35], GDB($B)': [390.28, 1198.48, 6988.47,
8900, 12680,14940]}, index=mIdx)
In [77]: ChinaUSDF.to_panel()
Out[77]:
<class 'pandas.core.panel.Panel'>
Dimensions: 2 (items) x 2 (major_axis) x 3 (minor_axis)
Items axis: Population(M) to GDB($B)
Major_axis axis: China to US
Minor_axis axis: 1990 to 2010
```

The sources of the US/China economic data are the following sites:

- `http://www.multpl.com/us-gdp-inflation-adjusted/table`
- `http://www.multpl.com/united-states-population/table`
- `http://en.wikipedia.org/wiki/Demographics_of_China`
- `http://www.theguardian.com/news/datablog/2012/mar/23/china-gdp-since-1980`

Other operations

Insertion, deletion, and itemwise operations behave the same as in the case of DataFrames. Panel structures can be rearranged by transposing them. The feature set of the operations of Panels is relatively underdeveloped and not as rich as for Series and DataFrames.

Summary

This chapter was a quick tour of the power of NumPy and showed a glimpse of how it makes life easier while working with pandas. Some of the highlights from the chapter were as follows:

- A NumPy array is a versatile data structure used for containing multidimensional homogeneous data.

- There are a variety of methods available for slicing/dicing, creating, and manipulating an array in the NumPy package.

- NumPy arrays have practical applications such as being the building blocks of linear algebra operations and a tool to manipulate multidimensional array data such as images and audio.

- Arrays (or matrices) are the computational blocks used in advanced mathematical models such as neural networks.

- NumPy arrays are the precursors of some of the essential data structures in pandas, namely Series.

- Series are very similar to arrays. Series are one-dimensional. A custom-index can be passed to Series. Arrays or lists can be converted to Series. An indexed Series can be converted to a DataFrame.

- Series, DataFrames, and Panels are other commonly used data structures in pandas, of which DataFrames are the most popular.

- Multi-indexed DataFrames can be created using a dictionary of tuples. Simple dictionaries or dictionaries of lists/arrays can also be used for creating DataFrames.

In the next chapter, we will focus on a variety of data sources for I/O operations in pandas. pandas supports a variety of data structures and sources to be read from and to be written to. We will learn about all that and more in the next chapter.

References

- https://opencv-python-tutroals.readthedocs.io/en/latest/index.html
- http://corochann.com/basic-image-processing-tutorial-1220.html

4

I/Os of Different Data Formats with pandas

A data scientist has to work on data that comes from a variety of sources and hence in a variety of formats. The most common are the ubiquitous spreadsheets, Excel sheets, and CSV and text files. But there are many others, such as URL, API, JSON, XML, HDF, Feather and so on, depending on where it is being accessed. In this chapter, we will cover the following topics among others:

- Data sources and pandas methods
- CSV and TXT
- URL and S3
- JSON
- Reading HDF formats

Let's get started!

Data sources and pandas methods

The data sources for a data science project can be clubbed into the following categories:

- **Databases**: Most of the CRM, ERP, and other business operations tools store data in a database. Depending on the volume, velocity, and variety, it can be a traditional or NoSQL database. To connect to most of the popular databases, we need JDBC/ODBC drivers from Python. Fortunately, there are such drivers available for all the popular databases. Working with data in such databases involves making a connection through Python to these databases, querying the data through Python, and then manipulating it using pandas. We will look at an example of how to do this later in this chapter.

- **Web services**: Many of the business operations tools, especially **Software as a Services (SaaS)** tools, make their data accessible through **Application Programming Interfaces (APIs)** instead of a database. This reduces the infrastructure cost of hosting a database permanently. Instead, data is made available as a service, as and when required. An API call can be made through Python, which returns packets of data in formats such as JSON or XML. This data is parsed and then manipulated using pandas for further usage.

- **Data files**: A lot of data for prototyping data science models comes as data files. One example of data being stored as a physical file is the data from IoT sensors – more often than not, the data from these sensors is stored in a flat file, a .txt file, or a .csv file. Another source for a data file is the sample data that's been extracted from a database and stored in such files. The output of many data science and machine learning algorithms are also stored in such files, such as CSV, Excel, and .txt files. Another example is that the trained weight matrices of a deep learning neural network model can be stored as an HDF file.

- **Web and document scraping**: Two other sources of data are the tables and text present on web pages. This data is gleaned from these pages using Python packages such as BeautifulSoup and Scrapy and are put into a data file or database to be used further. The tables and data that are present in another non-data format file, such as PDF or Docs, are also a major source of data. This is then extracted using Python packages such as Tesseract and Tabula-py.

In this chapter, we will look at how to read and write data to and from these formats/sources using pandas and ancillary libraries. We will also discuss a little bit about these formats, their utilities, and various operations that can be performed on them.

The following is a summary of the read and write methods in Python for some of the data formats we are going to discuss in this chapter:

Format Type	Data Description	Reader	Writer
text	CSV	read_csv	to_csv
text	JSON	read_json	to_json
text	HTML	read_html	to_html
text	Local clipboard	read_clipboard	to_clipboard
binary	MS Excel	read_excel	to_excel
binary	HDF5 Format	read_hdf	to_hdf
binary	Feather Format	read_feather	to_feather
binary	Parquet Format	read_parquet	to_parquet
binary	Msgpack	read_msgpack	to_msgpack
binary	Stata	read_stata	to_stata
binary	SAS	read_sas	
binary	Python Pickle Format	read_pickle	to_pickle
SQL	SQL	read_sql	to_sql
SQL	Google Big Query	read_gbq	to_gbq

Reader and writer methods in pandas for different types of data file formats and their sources

The section headers mean that we are dealing with I/O operations of that file type in that section.

CSV and TXT

CSV stands for comma-separated values, which means that the comma is the default delimiter for these files. However, they accept other delimiters as well.

CSVs are made of columns and rows and the cell value is arranged in a tabular format. They can come with or without column names and row indices. The primary reasons for a CSV file's existence include manually gathered data, data that's been extracted and downloaded from a database, a direct download from a tool or website, web scraping, and the result of running a data science algorithm.

Reading CSV and TXT files

`read_csv` is the go-to method for reading CSV files in `pandas`. It can also be used to read `txt` files. The syntax of using `read_csv` is shown in the following code:

```
pd.read_csv(filepath, sep=', ', dtype=None, header=None, names=None,
skiprows=None, index_col=None, skip_blank_lines=TRUE, na_filter=TRUE)
```

The parameters of the `read_csv` method are as follows:

- `filepath`: A string or filename with or without a filepath.
- `dtype`: Can be passed as a dictionary containing name and type as a key-value pair. Specifies the data type of the column name. Generally, pandas guesses the type of columns based on the first few rows.
- `header`: True/False. This specifies whether the first row in the data is a header or not.
- `names`: List. Specifies column names for all the columns of a dataset.
- `skiprows`: List. Skip certain rows of data by specifying row indices.
- `index_col`: Series/List. Specifies the column that can work as a row number/identifier.
- `skip_blank_lines`: True/False. Specifies whether to skip blank lines or not.
- `na_filter`: True/False. Specifies whether to filter NA values or not.
- `usecols`: List. Returns the subset of data with columns in the passed list.

The `read_csv` method returns a DataFrame. The following are some examples of reading files using the `read_csv` method.

Reading a CSV file

We can read a CSV file by using the following code:

```
import pandas as pd
import os
os.chdir(' ')
data=pd.read_csv('Hospital Cost.csv')
```

Specifying column names for a dataset

The following code will specify the column names for a dataset:

```
column_names=pd.read_csv('Customer Churn Columns.csv')
column_names_list=column_names['Column Names'].tolist()
data=pd.read_csv('Customer Churn
Model.txt',header=None,names=column_names_list)
```

Note that the column names are read from a file and then converted into a list to be passed to the names parameter in `read_csv`.

Reading from a string of data

Here's how we can use `read_csv` to create a DataFrame from a list of strings:

```
from io import StringIO
data = 'col1,col2,col3\na,b,1\na,b,2\nc,d,3\nc,e,4\ng,f,5\ne,z,6'
pd.read_csv(StringIO(data))
```

Skipping certain rows

We can also skip certain rows. Let's say that we only want the rows whose indices are multiples of 3:

```
from io import StringIO
data = 'col1,col2,col3\na,b,1\na,b,2\nc,d,3\nc,e,4\ng,f,5\ne,z,6'
pd.read_csv(StringIO(data),skiprows=lambda x: x % 3 != 0)
```

We get the following output:

	col1	col2	col3		col1	col2	col3
0	a	b	1	0	c	d	3
1	b	b	2	1	e	z	6
2	c	d	3				
3	c	e	4				
4	g	f	5				
5	e	z	6				

Demonstration of using the skiprows parameter in read_csv. The right-hand panel shows the data that's been filtered through skiprows (keeping only rows with row numbers that are multiples of 3)

The left-hand side diagram shows the resultant DataFrame without skipping any row, while the right-hand side shows the same DataFrame after filtering the rows whose indices are not multiples of 3. Note that this method considers the real index (3rd and 6th from the top, starting from 1) and not the Python index (starting from 0) for filtering the rows based on their index.

Row index

If a file has one more column of data than the number of column names, the first column will be used as the DataFrame's row names:

```
data = 'a,b,c\n4,apple,bat,5.7\n8,orange,cow,10'
pd.read_csv(StringIO(data), index_col=0)
```

We get the following output:

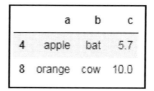

The column with values but no corresponding column name is used as a row index.

Reading a text file

`read_csv` can help read text files as well. Often, data is stored in `.txt` files with different kinds of delimiters. The `sep` parameter can be used to specify the delimiter of a particular file, as shown in the following code:

```
data=pd.read_csv('Tab Customer Churn Model.txt',sep='/t')
```

The preceding file has `Tab` as a delimiter, which is specified using the `sep` parameter.

Subsetting while reading

Only a selected list of columns can be subsetted and loaded using the `usecols` parameter while reading:

```
data=pd.read_csv('Tab Customer Churn Model.txt',sep='/t',usecols=[1,3,5])
data=pd.read_csv('Tab Customer Churn Model.txt',sep='/t',usecols=['VMail
Plan','Area Code'])
```

Numeric lists, as well as explicit lists with column names, can be used. Numeric indexing follows Python indexing, that is, starting from 0.

Reading thousand format numbers as numbers

If a dataset contains a numeric column that has thousand numbers formatted by a comma or any other delimiter, the default data type for such a column is a string or object. The problem is that it is actually a numeric field and it needs to be read as a numeric field to be used further:

```
pd.read_csv('tmp.txt',sep='|')
```

We get the following output:

	ID	level	category
0	Patient1	123,000	x
1	Patient2	23,000	y
2	Patient3	1,234,018	z

Data with a level column with thousand format numbers

```
data.level.dtype returns dtype('O')
```

To overcome this problem, the thousands parameter can be used while reading:

```
pd.read_csv('tmp.txt',sep='|',thousands=',')
data.level.dtype now returns dtype('int64')
```

Indexing and multi-indexing

index_col can be used to specify one column to provide row indices. A list of columns can be passed as indices, which leads to multi-indexing. Let's look at an example:

```
pd.read_csv('mindex.txt')
pd.read_csv('mindex.txt',index_col=[0,1])
```

Take a look at the following screenshot:

	year	indiv	zit	xit		year	indiv	zit	xit
0	1977	A	1.20	0.60		1977	A	1.20	0.60
1	1977	B	1.50	0.50			B	1.50	0.50
2	1977	C	1.70	0.80			C	1.70	0.80
3	1978	A	0.20	0.06		1978	A	0.20	0.06
4	1978	B	0.70	0.20			B	0.70	0.20
5	1978	C	0.80	0.30			C	0.80	0.30
6	1978	D	0.90	0.50			D	0.90	0.50
7	1978	E	1.40	0.90			E	1.40	0.90
8	1979	C	0.20	0.15		1979	C	0.20	0.15
9	1979	D	0.14	0.05			D	0.14	0.05
10	1979	E	0.50	0.15			E	0.50	0.15
11	1979	F	1.20	0.50			F	1.20	0.50
12	1979	G	3.40	1.90			G	3.40	1.90
13	1979	H	5.40	2.70			H	5.40	2.70
14	1979	I	6.40	1.20			I	6.40	1.20

Single index (left) and multi-index (right) on the same data

This kind of multi-indexing makes it easy to subset based on either an index or both:

```
data.loc[1977]
data.loc[(1977,'A')]
```

We get the following output:

	zit	xit
indiv		
A	1.2	0.6
B	1.5	0.5
C	1.7	0.8

```
zit    1.2
xit    0.6
Name: (1977, A), dtype: float64
```

Subsetting multi-indexed data using one index (left) and both indices (right)

Reading large files in chunks

Reading a large file in memory at once may consume the entire RAM of the computer and may cause it to throw an error. In such cases, it becomes pertinent to divide the data into chunks. These chunks can then be read sequentially and processed. This is achieved by using the chunksize parameter in read_csv.

The resulting chunks can be iterated over using a for loop. In the following code, we are printing the shape of the chunks:

```
for chunks in pd.read_csv('Chunk.txt',chunksize=500):
    print(chunks.shape)
```

These chunks can then be concatenated to each other using the concat method:

```
data=pd.read_csv('Chunk.txt',chunksize=500)
data=pd.concat(data,ignore_index=True)
print(data.shape)
```

Handling delimiter characters in column data

Sometimes, a column separate character is present as part of the data in one of the columns. This leads to incorrectly parsing data as this would split the column that was supposed to be read as one into two. To avoid such a situation, a quote character should be used around the data in the specified columns. This quote character forces read_csv to ignore the delimiter for the data that's present inside the quote character and not break it into two pieces.

The quote characters can be specified using the quotechar argument of read_csv. For example, consider the following dataset. Here, white space is used as a delimiter and double quotes have been used as a grouping element:

```
"Row Name"        "Column A"              "Column B"  "Column C"
"Row 1"  1 2 3
"Row 2"  4 5 6
"Row 3"  7 8 9
```

Usage of quotechar keyword 1—input dataset

To parse this, we would use the following code:

```
d1 =
pd.read_csv('t1.txt',index_col=0, delim_whitespace=True,quotechar="\"")
d1.head()
```

We would get the following output:

Row Name	Column A	Column B	Column C
Row 1	1	2	3
Row 2	4	5	6
Row 3	7	8	9

Usage of quotechar keyword 2—output dataset

Writing to a CSV

A DataFrame is an in-memory object. Often, DataFrames need to be saved as physical files for later use. In such cases, the DataFrames can be written as a CSV or TXT file.

Let's create a synthesized DataFrame using random numbers:

```
import numpy as np
import pandas as pd
a=['Male','Female']
b=['Rich','Poor','Middle Class']
gender=[]
seb=[]

for i in range(1,101):
    gender.append(np.random.choice(a))
    seb.append(np.random.choice(b))
    height=30*np.random.randn(100)+155
    weight=20*np.random.randn(100)+60
    age=10*np.random.randn(100)+35
    income=1500*np.random.randn(100)+15000

df=pd.DataFrame({'Gender':gender,'Height':height,'Weight':weight,'Age':age,
'Income':income,'Socio-Eco':seb})
```

This can be written to a .csv or .txt file using the to_csv method, as shown in the following code:

```
df.to_csv('data.csv')
df.to_csv('data.txt')
```

These files would be written to the current working directory.

A delimiter of choice can be provided while writing to a file:

```
df.to_csv('data.csv',sep='|')
df.to_csv('data.txt',sep='/')
```

There are many other useful options available, such as the following:

- `index`: True/False. Indicates whether we should have row indices or not.
- `index_label`: String/Column name. Column to be used as a row index.
- `header`: True/False. Specifies whether to write the column names.
- `na_rep`: String. A string representation for missing values.

Excel

Excel files are similar to CSV files but are different in the sense that they can have multiple sheets, formatted data and tables, charts, and formulas. In many cases, reading data from Excel files is required.

`xlrd` is the package of choice while working with Excel sheets. Some of the major functionalities of the `xlrd` package are summarized in the following table:

Code snippet	Goal achieved
`import xlrd`	Importing the xlrd library
`book=xlrd.open_workbook('SRS Career.xlsx')`	Reading the Excel workbook
`n=book.nsheets`	Finding the number of sheets in a workbook
`book.sheet_names()`	Finding the names of sheets in a workbook
`last_sheet=book.sheet_by_index(n-1)`	Reading the sheets by sheet index
`last_sheet.row_values(0)`	Getting the first row of a sheet
`last_sheet.cell(0,0)`	Getting the first cell of the sheet
`last_sheet.row_slice(rowx=0,start_colx=1,end_colx=5)`	Getting the 1st to the 5th columns of the first row

URL and S3

Sometimes, the data is directly available as a URL. In such cases, `read_csv` can be directly used to read from these URLs:

```
pd.read_csv('http://bit.ly/2cLzoxH').head()
```

Alternatively, to work with URLs in order to get data, we can use a couple of Python packages that we haven't used so far, such as `.csv` and `.urllib`. It would suffice to know that `.csv` provides a range of methods for handling `.csv` files and that `urllib` is used to navigate to and access information from the URL. Here is how we can do this:

```
import csv
import urllib2

url='http://archive.ics.uci.edu/ml/machine-learning-databases/iris/iris.dat
a'
response=urllib2.urlopen(url)
cr=csv.reader(response)

for rows in cr:
    print rows
```

`AWS S3` is a popular file-sharing and storage repository on the web. Many enterprises store their business operations data as files on S3, which needs to be read and processed directly or be moved to a database. Python allows us to directly read files from S3, as shown in the following code.

Python 3.4 and above use the `s3fs` package in addition to pandas to read files directly from S3. An AWS config file needs to be placed in the current working directory. The bucket name, as well as the path and filename, need to be passed for reading:

```
import os
import pandas as pd
from s3fs.core import S3FileSystem

os.environ['AWS_CONFIG_FILE'] = 'aws_config.ini'

s3 = S3FileSystem(anon=False)
key = 'path\to\your-csv.csv'
bucket = 'your-bucket-name'

df = pd.read_csv(s3.open('{}/{}'.format(bucket, key),
                         mode='rb')
                )
```

A DataFrame can be written to a CSV file and saved directly in S3 as follows:

```
import s3fs

bytes_to_write = df.to_csv(None).encode()
fs = s3fs.S3FileSystem(key=key, secret=secret)
with fs.open('s3://bucket/path/to/file.csv', 'wb') as f:
    f.write(bytes_to_write)
```

HTML

HTML is the popular file format for creating and wrapping web elements and pages. Sometimes, tabular data is stored in a file. In such cases, the read_html method is directly used to read such data. This function parses table elements from HTML files and reads the tables as DataFrames:

```
pd.read_html('http://www.fdic.gov/bank/individual/failed/banklist.html')
```

You can find all of the table elements containing a particular match word by using the following code:

```
match = 'Malta National Bank'
df_list =
pd.read_html('http://www.fdic.gov/bank/individual/failed/banklist.html',
match=match)
```

A DataFrame can be converted into an HTML table element so that it can be placed into an HTML file like so:

```
data=pd.read_csv('http://bit.ly/2cLzoxH')
print(data.to_html())
```

We get the following output:

```
<table border="1" class="dataframe">
  <thead>
    <tr style="text-align: right;">
      <th></th>
      <th>country</th>
      <th>year</th>
      <th>pop</th>
      <th>continent</th>
      <th>lifeExp</th>
      <th>gdpPercap</th>
    </tr>
  </thead>
  <tbody>
    <tr>
      <th>0</th>
      <td>Afghanistan</td>
      <td>1952</td>
      <td>8.425333e+06</td>
      <td>Asia</td>
```

HTML table element created from a DataFrame

A selected list of columns can be filtered and converted into HTML like so:

```
print(data.to_html(columns=['country','year']))
```

Writing to an HTML file

The HTML file can be saved as a physical file like so:

```
data=pd.read_csv('http://bit.ly/2cLzoxH')
print(data.to_html('test.html'))
```

Take a look at the following screenshot:

	country	year	pop	continent	lifeExp	gdpPercap
0	Afghanistan	1952	8.425333e+06	Asia	28.80100	779.445314
1	Afghanistan	1957	9.240934e+06	Asia	30.33200	820.853030
2	Afghanistan	1962	1.026708e+07	Asia	31.99700	853.100710
3	Afghanistan	1967	1.153797e+07	Asia	34.02000	836.197138
4	Afghanistan	1972	1.307946e+07	Asia	36.08800	739.981106
5	Afghanistan	1977	1.488037e+07	Asia	38.43800	786.113360
6	Afghanistan	1982	1.288182e+07	Asia	39.85400	978.011439
7	Afghanistan	1987	1.386796e+07	Asia	40.82200	852.395945
8	Afghanistan	1992	1.631792e+07	Asia	41.67400	649.341395
9	Afghanistan	1997	2.222742e+07	Asia	41.76300	635.341351
10	Afghanistan	2002	2.526840e+07	Asia	42.12900	726.734055
11	Afghanistan	2007	3.188992e+07	Asia	43.82800	974.580338
12	Albania	1952	1.282697e+06	Europe	55.23000	1601.056136
13	Albania	1957	1.476505e+06	Europe	59.28000	1942.284244

Subsetting multi-indexed data using one index (left) and both indices (right)

The row and column names are bold by default. This can be changed with the following code:

```
data.to_html('test.html',bold_rows=False)
```

JSON

JSON is a popular dictionary-like, key-value pair-based data structure that's suitable for exposing data as APIs from SaaS tools. address, postalCode, state, streetAddress, age, firstName, lastName, and phoneNumber are keys whose values are shown to the right of them. JSON files can be nested (the values of a key are JSON) as well. Here, address has nested values:

```
{u'address': {u'city': u'New York',
  u'postalCode': u'10021',
  u'state': u'NY',
  u'streetAddress': u'21 2nd Street'},
 u'age': 25,
 u'firstName': u'John',
 u'lastName': u'Smith',
 u'phoneNumber': [{u'number': u'212 555-1234', u'type': u'home'},
  {u'number': u'646 555-4567', u'type': u'fax'}]}
```

Example of JSON data (dictionary; key-value pairs)

DataFrames can be converted into JSON using `to_json`:

```
import numpy as np
pd.DataFrame(np.random.randn(5, 2), columns=list('AB')).to_json() "
```

Take a look at the following screenshot:

'{"A":{"0":0.873956251,"1":0.0829327443,"2":0.3289723511,"3":-0.7261613882,"4":1.0450163549},"B":{"0":-2.0288640507,"1":0.97613 81646,"2":-0.3547267738,"3":-1.7020589121,"4":0.2877029867}}'

Converting a DataFrame into JSON format

While converting the DataFrame into a JSON file, the orientation can be set.

If we want to keep the column name as the primary index and the row indices as the secondary index, then we can choose the orientation to be `columns`:

```
dfjo = pd.DataFrame(dict(A=range(1, 4), B=range(4, 7), C=range(7,
10)),columns=list('ABC'), index=list('xyz'))
dfjo.to_json(orient="columns")
```

We receive the following output:

'{"A":{"x":1,"y":2,"z":3},"B":{"x":4,"y":5,"z":6},"C":{"x":7,"y":8,"z":9}}'

Converting a DataFrame into JSON with the column orientation

If we want to keep the row indices as the primary index and the column names as the secondary index, then we can choose the orientation to be `index`:

```
dfjo = pd.DataFrame(dict(A=range(1, 4), B=range(4, 7), C=range(7,
10)),columns=list('ABC'), index=list('xyz'))
dfjo.to_json(orient="index")
```

We receive the following output:

'{"x":{"A":1,"B":4,"C":7},"y":{"A":2,"B":5,"C":8},"z":{"A":3,"B":6,"C":9}}'

Converting a DataFrame into JSON with the index orientation

Another option is to convert a DataFrame into an array of JSONs. This is useful while passing data to a visualization library, like so:

```
d3.js. dfjo = pd.DataFrame(dict(A=range(1, 4), B=range(4, 7), C=range(7,
10)),columns=list('ABC'), index=list('xyz')) dfjo.to_json(orient="records")
```

We receive the following output:

```
'[{"A":1,"B":4,"C":7},{"A":2,"B":5,"C":8},{"A":3,"B":6,"C":9}]'
```

Converting a DataFrame into JSON with the records orientation

We can also contain the bare-bones values as a list of values, without any row or column index:

```
dfjo = pd.DataFrame(dict(A=range(1, 4), B=range(4, 7), C=range(7,
10)),columns=list('ABC'), index=list('xyz')) dfjo.to_json(orient="values")
```

We receive the following output:

```
'[[1,4,7],[2,5,8],[3,6,9]]'
```

Converting a DataFrame into JSON with the values orientation

Finally, we can also orient the converted JSON in order to separate the row indices, column names, and data values:

```
dfjo = pd.DataFrame(dict(A=range(1, 4), B=range(4, 7), C=range(7,
10)),columns=list('ABC'), index=list('xyz')) dfjo.to_json(orient="split")
```

We receive the following output:

```
'{"columns":["A","B","C"],"index":["x","y","z"],"data":[[1,4,7],[2,5,8],[3,6,9]]}'
```

Converting a DataFrame into JSON with the split orientation

Writing a JSON to a file

JSON can be written to physical files like so:

```
import json with open('jsonex.txt','w') as outfile:
json.dump(dfjo.to_json(orient="columns"), outfile)
```

Reading a JSON

`json_loads` is used to read a physical file containing JSONs:

```
f=open('usagov_bitly.txt','r').readline() json.loads(f)
```

We get the following output:

```
{'a': 'Mozilla/5.0 (Windows NT 6.1; WOW64) AppleWebKit/535.11 (KHTML, like Gecko) Chrome/17.0.963.78 Safari/535.11',
 'c': 'US',
 'nk': 1,
 'tz': 'America/New_York',
 'gr': 'MA',
 'g': 'A6qOVH',
 'h': 'wfLQtf',
 'l': 'orofrog',
 'al': 'en-US,en;q=0.8',
 'hh': '1.usa.gov',
 'r': 'http://www.facebook.com/l/7AQEFzjSi/1.usa.gov/wfLQtf',
 'u': 'http://www.ncbi.nlm.nih.gov/pubmed/22415991',
 't': 1331923247,
 'hc': 1331822918,
 'cy': 'Danvers',
 'll': [42.576698, -70.954903]}
```

First record in a list of JSONs

The files can be read one JSON at a time using the `open` and `readline` methods:

```
records=[] f=open('usagov_bitly.txt','r') for i in range(1000):
fiterline=f.readline() d=json.loads(fiterline) records.append(d) f.close()
```

Now, `records` contains a list of JSONs from which all the values of a particular key can be pulled out. For example, here, we are pulling out all the `latlong` (`'ll'` column) wherever it has a non-zero value:

```
latlong=[rec['ll'] for rec in records if 'll' in rec]
```

Writing JSON to a DataFrame

A list of JSON objects can be converted into a DataFrame (much like a dictionary can). The records element we created previously is a list of JSONs (we can check this by using `records[0:3]` or `type(records)`):

```
df=pd.DataFrame(records)
df.head()
df['tz'].value_counts()
```

In the last line, we are trying to find the count of different time zones contained in the `'tz'` column.

Subsetting a JSON

Let's have a look at a new JSON file:

```
with open('product.json') as json_string:
    d=json.load(json_string)
d
```

We get the following output:

```
{'hits': {'hits': [{'_score': 1.0,
  '_type': 'product',
  '_id': '190242630612',
  '_source': {'item_id': '641113611',
   'price_id': 8143570,
   'r': {'wayfair': {'title': "9' Icarus Cantilever Umbrella Fabric: Texsilk Olefin - Sunflower",
     'product_url': 'http://www.shareasale.com/m-pr.cfm?merchantID=11035&userID=1272520&productID=641113611',
     'image_url': 'http://img.wfrcdn.com/lf/49/hash/38417/27558341/1/1/1.jpg',
     'price2': 3699.99,
     'price1': 3880.0,
     'affiliate_url': 'http://www.shareasale.com/m-pr.cfm?merchantID=11035&userID=1272520&productID=641113611'}},
   'upc': 190242630612,
   'title': "9' Icarus Cantilever Umbrella Fabric: Texsilk Olefin - Sunflower"},
  '_index': 'product_index'}],
 'total': 1,
 'max_score': 1.0},
 '_shards': {'successful': 5, 'failed': 0, 'total': 5},
 'took': 2,
 'timed_out': False}
```

Loading a JSON file with several degrees of nesting

This is a JSON with several degrees of nesting. The `hits` key contains a JSON as a value whose key value is `hits`. The value of this JSON is a list containing another JSON.

Let's say that we want to find out the score value from this JSON:

```
d['hits']['hits'][0]['_score']
```

Similarly, the image URL can be found as follows:

```
d['hits']['hits'][0]['_source']['r']['wayfair']['image_url']
```

Looping over JSON keys

JSON data can be looped on its keys and values:

```
for keys,values in d['hits']['hits'][0].items():
print(keys)
```

We receive the following output:

```
_score
_type
_id
_source
_index
```

Printing keys of the loaded JSON by looping over the keys and values

We can print both the keys and values together as well.

```
for keys,values in d['hits']['hits'][0].items():
  print(keys,values)
```

We receive the following output:

```
_score 1.0
_type product
_id 190242630612
_source {'item_id': '641113611', 'price_id': 8143570, 'r': {'wayfair': {'title': "9' Icarus Cantilever Umbrella Fabric: Texsilk
Olefin - Sunflower", 'product_url': 'http://www.shareasale.com/m-pr.cfm?merchantID=11035&userID=1272520&productID=641113611',
'image_url': 'http://img.wfrcdn.com/lf/49/hash/38417/27558341/1/1/1.jpg', 'price2': 3699.99, 'price1': 3880.0, 'affiliate_url':
'http://www.shareasale.com/m-pr.cfm?merchantID=11035&userID=1272520&productID=641113611'}}, 'upc': 190242630612, 'title': "9' I
carus Cantilever Umbrella Fabric: Texsilk Olefin - Sunflower"}
_index product_index
```

Printing keys and values of the loaded JSON by looping over the keys and values

Now, we will look at how to use reading and writing operations with exotic file formats.

Reading HDF formats

The **Hierarchical Data Format** (**HDF**) is efficient in handling large and complex data models. The versatility and flexibility of HDF in data storage make it a sought after format for storing scientific data. In fact, HDF was selected as the standard data and information system by NASA, for use in the Earth Observing System. HDF5 is the current technological suite used by the HDF file format and replaced the older HDF4.

The following are some unique features of HDF5:

- HDF5 has no set limits regarding file size and the objects in the file.
- HDF5 can group and link objects in the file, thereby facilitating as a supportive mechanism for complex relationships and dependencies in data.
- HDF5 also supports metadata.
- While accommodating a variety of predefined and user-defined data types, HDF5 also has the ability to store and share data type descriptions in HDF files.

For efficiency in the data transfer process, HDF5 incorporates Standard (Posix), Parallel, and Network I/O file drivers. Additional file drivers can also be developed and integrated with HDF5 for any custom data transfer and storage requirements. HDF5 makes data storage more optimized through techniques such as compression, extensibility, and chunking. Being able to perform data transformations, make changes to data types, and select subsets of data during data transfer makes the reading and writing processes efficient.

Now, let's read an HDF file using pandas:

```
pd.read_hdf('stat_df.h5','table')
```

We receive the following output:

	First_Name	Last_name	Entry_date	Score
0	Mike	K.	1989-06-23	0.692619
1	Val	K.	1995-06-16	0.503150
2	George	C.	1997-06-20	0.369661
3	Chris	B.	2005-06-25	0.898150
4	Benjamin	A.	2016-03-25	0.618379

Output of read_hdf

A subset of the data could be extracted during the reading process using the index argument:

```
pd.read_hdf('stat_df.h5', 'table', where=['index>=2'])
```

We receive the following output:

	First_Name	Last_name	Entry_date	Score
2	George	C.	1997-06-20	0.369661
3	Chris	B.	2005-06-25	0.898150
4	Benjamin	A.	2016-03-25	0.618379

Output of read_hdf with indexing

Reading feather files

The feather format is a binary file format for storing data that makes use of Apache Arrow, an in-memory columnar data structure. It was developed by Wes Mckinney and Hadley Wickham, chief scientists at RStudio as an initiative for a data sharing infrastructure across Python and R. The columnar serialization of data in feather files makes way for efficient read and write operations, making it far faster than CSV and JSON files where storage is record-wise.

Feather files have the following features:

- Fast I/O operations.
- Feather files can be read and written in languages other than R or Python, such as Julia and Scala.
- They have compatibility with all pandas datatypes, such as Datetime and Categorical.

Feather currently supports the following datatypes:

- All numeric datatypes
- Logical
- Timestamps
- Categorical
- UTF-8 encoded strings
- Binary

Since feather is merely a simplistic version of Arrow, it has several caveats associated with it. The following are some limitations of using a feather file:

- Not recommended for long-term data storage as their stability between versions cannot be guaranteed.
- Any index or multi-index, other than the default indexing scheme, is not supported in Feather format.
- Python data types such as Period are not supported.
- Duplicates in column names are not supported.

Reading a feather file in pandas is done like so:

```
pd.read_feather("sample.feather")
```

This results in the following output:

	First_Name	Last_name	Entry_date	Score
0	Mike	K.	1989-06-23	0.692619
1	Val	K.	1995-06-16	0.503150
2	George	C.	1997-06-20	0.369661
3	Chris	B.	2005-06-25	0.898150
4	Benjamin	A.	2016-03-25	0.618379

Output of read_feather

Reading parquet files

Apache Parquet is another file format that makes use of columnar compression for efficient read and write operations. It was designed to be compatible with big data ecosystems such as Hadoop and can handle nested data structures and sparsely populated columns. Though the parquet and feather formats share a similar base, parquet has a better compression routine than feather. The compressed file is smaller in parquet than it is in feather. Columns with similar data types use the same encoding for compression. The use of different encoding schemes for the compression of parquet makes it efficient. Just like feather, parquet is a binary file format that can work well with all pandas data types and is supported across several languages. Parquet can be used for the long-term storage of data.

The following are some limitations of the parquet file format:

- While parquet can accept multi-level indices, it requires that the index level name is in string format.
- Python data types such as Period are not supported.
- Duplicates in column names are not supported.
- When Categorical objects are serialized in a parquet file, they are deserialized as an object datatype.

Serialization or deserialization of parquet files t in pandas can take place in either of the `pyarrow` and `fastparquet` engines. These two engines have different dependencies. Pyarrow does not support Timedelta.

Let's read a parquet file using the `pyarrow` engine:

```
pd.read_parquet("sample.paraquet",engine='pyarrow')
```

This results in the following output:

	First_Name	Last_name	Entry_date	Score
0	Mike	K.	1989-06-23	0.692619
1	Val	K.	1995-06-16	0.503150
2	George	C.	1997-06-20	0.369661
3	Chris	B.	2005-06-25	0.898150
4	Benjamin	A.	2016-03-25	0.618379

Output of read_parquet

Parquet allows us to select columns when reading a file, which saves time:

```
pd.read_parquet("sample.paraquet",engine='pyarrow',columns=["First_Name","S
core"])
```

The same works for the `fastparquet` engine as well:

```
pd.read_parquet("sample.paraquet",engine='fastparquet')
```

Reading a SQL file

Interacting with a SQL database through pandas requires the sqlalchemy dependency to be installed.

First, let's define the engine from which connection parameters can be obtained:

```
engine = create_engine('sqlite:///:memory:')
```

Now, let's read the `data_sql` table from the SQL database:

```
with engine.connect() as conn, conn.begin():
    print(pd.read_sql_table('data_sql', conn))
```

This results in the following output:

```
   index First_Name Last_name Entry_date     Score
0      0       Mike        K. 1989-06-23  0.244067
1      1        Val        K. 1995-06-16  0.153420
2      2     George        C. 1997-06-20  0.755368
3      3      Chris        B. 2005-06-25  0.988560
4      4   Benjamin        A. 2016-03-25  0.697864
```

Output of read_sql_table

The `read_sql_table()` function reads an entire table for the given table name. A specific column can be set as the index when reading:

```
pd.read_sql_table('data_sql', engine, index_col='index')
```

This results in the following output:

index	First_Name	Last_name	Entry_date	Score
0	Mike	K.	1989-06-23	0.244067
1	Val	K.	1995-06-16	0.153420
2	George	C.	1997-06-20	0.755368
3	Chris	B.	2005-06-25	0.988560
4	Benjamin	A.	2016-03-25	0.697864

Output of read_sql_table with indexing

The columns argument lets us choose specific columns when reading data by passing the column names as a list. Any date columns can be parsed into a specific format during the read process, as shown in the following code:

```
pd.read_sql_table('data_sql', engine, parse_dates={'Entry_date': '%Y-%m-
%d'})
pd.read_sql_table('data_sql', engine, parse_dates={'Entry_date': {'format':
'%Y-%m-%d %H:%M:%S'}})
```

The `schema` argument in this function helps specify the schema from which the table is to be extracted.

Instead of reading the entire table, it is also possible to use a SQL query to get data in the necessary format. We can do this with the `read_sql_query()` function:

```
pd.read_sql_query("SELECT Last_name, Score FROM data_sql", engine)
```

This results in the following output:

	Last_name	Score
0	K.	0.244067
1	K.	0.153420
2	C.	0.755368
3	B.	0.988560
4	A.	0.697864

Output of read_sql_query

To run the `INSERT` and `CREATE` queries, which do not return any output, the `sql.execute()` function can be used. This requires an `sql` file of `pandas.io` to be imported:

```
from pandas.io import sql
sql.execute("INSERT INTO tablename VALUES (90, 100, 171)", engine)
```

With a `sqlite` database, the connection to the engine has to be defined as follows so that it can be used in the `read_sql_table()` or `read_sql_query()` functions. The `sqlite` module must be imported prior to this:

```
import sqlite3
conn = sqlite3.connect(':memory:')
```

Reading a SAS/Stata file

Pandas can read two file formats from SAS – SAS xports (.XPT) and SAS data files
(.sas7bdat).

The read_sas() function helps read SAS files. Here, a SAS data file has been read and
displayed as a pandas dataframe:

```
df = pd.read_sas('sample.sas7bdat')
df
```

This results in the following output:

	STATE	VOTE	INCOME	SCHOOL	URBAN	NORTHEAST	SOUTHEAST	MIDWEST	WEST
0	b'Alabama'	1.000240e+00	11.785000	12.2	61.799999	1.055269e-312	1.000047e+00	1.055296e-312	1.055286e-312
1	b'Alaska'	5.341279e-312	22.431999	12.7	43.700001	1.055269e-312	1.055660e-312	1.055658e-312	1.000047e+00
2	b'Arizona'	1.055295e-312	13.569000	12.6	74.699997	1.055268e-312	1.055269e-312	1.055299e-312	1.000047e+00
3	b'Arkansa'	1.000047e+00	10.106000	12.2	38.400002	1.055269e-312	1.055272e-312	1.000047e+00	1.055332e-312
4	b'California'	1.055295e-312	15.069000	12.7	92.699997	1.055270e-312	1.055660e-312	1.055656e-312	1.000047e+00
5	b'Colorado'	1.055273e-312	14.992000	12.8	80.599998	1.055395e-312	1.055333e-312	1.055655e-312	1.000047e+00

Output of read_sas

The chunksize and iterator arguments help in reading the SAS file in groups of the
same size. If the SAS data file that was used earlier is read with a chunksize of 10, then the
51 records will be divided into six groups, as shown in the following code:

```
rdr = pd.read_sas('sample.sas7bdat', chunksize=10)
for chunk in rdr:
print(chunk.shape)
```

Take a look at the following output:

```
(10, 9)
(10, 9)
(10, 9)
(10, 9)
(10, 9)
(1, 9)
```

Output of read_sas with chunksize

However, these SAS files cannot be written using pandas.

Pandas also provides support for reading and writing files that have been generated from Stata. Stata only supports limited datatypes: `int8`, `int16`, `int32`, `float32`, `float64`, and strings with a length less than 244. When writing a Stata data file through pandas, type conversion is applied wherever applicable.

Let's read a Stata datafile using pandas:

```
df = pd.read_stata('sample.dta')
df
```

Take a look at the following output:

	state	vote	income	school	urban	northeast	southeast	midwest	west
0	Alabama	1.0	11.785000	12.2	61.799999	0.0	1.0	0.0	0.0
1	Alaska	0.0	22.431999	12.7	43.700001	0.0	0.0	0.0	1.0
2	Arizona	0.0	13.569000	12.6	74.699997	0.0	0.0	0.0	1.0
3	Arkansa	1.0	10.106000	12.2	38.400002	0.0	0.0	1.0	0.0
4	California	0.0	15.069000	12.7	92.699997	0.0	0.0	0.0	1.0
5	Colorado	0.0	14.992000	12.8	80.599998	0.0	0.0	0.0	1.0

Output of read_stata

The `read_stata()` function also has `chunksize` and `iterator` arguments to read data in smaller groups. The following arguments are the available `stata` reader functions:

- `convert_categoricals`: Converts a suitable column into a categorical data type
- `index_col`: Identifies the column to be defined as an index
- `convert_missing`: Specifies whether to represent missing values as NaN or with a Stata missing value object
- `columns`: Columns to select from the dataset

Reading from Google BigQuery

BigQuery is an extremely powerful data warehousing solution provided by Google. Pandas can directly connect to BigQuery and bring your data to a Python environment for further analysis.

The following is an example of reading a dataset from BigQuery:

```
pd.read_gbq("SELECT urban_area_code, geo_code, name, area_type,
area_land_meters
FROM `bigquery-public-data.utility_us.us_cities_area` LIMIT 5", project_id,
dialect = "standard")
```

Take a look at the following output:

	urban_area_code	geo_code	name	area_type	area_land_meters
0	90946	90946	Visalia, CA	U	164293746
1	56251	56251	Merced, CA	U	122971428
2	28657	28657	Fairfield, CA	U	102312298
3	04951	04951	Bangor, ME	U	109957644
4	23500	23500	Denton--Lewisville, TX	U	376211292

Output of read_gbq

The read_gbq() function accepts the query and the Google Cloud project-id (which serves as a key) so that it can access the database and bring out the data. The dialect argument takes care of the SQL syntax to be used: BigQuery's legacy SQL dialect or the standard SQL dialect. In addition, there are arguments that allow the index column to be set (index_col), columns to be reordered (col_order), and reauthentication to be enabled (reauth).

Reading from a clipboard

This is a rather interesting feature in pandas. Any tabular data that has been copied onto the clipboard can be read as a DataFrame in pandas.

Let's copy the following tabular data with the usual *ctrl + C* keyboard command:

	Gender	Entry_Date	Flag
A	M	2012-01-19	True
B	F	2012-12-30	False
C	M	2012-05-05	False

Calling the `read_clipboard()` function makes this data available as a pandas DataFrame:

```
pd.read_clipboard()
```

Take a look at the following output:

```
   Gender  Entry_Date   Flag
A       M  2012-01-19   True
B       F  2012-12-30  False
C       M  2012-05-05  False
```

Output of read_clipboard

This function also recognizes the **Flag** column as a bool data type by default and assigns the unnamed column to be the index:

```
Gender         object
Entry_Date     object
Flag             bool
dtype: object
```

Data types after reading the clipboard

Managing sparse data

Sparse data refers to data structures such as arrays, series, DataFrames, and panels in which there is a very high proportion of missing data or NaNs.

Let's create a sparse DataFrame:

```
df = pd.DataFrame(np.random.randn(100, 3))
df.iloc[:95] = np.nan
```

This DataFrame has NaNs in 95% of the records. The memory usage of this data can be estimated with the following code:

```
df.memory_usage()
```

Take a look at the following output:

```
Index      80
0         800
1         800
2         800
dtype: int64
```

Memory usage of a DataFrame with 95% NaNs

As we can see, each element consumes 8 bytes of data, irrespective of whether it is actual data or a NaN. Pandas offers a memory-efficient solution for handling sparse data, as depicted in the following code:

```
sparse_df = df.to_sparse()
sparse_df.memory_usage()
```

Take a look at the following output:

```
Index      80
0          40
1          40
2          40
dtype: int64
```

Memory usage of sparse data

Now, the memory usage has come down, with memory not being allotted to NaNs. This can also be implemented by defining a `fill_value` instead of NaN:

```
df.fillna(0).to_sparse(fill_value = 0)
df.fillna(0).to_sparse(fill_value = 0).memory_usage()
```

Take a look at the following output:

```
Index     80
0         40
1         40
2         40
dtype: int64
```

Memory usage of sparse data after filling in the values

The sparse data can also be converted back into the original dense form, as shown in the following code:

```
sparse_df.to_dense()
```

This way of handling sparse data can be applied in a similar way to series, panels, and arrays.

Writing JSON objects to a file

The to_json() function allows any DataFrame object to be converted into a JSON string or written to a JSON file if the file path is specified:

```
df = pd.DataFrame({"Col1": [1, 2, 3, 4, 5], "Col2": ["A", "B", "B", "A",
"C"], "Col3": [True, False, False, True, True]})
df.to_json()
```

Take a look at the following output:

```
'{"Col1":{"0":1,"1":2,"2":3,"3":4,"4":5},"Col2":{"0":"A","1":"B","2":"B","3":"A","4":"C"},"Col3":{"0":true,"1":false,"2":false,"3":true,"4":true}}'
```

JSON output

The orientation of the data in the JSON can be altered. The to_json() function has an orient argument which can be set for the following modes: columns, index, record, value, and split. Columns is the default setting for orientation:

```
df.to_json(orient="columns")
```

Take a look at the following output:

```
'{"Col1":{"0":1,"1":2,"2":3,"3":4,"4":5},"Col2":{"0":"A","1":"B","2":"B","3":"A","4":"C"},"Col3":{"0":true,"1":false,"2":fals
e,"3":true,"4":true}}'
```

JSON output – column orientation

Orienting along the index acts like a transpose of the former case with a reversal of row and column indices in the JSON dictionary:

```
df.to_json(orient="index")
```

Take a look at the following output:

```
'{"0":{"Col1":1,"Col2":"A","Col3":true},"1":{"Col1":2,"Col2":"B","Col3":false},"2":{"Col1":3,"Col2":"B","Col3":false},"3":{"Col
1":4,"Col2":"A","Col3":true},"4":{"Col1":5,"Col2":"C","Col3":true}}'
```

JSON output – index orientation

Setting orient as records creates a JSON structure where each record or row from the original DataFrame retains its structural form:

```
df.to_json(orient="records")
```

Take a look at the following output:

```
'[{"Col1":1,"Col2":"A","Col3":true},{"Col1":2,"Col2":"B","Col3":false},{"Col1":3,"Col2":"B","Col3":false},{"Col1":4,"Col
2":"A","Col3":true},{"Col1":5,"Col2":"C","Col3":true}]'
```

JSON output – records orientation

When the orient option is set to values, both row indices and column indices vanish from the picture:

```
df.to_json(orient="values")
```

Take a look at the following output:

```
'[[1,"A",true],[2,"B",false],[3,"B",false],[4,"A",true],[5,"C",true]]'
```

JSON output – values orientation

The split orientation defines a JSON made up of entities such as column, index, and data:

```
df.to_json(orient="split")
```

Take a look at the following output:

'{"columns":["Col1","Col2","Col3"],"index":[0,1,2,3,4],"data":[[1,"A",true],[2,"B",false],[3,"B",false],[4,"A",true],[5,"C",tru e]]}'

JSON output—split orientation

Setting orient to table brings out aspects such as schema and field:

```
df.to_json(orient="table")
```

Take a look at the following output:

'{"schema": {"fields":[{"name":"index","type":"integer"},{"name":"Col1","type":"integer"},{"name":"Col2","type":"string"},{"nam e":"Col3","type":"boolean"}],"primaryKey":["index"],"pandas_version":"0.20.0"}, "data": [{"index":0,"Col1":1,"Col2":"A","Col3": true},{"index":1,"Col1":2,"Col2":"B","Col3":false},{"index":2,"Col1":3,"Col2":"B","Col3":false},{"index":3,"Col1":4,"Col 2":"A","Col3":true},{"index":4,"Col1":5,"Col2":"C","Col3":true}]}'

JSON output—table orientation

The `date_format` argument of `to_json()` allows timestamps in the DataFrame to be converted into either `epoch` format or `iso` format.

An unsupported datatype such as `complex` can be handled by specifying the type conversion to be followed through the `default_handler` argument.

Serialization/deserialization

Serialization is the process of translating `data structures` or `object` state into a format that can be stored (for example, in a `file` or memory `buffer`) or transmitted (for example, across a `network` connection link) and reconstructed later (possibly in a different computer environment).[1] When the resulting series of bits is reread according to the serialization format, it can be used to create a semantically identical clone of the original object.

Data structures such as JSON, arrays, DataFrames, and Series sometimes need to be stored as physical files or transmitted over a network. These serializations can be understood as a dump of data where data can be stored in any format (text, CSV, and so on) or structure but all the important data points can be recreated by loading/deserializing them.

Some examples of this are storing the parameters of the trained model object of a statistical model. This serialized file containing trained parameters can be loaded and the testing data can be passed through it for prediction. This is a popular method that's used to put statistical models to use.

Other uses of serialized data formats include transferring data through wires, storing objects in databases or HDDs, to make remote procedure calls, and to detect changes in time-varying data.

Let's create a sample DataFrame to understand the serialization of various file formats supported by Pandas:

```
df = pd.DataFrame({"First_Name":["Mike","Val","George","Chris","Benjamin"],
"Last_name":["K.","K.","C.","B.","A."],
"Entry_date":pd.to_datetime(["June 23,1989","June 16,1995","June
20,1997","June 25,2005","March 25,2016"],format= "%B %d,%Y"),
"Score":np.random.random(5)})
df
```

Take a look at the following output:

	First_Name	Last_name	Entry_date	Score
0	Mike	K.	1989-06-23	0.386284
1	Val	K.	1995-06-16	0.249500
2	George	C.	1997-06-20	0.807507
3	Chris	B.	2005-06-25	0.296101
4	Benjamin	A.	2016-03-25	0.722337

DataFrame for serialization

Writing to exotic file types

There are various formats that a data structure or object can be stored in. Let's go over a few of them.

to_pickle()

When a Python object is pickled, it gets saved to disk. Pickling serializes the object first, before writing it. It involves converting objects such as lists, Dicts, DataFrames, and trained machine learning models into a character stream.

Let's convert the DataFrame we defined earlier into pickle format:

```
df.to_pickle('pickle_filename.pkl')
```

It is also possible to compress pickle files before they are written. Compression schemes such as `gzip`, `bz2`, and `xz` are supported:

```
df.to_pickle("pickle_filename.compress", compression="gzip")
```

By default, the compression type is inferred from the extension that's provided:

```
df.to_pickle("pickle_filename.gz")
```

The `read_pickle()` function will deserialize the `pickle` file. Zip compression is only supported for reading a single file and not for writing.

to_parquet()

As we discussed in the *Reading parquet files* section, two engines can be used for deserialization as well:

```
df.to_parquet('sample_pyarrow.parquet', engine='pyarrow')
df.to_parquet('sample_fastparquet.parquet', engine='fastparquet')
```

to_hdf()

An HDF file is like a dictionary and it can store multiple objects. The `to_hdf()` function converts a Pandas object into an HDF file:

```
df.to_hdf('store.h5', append = True, format='table')
```

When all the columns of a row are NaNs, they are not automatically dropped. This can be done by setting the `dropna` argument to `True` when writing to HDF.

to_sql()

With support from the `sqlalchemy` package, data can be transferred to databases through pandas:

```
from sqlalchemy import create_engine
engine = create_engine('sqlite:///:memory:')
df.to_sql('data_sql',engine)
```

Data can also be pushed iteratively in batches by using the `chunksize` argument.

The data type of any column can also be changed when pushing to the database, as shown in the following code:

```
from sqlalchemy.types import String
df.to_sql('data_dtype', engine, dtype={'Score': String})
```

The `Timedelta` datatype, which is not supported across databases, is converted into its equivalent integral value in nanoseconds before being stored in the database.

to_feather()

Serializing a pandas object into feather format just requires the `to_feather()` function to be called:

```
df.to_feather('sample.feather')
```

to_html()

The `to_html()` function converts a DataFrame into a raw HTML format:

```
df.to_html()
```

This results in the following output:

```
'<table border="1" class="dataframe">\n  <thead>\n    <tr style="text-align: right;">\n      <th></th>\n      <th>First_Name</t
h>\n      <th>Last_name</th>\n      <th>Entry_date</th>\n      <th>Score</th>\n    </tr>\n  </thead>\n  <tbody>\n    <tr>\n
  <th>0</th>\n      <td>Mike</td>\n      <td>K.</td>\n      <td>1989-06-23</td>\n      <td>0.603962</td>\n    </tr>\n    <tr>\n
      <th>1</th>\n      <td>Val</td>\n      <td>K.</td>\n      <td>1995-06-16</td>\n      <td>0.297513</td>\n    </tr>\n    <tr
>\n      <th>2</th>\n      <td>George</td>\n      <td>C.</td>\n      <td>1997-06-20</td>\n      <td>0.487731</td>\n    </tr>\n
  <tr>\n      <th>3</th>\n      <td>Chris</td>\n      <td>B.</td>\n      <td>2005-06-25</td>\n      <td>0.415851</td>\n    </t
r>\n    <tr>\n      <th>4</th>\n      <td>Benjamin</td>\n      <td>A.</td>\n      <td>2016-03-25</td>\n      <td>0.766616</td>
\n    </tr>\n  </tbody>\n</table>'
```

DataFrame in HTML format

A horde of options in the `to_html()` function allow the raw HTML to be enriched. Being able to select columns and control escape sequences is possible through the use of the `columns` and `escape` arguments.

to_msgpack()

Msgpack offers fast and efficient binary serialization.

A single object can be directly converted into `msgpack` format like so:

```
df.to_msgpack("sample.msg")
```

If we have multiple objects, they can be serialized into a single `msgpack` file like so:

```
arr = np.random.randint(1,10,7)
lst = [10,20,40,60,60]
strg = "Data"
pd.to_msgpack("msg_all.msg",df,arr,lst,strg)
```

to_latex()

The `to_latex()` function takes a DataFrame and converts it into an aesthetic tabular structure that's compatible with `latex` documents:

```
df.to_latex()
```

Take a look at the following output:

```
'\\begin{tabular}{lllr}\n\\toprule\n{} & First\\_Name & Last\\_name & Entry\\_date &      Score \\\\\n\\midrule\n0 &       Mike
&        K. & 1989-06-23 &  0.244067 \\\\n1 &      Val &       K. & 1995-06-16 &  0.153420 \\\\n2 &     George &       C.
& 1997-06-20 &  0.755368 \\\\n3 &      Chris &       B. & 2005-06-25 &  0.988560 \\\\n4 &   Benjamin &      A. & 2016-03-2
5 &  0.697864 \\\\n\\bottomrule\n\\end{tabular}\n'
```

DataFrame in latex format

to_stata()

Pandas can help with creating `stata` data files with the `.dta` extension, as shown in the following code:

```
df.to_stata('stata_df.dta')
```

to_clipboard()

The `to_clipboard()` function transfers a DataFrame from a Python environment to the clipboard. From the clipboard, the object can be pasted elsewhere through the use of the *ctrl + V* keyboard command:

```
df.to_clipboard()
```

This DataFrame can also be sent to the clipboard in a format that's more compatible with CSV like so:

```
df.to_clipboard(excel=True,sep=",")
```

GeoPandas

GeoPandas is a Python package written on top of pandas that's used to work with geospatial data. It is designed to work with existing tools, such as desktop GIS, geospatial databases, web maps, and Python data tools.

GeoPandas allows you to easily perform operations in Python that would otherwise require a spatial database such as PostGIS.

What is geospatial data?

Spatial data, geospatial data, GIS data, and geodata are the names for numeric data that identifies the geographical location of a physical object such as a building, street, town, city, country, and so on according to a geographic coordinate system. Apart from the geographical location, geospatial data often also stores socioeconomic data, transaction data, and so on for each location.

Installation and dependencies

GeoPandas can be installed through pip or Anaconda, or directly through GitHub. The most common ways are through `pip` and Anaconda through a Terminal window:

```
pip install geopandas
conda install -c conda-forge geopandas
```

GeoPandas depends on the following Python libraries:

- `pandas`
- `numpy`
- `shapely`
- `fiona`
- `pyproj`
- `six`
- `rtree`

Working with GeoPandas

We can use the GeoPandas library to read many GIS file formats (relying on the `fiona` library, which is an interface to GDAL/OGR) using the `geopandas.read_file` function.

Data can be read through shapefiles as well. In this section, we will look at an example of working with GeoPandas. We will explain how to read a shapefile that contains geospatial data, performing aggregations on it, sorting it, and finally plotting the required Geo DataFrame.

Use the following code to call in the required prerequisites libraries:

```
import pandas as pd
import geopandas
import matplotlib as plt
```

Use the following code to read a shapefile that has geospatial information data:

```
countries = geopandas.read_file("ne_110m_admin_0_countries.shp")
```

Use the following code to access the first five rows of the dataset, just like we do with pandas:

```
countries.head(5)
```

The preceding code snippets result in the following output:

```
In [5]:   countries = geopandas.read_file("C:/Geopandas/ne_110m_admin_0_countries.shp")
          countries.head(5)
Out[5]:
```

	ABBREV	ABBREV_LEN	ADM0_A3	ADM0_A3_IS	ADM0_A3_UN	ADM0_A3_US	ADM0_A3_WB	ADM0_DIF	ADMIN	BRK_A3	...	WB_A2	WB_A3	WIKIDAT/
0	Fiji	4	FJI	FJI	-99	FJI	-99	0	Fiji	FJI	...	FJ	FJI	Q
1	Tanz.	5	TZA	TZA	-99	TZA	-99	0	United Republic of Tanzania	TZA	...	TZ	TZA	Q!
2	W. Sah.	7	SAH	MAR	-99	SAH	-99	0	Western Sahara	B28	...	-99	-99	Q6:
3	Can.	4	CAN	CAN	-99	CAN	-99	0	Canada	CAN	...	CA	CAN	(
4	U.S.A.	6	USA	USA	-99	USA	-99	1	United States of America	USA	...	US	USA	(

5 rows × 95 columns

A geospatial shape file read as a DataFrame

Let's plot a quick basic visualization of the data:

```
countries.plot()
```

This results in the following output:

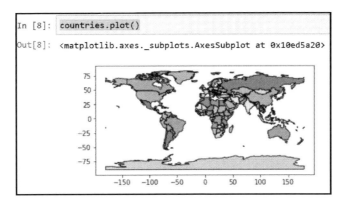

The countries in the shapefile plotted on a map

To check the data type of our geospatial data, we can use the following code:

```
type(countries)
```

This results in the following output:

```
In [9]:  type(countries)
Out[9]:  geopandas.geodataframe.GeoDataFrame
```

Asserting that the data type of the countries shapefile is a GeoDataFrame after conversion

Here, we can see that the DataFrame is a GeoDataFrame. Now, let's discuss what a GeoDataFrame is.

GeoDataFrames

A GeoDataFrame contains a geospatial dataset. It is just like a pandas DataFrame but with some additional functionality for working with geospatial data. This additional functionality is as follows:

- A .geometry attribute that always returns the column that includes geometry information (returning a GeoSeries). The column name itself does not necessarily need to be .geometry, but it will always be accessible as the .geometry attribute.
- It has some extra methods for working with spatial data (area, distance, buffer, intersection, and so on), all of which we will look at in later chapters.

GeoDataFrame is still a DataFrame, so we have all the functionalities that we have available for DataFrames. We can perform aggregation, sorting, filtering, and so on in GeoDataFrames as well.

Use the following code to perform a simple aggregation with GeoPandas:

```
countries['POP_EST'].mean()
```

POP_EST is a column in the countries GeoDataFrame and is of the numeric type. This results in the following output:

```
In [13]:  countries['POP_EST'].mean()
Out[13]:  41712369.84180791
```

Aggregating a numeric column in a GeoDataFrame shows that it works exactly the same way as a normal DataFrame

Alternatively, we can use boolean filtering to select a subset of the DataFrame based on a condition:

```
africa = countries[countries['CONTINENT'] == 'Africa']
```

Now, we will try to plot the filtered GeoDataFrame by using the `plot()` function:

```
africa.plot()
```

This results in the following output:

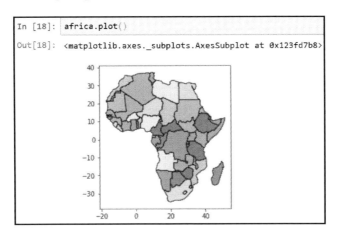

Subsetting one continent and plotting it for better visibility

GeoPandas also helps in converting an ordinary DataFrame into a GeoDataFrame, provided that you have `Latitude` and `Longitude` coordinates. Let's take a look at this.

Let's assume that we have a simple DataFrame, like this:

```
df = pd.DataFrame(
{'City': ['Buenos Aires', 'Brasilia', 'Santiago', 'Bogota', 'Caracas'],
'Country': ['Argentina', 'Brazil', 'Chile', 'Colombia', 'Venezuela'],
'Latitude': [-34.58, -15.78, -33.45, 4.60, 10.48],
'Longitude': [-58.66, -47.91, -70.66, -74.08, -66.86]})
```

The preceding code results in the following output:

	City	Country	Latitude	Longitude
0	Buenos Aires	Argentina	-34.58	-58.66
1	Brasilia	Brazil	-15.78	-47.91
2	Santiago	Chile	-33.45	-70.66
3	Bogota	Colombia	4.60	-74.08
4	Caracas	Venezuela	10.48	-66.86

Creating a normal DataFrame of country capitals with latitude and longitude

Let's append a new column called `'Coordinates'` which concatenates the latitude and longitude columns:

```
df['Coordinates']  = list(zip(df.Longitude, df.Latitude))
```

This results in the following output:

	City	Country	Latitude	Longitude	Coordinates
0	Buenos Aires	Argentina	-34.58	-58.66	(-58.66, -34.58)
1	Brasilia	Brazil	-15.78	-47.91	(-47.91, -15.78)
2	Santiago	Chile	-33.45	-70.66	(-70.66, -33.45)
3	Bogota	Colombia	4.60	-74.08	(-74.08, 4.6)
4	Caracas	Venezuela	10.48	-66.86	(-66.86, 10.48)

A normal DataFrame with latitude and longitude zipped in one column

Using the `Point` function from the shapely package, we can correctly identify these as positional coordinates or point tuple parameters, which are the vertebra of a GeoDataFrame:

```
from shapely.geometry import Point
    df['Coordinates'] = df['Coordinates'].apply(Point)
```

This results in the following output:

	City	Country	Latitude	Longitude	Coordinates
0	Buenos Aires	Argentina	-34.58	-58.66	POINT (-58.66 -34.58)
1	Brasilia	Brazil	-15.78	-47.91	POINT (-47.91 -15.78)
2	Santiago	Chile	-33.45	-70.66	POINT (-70.66 -33.45)
3	Bogota	Colombia	4.60	-74.08	POINT (-74.08 4.6)
4	Caracas	Venezuela	10.48	-66.86	POINT (-66.86 10.48)

Converting the zipped latitude and longitude into a point so that it is usable by geopandas for converting it into a GeoDataFrame

Now that everything is in place, let's convert this to a GeoDataFrame:

```
gdf = geopandas.GeoDataFrame(df, geometry='Coordinates')
```

Let's print the type as `gdf` to see its GeodataFrame type:

```
type(gdf)
```

This results in the following output:

```
In [16]: type(gdf)
Out[16]: geopandas.geodataframe.GeoDataFrame
```

Asserting that the type of the newly created DataFrame is a GeoDataFrame

This has given us a basic idea about GeoPandas and how it works. Its wings are so widespread that you can glide across the various features of it and get benefits from it.

Open source APIs – Quandl

Python can be used to fetch data from open source and commercial APIs. We can use it to fetch data in several formats. Some of them output data in JSON format, some in XML, and some in tabular formats such as CSV and DataFrames. Once converted into DataFrames, this data is generally processed in pandas.

In this section, we will look at an example of fetching data from the Quandl API, which is an open source API that contains data on a variety of topics such as financial, economic, and alternative data. You can have a look at this famous data repository here: `https://www.quandl.com/`.

An `api` key is an application programming interface that acts as a mediator between a developer or any other user who wishes to access the data within the website using a computer code. An `api` key is a piece of code that identifies the user and their associated account.

To get started with this example, you will need to sign up for a Quandl account, which is free. Post signup, the API key can be found under the Account setting options, which will be available under the dropdown of the profile image.

Python has made it easier to work with the Quandl API by providing us with a package that can be used to interact with the latest version of the Quandl data repository. This package is compatible with Python version 2.7 and above.

First things first, you need to install the Quandl package through `pip` or `conda` using the following command:

```
pip install quandl
conda install quandl
```

You can fetch any dataset you wish to use. Here, I am using the Brazilian Real Futures, July 2022 dataset for illustration purposes. You will need to find the data code for the dataset you want to download. This can be obtained from the Quandl website and is shown in the following screenshot:

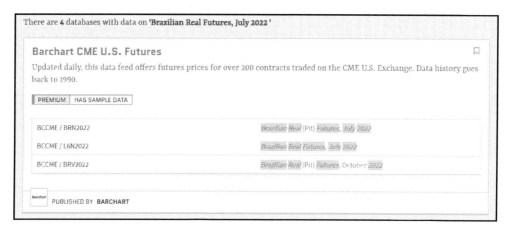

Finding the data code for a dataset on the Quandl website

Now, let's look at how we can use the Quandl API to fetch the data we want:

```
# import quandl into your code
import quandl
# setting your api key
quandl.ApiConfig.api_key = "[YOUR API KEY]"
# BCCME/L6N2022 is the code for the dataset and you can see it on the
right below the table
data = quandl.get("BCCME/L6N2022", start_date="2015-12-31",
end_date="2019-06-23")
data.head()
```

This results in the following output:

Date	Open	High	Low	Close	Volume	Prev Day OI	Prev Day Volume
2015-12-31	0.13490	0.13490	0.13490	0.13490	0.0	0.0	0.0
2016-01-04	0.13380	0.13380	0.13380	0.13380	0.0	0.0	0.0
2016-01-05	0.13755	0.13755	0.13755	0.13755	0.0	0.0	0.0
2016-01-06	0.13655	0.13655	0.13655	0.13655	0.0	0.0	0.0
2016-01-07	0.13470	0.13470	0.13470	0.13470	0.0	0.0	0.0

Brazilian Real Futures data fetched via the Quandl API

The API can also be used to fetch a subset of data and not all of it at once. For example, here, we have filtered the data for a given date range:

```
transform =  quandl.get("BCCME/L6N2022", start_date="2015-12-31",
end_date="2019-06-23",transformation='diff')
transform.head()
```

This results in the following output:

Date	Open	High	Low	Close	Volume	Prev Day OI	Prev Day Volume
2016-01-04	-0.00110	-0.00110	-0.00110	-0.00110	0.0	0.0	0.0
2016-01-05	0.00375	0.00375	0.00375	0.00375	0.0	0.0	0.0
2016-01-06	-0.00100	-0.00100	-0.00100	-0.00100	0.0	0.0	0.0
2016-01-07	-0.00185	-0.00185	-0.00185	-0.00185	0.0	0.0	0.0
2016-01-08	0.00120	0.00120	0.00120	0.00120	0.0	0.0	0.0

Brazilian Real Futures data fetched via the Quandl API with a date range filter

Once the data has been read, pandas can be used to perform all the transformations on the data, which will be helpful for further analysis.

Datasets can also be downloaded by providing the URLs of the dataset. This can be checked by downloading a file that will list the available datasets. Let's try downloading a file from the URL through Python's `urllib` package rather than following the `Quandl` package method.

To get the URL that can be used in this method, follow these steps:

1. Click on the dataset header/link (marked in the red box):

Data topic link to get more details about the topic

2. Clicking on the link will take you to the next page, where you would see these options. Select API under the Usage option, as shown in the following screenshot:

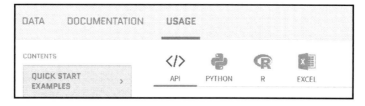

Data topic documentation

3. After this selection, you should scroll down a bit to find the following URLs, which can be used in the code to fetch the data:

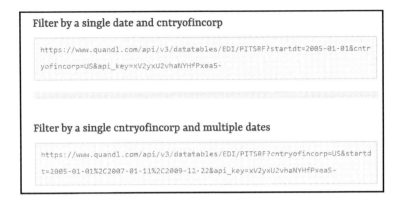

Filter by a single date and cntryofincorp

```
https://www.quandl.com/api/v3/datatables/EDI/PITSRF?startdt=2005-01-01&cntr
yofincorp=US&api_key=xV2yxU2vhaNYHfPxea5-
```

Filter by a single cntryofincorp and multiple dates

```
https://www.quandl.com/api/v3/datatables/EDI/PITSRF?cntryofincorp=US&startd
t=2005-01-01%2C2007-01-11%2C2009-12-22&api_key=xV2yxU2vhaNYHfPxea5-
```

API links for Quandl data that were obtained from the Data topic documentation

4. Since one topic may contain multiple datasets, the topic is downloaded as a `.zip` file containing all the datasets. It provides a metadata table, as well as the details (including the dataset key) of each dataset:

```
import urllib.request
print('Beginning file download with urllib...')
url =
'https://www.quandl.com/api/v3/databases/EOD/metadata?api_key=[YOUR API
KEY]'
urllib.request.urlretrieve(url,'file location.zip')
# We will read the zip file contents through the zipfile package.
import zipfile
archive = zipfile.ZipFile('[Name of the zip file].zip', 'r')
# lists the contents of the zip file
archive.namelist()
['EOD_metadata.csv']
df = pd.read_csv(archive.open('EOD_metadata.csv'))
df.head()
```

This results in the following output:

	code	name	description	refreshed_at	from_date	to_date
0	A	Agilent Technologies Inc. (A) Stock Prices, Di...	\<p>\Ticker\: A\</p> \<p>\Exchange\: NY...	2019-06-22 00:49:37	1999-11-18	2019-06-21
1	AA	Alcoa Corporation (AA) Stock Prices, Dividends...	\<p>\Ticker\: AA\</p> \<p>\Exchange\: N...	2019-06-22 00:49:57	2016-11-01	2019-06-21
2	AAAP	Advanced Accelerator Applications S.A. (AAAP) ...	\<p>\Ticker\: AAAP\</p> \<p>\Exchange\:...	2018-04-08 09:22:56	2015-11-11	2018-02-09
3	AAAU	Perth Mint Physical Gold (AAAU) Stock Prices, ...	\<p>\Ticker\: AAAU\</p> \<p>\Exchange\:...	2019-06-22 00:50:16	2018-08-15	2019-06-21
4	AABA	Altaba Inc. (AABA) Stock Prices, Dividends and...	\<p>\Ticker\: AABA\</p> \<p>\Exchange\:...	2019-06-22 00:49:36	1996-04-12	2019-06-21

Output of the metadata table of the downloaded data topic

read_sql_query

Python supports a lot of database operations using libraries such as `psycopg2` and `sqlalchemy`. Both of them are quite comprehensive and useful when working with databases from a Python interface. However, they have their own paraphernalia, which sometimes gets too much information for simple querying tasks. Fortunately, there is a hidden gem in pandas called `read_sql_query` method. It does the following:

- Runs simple queries involving select, where, and so on.
- Runs all the queries that return a table or its subset in a tabular form.
- Can't use the INSERT, UPDATE, and DELETE statements.
- The output is a DataFrame and hence all the pandas methods can be used for further data processing.

Let's look at how we can make use of this method. To illustrate this, we will insert a dataset as a table into a database. To do this, you will need to install a PostgreSQL or SQL database to your local directory. If you already have a database set up, you can ignore the table creation process and jump to the queries process.

Let's download the World Happiness 2019 dataset from Kaggle, push it to a `db`, and perform various DB and pandas operations on it:

```
import pandas as pd
df = pd.read_csv('F:/world-happiness-report-2019.csv')
df.head()
```

The following data shows us the World Happiness report as a DataFrame:

	Country (region)	Ladder	SD of Ladder	Positive affect	Negative affect	Social support	Freedom	Corruption	Generosity	Log of GDP per capita	Healthy life expectancy
0	Finland	1	4	41.0	10.0	2.0	5.0	4.0	47.0	22.0	27.0
1	Denmark	2	13	24.0	26.0	4.0	6.0	3.0	22.0	14.0	23.0
2	Norway	3	8	16.0	29.0	3.0	3.0	8.0	11.0	7.0	12.0
3	Iceland	4	9	3.0	3.0	1.0	7.0	45.0	3.0	15.0	13.0
4	Netherlands	5	1	12.0	25.0	15.0	19.0	12.0	7.0	12.0	18.0

World Happiness report as a DataFrame

Since we are going to directly create a table from the DataFame that we generated previously, it is necessary to change the column name to postgresql since it does not support column names with spaces:

```
# rename Country (region) to region
df= df.rename(columns={'Country (region)':'region'})
# push the dataframe to postgresql using sqlalchemy
# Syntax:engine =
db.create_engine('dialect+driver://user:pass@host:port/db')
from sqlalchemy import create_engine
engine =
create_engine('postgresql://postgres:1128@127.0.0.1:5433/postgres')
df.to_sql('happy', engine,index=False)
```

In order to use the `read_sql_query` method, we need to make a connection with the database using either `psycopg2` or `sqlalchemy`. Once the connection has been established, `read_sql_query` can be used in its full form:

```
import psycopg2
try:
    connection = psycopg2.connect(user="[db-user_name]",
                                  password="[db-pwd]",
                                  host="127.0.0.1",
                                  port="5433",
                                  database="postgres")
        happy= pd.read_sql_query("select * from
happy;",con=connection).head()
```

This results in the following output:

	region	Ladder	SD of Ladder	Positive affect	Negative affect	Social support	Freedom	Corruption	Generosity	Log of GDP per capita	Healthy life expectancy
0	Finland	1	4	41.0	10.0	2.0	5.0	4.0	47.0	22.0	27.0
1	Denmark	2	13	24.0	26.0	4.0	6.0	3.0	22.0	14.0	23.0
2	Norway	3	8	16.0	29.0	3.0	3.0	8.0	11.0	7.0	12.0
3	Iceland	4	9	3.0	3.0	1.0	7.0	45.0	3.0	15.0	13.0
4	Netherlands	5	1	12.0	25.0	15.0	19.0	12.0	7.0	12.0	18.0

World Happiness report data as a DataFrame queried from the table in the PostgreSQL DB

Take a look at the following code. This helps in running a SQL query.

```
posgrt40 = pd.read_sql_query('select * from happy where "Positive affect" >
40;',con=connection).head()
```

This results in the following output:

	region	Ladder	SD of Ladder	Positive affect	Negative affect	Social support	Freedom	Corruption	Generosity	Log of GDP per capita	Healthy life expectancy
0	Finland	1	4	41.0	10.0	2.0	5.0	4.0	47.0	22.0	27.0
1	Switzerland	6	11	44.0	21.0	13.0	11.0	7.0	16.0	8.0	4.0
2	Austria	10	10	64.0	24.0	31.0	26.0	19.0	25.0	16.0	15.0
3	Australia	11	26	47.0	37.0	7.0	17.0	13.0	6.0	18.0	10.0
4	Israel	13	14	104.0	69.0	38.0	93.0	74.0	24.0	31.0	11.0

World Happiness report data with filters as a DataFrame queried from the table in the PostgreSQL DB

```
except (Exception, psycopg2.Error) as error :
print ("Error while fetching data from PostgreSQL", error)
```

The pd.read_sql_query() method returns the table as a DataFrame rather than requiring the programmer to intervene and convert the data into the necessary format.

Pandas plotting

A picture is worth a thousand words. This is why graphs are commonly used to visually illustrate relationships in data. The purpose of a graph is to present data that is too numerous or complicated to be described adequately in terms of text and in less space. With Python's **plotting function**, it takes far less than a few words of code to create a production-quality graphic.

We will begin by installing the necessary packages:

```
import pandas as pd
import numpy as np
```

We are using the `mtcars` data here to explain the plots:

```
mtcars = pd.DataFrame({
        'mpg':[21,21,22.8,21.4,18.7,18.1,18.3,24.4,22.8,19.2],
        'cyl':[6,6,4,6,8,6,8,4,4,4],
        'disp':[160,160,108,258,360,225,360,146.7,140.8,167.7],
   'hp':[110,110,93,110,175,105,245,62,95,123],
'category':['SUV','Sedan','Sedan','Hatchback','SUV','Sedan','SUV','Hatchbac
k','SUV','Sedan']
        })
mtcars
```

This results in the following output:

	Category	Cylinder	Displacement	Horse Power	Miles Per Gallon
0	SUV	6	160.0	110	21.0
1	Sedan	6	160.0	110	21.0
2	Sedan	4	108.0	93	22.8
3	Hatchback	6	258.0	110	21.4
4	SUV	8	360.0	175	18.7
5	Sedan	6	225.0	105	18.1
6	SUV	8	360.0	245	18.3
7	Hatchback	4	146.7	62	24.4
8	SUV	4	140.8	95	22.8
9	Sedan	4	167.7	123	19.2

mtcars DataFrame

Let's discuss the various plots in `pandas.plotting` in detail.

Andrews curves

Andrews curve is a method that's used to visualize multidimensional data. It does this by mapping each observation onto a function. Here, each color that's used represents a class and we can easily note that the lines that represent samples from the same class have similar curves. This curve is very useful in analyzing time series and signal data.

Basically, each data point is sent through a Fourier transform according to the Fourier function. Each line in the following chart represents a separate data point. It can be plotted using the snippet below.

```
andrew = pd.plotting.andrews_curves(mtcars,'Category')
```

The following is the graph:

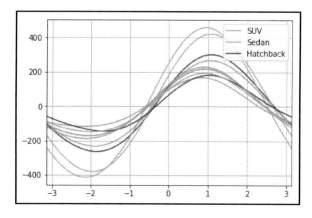

Andrews curve plot

Parallel plot

Parallel plots are best used when we need to compare many variables for each point and to understand the relationship between them, for example, if you need to compare an array of variables with the same attributes but differing values (for example, comparing motorcycle specs across different models).

Each connected line represents one data point. The vertical lines represent the columns or variables whose values have been plotted for each data point. The inflection point (marked in red) represents the values of those variables for those points. A parallel chart can be plotted very easily using pandas, as shown in the following code:

```
parallel = pd.plotting.parallel_coordinates(mtcars,'Category')
```

This results in the following output:

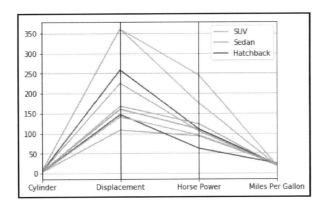

Parallel plot

Radviz plots

Radviz plots allow for the exploration of multi-task classification problems. It displays data of three or more variables in a two-dimensional projection. This plot is like a circle with data points inside it. The variables are present around the perimeter of the circle.

The position of each point is determined by the values of all the variable values that make it. An imaginary circle is created and the variables are placed on this circle. The points are placed within the perimeter of the circle. The exact position of the point is determined by the position where the force that's exerted on it by each variable sums to zero. The force that's applied by each variable can be thought of as a spring force and is governed by Hook's law (F = kx):

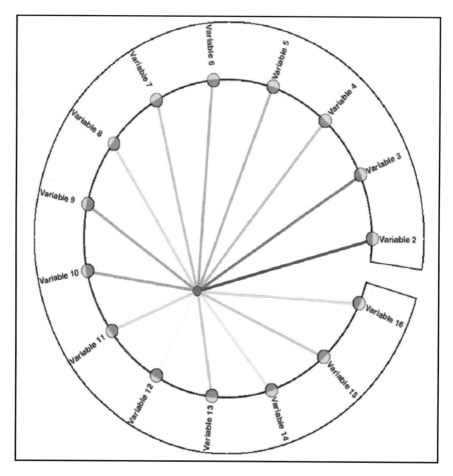

Radviz plot explanation

The plot above can be obtained by running the snippet below.

```
rad_viz = pd.plotting.radviz(mtcars, 'Category')
```

This results in the following output:

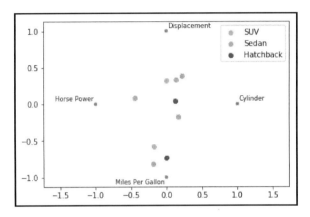

Radviz plot

Scatter matrix plot

A scatter matrix plot consists of several plots of variables, all of which are present in a matrix format. Basically, a 2 x 2 matrix of variables is created where each cell represents a combination of two variables. Then, a scatter plot is generated for each combination. It can be used to determine the correlation between variables. It is used in a lot of dimension reduction cases:

```
scatter = pd.plotting.scatter_matrix(mtcars,alpha = 0.5)
```

This results in the following output:

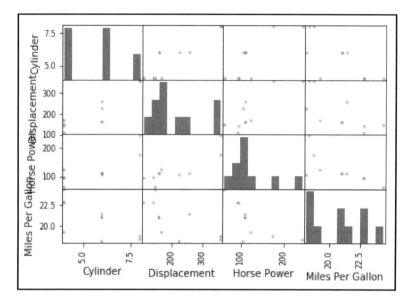

Scatter matrix plot

Lag plot

A lag plot is a special type of scatter plot with variables (X, X-lagged, and so on).

X -lagged is the variable that's derived from X with a time lag. The graph is plotted among two variables and the plot is used to determine the randomness, model suitability, outliers, and serial correlation in the data – especially time series data:

```
s = pd.Series(np.random.uniform(size=100))
```

This results in the following output:

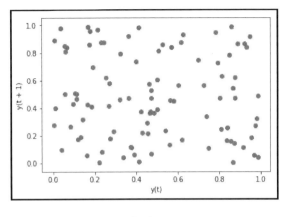

Lag plot

Bootstrap plot

A bootstrap plot is used to determine the uncertainty of statistics such as mean, median, midrange, and so on. It relies on the random sampling method with replacement. Calculating a statistic by randomly sampling from the same data multiple times and then averaging the individual result from each sample is called bootstrapping. A bootstrapping plot basically plots all the resultant values that were obtained from each random sample. It calculates the mean, median, and mode for all the samples and plots them as bar and line charts.

A random sample is selected from the data and the process is repeated a specified number of times to obtain the required metrics. The resulting plot that's obtained is a bootstrap plot:

```
fig = pd.plotting.bootstrap_plot(s)
```

This results in the following output:

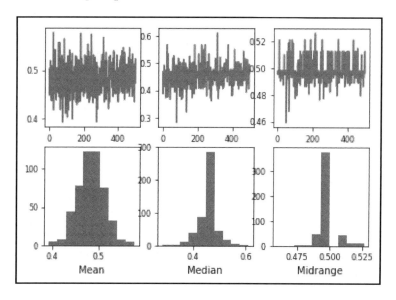

Lag plot

pandas-datareader

We can use pandas to not only read data from local CSV or text files but also from various popular remote data sources such as Yahoo Finance, World Bank, and so on. Without any support from pandas, this would have been tedious and we would have to resort to web scraping. This simple and powerful functionality is provided through the `pandas-datareader`.

It provides us with a direct way of connecting through various data sources from the comfort of the pandas ecosystem without having to delve into the complexity of HTML/JavaScript code where data is enmeshed. These data sources can be accessed by providing the source name and data code. Only a subset of the data can be obtained.

Let's delve deeper and see how we can use it:

1. Install `pandas-datareader` through `pip` using the following command:

   pip install pandas-datareader

   You can also install it through `conda` using the following set of commands

2. First, we have to add `conda-forge` to our channel:

   conda config --add channels conda-forge

3. After enabling `pandas-datareader`, it can be installed with the following code:

   conda install pandas-datareader

Now, let's get hands-on with some of the remote data sources and perform various functions provided by the pandas library to get an idea of how it works.

Yahoo Finance

If you are interested in knowing about the trends of the business world and have a thirst to get updates about `stocks` and `bonds`, or if you are the one who has invested in them, then you may crave an update that occurs every minute. Google Finance is a financial website that was developed by Google that's made this straightforward by providing the required information and also letting us customize our needs according to our interests.

Google's API became less reliable during 2017 and has become highly deprecated because of the unavailability of a stable replacement due to large breaks in the API.

An alternative to it is **Yahoo** Finance, which is similar to Google Finance, and is popular among users for its robust data and consistency.

Now let's use `pandas-datareader` to get information related to stocks, mutual funds, and anything related to finance using the Google Finance API.

```
import pandas as pd
from pandas_datareader import data
symbols=['AAPL','GOOGL','FB','TWTR']
# initializing a dataframe
get_data = pd.DataFrame()
stock = pd.DataFrame()
for ticker in symbols:
    get_data = get_data.append(data.DataReader(ticker,
                        start='2015-1-1',
```

```
                          end='2019-6-23', data_source='yahoo'))
        for line in get_data:
            get_data['symbol'] = ticker
        stock = stock.append(get_data)
        get_data = pd.DataFrame()
    stock.head()
```

The preceding code results in the following output:

Date	High	Low	Open	Close	Volume	Adj Close	symbol
2014-12-31	113.129997	110.209999	112.820000	110.379997	41403400.0	102.110046	AAPL
2015-01-02	111.440002	107.349998	111.389999	109.330002	53204600.0	101.138702	AAPL
2015-01-05	108.650002	105.410004	108.290001	106.250000	64285500.0	98.289474	AAPL
2015-01-06	107.430000	104.629997	106.540001	106.260002	65797100.0	98.298729	AAPL
2015-01-07	108.199997	106.699997	107.199997	107.750000	40105900.0	99.677094	AAPL

Date filtered stock data for Apple, Google, Facebook, and Twitter

```
stock.describe()
```

This results in the following output:

	High	Low	Open	Close	Volume	Adj Close
count	4504.000000	4504.000000	4504.000000	4504.000000	4.504000e+03	4504.000000
mean	302.697999	297.150684	299.999678	300.020391	2.129974e+07	298.871501
std	363.983370	357.617967	360.916652	360.927581	1.904314e+07	361.466151
min	14.220000	13.730000	13.950000	14.010000	5.206000e+05	14.010000
25%	69.495002	66.987500	68.860001	68.755002	6.498700e+06	68.755002
50%	139.985001	138.455002	139.154999	139.330002	1.842245e+07	138.701065
75%	300.172501	295.062500	297.894997	298.317505	2.867828e+07	296.309067
max	1296.969971	1271.709961	1289.119995	1296.199951	1.924153e+08	1296.199951

Summary statistics of the stock data

Take a look at the following code:

```
# get the list of column names
cols = [ col for col in stock.columns]
cols
```

This results in the following output:

```
['High', 'Low', 'Open', 'Close', 'Volume', 'Adj Close', 'symbol']
```

Take a look at the following code:

```
# returns the symbol of the highest traded value among the symbols
stock.loc[stock['High']==stock['High'].max(), 'High']
```

This results in the following output:

```
Date
2019-04-29    1296.969971
Name: High, dtype: float64
```

The preceding code will return a DataFrame that gives you full details about the stock prices for each and every day between the two dates for `Apple[AAPL]`, `Google[GOOGL]`, `FB[FB]`, and `Twitter[TWTR]`.

It is important to get to know your data before performing any kind of analysis. Please take the following things into account:

- High is the highest price that the stock was traded for on that particular date.
- Low is the lowest price that the stock was traded for on that particular date.
- Open is the price that the stock was when the date started.
- Close is the price that the stock was when the market closed for that date.
- Volume is the number of physical shares that were traded for that particular stock.
- Adj Close is the price that the stock was after the market closed.

World Bank

The World Bank is an organization that provides financial advice and helps various nations in terms of their economical state. It also provides a variety of data, including time series, geospatial, financial data, and so on, all of which will be helpful for analysis.

Before we start fetching data from the World Bank website, we must sign up to it. This allows us to get the indicator code for the dataset that we want to download. Signing up for the World Bank is free and doesn't take much time.

For the purpose of this example, I have used the World Development Indicators dataset. You can choose any dataset of your choice and start working on it:

```
from pandas_datareader import wb
```

To get the indicator code, select the **Databank** tab and choose **Metadata Glossary** from the list that's displayed on the left-hand pane. You can find the indicator below each dataset, on the left-hand side of the panel (marked in red in the attached screenshot):

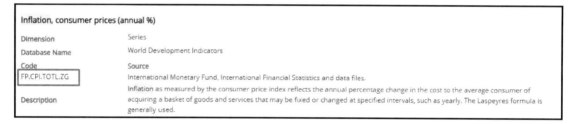

Indicator code for the dataset, which is required for fetching data

```
dat = wb.download(indicator='FP.CPI.TOTL.ZG', start=2005, end=2019)
```

The DataFrame is returned in a multi-index row format:

```
dat.head()
```

This results in the following output:

country	year	FP.CPI.TOTL.ZG
Canada	2018	NaN
	2017	1.596884
	2016	1.428760
	2015	1.125241
	2014	1.906636

Multi-indexed DataFrame output of the World Bank indicator data

Now, let's display the data for one particular country, like so:

```
dat.loc['Canada']
```

This results in the following output:

year	FP.CPI.TOTL.ZG
2018	NaN
2017	1.596884
2016	1.428760
2015	1.125241
2014	1.906636
2013	0.938292
2012	1.515678
2011	2.912135
2010	1.776872
2009	0.299467
2008	2.370271
2007	2.138384
2006	2.002025
2005	2.213552

Multi-indexed DataFrame output of the World Bank indicator data for one country. It becomes single indexed.

We can also return the price inflation data related to only one particular year for a particular country, like so:

```
dat.loc['Canada'].loc['2015']
```

This results in the following output:

```
FP.CPI.TOTL.ZG    1.125241
Name: 2015, dtype: float64
```

Data subsetted by both indices

Summary

After reading this chapter, the following points have been observed:

- pandas provides powerful methods so that we can read from and write to a variety of data structures and a variety of sources.
- The read_csv method in pandas can be used for reading CSV files, TXT files, and tables. This method has a multitude of arguments in order to specify delimiters, which rows to skip while reading, reading a file in smaller chunks, and so on.
- pandas can be used to read data directly from URLs or S3.
- DataFrames can be converted into JSON and vice versa. JSON can be stored in text files that can be read.
- JSONs have dictionary-like structures that can be nested an infinite number of times. This nested data can be subsetted just like a dictionary with keys.
- Pandas provide methods so that we can read data from the HD5, HTML, SAS, SQL, parquet, feather, and Google BigQuery data formats.
- Serialization helps in dumping data structures or objects to physical files, storing them in a database, or transmitting them through a message.

In the next chapter, we will learn how to access and select data from panda data structures. We will also look in detail at basic indexing and label-, integer-, and mixed indexing.

Section 3: Mastering Different Data Operations in pandas

3

This section introduces you to the different data analysis tasks you can perform with the power of pandas. These highly practical chapters will make you an expert in the different data manipulation techniques that pandas has to offer, from accessing and selecting data to merging and grouping it with other data. All this is absolutely essential if you want to gain a mastery of using pandas for expert data analysis.

This section is comprised of the following chapters:

- Chapter 5, *Indexing and Selecting in pandas*
- Chapter 6, *Grouping, Merging, and Reshaping Data in pandas*
- Chapter 7, *Special Data Operations in pandas*
- Chapter 8, *Time Series and Plotting Using Matplotlib*

5
Indexing and Selecting in pandas

In the previous chapter, you learned how pandas makes it possible to read from any source and store structured data as a pandas object—Series, DataFrame, or panel. This chapter elaborates on how to slice and dice these objects. The row labels and column labels serve as identifiers that help us with selecting a subset of the data. Instead of a label, positional identifiers such as the row index and column index can also be used. Indexing and selecting are the most fundamental yet vital operations performed on data. The topics that will be addressed in this chapter include the following:

- Basic indexing
- Labels, integer, and mixed indexing
- Multi-indexing
- Boolean indexing
- Operations on indexes

Basic indexing

If you have come across lists in Python, you will know that a pair of square brackets ([ ]) is used to index and subset a list. This square bracket operator is also useful in slicing NumPy arrays. The square bracket [ ] is the basic indexing operator in pandas as well.

Let's create a Series, DataFrame, and panel to understand how the square bracket operator is used in pandas:

```
# Creating a series with 6 rows and user-defined index
ser = pd.Series(["Numpy", "Pandas", "Sklearn", "Tensorflow", "Scrapy",
"Keras"],
index = ["A", "B", "C", "D", "E", "F"])

# Creating a 6X3 dataframe with defined row and column labels
df = pd.DataFrame(np.random.randn(6, 3), columns = ["colA", "colB",
"colC"],
index = ["R1", "R2", "R3", "R4", "R5", "R6"])

# Creating a panel with 3 items
pan = pd.Panel({"Item1": df+1, "Item2": df, "Item3": df*2})
```

For a Series, the square bracket operator can be used to slice by specifying the label or the positional index. Both use cases are shown in the following code block:

```
# Subset using the row-label
In: ser["D"]
Out: 'Tensorflow'

# Subset using positional index
In: ser[1]
Out: 'Pandas'
```

The use of the square bracket operator in a DataFrame does have some restrictions. It allows only the column label to be passed and not the positional index or even the row label. Passing any other string that does not represent a column name raises KeyError:

```
# Subset a single column by column name
df["colB"]
```

This results in the following output:

```
R1     0.037022
R2     0.320217
R3     0.322619
R4     0.314157
R5    -0.187626
R6    -1.441116
Name: colB, dtype: float64
```

Subset of a single column by column name

A sequence of square bracket operators can be used to specify the row index or row label following the column attribute:

```
# Accessing a single element in a DataFrame
df["colB"]["R3"], df["colB"][1]
```

This results in the following output:

```
(0.3226187490246503, 0.32021698017618827)
```

Slicing a single element using the square bracket operator

The rules that apply to a DataFrame apply to a panel as well—each item can be sliced from the panel by specifying the item name. The square bracket operator accepts only a valid item name:

```
# Subset a panel
pan["Item1"]
```

This results in the following output:

	colA	colB	colC
R1	0.602401	1.037022	-1.198529
R2	2.185997	1.320217	0.514537
R3	1.001112	1.322619	1.461976
R4	0.020544	1.314157	-0.244565
R5	2.332869	0.812374	2.654282
R6	-0.357020	-0.441116	-0.533661

Subset of a panel

To subset multiple values, a list of the labels of the entities to be subset should be passed into the square bracket operator. Let's examine this using the DataFrame. This holds good for Series and Panels as well:

```
df[["colA", "colB"]]
```

This results in the following output:

	colA	colB
R1	1.153329	-0.853382
R2	-0.023922	0.580591
R3	-0.282767	0.214133
R4	0.742148	-1.771625
R5	-0.634333	0.033427
R6	1.846869	-0.441400

Slicing multiple columns from a DataFrame

When a string that is not a column name is passed in, it raises an exception. This can be overcome by using the `get ()` method:

```
In: df.get("columnA", "NA")
Out: 'NA'
```

The square bracket operator is also useful for inserting a new column in a DataFrame, as shown in the following code block:

```
# Add new column "colD"
df["colD"] = list(range(len(df)))
df
```

This results in the following output:

	colA	colB	colC	colD
R1	-0.377364	0.166759	0.682802	0
R2	1.921379	-0.197037	-0.759879	1
R3	-2.089066	-0.036373	-1.217749	2
R4	-1.428905	-0.170528	1.160940	3
R5	-1.061140	-1.408500	0.839550	4
R6	-0.099625	-1.736265	-0.307186	5

Adding a new column to a DataFrame

New values can be added to Series and Panels as well, via the method shown here.

Accessing attributes using the dot operator

To access a single entity (a column, value, or item), the square bracket operator can be replaced by the dot operator. Let's subset `colA` in the DataFrame using the dot (`.`) operator:

```
df.colA
```

This results in the following output:

```
R1    -0.377364
R2     1.921379
R3    -2.089066
R4    -1.428905
R5    -1.061140
R6    -0.099625
Name: colA, dtype: float64
```

Slicing a column with the dot operator

By using two dot operators in a chain, an individual element can be accessed:

```
In: df.colA.R3
Out: -2.089066
```

This is also applicable to Panels and Series. However, unlike the square bracket operator in Series, the positional index cannot be used here. For the dot operator to be used, the row labels or column labels must have valid names. A valid Python identifier must follow the following lexical convention:

```
identifier::= (letter|"_") (letter | digit | "_")*
Thus, a valid Python identifier cannot contain a space. See the Python
Lexical Analysis documents for more details at
http://docs.python.org/2.7/reference/lexical_analysis.html#identifiers.
```

Using the dot operator, the values of existing columns can be changed. However, new columns cannot be created.

Range slicing

Slicing by supplying the start and end position to subset a range of values can be done in pandas objects, just as in NumPy arrays. The [:] operator helps in range slicing.

Let's slice the Series that we created earlier to subset the second, third, and fourth rows:

```
ser[1:4]
```

This results in the following output:

```
B            Pandas
C           Sklearn
D        Tensorflow
dtype: object
```

Slicing a Series with a range of indexes

As always with a range in Python, the value after the colon is excluded when slicing.

Range slicing can be done by providing either the start or end index. If the end index is not provided, values are sliced from the given starting index to the end of the data structure. Likewise, when only the end index is given, the first row is considered as the starting position for slicing:

```
# End provided for range slicing
df[:2]
```

This results in the following output:

	colA	colB	colC
R1	1.049545	1.663777	0.603633
R2	0.231452	0.368404	-0.497894

Range slicing with the posterior end of the range defined

When the starting index is given, the row corresponding to that index value is chosen as the starting position for slicing:

```
# Start provided for range slicing
df[2:]
```

This results in the following output:

	colA	colB	colC
R3	1.567452	0.469145	0.545377
R4	-0.331197	-0.960112	-0.854184
R5	1.676691	-0.461345	0.253380
R6	0.760322	0.283970	-0.469825

Range slicing with the anterior end of the range defined

Range slicing can be made even more interesting through a property to select rows at evenly spaced intervals. For instance, you can select only the odd-numbered rows or even-numbered rows this way:

```
# Select odd rows
df[::2]
```

This results in the following output:

	colA	colB	colC
R1	1.049545	1.663777	0.603633
R3	1.567452	0.469145	0.545377
R5	1.676691	-0.461345	0.253380

Range slicing to select odd-numbered rows

To select even rows, you can use the following code:

```
# Select even rows
df[1::2]
```

This results in the following output:

	colA	colB	colC
R2	0.231452	0.368404	-0.497894
R4	-0.331197	-0.960112	-0.854184
R6	0.760322	0.283970	-0.469825

Range slicing to select even-numbered rows

If you want to reverse the order of the rows, you can use the following command:

```
# Reverse the rows
df[::-1]
```

This results in the following output:

	colA	colB	colC
R6	0.760322	0.283970	-0.469825
R5	1.676691	-0.461345	0.253380
R4	-0.331197	-0.960112	-0.854184
R3	1.567452	0.469145	0.545377
R2	0.231452	0.368404	-0.497894
R1	1.049545	1.663777	0.603633

Range slicing to reverse the order of rows

Labels, integer, and mixed indexing

In addition to the standard indexing operator, `[]`, and attribute operator, there are operators provided in pandas to make the job of indexing easier and more convenient. By label indexing, we generally mean indexing by a header name, which tends to be a string value in most cases. These operators are as follows:

- **The** `.loc` **operator**: This allows label-oriented indexing.
- **The** `.iloc` **operator**: This allows integer-based indexing.
- **The** `.ix` **operator**: This allows mixed label and integer-based indexing.

We'll now turn our attention to these operators.

Label-oriented indexing

The `.loc` operator supports pure label-based indexing. It accepts the following as valid inputs:

- A single label such as `["colC"]`, `[2]`, or `["R1"]`—note that in cases where the label is an integer, it doesn't refer to the integer position of the index, but the integer is itself a label.

- A list or array of labels, for example, ["colA", "colB"].
- A slice object with labels, for example, "colB":"colD".
- A Boolean array.

Let's examine each of these four cases with respect to the following two Series—one with an integer-based label and another with a string-based label:

```
ser_loc1 = pd.Series(np.linspace(11, 15, 5))
ser_loc2 = pd.Series(np.linspace(11, 15, 5), index = list("abcde"))

# Indexing with single label
In: ser_loc1.loc[2]
Out: 13.0
In: ser_loc2.loc["b"]
Out: 12.0

# Indexing with a list of labels
ser_loc1.loc[[1, 3, 4]]
```

This results in the following output:

```
1        12.0
3        14.0
4        15.0
dtype: float64
```

Output of loc1.loc with a list of integer labels

```
ser_loc2.loc[["b", "c", "d"]]
```

```
b        12.0
c        13.0
d        14.0
dtype: float64
```

Output of loc2.loc with a list of labels

```
# Indexing with range slicing
ser_loc1.loc[1:4]
```

```
1       12.0
2       13.0
3       14.0
4       15.0
dtype: float64
```

Output of loc with range slicing (integer labels)

```
ser_loc2.loc["b":"d"]
```

```
b       12.0
c       13.0
d       14.0
dtype: float64
```

Output of loc with range slicing

Notice that, unlike the ranges in Python where the posterior end is excluded, here, both the exteriors are included in the selected data. pandas objects can also be filtered based on logical conditions applied to values within the objects:

```
# Indexing with Boolean arrays
ser_loc1.loc[ser_loc1 > 13]
```

```
3       14.0
4       15.0
dtype: float64
```

Output of loc with a Boolean array for indexing

Now, these techniques for slicing can be applied to a DataFrame. It works the same, except for the fact that there is a provision to supply two sets of labels—one for each axis:

```
# Create a dataframe with default row-labels
df_loc1 = pd.DataFrame(np.linspace(1, 25, 25).reshape(5, 5), columns =
["Asia", "Europe", "Africa", "Americas", "Australia"])
```

```
# Create a dataframe with custom row labels
df_loc2 = pd.DataFrame(np.linspace(1, 25, 25).reshape(5, 5), columns =
["Asia", "Europe", "Africa", "Americas", "Australia"], index = ["2011",
"2012", "2013", "2014", "2015"])
```

```
# Indexing with single label
df_loc1.loc[:,"Asia"]
```

```
0     1.0
1     6.0
2    11.0
3    16.0
4    21.0
Name: Asia, dtype: float64
```

Output of loc for slicing a single column

```
df_loc1.loc[2, :]
```

```
Asia         11.0
Europe       12.0
Africa       13.0
Americas     14.0
Australia    15.0
Name: 2, dtype: float64
```

Output of loc for slicing a single row (integer label)

In the preceding case, "2" did not represent the position, but the index label:

```
df_loc2.loc["2012", :]
```

```
Asia          6.0
Europe        7.0
Africa        8.0
Americas      9.0
Australia    10.0
Name: 2012, dtype: float64
```

Output of loc for slicing a single row

```
# Indexing with a list of labels
df_loc1.loc[:,["Africa", "Asia"]]
```

	Africa	Asia
0	3.0	1.0
1	8.0	6.0
2	13.0	11.0
3	18.0	16.0
4	23.0	21.0

Output of loc for selecting through a list of labels

```
# Indexing with range slicing
df_loc1.loc[:,"Europe":"Americas"]
```

	Europe	Africa	Americas
0	2.0	3.0	4.0
1	7.0	8.0	9.0
2	12.0	13.0	14.0
3	17.0	18.0	19.0
4	22.0	23.0	24.0

Output of loc for range slicing

```
# Indexing with Boolean array
df_loc2.loc[df_loc2["Asia"] > 11, :]
```

	Asia	Europe	Africa	Americas	Australia
2014	16.0	17.0	18.0	19.0	20.0
2015	21.0	22.0	23.0	24.0	25.0

Output of loc for slicing based on a Boolean array

Integer-oriented indexing

Integer-oriented indexing can be implemented for the same four cases as label-oriented indexing: single labels, a list of labels, range slicing, and Boolean arrays.

Let's use the same DataFrames as in the previous session to understand integer-oriented indexing. Here, let's use two values—one for each axis—to examine integer-based indexing. Passing an index for one axis is also permissible. This can also be done with the `loc` operator by passing in both the row and column labels:

```
# Indexing with single values.
In: df_loc1.iloc[3, 2]
Out: 18.0

# Indexing with list of indices
df_loc1.iloc[[1, 4], [0, 2, 3]]
```

	Asia	Africa	Americas
1	6.0	8.0	9.0
4	21.0	23.0	24.0

Output of iloc for slicing with a list of indices

```
# Indexing with ranged slicing
df_loc2.iloc[3:,:3]
```

	Asia	Europe	Africa
2014	16.0	17.0	18.0
2015	21.0	22.0	23.0

Output of iloc for ranged slicing

```
# Indexing with Boolean array
df_loc2.iloc[(df_loc2["Asia"] > 11).values, :]
```

	Asia	Europe	Africa	Americas	Australia
2014	16.0	17.0	18.0	19.0	20.0
2015	21.0	22.0	23.0	24.0	25.0

Output of iloc for slicing with a Boolean array

For Boolean array-based indexing with the `iloc` operator, the array must be extracted using logical conditions around array values.

The .iat and .at operators

The `.iat` and `.at` operators are equivalent to `.iloc` and `.loc` operators—the former is for position-based indexing and the latter for label-based indexing. While `.loc` and `.iloc` support the selection of multiple values, `.at` and `.iat` can only extract a single scalar value. Hence they require row and column indices for slicing:

```
In: df_loc2.at["2012", "Americas"]
Out: 9.0

In: df_loc1.iat[2, 3]
Out: 14.0
```

The `.iat` and `.at` operators are considerably faster in performance than `.iloc` and `.loc`:

```
%timeit df_loc1.iat[2, 3]

  4.72 µs ± 132 ns per loop (mean ± std. dev. of 7 runs, 100000 loops each)

%timeit df_loc1.iloc[2, 3]

  8.5 µs ± 762 ns per loop (mean ± std. dev. of 7 runs, 100000 loops each)
```

Benchmarking .iat with respect to .iloc

Mixed indexing with the .ix operator

The `.ix` operator accepts both label-based and position-based indexing and is considered to be a more generic version of the `.loc` and `.iloc` operators. Due to ambiguity, this operator is deprecated and will not be available in a future version. Hence, it is advised not to use the `.ix` operator. Let's get an understanding of the `.ix` operator.

Here, the row index is label-based and the column index is position-based:

```
df_loc2.ix["2012":"2014", 0:2]
```

	Asia	Europe
2012	6.0	7.0
2013	11.0	12.0
2014	16.0	17.0

Mixed indexing with .ix in a DataFrame

Multi-indexing

We'll now turn to the topic of multi-indexing. Multi-level or hierarchical indexing is useful because it enables pandas users to select and massage data in multiple dimensions by using data structures such as Series and DataFrames. In order to start, let's save the following data to a file, `stock_index_prices.csv`, and read it in:

```
In[950]:sharesIndexDataDF=pd.read_csv('./stock_index_prices.csv')
In [951]: sharesIndexDataDF
Out[951]:
    TradingDate  PriceType   Nasdaq     S&P 500    Russell 2000
0   2014/02/21   open       4282.17    1841.07     1166.25
1   2014/02/21   close      4263.41    1836.25     1164.63
2   2014/02/21   high       4284.85    1846.13     1168.43
3   2014/02/24   open       4273.32    1836.78     1166.74
4   2014/02/24   close      4292.97    1847.61     1174.55
5   2014/02/24   high       4311.13    1858.71     1180.29
6   2014/02/25   open       4298.48    1847.66     1176.00
7   2014/02/25   close      4287.59    1845.12     1173.95
8   2014/02/25   high       4307.51    1852.91     1179.43
9   2014/02/26   open       4300.45    1845.79     1176.11
10  2014/02/26   close      4292.06    1845.16     1181.72
11  2014/02/26   high       4316.82    1852.65     1188.06
12  2014/02/27   open       4291.47    1844.90     1179.28
13  2014/02/27   close      4318.93    1854.29     1187.94
14  2014/02/27   high       4322.46    1854.53     1187.94
15  2014/02/28   open       4323.52    1855.12    1189.19
16  2014/02/28   close      4308.12    1859.45    1183.03
17  2014/02/28   high       4342.59    1867.92    1193.50
```

Here, we create a multi-index from the `TradingDate` and `PriceType` columns:

```
In[958]:sharesIndexDF=sharesIndexDataDF.set_index(['TradingDate','PriceType
'])

In [959]: mIndex=sharesIndexDF.index; mIndex

Out[959]: MultiIndex
        [(u'2014/02/21', u'open'), (u'2014/02/21', u'close'),
(u'2014/02/21', u'high'), (u'2014/02/24', u'open'), (u'2014/02/24',
u'close'), (u'2014/02/24', u'high'), (u'2014/02/25', u'open'),
(u'2014/02/25', u'close'), (u'2014/02/25', u'high'), (u'2014/02/26',
u'open'), (u'2014/02/26', u'close'), (u'2014/02/26', u'high'),
(u'2014/02/27', u'open'), (u'2014/02/27', u'close'), (u'2014/02/27',
u'high'), (u'2014/02/28', u'open'), (u'2014/02/28', u'close'),
(u'2014/02/28', u'high')]
In [960]: sharesIndexDF
Out[960]: Nasdaq   S&P 500    Russell 2000 TradingDate PriceType
2014/02/21 open    4282.17   1841.07    1166.25
           close   4263.41   1836.25    1164.63
           high    4284.85   1846.13    1168.43
2014/02/24 open              4273.32    1836.78   1166.74
           close             4292.97    1847.61   1174.55
           high              4311.13    1858.71   1180.29
2014/02/25 open              4298.48    1847.66   1176.00
           close             4287.59    1845.12   1173.95
           high              4307.51    1852.91   1179.43
2014/02/26 open              4300.45    1845.79   1176.11
           close             4292.06    1845.16   1181.72
           high              4316.82    1852.65   1188.06
2014/02/27 open              4291.47    1844.90   1179.28
           close             4318.93    1854.29   1187.94
           high              4322.46    1854.53   1187.94
2014/02/28 open              4323.52    1855.12   1189.19
           close             4308.12    1859.45   1183.03
           high              4342.59    1867.92   1193.50
```

Upon inspection, we see that the multi-index consists of a list of tuples. Applying the `get_level_values` function with the appropriate argument produces a list of the labels for each level of the index:

```
In [962]: mIndex.get_level_values(0)
Out[962]: Index([u'2014/02/21', u'2014/02/21', u'2014/02/21',
u'2014/02/24', u'2014/02/24', u'2014/02/24', u'2014/02/25', u'2014/02/25',
u'2014/02/25', u'2014/02/26', u'2014/02/26', u'2014/02/26', u'2014/02/27',
u'2014/02/27', u'2014/02/27', u'2014/02/28', u'2014/02/28', u'2014/02/28'],
dtype=object)
In [963]: mIndex.get_level_values(1)
```

```
Out[963]: Index([u'open', u'close', u'high', u'open', u'close',
   u'high', u'open', u'close', u'high', u'open', u'close', u'high', u'open',
   u'close', u'high', u'open', u'close', u'high'], dtype=object)
```

`IndexError` **will be thrown if the value passed to** `get_level_values()` **is invalid or out of range:**

```
In [88]: mIndex.get_level_values(2)
---------------------------------------------------------
IndexError                        Traceback (most recent call last)
...
```

You can achieve hierarchical indexing with a multi-indexed DataFrame:

```
In [971]: sharesIndexDF.ix['2014/02/21']
Out[971]:        Nasdaq    S&P 500    Russell 2000
   PriceType
   open        4282.17   1841.07    1166.25
   close       4263.41   1836.25    1164.63
   high        4284.85   1846.13    1168.43
In [976]: sharesIndexDF.ix['2014/02/21','open']
Out[976]: Nasdaq          4282.17
    S&P 500         1841.07
    Russell 2000    1166.25
    Name: (2014/02/21, open), dtype: float64
```

We can slice using a multi-index:

```
In [980]: sharesIndexDF.ix['2014/02/21':'2014/02/24']
Out[980]:        Nasdaq    S&P 500    Russell 2000
   TradingDate  PriceType
   2014/02/21   open  4282.17   1841.07    1166.25
         close  4263.41   1836.25    1164.63
         high   4284.85   1846.13    1168.43
   2014/02/24   open  4273.32   1836.78    1166.74
         close  4292.97   1847.61    1174.55
         high   4311.13   1858.71    1180.29
```

We can try slicing at a lower level:

```
In [272]:
sharesIndexDF.ix[('2014/02/21','open'):('2014/02/24','open')]
---------------------------------------------------------
KeyError                                Traceback (most recent call
last)
<ipython-input-272-65bb3364d980> in <module>()
----> 1 sharesIndexDF.ix[('2014/02/21','open'):('2014/02/24','open')]
...
```

```
    KeyError: 'Key length (2) was greater than MultiIndex lexsort depth
(1)'
```

However, this results in `KeyError` with a rather strange error message. The key lesson to be learned here is that the current incarnation of multi-index requires the labels to be sorted for the lower-level slicing routines to work correctly.

In order to do this, you can utilize the `sortlevel()` method, which sorts the labels of an axis within a multi-index. To be on the safe side, sort first before slicing with a multi-index. Thus, we can do the following:

```
In [984]:
sharesIndexDF.sortlevel(0).ix[('2014/02/21','open'):('2014/02/24','open')]
Out[984]:            Nasdaq    S&P 500   Russell 2000
     TradingDate  PriceType
     2014/02/21   open      4282.17   1841.07   1166.25
     2014/02/24   close     4292.97   1847.61   1174.55
         high     4311.13   1858.71   1180.29
         open     4273.32   1836.78   1166.74
```

We can also pass a list of tuples:

```
In [985]: sharesIndexDF.ix[[('2014/02/21','close'),('2014/02/24','open')]]
Out[985]: Nasdaq S&P 500 Russell 2000 TradingDate PriceType 2014/02/21
close 4263.41 1836.25 1164.63 2014/02/24 open 4273.32 1836.78 1166.74 2
rows × 3 columns
```

Note that by specifying a list of tuples instead of a range, as in the previous example, we display only the values of open `PriceType` rather than all three for `TradingDate` = `2014/02/24`.

Swapping and re-ordering levels

The `swaplevel` function enables levels within the multi-index to be swapped:

```
In [281]: swappedDF=sharesIndexDF[:7].swaplevel(0, 1, axis=0)
          swappedDF
Out[281]:            Nasdaq    S&P 500   Russell 2000
   PriceType  TradingDate
   open       2014/02/21   4282.17   1841.07   1166.25
   close      2014/02/21   4263.41   1836.25   1164.63
   high       2014/02/21   4284.85   1846.13   1168.43
   open       2014/02/24   4273.32   1836.78   1166.74
   close      2014/02/24   4292.97   1847.61   1174.55
   high       2014/02/24   4311.13   1858.71   1180.29
```

```
open            2014/02/25    4298.48   1847.66   1176.00
7 rows × 3 columns
```

The `reorder_levels` function is more general, allowing you to specify the order of the levels:

```
In [285]: reorderedDF=sharesIndexDF[:7].reorder_levels(['PriceType',
'TradingDate'],axis=0)
reorderedDF
    Out[285]:              Nasdaq     S&P 500   Russell 2000
    PriceType   TradingDate
    open       2014/02/21    4282.17   1841.07   1166.25
    close      2014/02/21    4263.41   1836.25   1164.63
    high       2014/02/21    4284.85   1846.13   1168.43
    open       2014/02/24    4273.32   1836.78   1166.74
    close      2014/02/24    4292.97   1847.61   1174.55
    high       2014/02/24    4311.13   1858.71   1180.29
    open       2014/02/25    4298.48   1847.66   1176.00
    7 rows × 3 columns
```

Cross-sections

The `xs` method provides a shortcut means of selecting data based on a particular index-level value:

```
In [287]: sharesIndexDF.xs('open',level='PriceType')
Out[287]:
        Nasdaq     S&P 500   Russell 2000
    TradingDate
    2014/02/21   4282.17   1841.07   1166.2x5
    2014/02/24   4273.32   1836.78   1166.74
    2014/02/25   4298.48   1847.66   1176.00
    2014/02/26   4300.45   1845.79   1176.11
    2014/02/27   4291.47   1844.90   1179.28
    2014/02/28   4323.52   1855.12   1189.19
    6 rows × 3 columns
```

The more long-winded alternative to the preceding command would be to use `swaplevel` to switch between the `TradingDate` and `PriceType` levels and then perform the selection as follows:

```
In [305]: sharesIndexDF.swaplevel(0, 1, axis=0).ix['open']
Out[305]:      Nasdaq    S&P 500   Russell 2000
    TradingDate
    2014/02/21   4282.17   1841.07   1166.25
    2014/02/24   4273.32   1836.78   1166.74
```

```
2014/02/25    4298.48    1847.66    1176.00
2014/02/26    4300.45    1845.79    1176.11
2014/02/27    4291.47    1844.90    1179.28
2014/02/28    4323.52    1855.12    1189.19
6 rows × 3 columns
```

Using `.xs` achieves the same effect as obtaining a cross-section in the previous section on integer-oriented indexing.

Boolean indexing

We use Boolean indexing to filter or select parts of the data. The operators are as follows:

Operators	Symbol
OR	|
AND	&
NOT	~

These operators must be grouped using parentheses when used together. Using the earlier DataFrame from the previous section, here we display the trading dates for which NASDAQ closed above 4,300:

```
In [311]: sharesIndexDataDF.ix[(sharesIndexDataDF['PriceType']=='close')
& \
                          (sharesIndexDataDF['Nasdaq']>4300) ]
Out[311]:          PriceType    Nasdaq    S&P 500    Russell 2000
     TradingDate
     2014/02/27    close    4318.93    1854.29    1187.94
     2014/02/28    close    4308.12    1859.45    1183.03
     2 rows × 4 columns
```

You can also create Boolean conditions in which you use arrays to filter out parts of the data, as shown in the following code:

```
highSelection=sharesIndexDataDF['PriceType']=='high'
NasdaqHigh=sharesIndexDataDF['Nasdaq']<4300
sharesIndexDataDF.ix[highSelection & NasdaqHigh]
    Out[316]: TradingDate    PriceType    Nasdaq    S&P 500    Russell 2000
        2014/02/21          high    4284.85    1846.13    1168.43
```

Thus, the preceding code snippet displays the only date in the dataset for which the NASDAQ Composite index stayed below the 4,300 level for the entire trading session.

The isin and any all methods

These methods enable the user to achieve more with Boolean indexing than the standard operators used in the preceding sections. The `isin` method takes a list of values and returns a Boolean array with `True` at the positions within the Series or DataFrame that match the values in the list. This enables the user to check for the presence of one or more elements within a Series. Here is an illustration using `Series`:

```
In[317]:stockSeries=pd.Series(['NFLX','AMZN','GOOG','FB','TWTR'])
        stockSeries.isin(['AMZN','FB'])
Out[317]:0     False
         1     True
         2     False
         3     True
         4     False
         dtype: bool
```

Here, we use the Boolean array to select a sub-series containing the values that we're interested in:

```
In [318]: stockSeries[stockSeries.isin(['AMZN','FB'])]
Out[318]: 1     AMZN
          3     FB
          dtype: object
```

For our DataFrame example, we switch to a more interesting dataset for those of us who are of a biological anthropology bent—that of classifying Australian mammals (a pet interest of mine):

```
In [324]: australianMammals=
              {'kangaroo': {'Subclass':'marsupial',
                            'Species Origin':'native'},
               'flying fox' : {'Subclass':'placental',
                            'Species Origin':'native'},
               'black rat': {'Subclass':'placental',
                            'Species Origin':'invasive'},
               'platypus' : {'Subclass':'monotreme',
                            'Species Origin':'native'},
               'wallaby' :  {'Subclass':'marsupial',
                            'Species Origin':'native'},
        'palm squirrel' : {'Subclass':'placental',
                            'Origin':'invasive'},
```

```
           'anteater':        {'Subclass':'monotreme', 'Origin':'native'},
           'koala':           {'Subclass':'marsupial', 'Origin':'native'}
}
```

 Some more information on mammals: Marsupials are pouched mammals, monotremes are egg-laying, and placentals give birth to live young. The source of this information is the following:

http://en.wikipedia.org/wiki/List_of_mammals_of_Australia.

The source of the preceding image is Bennett's wallaby at http://bit.ly/NG4R7N.

Let's read the Australian Mammals dataset, convert that to a DataFrame, and transpose it before using it:

```
In [328]: ozzieMammalsDF=pd.DataFrame(australianMammals)
In [346]: aussieMammalsDF=ozzieMammalsDF.T; aussieMammalsDF
Out[346]:        Subclass   Origin
  anteater       monotreme      native
  black rat      placental  invasive
  flying fox     placental  native
  kangaroo       marsupial  native
  koala            marsupial    native
  palm squirrel placental  invasive
  platypus       monotreme      native
  wallaby    marsupial    native
8 rows × 2 columns
```

Let's try to select mammals that are native to Australia:

```
     In [348]:
aussieMammalsDF.isin({'Subclass':['marsupial'],'Origin':['native']})
     Out[348]:     Subclass Origin
       anteater     False    True
       black rat    False    False
       flying fox   False    True
       kangaroo     True     True
       koala        True     True
       palm squirrel False False
       platypus     False    True
       wallaby      True     True
       8 rows x 2 columns
```

The set of values passed to `isin` can be an array or a dictionary. That works to some extent, but we can achieve better results by creating a mask as a combination of the `isin` and `all()` methods:

```
     In [349]: nativeMarsupials={'Mammal Subclass':['marsupial'],
                                 'Species Origin':['native']}
   nativeMarsupialMask=aussieMammalsDF.isin(nativeMarsupials).all(True)
          aussieMammalsDF[nativeMarsupialMask]
     Out[349]:      Subclass    Origin
       kangaroo   marsupial   native
       koala      marsupial   native
       wallaby    marsupial   native
       3 rows x 2 columns
```

Thus, we see that kangaroo, koala, and wallaby are the native marsupials in our dataset. The `any()` method returns whether any element is `True` in a Boolean DataFrame. The `all()` method filters return whether all elements are `True` in a Boolean DataFrame.

More can be read about the pandas methods from their official documentation page: `http://pandas.pydata.org/pandas-docs/stable/generated/pandas.DataFrame.any.html`.

Using the where() method

The `where()` method is used to ensure that the result of Boolean filtering is the same shape as the original data. First, we set the random number generator seed to 100 so that the user can generate the same values, as shown next:

```
In [379]: np.random.seed(100)
          normvals=pd.Series([np.random.normal() for i in np.arange(10)])
          normvals
Out[379]: 0    -1.749765
          1     0.342680
          2     1.153036
          3    -0.252436
          4     0.981321
          5     0.514219
          6     0.221180
          7    -1.070043
          8    -0.189496
          9     0.255001
          dtype: float64
In [381]: normvals[normvals>0]
Out[381]: 1     0.342680
          2     1.153036
          4     0.981321
          5     0.514219
          6     0.221180
          9     0.255001
          dtype: float64
In [382]: normvals.where(normvals>0)
Out[382]: 0          NaN
          1     0.342680
          2     1.153036
          3          NaN
          4     0.981321
          5     0.514219
          6     0.221180
          7          NaN
          8          NaN
          9     0.255001
          dtype: float64
```

This method seems to be useful only in the case of a Series, as we get this behavior for free in the case of a DataFrame:

```
In [393]: np.random.seed(100)
          normDF=pd.DataFrame([[round(np.random.normal(),3) for i in
np.arange(5)] for j in range(3)],
```

```
                    columns=['0','30','60','90','120'])
         normDF
Out[393]:   0     30      60      90      120
    0   -1.750   0.343   1.153  -0.252   0.981
    1    0.514   0.221  -1.070  -0.189   0.255
    2   -0.458   0.435  -0.584   0.817   0.673
    3 rows × 5 columns
In [394]: normDF[normDF>0]
Out[394]:   0     30      60      90      120
    0    NaN    0.343   1.153    NaN    0.981
    1   0.514   0.221    NaN     NaN    0.255
    2    NaN    0.435    NaN    0.817   0.673
    3 rows × 5 columns
In [395]: normDF.where(normDF>0)
Out[395]:   0     30      60      90      120
    0    NaN    0.343   1.153    NaN    0.981
    1   0.514   0.221    NaN     NaN    0.255
    2    NaN    0.435    NaN    0.817   0.673
    3 rows × 5 columns
```

The inverse operation of the `where` method is `mask`:

```
In [396]: normDF.mask(normDF>0)
Out[396]:   0     30      60      90      120
    0  -1.750   NaN     NaN   -0.252    NaN
    1    NaN    NaN   -1.070  -0.189    NaN
    2  -0.458   NaN   -0.584    NaN     NaN
    3 rows × 5 columns
```

Operations on indexes

To complete this chapter, we'll discuss operations on indexes. We sometimes need to operate on indexes when we wish to realign our data or select it in different ways. There are various operations:

Note that `set_index` allows the creation of an index on an existing DataFrame and returns an indexed DataFrame, as we have seen before:

```
In [939]: stockIndexDataDF=pd.read_csv('./stock_index_data.csv')
In [940]: stockIndexDataDF
Out[940]:    TradingDate   Nasdaq    S&P 500   Russell 2000
    0        2014/01/30   4123.13   1794.19    1139.36
    1        2014/01/31   4103.88   1782.59    1130.88
    2        2014/02/03   3996.96   1741.89    1094.58
    3        2014/02/04   4031.52   1755.20    1102.84
    4        2014/02/05   4011.55   1751.64    1093.59
```

```
    5    2014/02/06    4057.12   1773.43   1103.93
```

Now, we can set the index as follows:

```
In [941]: stockIndexDF=stockIndexDataDF.set_index('TradingDate')
In [942]: stockIndexDF
Out[942]:      Nasdaq    S&P 500   Russell 2000
    TradingDate
    2014/01/30  4123.13   1794.19   1139.36
    2014/01/31    4103.88   1782.59   1130.88
    2014/02/03  3996.96   1741.89   1094.58
    2014/02/04  4031.52   1755.20   1102.84
    2014/02/05  4011.55   1751.64   1093.59
    2014/02/06  4057.12   1773.43   1103.93
```

Furthermore, `reset_index` **reverses** `set_index`:

```
In [409]: stockIndexDF.reset_index()
Out[409]:
        TradingDate    Nasdaq    S&P 500    Russell 2000
    0    2014/01/30    4123.13   1794.19      1139.36
    1    2014/01/31    4103.88   1782.59      1130.88
    2    2014/02/03    3996.96   1741.89      1094.58
    3    2014/02/04    4031.52   1755.20      1102.84
    4    2014/02/05    4011.55   1751.64      1093.59
    5    2014/02/06    4057.12   1773.43      1103.93
    6 rows × 4 columns
```

After reading this chapter, you have come a long way in wrangling data using pandas. We will continue to learn about useful tools for data wrangling in the next chapter.

Summary

In this chapter, we learned how to access and select data from panda data structures. We also looked in detail at basic indexing and label-oriented, integer-oriented, and mixed indexing. We also learned how to use a Boolean/logical index as well. At the end of the chapter, we discussed the index operations.

For further references about indexing in pandas, please take a look at the official documentation at `http://pandas.pydata.org/pandas-docs/stable/indexing.html`.

In the next chapter, we will examine the topics of grouping, reshaping, and merging data using pandas.

6
Grouping, Merging, and Reshaping Data in pandas

In this chapter, we'll tackle the question of rearranging and reshaping data in our data structures. We'll examine the various functions that enable us to rearrange data by utilizing them on real-world datasets. Such functions include `groupby`, `concat`, `aggregate`, `append`, and so on.

The topics that we'll discuss in this chapter are as follows:

- Aggregating/grouping data
- Merging and concatenating data
- Reshaping data
- Other methods for reshaping DataFrames

Grouping data

Grouping data is vital to arrive at key conclusions at an initial exploratory analysis phase. For example, when you deal with a retail dataset with variables such as *OrderID, CustomerID, Shipping Date, Product Category, Sales Region, Quantity Ordered, Cancelation Status, Total Sales, Profit, Discount,* and others,grouping the data and aggregating it helps you to arrive at answers to questions such as those that follow:

- Which region was the most profitable?
- Which product category had the most cancelations?
- What percent of customers contribute to 80% of the profit?

Grouping involves aggregating across each category. Aggregation may involve operations such as count, sum, exponent, or implementing a complex user-defined function. The `groupby` function of pandas helps with grouping. This is not much different from the `groupby` query in SQL.

The groupby operation

Through a `groupby` function, a chain of actions gets executed: splitting, applying, and combining. Splitting segments each category from the desired grouping variable to perform further operations with it. Then, functions can be individually applied across each of these split groups. These functions might involve aggregation (sum across a group or mean across a group), transformation (filling NAs within a group or sorting), filtration (applying conditions within a group to drop rows), or even a combination of these three operations. Finally, the results obtained after the functions are applied across each of the split groups are combined together.

Let's use sample data from a fictitious global retailer. The data available as CSV is read as a pandas DataFrame:

```
sales_data = pd.read_csv("salesdata.csv", encoding = "ISO-8859-1")
```

The `head` function will give us a quick glimpse of the dataset we just imported:

```
sales_data.head()
```

The following will be the output:

	Order ID	Order Date	Ship Date	Ship Mode	Customer Name	Segment	Country	Region	Product ID	Category	Sub-Category	Sales	Quantity	Discount	Profit
0	CA-2012-124891	31-07-2012	31-07-2012	Same Day	Rick Hansen	Consumer	United States	East	TEC-AC-10003033	Technology	Accessories	2309.650	7	0.0	762.1845
1	IN-2013-77878	05-02-2013	07-02-2013	Second Class	Justin Ritter	Corporate	Australia	Oceania	FUR-CH-10003950	Furniture	Chairs	3709.395	9	0.1	-288.7650
2	IN-2013-71249	17-10-2013	18-10-2013	First Class	Craig Reiter	Consumer	Australia	Oceania	TEC-PH-10004664	Technology	Phones	5175.171	9	0.1	919.9710
3	ES-2013-1579342	28-01-2013	30-01-2013	First Class	Katherine Murray	Home Office	Germany	Central	TEC-PH-10004583	Technology	Phones	2892.510	5	0.1	-96.5400
4	SG-2013-4320	05-11-2013	06-11-2013	Same Day	Rick Hansen	Consumer	Senegal	Africa	TEC-SHA-10000501	Technology	Copiers	2832.960	8	0.0	311.5200

Snapshot of sample sales data

While a sample of five rows has been shown in the preceding output, the data contains 51,290 rows and 15 columns.

Now, to understand how `groupby` splits the data, let's split it by the `Category` variable. The object created is not a DataFrame but rather an object type unique to the `groupby` function:

```
category_grouped = sales_data.groupby("Category")
type(category_grouped)
pandas.core.groupby. DataFrameGroupBy
```

The grouping object is referred to as the key. Here, `Category` is the key. The groups under the `groupby` object created in the previous step are shown here. You can see that each group in `Category` is mapped to the row-index labels covered by each category:

```
category_grouped.groups
```

The following will be the output:

```
{'Furniture': Int64Index([    1,     6,     7,     9,    11,    13,    20,    22,    25,
            26,
            ...
            51136, 51157, 51165, 51186, 51200, 51232, 51239, 51242, 51246,
            51254],
           dtype='int64', length=9876),
 'Office Supplies': Int64Index([    8,    10,    14,    15,    17,    19,    23,    27,    33,
            44,
            ...
            51280, 51281, 51282, 51283, 51284, 51285, 51286, 51287, 51288,
            51289],
           dtype='int64', length=31273),
 'Technology': Int64Index([    0,     2,     3,     4,     5,    12,    16,    18,    21,
            24,
            ...
            51021, 51058, 51087, 51095, 51143, 51151, 51178, 51219, 51237,
            51259],
           dtype='int64', length=10141)}
```

Information for each group

The data has four quantitative variables: Quantity, Sales, Discount, and Profit. Using groupby, let's compute the sum of all these four variables across each Category. This is an application of aggregation with groupby:

```
sales_data.groupby("Category").sum()
```

The following will be the output:

Category	Sales	Quantity	Discount	Profit
Furniture	4.110874e+06	34954	1660.030	285204.72380
Office Supplies	3.787070e+06	108182	4297.190	518473.83430
Technology	4.744557e+06	35176	1372.508	663778.73318

Results of groupby and summing

Modify the code slightly, as shown here, to compute only the sum of sales. This involves subsetting the data right before applying `groupby`:

```
sales_data[["Category", "Sales"]].groupby("Category").sum()
```

The following will be the output:

Category	Sales
Furniture	4.110874e+06
Office Supplies	3.787070e+06
Technology	4.744557e+06

groupby and sum across one variable

Aggregation need not be applied across only a quantitative variable. Now, using `groupby`, let's find the `Country` in which each category was first ordered:

```
sales_data[["Category", "Country"]].groupby("Category").first()
```

The following will be the output:

Category	Country
Furniture	Australia
Office Supplies	United States
Technology	United States

Using the aggregate first along with groupby

The `size()` function helps to find the number of occurrences of each `Category`. After computing `size`, let's explore the transformation ability of `groupby` by sorting the results:

```
sales_data.groupby("Category").size().sort_values(ascending = True)
```

The following will be the output:

```
Category
Furniture           9876
Technology         10141
Office Supplies    31273
dtype: int64
```

Aggregation of size after sorting

The key or grouping object need not necessarily be an existing column; it can also be a function defining a grouping rule. For example, from `OrderDate`, we can extract the year and then `groupby` the year in which orders were placed. For this, the index is first set to `OrderDate`:

```
index_by_date = sales_data.set_index('OrderDate')
index_by_date.groupby(lambda OrderDate: OrderDate.split('-')[2]).sum()
```

The following will be the output:

	Sales	Quantity	Discount	Profit
2011	2.259451e+06	31443	1333.394	248940.81154
2012	2.677439e+06	38111	1548.774	307415.27910
2013	3.405746e+06	48136	1935.522	406935.23018
2014	4.299866e+06	60622	2512.038	504165.97046

Groupby to group variables created via a custom& function

It is also possible to group by more than one key. Here, let's group by `ShipMode` and `Category` to aggregate by the number of observations. The `groupby` function accepts multiple variables as a list:

```
sales_data.groupby(["ShipMode","Category"]).size()
```

The following will be the output:

```
ShipMode        Category
First Class     Furniture          1431
                Office Supplies     4598
                Technology         1476
Same Day        Furniture           508
                Office Supplies     1675
                Technology          518
Second Class    Furniture          1968
                Office Supplies     6311
                Technology         2030
Standard Class  Furniture          5969
                Office Supplies    18689
                Technology         6117
dtype: int64
```

Aggregate of size across two grouping variables

The `get_group()` attribute of the `groupby` function allows data to be filtered by one category out of all of the categories available in the group:

```
sales_data.groupby("ShipMode").get_group("Same Day")
```

The following will be the output:

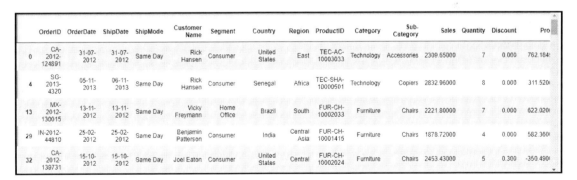

	OrderID	OrderDate	ShipDate	ShipMode	Customer Name	Segment	Country	Region	ProductID	Category	Sub-Category	Sales	Quantity	Discount	Pro
0	CA-2012-124891	31-07-2012	31-07-2012	Same Day	Rick Hansen	Consumer	United States	East	TEC-AC-10003033	Technology	Accessories	2309.65000	7	0.000	762.184
4	SG-2013-4320	05-11-2013	06-11-2013	Same Day	Rick Hansen	Consumer	Senegal	Africa	TEC-SHA-10000501	Technology	Copiers	2832.96000	8	0.000	311.520
13	MX-2012-130015	13-11-2012	13-11-2012	Same Day	Vicky Freymann	Home Office	Brazil	South	FUR-CH-10002033	Furniture	Chairs	2221.80000	7	0.000	622.020
29	IN-2012-44810	25-02-2012	25-02-2012	Same Day	Benjamin Patterson	Consumer	India	Central Asia	FUR-CH-10001415	Furniture	Chairs	1878.72000	4	0.000	582.360
32	CA-2012-139731	15-10-2012	15-10-2012	Same Day	Joel Eaton	Consumer	United States	Central	FUR-CH-10002024	Furniture	Chairs	2453.43000	5	0.300	-350.490

The `get_group` attribute of groupby

The `groupby` object produced by the `groupby` function is iterable. Let's iterate over a simple `groupby` object:

```
for name, group in sales_data.groupby("ShipMode"):
print(name)
print(group.iloc[0:5,0:5])
```

The following will be the output:

```
First Class
            OrderID    OrderDate      ShipDate      ShipMode     Customer Name
2       IN-2013-71249  17-10-2013   18-10-2013   First Class      Craig Reiter
3     ES-2013-1579342  28-01-2013   30-01-2013   First Class  Katherine Murray
6       IN-2011-81826  07-11-2011   09-11-2011   First Class      Toby Swindell
11      ID-2012-28402  19-04-2012   22-04-2012   First Class    Anthony Jacobs
18      IN-2014-11763  31-01-2014   01-02-2014   First Class          Jim Sink
Same Day
            OrderID    OrderDate      ShipDate   ShipMode       Customer Name
0      CA-2012-124891  31-07-2012   31-07-2012   Same Day         Rick Hansen
4        SG-2013-4320  05-11-2013   06-11-2013   Same Day         Rick Hansen
13     MX-2012-130015  13-11-2012   13-11-2012   Same Day      Vicky Freymann
29      IN-2012-44810  25-02-2012   25-02-2012   Same Day   Benjamin Patterson
32     CA-2012-139731  15-10-2012   15-10-2012   Same Day          Joel Eaton
Second Class
            OrderID    OrderDate      ShipDate      ShipMode      Customer Name
1       IN-2013-77878  05-02-2013   07-02-2013   Second Class      Justin Ritter
5       IN-2013-42360  28-06-2013   01-07-2013   Second Class        Jim Mitchum
9      CA-2012-116638  28-01-2012   31-01-2012   Second Class        Joseph Holt
10     CA-2011-102988  05-04-2011   09-04-2011   Second Class       Greg Maxwell
12       SA-2011-1830  27-12-2011   29-12-2011   Second Class   Magdelene Morse
Standard Class
            OrderID    OrderDate      ShipDate       ShipMode      Customer Name
7       IN-2012-86369  14-04-2012   18-04-2012   Standard Class        Mick Brown
8      CA-2014-135909  14-10-2014   21-10-2014   Standard Class         Jane Waco
17    ES-2014-1651774  08-09-2014   14-09-2014   Standard Class      Patrick Jones
38    ES-2014-2637201  14-01-2014   18-01-2014   Standard Class  Patrick O'Donnell
40      ID-2013-63976  22-08-2013   26-08-2013   Standard Class         Joy Bell-
```

Iterating through the groupby object

Instead of grouping by a column name, an index can also be used. When using an index, the level can be specified in place of the index name. Let's set `Region` as an index to demonstrate this:

```
region_index_df = sales_data.set_index("Region", drop = True)
region_index_df.groupby(level = 0).sum()
```

The following will be the output:

Region	Sales	Quantity	Discount	Profit
Africa	7.837732e+05	10564	718.800	88871.63100
Canada	6.692817e+04	833	0.000	17817.39000
Caribbean	3.242809e+05	6299	229.420	34571.32104
Central	2.822303e+06	41762	1543.610	311403.98164
Central Asia	7.528266e+05	7715	138.200	132480.18700
EMEA	8.061613e+05	11517	986.100	43897.97100
East	6.787812e+05	10618	414.000	91522.78000
North	1.248166e+06	18021	459.630	194597.95252
North Asia	8.483098e+05	8851	113.900	165578.42100
Oceania	1.100185e+06	12838	534.100	120089.11200
South	1.600907e+06	25206	990.438	140355.76618
Southeast Asia	8.844232e+05	11822	851.330	17852.32900
West	7.254578e+05	12266	350.200	108418.44890

Grouping with index

`groupby` aggregations need not always occur along a column. If required, items can be grouped and aggregated along a row by changing the `axis` argument. The default setting of the `axis` argument is 0. Changing it to `axis = 1` groups items along a row:

```
sales_data.groupby("ShipMode", axis = 0).size()
```

Using groupby with a MultiIndex

Let's explore how the `groupby` function works for hierarchically indexed data.

To start with, we can assign two indices to the sample sales data, as shown:

```
multiindex_df = sales_data.set_index(["ShipMode", "Category"])
multiindex_df.head()
```

The following will be the output:

ShipMode	Category	OrderID	OrderDate	ShipDate	Customer Name	Segment	Country	Region	ProductID	Sub-Category	Sales	Quantity	Discount	Profit
Same Day	Technology	CA-2012-124891	31-07-2012	31-07-2012	Rick Hansen	Consumer	United States	East	TEC-AC-10003033	Accessories	2309.650	7	0.0	762.1845
Second Class	Furniture	IN-2013-77878	05-02-2013	07-02-2013	Justin Ritter	Corporate	Australia	Oceania	FUR-CH-10003950	Chairs	3709.395	9	0.1	-288.7650
First Class	Technology	IN-2013-71249	17-10-2013	18-10-2013	Craig Reiter	Consumer	Australia	Oceania	TEC-PH-10004664	Phones	5175.171	9	0.1	919.9710
	Technology	ES-2013-1579342	28-01-2013	30-01-2013	Katherine Murray	Home Office	Germany	Central	TEC-PH-10004583	Phones	2892.510	5	0.1	-96.5400
Same Day	Technology	SG-2013-4320	05-11-2013	06-11-2013	Rick Hansen	Consumer	Senegal	Africa	TEC-SHA-10000501	Copiers	2832.960	8	0.0	311.5200

Snapshot of multi-indexed data

Grouping by an index can be done by specifying either the level number or the index name:

```
multiindex_df.groupby(level = 0).sum()
```

The following will be the output:

ShipMode	Sales	Quantity	Discount	Profit
First Class	1.830976e+06	26039	1117.478	208104.67520
Same Day	6.672020e+05	9230	387.662	76173.06780
Second Class	2.565672e+06	35724	1449.656	292583.52708
Standard Class	7.578652e+06	107319	4374.932	890596.02120

The level attribute of groupby

The `level` parameter can take names as well instead of numbers as follows:

```
multiindex_df.groupby(level = "Category").sum()
```

The following will be the output:

	Sales	Quantity	Discount	Profit
Category				
Furniture	4.110874e+06	34954	1660.030	285204.72380
Office Supplies	3.787070e+06	108182	4297.190	518473.83430
Technology	4.744557e+06	35176	1372.508	663778.73318

Using the level name to group by

Index names can be used directly as keys, as shown:

```
multiindex_df.groupby("Category").sum()
```

This results in the following output:

	Sales	Quantity	Discount	Profit
Category				
Furniture	4.110874e+06	34954	1660.030	285204.72380
Office Supplies	3.787070e+06	108182	4297.190	518473.83430
Technology	4.744557e+06	35176	1372.508	663778.73318

Providing index names as the key

Multiple indices can also be passed through the level argument of groupby to obtain the same result as the preceding one:

```
multiindex_df.groupby(level = ["ShipMode", "Category"]).sum()
```

The following will be the output:

ShipMode	Category	Sales	Quantity	Discount	Profit
First Class	Furniture	5.875523e+05	5034	237.960	45807.50020
	Office Supplies	5.574531e+05	15922	665.020	71015.18220
	Technology	6.859707e+05	5083	214.498	91281.99280
Same Day	Furniture	1.998643e+05	1801	83.620	18797.42350
	Office Supplies	1.964628e+05	5638	223.790	28335.00450
	Technology	2.708749e+05	1791	80.252	29040.63980
Second Class	Furniture	8.175204e+05	6891	344.610	42716.61010
	Office Supplies	8.012851e+05	21637	840.420	111871.66700
	Technology	9.468661e+05	7196	264.626	137995.24998
Standard Class	Furniture	2.505937e+06	21228	993.840	177883.19000
	Office Supplies	2.231869e+06	64985	2567.960	307251.98060
	Technology	2.840846e+06	21106	813.132	405460.85060

Groupby for multiple indexes

When grouping by index, the aggregation functions can directly take up the `level` parameter to enable splitting across groups. Here, we have grouped across both levels by specifying the `level` number. Instead of the `level` number, the index name can also be specified:

```
multiindex_df.sum(level = [0, 1])
```

The following will be the output:

		Sales	Quantity	Discount	Profit
ShipMode	**Category**				
Same Day	Technology	2.708749e+05	1791	80.252	29040.63980
Second Class	Furniture	8.175204e+05	6891	344.610	42716.61010
First Class	Technology	6.859707e+05	5083	214.498	91281.99280
Second Class	Technology	9.468661e+05	7196	264.626	137995.24998
First Class	Furniture	5.875523e+05	5034	237.960	45807.50020
Standard Class	Furniture	2.505937e+06	21228	993.840	177883.19000
	Office Supplies	2.231869e+06	64985	2567.960	307251.98060
Second Class	Office Supplies	8.012851e+05	21637	840.420	111871.66700
Same Day	Furniture	1.998643e+05	1801	83.620	18797.42350
Standard Class	Technology	2.840846e+06	21106	813.132	405460.85060
First Class	Office Supplies	5.574531e+05	15922	665.020	71015.18220
Same Day	Office Supplies	1.964628e+05	5638	223.790	28335.00450

Multi-index grouping with the level parameter

To group by both index and column name, the following method can be used. The level number provided here can also be replaced with the level name. Instead of using the Grouper function, the index name and column name can be provided as a list of keys:

```
multiindex_df.groupby([pd.Grouper(level = 1), "Region"]).size()
multiindex_df.groupby(["Category", "Region"]).size()
```

The following will be the output:

```
Category        Region
Furniture       Africa           631
                Canada            42
                Caribbean        376
                Central         2046
                Central Asia     478
                EMEA             770
                East             601
                North            945
                North Asia       522
                Oceania          742
                South           1329
                Southeast Asia   687
                West             707
Office Supplies Africa          3045
                Canada           277
                Caribbean        973
                Central         6936
                Central Asia    1111
                EMEA            3297
                East            1712
                North           2914
                North Asia      1332
                Oceania         1961
                South           4045
                Southeast Asia  1773
                West            1897
Technology      Africa           911
                Canada            65
                Caribbean        341
                Central         2135
                Central Asia     459
                EMEA             962
                East             535
                North            926
                North Asia       484
                Oceania          784
                South           1271
                Southeast Asia   669
                West             599
dtype: int64
```

Using normal columns and index columns together for grouping

Let's take `groupby` a notch further and apply some data transformation to the results. We will begin by computing the ratio of total sales, quantity, profit, and discount with respect to the overall `Sales`, `Quantity`, `Profit`, and `Discount`:

```
sum_all = multiindex_df.groupby(level = 1).sum()

sum_all.ix["Furniture"]/(sum_all.ix["Furniture"] + sum_all.ix["Technology"]
+ sum_all.ix["Office Supplies"])
```

The following will be the output:

```
Sales        0.325163
Quantity     0.196027
Discount     0.226479
Profit       0.194353
dtype: float64
```

Groupby to evaluate complex calculations

This results in a series. Remember the `transpose` function from NumPy? Similarly, a DataFrame can be transposed as well. However, the output just obtained is a series and not a DataFrame. Before transposing, the series has to be converted to a DataFrame:

```
furniture_ratio = sum_all.ix["Furniture"]/(sum_all.ix["Furniture"] +
sum_all.ix["Technology"] + sum_all.ix["Office Supplies"])

pd.DataFrame(furniture_ratio).T
```

The following will be the output:

	Sales	Quantity	Discount	Profit
0	0.325163	0.196027	0.226479	0.194353

Intermediate result of data transformation

The index label in the result is 0. Let's rename it to a more appropriate label using the following snippet. The output is also shown in the screenshot that follows:

```
furniture_ratio_df = pd.DataFrame(furniture_ratio).T
furniture_ratio_df.rename(index = {0 : "FurniturePercent"})
```

Take a look at the following screenshot:

	Sales	Quantity	Discount	Profit
FurniturePercent	0.325163	0.196027	0.226479	0.194353

Result of data transformation

Using the aggregate method

In all of the previous use cases, we used sum aggregation. We were directly able to use `sum` without going through the `aggregate` function of Python. The `sum()` function that we used is a Cython-optimized implementation. Some other Cython-optimized implementations are `mean`, `std`, and `sem` (standard error of the mean). To implement other functions or a combination of aggregations, the `aggregate` function comes in handy:

```
sales_data.groupby("Category").aggregate(np.sum)
```

The following will be the output:

Category	Sales	Quantity	Discount	Profit
Furniture	4.110874e+06	34954	1660.030	285204.72380
Office Supplies	3.787070e+06	108182	4297.190	518473.83430
Technology	4.744557e+06	35176	1372.508	663778.73318

Use of the aggregate function

All the rules discussed in the sections on handling multiple keys and indices are applicable here as well.

Please note that when using multiple keys or Multiindex, the result has a hierarchical ordering in indices. To overcome this, you can use the `reset_index` attribute of DataFrames:

```
sales_data.groupby(["ShipMode", "Category"]).aggregate(np.sum)
```

The following will be the output:

ShipMode	Category	Sales	Quantity	Discount	Profit
First Class	Furniture	5.875523e+05	5034	237.960	45807.50020
	Office Supplies	5.574531e+05	15922	665.020	71015.18220
	Technology	6.859707e+05	5083	214.498	91281.99280
Same Day	Furniture	1.998643e+05	1801	83.620	18797.42350
	Office Supplies	1.964628e+05	5638	223.790	28335.00450
	Technology	2.708749e+05	1791	80.252	29040.63980
Second Class	Furniture	8.175204e+05	6891	344.610	42716.61010
	Office Supplies	8.012851e+05	21637	840.420	111871.66700
	Technology	9.468661e+05	7196	264.626	137995.24998
Standard Class	Furniture	2.505937e+06	21228	993.840	177883.19000
	Office Supplies	2.231869e+06	64985	2567.960	307251.98060
	Technology	2.840846e+06	21106	813.132	405460.85060

The aggregate function for multiple columns

The index of the output can be reset using the following snippet:

```
sales_data.groupby(["ShipMode",
"Category"]).aggregate(np.sum).reset_index()
```

The following will be the output:

	ShipMode	Category	Sales	Quantity	Discount	Profit
0	First Class	Furniture	5.875523e+05	5034	237.960	45807.50020
1	First Class	Office Supplies	5.574531e+05	15922	665.020	71015.18220
2	First Class	Technology	6.859707e+05	5083	214.498	91281.99280
3	Same Day	Furniture	1.998643e+05	1801	83.620	18797.42350
4	Same Day	Office Supplies	1.964628e+05	5638	223.790	28335.00450
5	Same Day	Technology	2.708749e+05	1791	80.252	29040.63980
6	Second Class	Furniture	8.175204e+05	6891	344.610	42716.61010
7	Second Class	Office Supplies	8.012851e+05	21637	840.420	111871.66700
8	Second Class	Technology	9.468661e+05	7196	264.626	137995.24998
9	Standard Class	Furniture	2.505937e+06	21228	993.840	177883.19000
10	Standard Class	Office Supplies	2.231869e+06	64985	2567.960	307251.98060
11	Standard Class	Technology	2.840846e+06	21106	813.132	405460.85060

The aggregate function for multiple grouping variables

To achieve the same results, in place of `reset_index`, the `as_index` parameter of `groupby` can be set to `False`:

```
sales_data.groupby(["ShipMode", "Category"], as_index =
False).aggregate(np.sum)
```

Like the implementation of the `sum` function, the following is a list of other functions that can be applied to `groupby` objects:

Function	Description
mean()	Compute mean of groups
sum()	Compute sum of group values
size()	Compute group sizes
count()	Compute count of group
std()	Standard deviation of groups
var()	Compute variance of groups
sem()	Standard error of the mean of groups
describe()	Generate descriptive statistics
first()	Compute first of group values
last()	Compute last of group values
nth()	Take nth value, or a subset if n is a list
min()	Compute min of group values
max()	Compute max of group values

Table 6.1: List of all aggregate functions

Applying multiple functions

For any DataFrame, a list of aggregations can be performed after applying `groupby`. In the following example, the mean and standard deviation have been computed for `Sales` and `Quantity`:

```
sales_data[["Sales", "Quantity",
"Category"]].groupby("Category").agg([np.mean, np.std])
```

The following will be the output:

	Sales		Quantity	
	mean	std	mean	std
Category				
Furniture	416.248905	553.066417	3.539287	2.260945
Office Supplies	121.097120	299.321405	3.459278	2.288316
Technology	467.858939	708.972701	3.468691	2.265671

Multiple aggregations

Note that hierarchy has also been introduced in the column index. `agg` is a short form of aggregate. These aggregations will exclude any NAs found for computation.

In the preceding example, columns were created with the `mean` and `std` labels. Let's try renaming them. The `rename` argument maps the new name onto the old name:

```
sales_data[["Sales", "Quantity",
"Category"]].groupby("Category").agg([np.mean, np.std]).rename(columns =
{"mean": "Mean", "std": "SD"})
```

The following will be the output:

	Sales		Quantity	
	Mean	SD	Mean	SD
Category				
Furniture	416.248905	553.066417	3.539287	2.260945
Office Supplies	121.097120	299.321405	3.459278	2.288316
Technology	467.858939	708.972701	3.468691	2.265671

Different aggregates for each column

To apply selected functions to selected columns, the following convention can be used. For example, here, the sum of `Sales` and the mean of `Quantity` have been computed:

```
sales_data[["Sales", "Quantity",
"Category"]].groupby("Category").agg({"Sales":"sum", "Quantity":"mean"})
```

The following is the output:

Category	Sales	Quantity
Furniture	4.110874e+06	3.539287
Office Supplies	3.787070e+06	3.459278
Technology	4.744557e+06	3.468691

Renaming columns after aggregation

The transform() method

The `transform` function in `groupby` is used to perform transformation operations on a `groupby` object. For example, we could replace NaN values in the `groupby` object using the `fillna` method. The resultant object after using `transform` has the same size as the original `groupby` object.

Let's introduce NAs into the sample sales data. The following code injects NAs into 25% of the records:

```
na_df = sales_data[["Sales", "Quantity", "Discount", "Profit",
"Category"]].set_index("Category").mask(np.random.random(sales_data[["Sales
", "Quantity", "Discount", "Profit"]].shape) &lt; .25)

na_df.head(10)
```

The following will be the output:

Category	Sales	Quantity	Discount	Profit
Technology	2309.650	7.0	NaN	762.1845
Furniture	3709.395	9.0	NaN	NaN
Technology	5175.171	NaN	NaN	919.9710
Technology	NaN	5.0	0.10	-96.5400
Technology	2832.960	NaN	0.00	311.5200
Technology	NaN	5.0	0.10	763.2750
Furniture	1822.080	4.0	0.00	564.8400
Furniture	5244.840	6.0	NaN	996.4800
Office Supplies	5083.960	5.0	0.20	1906.4850
Furniture	4297.644	13.0	0.40	-1862.3124

Snapshot of data with NAs inserted

Now, the four quantitative variables contain NAs in 25% of the rows, and `Category` is set as the index. A simple `groupby` and `count` aggregation will give the number of non-NA values in each column for each category:

```
na_df.groupby("Category").count()
```

The following will be the output:

Category	Sales	Quantity	Discount	Profit
Furniture	7424	7494	7425	7395
Office Supplies	23424	23478	23385	23510
Technology	7627	7644	7572	7564

Count of non-NA values

The `transform()` function fills the NAs with the mean of each group:

```
transformed = na_df.groupby("Category").transform(lambda x:
x.fillna(x.mean()))
transformed.head(10)
```

The following will be the output:

Category	Sales	Quantity	Discount	Profit
Technology	2309.650000	7.000000	0.135326	762.1845
Furniture	3709.395000	9.000000	0.165502	29.1085
Technology	5175.171000	3.451977	0.135326	919.9710
Technology	474.264323	5.000000	0.100000	-96.5400
Technology	2832.960000	3.451977	0.000000	311.5200
Technology	474.264323	5.000000	0.100000	763.2750
Furniture	1822.080000	4.000000	0.000000	564.8400
Furniture	5244.840000	6.000000	0.165502	996.4800
Office Supplies	5083.960000	5.000000	0.200000	1906.4850
Furniture	4297.644000	13.000000	0.400000	-1862.3124

Using transform to fill NAs

The result shows that `transform()` performs group-specific NA handling. The count of non-NAs can be seen to have increased:

```
transformed.groupby("Category").count()
```

The following will be the output:

Category	Sales	Quantity	Discount	Profit
Furniture	9876	9876	9876	9876
Office Supplies	31273	31273	31273	31273
Technology	10141	10141	10141	10141

Count of non-NAs after transformation

To verify the operation, let's compare averages of the groups before and after transformation. The outputs from the two methods are found to be equal as shown following:

```
na_df.groupby("Category").mean()
```

The following will be the output:

Category	Sales	Quantity	Discount	Profit
Furniture	417.178827	3.551084	0.165502	29.108500
Office Supplies	122.121329	3.443105	0.137629	15.754366
Technology	474.264323	3.451977	0.135326	66.237839

Group means before transformation

Calculating the mean using the object obtained from the transform method can be done as follows:

```
transformed.groupby("Category").mean()
```

The following will be the output:

Category	Sales	Quantity	Discount	Profit
Furniture	417.178827	3.551084	0.165502	29.108500
Office Supplies	122.121329	3.443105	0.137629	15.754366
Technology	474.264323	3.451977	0.135326	66.237839

Group means after transformation

Some functions, such as `bfill()` (backward fill), `ffill()` (forward fill), `fillna()`, and `shift()` can perform transformation by themselves, without the need for the `transform()` function:

```
na_df.groupby("Category").bfill()
```

The following will be the output:

	Category	Sales	Quantity	Discount	Profit
Category					
Technology	Technology	2309.650	7.0	0.10	762.1845
Furniture	Furniture	3709.395	9.0	0.00	564.8400
Technology	Technology	5175.171	5.0	0.10	919.9710
Technology	Technology	2832.960	5.0	0.10	-96.5400
Technology	Technology	2832.960	5.0	0.00	311.5200
Technology	Technology	2565.594	5.0	0.10	763.2750
Furniture	Furniture	1822.080	4.0	0.00	564.8400
Furniture	Furniture	5244.840	6.0	0.40	996.4800
Office Supplies	Office Supplies	5083.960	5.0	0.20	1906.4850
Furniture	Furniture	4297.644	13.0	0.40	-1862.3124

Transformation with backward fill

Operations such as `rolling()`, `resample()`, and `expanding()` can also be used as methods on `groupby`. `rolling()` aggregates values in moving windows, `expanding()` cumulates the aggregates, and `resample()` helps to bring regular frequency to time-series data with forward fill or backward fill:

```
sales_data[["Sales", "Category"]].groupby("Category").expanding().sum()
```

The preceding example of `expanding()` calculates a cumulative sum within each group.

Filtering

The `filter` method enables us to apply filtering to a `groupby` object to result in a subset of the initial object.

Let's apply `filter` to the sample sales data to compute only the sums of those groups whose length is more than `10000`, when grouped across `Category`:

```
filtered_df = sales_data[["Category",
"Quantity"]].set_index("Category").groupby("Category").filter(lambda x:
len(x) &amp;gt; 10000)
filtered_df.groupby("Category").sum()
```

The following will be the output:

	Quantity
Category	
Office Supplies	108182
Technology	35176

Filtering with groupby

Now, as you can see, filtering removes the `Furniture` category, whose length is less than `10000`.

Merging and joining

There are various functions that can be used to merge and join pandas data structures, which include the following functions:

- `concat`
- `append`
- `join`

The concat function

The `concat` function is used to join multiple pandas data structures along a specified axis and possibly perform union or intersection operations along other axes. The following command explains the `concat` function:

```
concat(objs, axis=0, , join='outer', join_axes=None, ignore_index=False,
keys=None, levels=None, names=None, verify_integrity=False)
```

The elements of the `concat` function can be summarized as follows:

- The `objs` function: A list or dictionary of Series, DataFrame, or Panel objects to be concatenated.
- The `axis` function: The axis along which the concatenation should be performed. 0 is the default value.

- The `join` function: The type of join to perform when handling indexes on other axes. The `'outer'` function is the default.
- The `join_axes` function: This is used to specify exact indexes for the remaining indexes instead of doing an outer/inner join.
- The `keys` function: This specifies a list of keys to be used to construct a MultiIndex.

For an explanation of the remaining options, please refer to the documentation at `http://pandas.pydata.org/pandas-docs/stable/merging.html`.

Here is an illustration of the workings of `concat` using our stock price examples from earlier chapters:

```
In [53]: stockDataDF=pd.read_csv('./tech_stockprices.csv').set_index(
['Symbol']);stockDataDF
Out[53]:
        Closing price  EPS  Shares Outstanding(M) P/E Market Cap(B) Beta
Symbol
AAPL    501.53  40.32   892.45              12.44  447.59    0.84
AMZN    346.15  0.59    459.00             589.80  158.88    0.52
FB      61.48           0.59   2450.00     104.93  150.92    NaN
GOOG    1133.43 36.05   335.83              31.44  380.64    0.87
TWTR    65.25          -0.30    555.20         NaN  36.23    NaN
YHOO    34.90   1.27   1010.00              27.48   35.36    0.66
```

We now take various slices of the data:

```
In [83]: A=stockDataDF.ix[:4, ['Closing price', 'EPS']]; A
Out[83]:   Closing price  EPS
 Symbol
  AAPL      501.53       40.32
  AMZN      346.15        0.59
  FB        61.48    0.59
   GOOG     1133.43      36.05
In [84]: B=stockDataDF.ix[2:-2, ['P/E']];B
Out[84]:         P/E
       Symbol
       FB    104.93
       GOOG   31.44
In [85]: C=stockDataDF.ix[1:5, ['Market Cap(B)']];C
Out[85]:       Market Cap(B)
       Symbol
       AMZN   158.88
       FB     150.92
       GOOG   380.64
       TWTR    36.23
```

Here, we perform concatenation by specifying an outer join, which concatenates and performs a union on all three DataFrames and includes entries that do not have values for all the columns by inserting NaN for such columns:

```
In [86]: pd.concat([A,B,C],axis=1) # outer join
Out[86]:  Closing price  EPS    P/E    Market Cap(B)
  AAPL    501.53       40.32  NaN    NaN
  AMZN    346.15        0.59  NaN    158.88
   FB     61.48               0.59  104.93 150.92
   GOOG   1133.43             36.05  31.44 380.64
   TWTR   NaN                 NaN    NaN    36.23
```

We can also specify an inner join that performs concatenation but only includes rows that contain values for all the columns in the final DataFrame by throwing out rows with missing columns; that is, it takes the intersection:

```
In [87]: pd.concat([A,B,C],axis=1, join='inner') # Inner join
Out[87]:         Closing price  EPS    P/E    Market Cap(B)
        Symbol
          FB          61.48     0.59 104.93   150.92
        GOOG        1133.43    36.05  31.44   380.64
```

The third case enables us to use the specific index from the original DataFrame to join on:

```
In [102]: pd.concat([A,B,C], axis=1, join_axes=[stockDataDF.index])
Out[102]:         Closing price  EPS    P/E    Market Cap(B)
        Symbol
          AAPL    501.53       40.32  NaN    NaN
          AMZN    346.15        0.59  NaN    158.88
          FB      61.48                0.59  104.93 150.92
          GOOG    1133.43             36.05  31.44 380.64
          TWTR    NaN                 NaN    NaN    36.23
          YHOO    NaN                 NaN    NaN    NaN
```

In this last case, we see that the YHOO row was included even though it wasn't contained in any of the slices that were concatenated. In this case, however, the values for all the columns are NaN. Here is another illustration of concat, but this time, it is on random statistical distributions. Note that in the absence of an axis argument, the default axis of concatenation is 0:

```
In[135]: np.random.seed(100)
         normDF=pd.DataFrame(np.random.randn(3,4));normDF
Out[135]:      0         1         2         3
  0  -1.749765  0.342680  1.153036  -0.252436
  1   0.981321  0.514219  0.221180  -1.070043
  2  -0.189496  0.255001 -0.458027   0.435163
In [136]:
```

```
binomDF=pd.DataFrame(np.random.binomial(100,0.5,(3,4)));binomDF
Out[136]:  0  1  2  3
   0  57  50  57    50
   1  48  56  49    43
   2  40  47  49    55
In [137]:
poissonDF=pd.DataFrame(np.random.poisson(100,(3,4)));poissonDF
Out[137]:  0  1  2  3
   0  93  96  96  89
   1  76  96  104  103
   2  96  93  107   84
In [138]: rand_distribs=[normDF,binomDF,poissonDF]
In [140]: rand_distribsDF=pd.concat(rand_distribs,keys=['Normal',
'Binomial', 'Poisson']);rand_distribsDF
Out[140]:            0           1          2          3
  Normal     0  -1.749765    0.342680   1.153036  -0.252436
          1   0.981321    0.514219   0.221180  -1.070043
          2  -0.189496    0.255001  -0.458027   0.435163
  Binomial 0    57.00       50.00      57.00      50.00
          1   48.00       56.00      49.00      43.00
          2   40.00       47.00      49.00      55.00
  Poisson  0   93.00       96.00      96.00      89.00
          1   76.00       96.00     104.00     103.00
          2   96.00       93.00     107.00      84.00
```

Using append

append is a simpler version of concat that concatenates along axis=0. Here is an illustration of its use, where we slice out the first two rows and the first three columns of the stockData DataFrame:

```
In [145]: stockDataA=stockDataDF.ix[:2,:3]
              stockDataA
Out[145]:  Closing price   EPS   Shares Outstanding(M)
  Symbol
  AAPL      501.53       40.32     892.45
  AMZN      346.15        0.59     459.00
```

And the remaining rows can be obtained as shown following:

```
In [147]: stockDataB=stockDataDF[2:]
          stockDataB
Out[147]:
      Closing price EPS Shares Outstanding(M)  P/E  Market Cap(B) Beta
  Symbol
  FB    61.48         0.59 2450.00              104.93 150.92   NaN
```

GOOG	1133.43	36.05	335.83	31.44	380.64	0.87
TWTR	65.25	-0.30	555.20	NaN	36.23	NaN
YHOO	34.90	1.27	1010.00	27.48	35.36	0.66

Now, we use `append` to combine the two DataFrames from the preceding commands:

```
In [161]:stockDataA.append(stockDataB)
Out[161]:
     Beta Closing price EPS MarketCap(B) P/E     Shares Outstanding(M)
Symbol
AMZN NaN   346.15       0.59 NaN        NaN       459.00
GOOG NaN   1133.43      36.05 NaN       NaN       335.83
FB   NaN   61.48        0.59 150.92 104.93 2450.00
YHOO 27.48 34.90        1.27 35.36      0.66      1010.00
TWTR NaN   65.25        -0.30 36.23     NaN       555.20
AAPL 12.44 501.53       40.32 0.84      447.59 892.45
```

In order to maintain the order of columns similar to the original DataFrame, we can apply the `reindex_axis` function:

```
In [151]:
stockDataA.append(stockDataB).reindex_axis(stockDataDF.columns, axis=1)
Out[151]:
     Closing price EPS Shares Outstanding(M)   P/E Market Cap(B) Beta
Symbol
AAPL    501.53 40.32 892.45          NaN NaN        NaN
AMZN    346.15  0.59 459.00          NaN NaN        NaN
FB      61.48   0.59 2450.00         104.93 150.92     NaN
GOOG    1133.43 36.05 335.83         31.44 380.64     0.87
TWTR    65.25  -0.30 555.20          NaN  36.23      NaN
YHOO    34.90   1.27 1010.00         27.48 35.36    0.66
```

Note that, for the first two rows, the value of the last two columns is NaN since the first DataFrame only contained the first three columns. The `append` function does not work in places, but it returns a new DataFrame with the second DataFrame appended to the first.

Appending a single row to a DataFrame

We can append a single row to a DataFrame by passing a series or dictionary to the `append` method:

```
In [152]:
algos={'search':['DFS','BFS','Binary Search','Linear'],
       'sorting': ['Quicksort','Mergesort','Heapsort','Bubble Sort'],
       'machine learning':['RandomForest','K Nearest
Neighbor','Logistic Regression','K-Means Clustering']}
```

```
algoDF=pd.DataFrame(algos);algoDF
Out[152]: machine learning      search        sorting
0      RandomForest          DFS       Quicksort
1      K Nearest Neighbor    BFS        Mergesort
2      Logistic Regression  Binary Search Heapsort
3      K-Means Clustering    Linear         Bubble Sort
In [154]:
moreAlgos={'search': 'ShortestPath'  , 'sorting': 'Insertion Sort',
           'machine learning': 'Linear Regression'}
    algoDF.append(moreAlgos,ignore_index=True)


Out[154]: machine learning      search        sorting
0      RandomForest          DFS       Quicksort
1      K Nearest Neighbor    BFS        Mergesort
2      Logistic Regression Binary Search Heapsort
3      K-Means Clustering    Linear         Bubble Sort
4      Linear Regression     ShortestPath  Insertion Sort
```

In order for this to work, you must pass the `ignore_index=True` argument so that the index `[0,1,2,3]` in `algoDF` is ignored.

SQL-like merging/joining of DataFrame objects

The `merge` function is used to join two DataFrame objects similar to those used in SQL database queries. It results in a merged DataFrame. DataFrame objects are analogous to SQL tables. The following command explains this:

```
merge(left, right, how='inner', on=None, left_on=None,
      right_on=None, left_index=False, right_index=False,
      sort=True, suffixes=('_x', '_y'), copy=True)
```

The following is a summary of the `merge` function:

- The `left` argument: This is the first DataFrame object.
- The `right` argument: This is the second DataFrame object.
- The `how` argument: This is the type of join and can be inner, outer, left, or right. The default is inner.
- The `on` argument: This shows the names of columns to join on as join keys.
- The `left_on` and `right_on` arguments: These show the left and right DataFrame column names to join on.

- The `left_index` and `right_index` arguments: These have a Boolean value. If this is `True`, use the left or right `DataFrame` index/row labels to join on.
- The `sort` argument: This has a Boolean value. The default `True` setting results in a lexicographical sort. Setting the default value to `False` may improve performance.
- The `suffixes` argument: The tuple of string suffixes to be applied to overlapping columns. The defaults are `'_x'` and `'_y'`.
- The `copy` argument: The default `True` value causes data to be copied from the passed `DataFrame` objects.

The source of the preceding information is `http://pandas.pydata.org/pandas-docs/stable/merging.html`.

Let's create two DataFrames – left and right – to understand merging:

```
left
```

The following will be the output:

	Category	Region	Sales	Quantity
0	Technology	Central	1.038450e+06	7979
1	Technology	Caribbean	1.163330e+05	1245
2	Technology	Canada	2.629881e+04	142
3	Office Supplies	Oceania	2.817136e+05	7204
4	Office Supplies	Canada	3.003408e+04	613

Left DataFrame for merge

The right dataframe can be viewed using the following:

```
right
```

The following will be the output:

	Category	Region	Discount	Profit
0	Office Supplies	Oceania	302.4	33306.1860
1	Office Supplies	Canada	0.0	7957.5300
2	Furniture	North	224.0	30922.0680
3	Technology	Central Asia	33.0	56439.9750
4	Office Supplies	East	244.7	41014.5791

Right dataframe for merge

The DataFrames have five rows each, with `Category` and `Region` as the keys. Of these five rows, two rows from each DataFrame share the same set of keys. Let's perform a merge on both keys:

```
pd.merge(left, right, on = ["Category", "Region"])
```

The following will be the output:

	Category	Region	Sales	Quantity	Discount	Profit
0	Office Supplies	Oceania	281713.626	7204	302.4	33306.186
1	Office Supplies	Canada	30034.080	613	0.0	7957.530

Default inner merge

By default, the `how` argument is set to `inner`, hence, in this scenario, an inner join is performed. Now, let's perform a `left` join:

```
pd.merge(left, right, how = "left", on = ["Category", "Region"])
```

The following will be the output:

	Category	Region	Sales	Quantity	Discount	Profit
0	Technology	Central	1.038450e+06	7979	NaN	NaN
1	Technology	Caribbean	1.163330e+05	1245	NaN	NaN
2	Technology	Canada	2.629881e+04	142	NaN	NaN
3	Office Supplies	Oceania	2.817136e+05	7204	302.4	33306.186
4	Office Supplies	Canada	3.003408e+04	613	0.0	7957.530

Left merge

In a left join, all the rows found in the left DataFrame are included in the result. The rows of `left` not found in `right` get NAs appended to the columns originating from the right DataFrame – `Discount` and `Profit` – for which keys do not exist in the left DataFrame. A right join would be the exact opposite: the result would contain all the rows from the right dataframe and NAs would be appended to `Sales` and `Quantity` for cases where keys are found in `left` but not in the right DataFrame:

```
pd.merge(left, right, how = "right", on = ["Category", "Region"])
```

The following will be the output:

	Category	Region	Sales	Quantity	Discount	Profit
0	Office Supplies	Oceania	281713.626	7204.0	302.4	33306.1860
1	Office Supplies	Canada	30034.080	613.0	0.0	7957.5300
2	Furniture	North	NaN	NaN	224.0	30922.0680
3	Technology	Central Asia	NaN	NaN	33.0	56439.9750
4	Office Supplies	East	NaN	NaN	244.7	41014.5791

Right merge

In the case of an outer join, no rows are excluded and NAs are appended as necessary for missing values:

```
pd.merge(left, right, how = "outer", on = ["Category", "Region"])
```

The following will be the output:

	Category	Region	Sales	Quantity	Discount	Profit
0	Technology	Central	1.038450e+06	7979.0	NaN	NaN
1	Technology	Caribbean	1.163330e+05	1245.0	NaN	NaN
2	Technology	Canada	2.629881e+04	142.0	NaN	NaN
3	Office Supplies	Oceania	2.817136e+05	7204.0	302.4	33306.1860
4	Office Supplies	Canada	3.003408e+04	613.0	0.0	7957.5300
5	Furniture	North	NaN	NaN	224.0	30922.0680
6	Technology	Central Asia	NaN	NaN	33.0	56439.9750
7	Office Supplies	East	NaN	NaN	244.7	41014.5791

Outer merge

Let's investigate the behavior of an outer merge when duplicate entries of a key are found. The following command duplicates the last key combination of the `left` DataFrame. The keys with the `Office Supplies` category and the `Canada` region occur twice:

```
left.loc[5,:] =["Office Supplies", "Canada", 111, 111]
left
```

The following will be the output:

	Category	Region	Sales	Quantity
0	Technology	Central	1.038450e+06	7979.0
1	Technology	Caribbean	1.163330e+05	1245.0
2	Technology	Canada	2.629881e+04	142.0
3	Office Supplies	Oceania	2.817136e+05	7204.0
4	Office Supplies	Canada	3.003408e+04	613.0
5	Office Supplies	Canada	1.110000e+02	111.0

Inserting duplicates in the left DataFrame

The result of the outer merge is as follows:

```
pd.merge(left, right, how = "outer", on = ["Category", "Region"])
```

The following will be the output:

	Category	Region	Sales	Quantity	Discount	Profit
0	Technology	Central	1.038450e+06	7979.0	NaN	NaN
1	Technology	Caribbean	1.163330e+05	1245.0	NaN	NaN
2	Technology	Canada	2.629881e+04	142.0	NaN	NaN
3	Office Supplies	Oceania	2.817136e+05	7204.0	302.4	33306.1860
4	Office Supplies	Canada	3.003408e+04	613.0	0.0	7957.5300
5	Office Supplies	Canada	1.110000e+02	111.0	0.0	7957.5300
6	Furniture	North	NaN	NaN	224.0	30922.0680
7	Technology	Central Asia	NaN	NaN	33.0	56439.9750
8	Office Supplies	East	NaN	NaN	244.7	41014.5791

Outer merge for data with duplicates

As you can see, the `right` DataFrame gets merged on the `left` DataFrame for each occurrence of the key and duplicates are not dropped. This behavior may not be desirable in huge datasets. It may be necessary to drop duplicates before merging. For such instances, the `validate` argument of `merge` helps to keep a check to support only one-to-one merges:

```
pd.merge(left, right, how = "outer", on = ["Category", "Region"], validate
= "one_to_one")
```

The following will be the output:

```
MergeError: Merge keys are not unique in left dataset; not a one-to-one merge
```

Error indicating duplicates in the DataFrame when merging

The `indicator` argument of merge indicates the source of a row – `left`, `right`, or both:

```
pd.merge(left, right, how = "outer", on = ["Category", "Region"], indicator
= "Indicator")
```

The following will be the output:

	Category	Region	Sales	Quantity	Discount	Profit	Indicator
0	Technology	Central	1.038450e+06	7979.0	NaN	NaN	left_only
1	Technology	Caribbean	1.163330e+05	1245.0	NaN	NaN	left_only
2	Technology	Canada	2.629881e+04	142.0	NaN	NaN	left_only
3	Office Supplies	Oceania	2.817136e+05	7204.0	302.4	33306.1860	both
4	Office Supplies	Canada	3.003408e+04	613.0	0.0	7957.5300	both
5	Office Supplies	Canada	1.110000e+02	111.0	0.0	7957.5300	both
6	Furniture	North	NaN	NaN	224.0	30922.0680	right_only
7	Technology	Central Asia	NaN	NaN	33.0	56439.9750	right_only
8	Office Supplies	East	NaN	NaN	244.7	41014.5791	right_only

The indicator parameter of merge

The join function

The `DataFrame.join` function is used to combine two DataFrames that have different columns with nothing in common. Essentially, this does a longitudinal join of two DataFrames. Here is an example:

```
df_1 = sales_data.iloc[0:5, 0:3]
df_2 = sales_data.iloc[3:8, 3:6]
df_1.join(df_2)
```

The following will be the output:

	OrderID	OrderDate	ShipDate	ShipMode	Customer Name	Segment
0	CA-2012-124891	31-07-2012	31-07-2012	NaN	NaN	NaN
1	IN-2013-77878	05-02-2013	07-02-2013	NaN	NaN	NaN
2	IN-2013-71249	17-10-2013	18-10-2013	NaN	NaN	NaN
3	ES-2013-1579342	28-01-2013	30-01-2013	First Class	Katherine Murray	Home Office
4	SG-2013-4320	05-11-2013	06-11-2013	Same Day	Rick Hansen	Consumer

Default left join

`join` is almost identical to `merge`, the difference being that, while merge works for DataFrames that share identical keys, `join` combines DataFrames by the row-index. By default, the `join` function performs a left join. The other types of join can be specified through the `how` parameter:

```
df_1.join(df_2, how = "right")
```

The following will be the output:

	OrderID	OrderDate	ShipDate	ShipMode	Customer Name	Segment
3	ES-2013-1579342	28-01-2013	30-01-2013	First Class	Katherine Murray	Home Office
4	SG-2013-4320	05-11-2013	06-11-2013	Same Day	Rick Hansen	Consumer
5	NaN	NaN	NaN	Second Class	Jim Mitchum	Corporate
6	NaN	NaN	NaN	First Class	Toby Swindell	Consumer
7	NaN	NaN	NaN	Standard Class	Mick Brown	Consumer

Right join

The inner join can be performed as shown following:

```
df_1.join(df_2, how = "inner")
```

The following will be the output:

	OrderID	OrderDate	ShipDate	ShipMode	Customer Name	Segment
3	ES-2013-1579342	28-01-2013	30-01-2013	First Class	Katherine Murray	Home Office
4	SG-2013-4320	05-11-2013	06-11-2013	Same Day	Rick Hansen	Consumer

Inner join

The outer join can be performed as shown following:

```
df_1.join(df_2, how = "outer")
```

The following will be the output:

	OrderID	OrderDate	ShipDate	ShipMode	Customer Name	Segment
0	CA-2012-124891	31-07-2012	31-07-2012	NaN	NaN	NaN
1	IN-2013-77878	05-02-2013	07-02-2013	NaN	NaN	NaN
2	IN-2013-71249	17-10-2013	18-10-2013	NaN	NaN	NaN
3	ES-2013-1579342	28-01-2013	30-01-2013	First Class	Katherine Murray	Home Office
4	SG-2013-4320	05-11-2013	06-11-2013	Same Day	Rick Hansen	Consumer
5	NaN	NaN	NaN	Second Class	Jim Mitchum	Corporate
6	NaN	NaN	NaN	First Class	Toby Swindell	Consumer
7	NaN	NaN	NaN	Standard Class	Mick Brown	Consumer

Outer join

If the two DataFrames being joined have a common column over which the join should be performed, the key or list of keys can be mentioned in the `on` parameter of the `join` function. This is just the same as a `merge` function.

Pivots and reshaping data

This section deals with how you can reshape data. Sometimes, data is stored in what is known as a *stacked* format. Here is an example of stacked data using the `PlantGrowth` dataset:

```
In [344]: plantGrowthRawDF=pd.read_csv('./PlantGrowth.csv')
        plantGrowthRawDF
Out[344]:   observation   weight   group
        0    1           4.17    ctrl
        1    2           5.58    ctrl
        2    3           5.18    ctrl
        ...
        10   1           4.81    trt1
        11   2           4.17    trt1
        12   3           4.41    trt1
        ...
        20   1           6.31    trt2
        21   2           5.12    trt2
        22   3           5.54    trt2
```

This data consists of results from an experiment that compared the dried weight yields of plants that were obtained under a **control** (**ctrl**) and two different treatment conditions (**trt1** and **trt2**). Suppose we wanted to do some analysis on this data by group value. One way to do this would be to use a logical filter on the DataFrame:

```
In [346]: plantGrowthRawDF[plantGrowthRawDF['group']=='ctrl']
Out[346]:    observation   weight   group
         0        1          4.17    ctrl
         1        2          5.58    ctrl
         2        3          5.18    ctrl
         3        4          6.11    ctrl
         ...
```

This can be tedious, so we would instead like to pivot/unstack this data and display it in a form that is more conducive to analysis. We can do this using the DataFrame.pivot function as follows:

```
In [345]:
plantGrowthRawDF.pivot(index='observation',columns='group',values='weight')
Out[345]: weight
              group    ctrl  trt1  trt2
          observation
              1        4.17  4.81  6.31
              2        5.58  4.17  5.12
              3        5.18  4.41  5.54
              4        6.11  3.59  5.50
              5        4.50  5.87  5.37
              6        4.61  3.83  5.29
              7        5.17  6.03  4.92
              8        4.53  4.89  6.15
              9        5.33  4.32  5.80
             10        5.14  4.69  5.26
```

Here, a DataFrame is created with columns corresponding to the different values of a group, or, in statistical parlance, levels of the factor.

Some more examples of pivoting on salesdata.csv are as follows:

```
datastr=pd.read_csv('salesdata.csv')
table=pd.pivot_table(datastr,index=['Customer Segment'])# the aggregate
values are average by default
```

The following will be the output. This gives the results for all the columns:

	Discount	Order ID	Order Quantity	Product Base Margin	Profit	Row ID	Sales	Shipping Cost	Unit Price
Customer Segment									
Consumer	0.049903	29651.300788	25.324439	0.512905	174.627010	4155.625834	1857.859965	13.024748	102.436404
Corporate	0.049841	29526.969766	25.525683	0.512783	194.975943	4138.810793	1787.680389	12.698911	87.316284
Home Office	0.049444	30227.655020	25.987697	0.513608	156.670290	4237.240650	1754.312931	12.771757	88.301412
Small Business	0.049403	30776.489647	25.391596	0.510258	192.270408	4313.104750	1698.124841	12.995840	81.296127

If we specify a `columns` parameter with a variable name, all the categories in that variable become separate columns:

```
table2=pd.pivot_table(datastr,values='Sales',index=['Customer
Segment'],columns=['Region'])
```

For example, the output of the preceding code would be as shown following:

Region	Atlantic	Northwest Territories	Nunavut	Ontario	Prarie	Quebec	West	Yukon
Customer Segment								
Consumer	2191.276783	2052.510621	2271.586667	1478.099014	1519.745182	2082.320233	2068.721678	1964.666187
Corporate	1643.961467	1976.408073	1742.229000	1751.318412	1872.082308	1996.559045	1772.304088	1548.871968
Home Office	2113.716464	2204.625398	997.452978	1811.414706	1417.655288	2093.104754	1589.417233	1970.877118
Small Business	1631.070976	1970.896366	577.556667	1528.490906	1682.845591	1567.529777	1851.106647	1983.969563

Multi-indexed pivots are also possible, as shown:

```
table4=pd.pivot_table(datastr,values='Sales',index=['Customer
Segment','Ship Mode'],columns=['Region'])
```

The following will be the output:

Customer Segment	Ship Mode	Atlantic	Northwest Territories	Nunavut	Ontario	Prarie	Quebec	West	Yukon
	Region								
Consumer	Delivery Truck	4791.027488	6562.887500	12173.420000	4918.616421	5132.905304	6178.034000	6455.878235	6080.114250
	Express Air	1528.610419	1405.924750	173.120000	925.680163	863.624792	1502.519719	1232.537128	987.056667
	Regular Air	1739.560827	1434.304060	341.834286	1041.422888	949.405056	1094.541061	1467.925878	1252.615467
Corporate	Delivery Truck	4863.889231	5096.620593	4596.030000	5872.541093	6145.793646	6679.263586	5549.020917	4957.745800
	Express Air	929.865040	873.736500	1133.937500	1293.076480	1126.284304	1310.311156	1420.634506	1233.630727
	Regular Air	1173.492102	1526.387851	1287.004423	1076.549469	1189.833286	1330.836827	1120.004281	981.426089

A different aggregate function, other than default average, or a custom function can be applied for aggregation as shown in the example following:

```
table5=pd.pivot_table(datastr,values='Sales',index=['Customer
Segment','Ship Mode'],columns=['Region'],aggfunc=sum)
```

The following will be the output:

Customer Segment	Ship Mode	Atlantic	Northwest Territories	Nunavut	Ontario	Prarie	Quebec	West	Yukon
	Region								
Consumer	Delivery Truck	206014.1820	26251.5500	24346.8400	186907.4240	236113.6440	185341.0200	329249.7900	97281.8280
	Express Air	47386.9230	5623.6990	519.3600	39804.2470	31090.4925	24040.3155	57929.2450	11844.6800
	Regular Air	351391.2870	35857.6015	2392.8400	255148.6075	237351.2640	125872.2220	450653.2445	95198.7755
Corporate	Delivery Truck	252922.2400	137608.7560	22980.1500	505038.5340	589996.1900	193698.6440	532706.0080	148732.3740
	Express Air	46493.2520	13979.7840	4535.7500	95687.6595	88976.4600	41929.9570	120753.9330	27139.8760
	Regular Air	328577.7885	225905.4020	33462.1150	511360.9980	612764.1425	227573.0975	571202.1835	164879.5830

Some more important tips and tricks to keep in mind while using `pivot_tables` are listed following:

- If you expect missing values in your pivot table, then use `fill.values=0`:

```
table4=pd.pivot_table(datastr,values='Sales',index=['Customer
Segment','Ship Mode'],columns=['Region'],fill_values=0)
```

- If you want totals at the end, use `margins=TRUE`:

```
table4=pd.pivot_table(datastr,values='Sales',index=['Customer
Segment','Ship Mode'],columns=['Region'],fill_values=0,margins=TRUE)
```

- You can pass different aggregate functions to different value columns:

```
table6=pd.pivot_table(datastr,values=['Sales','Unit
Price'],index=['Customer Segment','Ship
Mode'],columns=['Region'],aggfunc={"Sales":sum,"Unit Price":len})
```

Stacking and unstacking

In addition to pivot functions, the stack and unstack functions are also available on Series and DataFrames, which work on objects containing MultiIndex.

The stack() function

When stacking, a set of column labels get converted to an index level. To explore stacking further, let's use a DataFrame with a MultiIndex along the row-index and column-index:

```
multi_df = sales_data[["Sales", "Quantity", "Category",
"ShipMode"]].groupby(["Category", "ShipMode"]).agg([np.sum, np.mean])
multi_df
```

The following will be the output:

		Sales		Quantity	
		sum	mean	sum	mean
Category	ShipMode				
Furniture	First Class	5.875523e+05	410.588620	5034	3.517820
	Same Day	1.998643e+05	393.433729	1801	3.545276
	Second Class	8.175204e+05	415.406714	6891	3.501524
	Standard Class	2.505937e+06	419.825285	21228	3.556375
Office Supplies	First Class	5.574531e+05	121.238165	15922	3.462810
	Same Day	1.964628e+05	117.291198	5638	3.365970
	Second Class	8.012851e+05	126.966427	21637	3.428458
	Standard Class	2.231869e+06	119.421546	64985	3.477179
Technology	First Class	6.859707e+05	464.749824	5083	3.443767
	Same Day	2.708749e+05	522.924505	1791	3.457529
	Second Class	9.468661e+05	466.436525	7196	3.544828
	Standard Class	2.840846e+06	464.418133	21106	3.450384

Hierarchical data for stacking and unstacking

Applying `stack()` makes a wide DataFrame longer. Let's apply `stack()` on the preceding DataFrame. The column labels on the last level get added to the MultiIndex:

```
multi_df.stack()
```

The following will be the output:

Category	ShipMode		Sales	Quantity
Furniture	First Class	sum	5.875523e+05	5034.000000
		mean	4.105886e+02	3.517820
	Same Day	sum	1.998643e+05	1801.000000
		mean	3.934337e+02	3.545276
	Second Class	sum	8.175204e+05	6891.000000
		mean	4.154067e+02	3.501524
	Standard Class	sum	2.505937e+06	21228.000000
		mean	4.198253e+02	3.556375
Office Supplies	First Class	sum	5.574531e+05	15922.000000
		mean	1.212382e+02	3.462810
	Same Day	sum	1.964628e+05	5638.000000
		mean	1.172912e+02	3.365970
	Second Class	sum	8.012851e+05	21637.000000
		mean	1.269664e+02	3.428458
	Standard Class	sum	2.231869e+06	64985.000000
		mean	1.194215e+02	3.477179
Technology	First Class	sum	6.859707e+05	5083.000000
		mean	4.647498e+02	3.443767
	Same Day	sum	2.708749e+05	1791.000000
		mean	5.229245e+02	3.457529
	Second Class	sum	9.468661e+05	7196.000000
		mean	4.664365e+02	3.544828
	Standard Class	sum	2.840846e+06	21106.000000
		mean	4.644181e+02	3.450384

Result of stacking

The stack() function accepts a level argument. In this case, the default level setting is 1. Let's try stacking at level 0:

```
multi_df.stack(level = 0)
```

The following will be the output:

			mean	sum
Category	ShipMode			
Furniture	First Class	Quantity	3.517820	5.034000e+03
		Sales	410.588620	5.875523e+05
	Same Day	Quantity	3.545276	1.801000e+03
		Sales	393.433729	1.998643e+05
	Second Class	Quantity	3.501524	6.891000e+03
		Sales	415.406714	8.175204e+05
	Standard Class	Quantity	3.556375	2.122800e+04
		Sales	419.825285	2.505937e+06
Office Supplies	First Class	Quantity	3.462810	1.592200e+04
		Sales	121.238165	5.574531e+05
	Same Day	Quantity	3.365970	5.638000e+03
		Sales	117.291198	1.964628e+05
	Second Class	Quantity	3.428458	2.163700e+04
		Sales	126.966427	8.012851e+05
	Standard Class	Quantity	3.477179	6.498500e+04
		Sales	119.421546	2.231869e+06
Technology	First Class	Quantity	3.443767	5.083000e+03
		Sales	464.749824	6.859707e+05
	Same Day	Quantity	3.457529	1.791000e+03
		Sales	522.924505	2.708749e+05
	Second Class	Quantity	3.544828	7.196000e+03
		Sales	466.436525	9.468661e+05
	Standard Class	Quantity	3.450384	2.110600e+04
		Sales	464.418133	2.840846e+06

Stacking using the level parameter

Instead of specifying level numbers, level names can also be specified when stacking. To stack multiple levels, a list of level names or level numbers can be passed to the `level` argument. However, the list cannot be a combination of both level names and level numbers:

```
multi_df.stack(level = [0,1])
```

The following will be the output:

```
Category           ShipMode
Furniture          First Class    Quantity  mean     3.517820e+00
                                             sum      5.034000e+03
                                   Sales     mean     4.105886e+02
                                             sum      5.875523e+05
                   Same Day        Quantity  mean     3.545276e+00
                                             sum      1.801000e+03
                                   Sales     mean     3.934337e+02
                                             sum      1.998643e+05
                   Second Class    Quantity  mean     3.501524e+00
                                             sum      6.891000e+03
                                   Sales     mean     4.154067e+02
                                             sum      8.175204e+05
                   Standard Class  Quantity  mean     3.556375e+00
                                             sum      2.122800e+04
                                   Sales     mean     4.198253e+02
                                             sum      2.505937e+06
Office Supplies    First Class     Quantity  mean     3.462810e+00
                                             sum      1.592200e+04
                                   Sales     mean     1.212382e+02
                                             sum      5.574531e+05
                   Same Day        Quantity  mean     3.365970e+00
                                             sum      5.638000e+03
                                   Sales     mean     1.172912e+02
                                             sum      1.964628e+05
                   Second Class    Quantity  mean     3.428458e+00
                                             sum      2.163700e+04
                                   Sales     mean     1.269664e+02
                                             sum      8.012851e+05
```

Stacking multiple levels at once

Let's explore the attributes of the index after stacking. The `index` attribute of a DataFrame helps us understand the various levels, labels, and names of each index:

```
multi_df.stack(level = 0).index
```

The following will be the output:

```
MultiIndex(levels=[['Furniture', 'Office Supplies', 'Technology'], ['First Class', 'Same Day', 'Second Class', 'Standard Clas
s'], ['Quantity', 'Sales']],
        labels=[[0, 0, 0, 0, 0, 0, 0, 0, 1, 1, 1, 1, 1, 1, 1, 1, 2, 2, 2, 2, 2, 2, 2, 2], [0, 0, 1, 1, 2, 2, 3, 3, 0, 0, 1,
1, 2, 2, 3, 3, 0, 0, 1, 1, 2, 2, 3, 3], [0, 1, 0, 1, 0, 1, 0, 1, 0, 1, 0, 1, 0, 1, 0, 1, 0, 1, 0, 1, 0, 1, 0, 1]],
        names=['Category', 'ShipMode', None])
```

Index properties after stacking

At times, stacking introduces missing values when there are no values for a certain combination of index and column name. Consider the following DataFrame:

```
multicol = pd.MultiIndex.from_tuples([('Male', 'M'),
('Female', 'F')])
missing_info = pd.DataFrame([[20, None], [34, 78]],
index=['ClassA', 'ClassB'],
columns=multicol)
missing_info
```

The following will be the output:

		Female	Male
ClassA	M	NaN	20.0
ClassB	F	78.0	NaN
	M	NaN	34.0

Handling missing values when stacking

Upon stacking, the `dropna` parameter of the `stack` function, which is set to `True` by default, automatically drops all NAs:

```
missing_info.stack(dropna = False)
```

The following will be the output:

		Female	Male
ClassA	F	NaN	NaN
	M	NaN	20.0
ClassB	F	78.0	NaN
	M	NaN	34.0

dropna set to False when stacking

By default, it will drop the rows with all missing values, as shown following:

```
missing_info.stack()
```

The following will be the output:

		Female	Male
ClassA	M	NaN	20.0
ClassB	F	78.0	NaN
	M	NaN	34.0

Dropping NAs by default when stacking

The unstack() function

The `unstack` function performs the reverse operation of the `stack` function. It converts long DataFrames to a wider format. Let's unstack the multi-level indexed sales data. The last level is unstacked by default:

```
multi_df.unstack()
```

The following will be the output:

	Sales								Quantity				
	sum				mean				sum				mean
ShipMode	First Class	Same Day	Second Class	Standard Class	First Class	Same Day	Second Class	Standard Class	First Class	Same Day	Second Class	Standard Class	First Class
Category													
Furniture	587552.3157	199864.3341	817520.41310	2.505937e+06	410.588620	393.433729	415.406714	419.825285	5034	1801	6891	21228	3.51782
Office Supplies	557453.0821	196462.7563	801285.12240	2.231869e+06	121.238165	117.291198	126.966427	119.421546	15922	5638	21637	64985	3.46281
Technology	685970.7404	270874.8935	946866.14558	2.840846e+06	464.749824	522.924505	466.436525	464.418133	5083	1791	7196	21106	3.44376

Unstacking

Just like `stack`, `unstack` has a `level` parameter. This `level` parameter accepts a level number, a level name, or a list of level names/level numbers.

Any missing values created when unstacking can be handled using the `fill_value` argument of the `unstack` function. Consider the following DataFrame:

```
multi_df.iloc[[0,5,6],[0,2]]
```

The following will be the output:

Category	ShipMode	Sales sum	Quantity sum
Furniture	First Class	587552.3157	5034
Office Supplies	Same Day	196462.7563	5638
	Second Class	801285.1224	21637

Snapshot of data

Unstacking the preceding DataFrame introduces NAs:

```
multi_df.iloc[[0,5,6],[0,2]].unstack()
```

The following will be the output:

Category	Sales sum First Class	Same Day	Second Class	Quantity sum First Class	Same Day	Second Class
Furniture	587552.3157	NaN	NaN	5034.0	NaN	NaN
Office Supplies	NaN	196462.7563	801285.1224	NaN	5638.0	21637.0

Unstacking without handling missing data

We can impute the missing cells with a value of our choice using the `fill_value` method. Following are the missing values have been replaced by 0:

```
multi_df.iloc[[0,5,6],[0,2]].unstack(fill_value = 0)
```

	Sales			Quantity		
	sum			sum		
ShipMode	First Class	Same Day	Second Class	First Class	Same Day	Second Class
Category						
Furniture	587552.3157	0.0000	0.0000	5034	0	0
Office Supplies	0.0000	196462.7563	801285.1224	0	5638	21637

Filling NAs with 0 when unstacking

Other methods for reshaping DataFrames

There are various other methods that are related to reshaping DataFrames; we'll discuss them here.

Using the melt function

The `melt` function enables us to transform a DataFrame by designating some of its columns as ID columns, ensuring they remain as columns with the remaining non-ID columns treated as *variable* columns and are pivoted and become part of a name-value two-column scheme. ID columns uniquely identify a row in a DataFrame.

The names of those non-ID columns can be customized by supplying the `var_name` and `value_name` parameters. The use of `melt` is perhaps best illustrated by an example, as follows:

```
In [385]: from pandas.core.reshape import melt
In [401]: USIndexDataDF[:2]

Out[401]:   TradingDate   Nasdaq   S&amp;P 500   Russell 2000   DJIA
        0     2014/01/30   4123.13    1794.19       1139.36   15848.61
        1     2014/01/31   4103.88    1782.59       1130.88   15698.85
In [402]: melt(USIndexDataDF[:2], id_vars=['TradingDate'],
var_name='Index Name', value_name='Index Value')
```

```
Out[402]:
       TradingDate      Index Name      Index value
    0   2014/01/30      Nasdaq          4123.13
    1   2014/01/31      Nasdaq          4103.88
    2   2014/01/30      S&amp;P 500         1794.19
    3   2014/01/31      S&amp;P 500         1782.59
    4   2014/01/30      Russell 2000    1139.36
    5   2014/01/31      Russell 2000    1130.88
    6   2014/01/30      DJIA               15848.61
    7   2014/01/31      DJIA               15698.85
```

The pandas.get_dummies() function

This function is used to convert a categorical variable into an indicator DataFrame, which is essentially a truth table of possible values of the categorical variable. An example of this is the following command:

```
In [408]: melted=melt(USIndexDataDF[:2], id_vars=['TradingDate'],
var_name='Index Name', value_name='Index Value')

melted

Out[408]: TradingDate     Index Name   Index Value
    0      2014/01/30      Nasdaq          4123.13
    1      2014/01/31      Nasdaq          4103.88
    2      2014/01/30      S&amp;P 500         1794.19
    3      2014/01/31      S&amp;P 500         1782.59
    4      2014/01/30      Russell 2000    1139.36
    5      2014/01/31      Russell 2000    1130.88
    6      2014/01/30      DJIA               15848.61
    7      2014/01/31      DJIA               15698.85
In [413]: pd.get_dummies(melted['Index Name'])

Out[413]:             DJIA  Nasdaq   Russell 2000   S&amp;P 500
        0   0   1       0               0
        1   0   1       0               0
        2   0   0       0               1
        3   0   0       0               1
        4   0   0       1               0
        5   0   0       1               0
        6   1   0       0               0
        7   1   0       0               0
```

The source of the preceding data
is http://vincentarelbundock.github.io/Rdatasets/csv/datasets/PlantGrowth.csv.

pivot table

The pandas `pivot_table` function is more advanced than the `pivot` function in several ways. Let's discuss some interesting parameters of the `pivot_table` function:

- `data`: The DataFrame object that is to be reshaped
- `values`: A column or a list of columns that are to be aggregated
- `index`: The key across which grouping of pivot index occurs
- `columns`: The key with respect to which grouping of the `pivot` column occurs
- `aggfunc`: The function to use for aggregation, such as `np.mean`

Let's pivot the sample sales data to slice and dice `Sales` across `Category` and `ShipMode`. Note that when `aggfunc` is empty, the mean is calculated:

```
pd.pivot_table(sales_data, values = "Sales", index = "Category", columns =
"ShipMode")
```

The following will be the output:

ShipMode	First Class	Same Day	Second Class	Standard Class
Category				
Furniture	410.588620	393.433729	415.406714	419.825285
Office Supplies	121.238165	117.291198	126.966427	119.421546
Technology	464.749824	522.924505	466.436525	464.418133

Pivot table from pandas

Now, it is possible to have multiple values for `values`, `index`, `column`, or `aggfunc`. Those multiple values can be passed as a list. Let's calculate `mean` for `Sales` and `sum` for `Quantity`:

```
pd.pivot_table(sales_data, values = ["Sales", "Quantity"], index =
"Category", columns = "ShipMode", aggfunc = {"Sales": np.mean, "Quantity":
np.sum})
```

The following will be the output:

ShipMode	Quantity				Sales			
	First Class	Same Day	Second Class	Standard Class	First Class	Same Day	Second Class	Standard Class
Category								
Furniture	5034	1801	6891	21228	410.588620	393.433729	415.406714	419.825285
Office Supplies	15922	5638	21637	64985	121.238165	117.291198	126.966427	119.421546
Technology	5083	1791	7196	21106	464.749824	522.924505	466.436525	464.418133

Pivot table with multiple aggregations

Through `pivot_table`, DataFrames with hierarchical indices can be created. The `fill_value` and `dropna` parameters of the `pivot_table` function help in handling missing values.

Transpose in pandas

The `transpose` function in pandas is similar to that of NumPy. It interchanges rows and columns. Let's find the transpose of the following DataFrame:

```
sales_data.groupby("Category").sum()
```

The following will be the output:

Category	Sales	Quantity	Discount	Profit
Furniture	4.110874e+06	34954	1660.030	285204.72380
Office Supplies	3.787070e+06	108182	4297.190	518473.83430
Technology	4.744557e+06	35176	1372.508	663778.73318

Data to be transposed

In the transpose of the DataFrame, the column labels and row indices are swapped:

```
sales_data.groupby("Category").sum().transpose()
```

The following will be the output:

Category	Furniture	Office Supplies	Technology
Sales	4.110874e+06	3.787070e+06	4.744557e+06
Quantity	3.495400e+04	1.081820e+05	3.517600e+04
Discount	1.660030e+03	4.297190e+03	1.372508e+03
Profit	2.852047e+05	5.184738e+05	6.637787e+05

Output of transpose

`T` acts as an accessor to the `transpose` function and can be used as shown:

```
sales_data.groupby("Category").sum().T
```
Swaplevel and swapaxes

The `swaplevel` function helps to interchange the levels within any axis. Consider the following DataFrame:

```
multi_df
```

The following will be the output:

Category	ShipMode	Sales		Quantity	
		sum	mean	sum	mean
Furniture	First Class	5.875523e+05	410.588620	5034	3.517820
	Same Day	1.998643e+05	393.433729	1801	3.545276
	Second Class	8.175204e+05	415.406714	6891	3.501524
	Standard Class	2.505937e+06	419.825285	21228	3.556375
Office Supplies	First Class	5.574531e+05	121.238165	15922	3.462810
	Same Day	1.964628e+05	117.291198	5638	3.365970
	Second Class	8.012851e+05	126.966427	21637	3.428458
	Standard Class	2.231869e+06	119.421546	64985	3.477179
Technology	First Class	6.859707e+05	464.749824	5083	3.443767
	Same Day	2.708749e+05	522.924505	1791	3.457529
	Second Class	9.468661e+05	466.436525	7196	3.544828
	Standard Class	2.840846e+06	464.418133	21106	3.450384

Data for swaplevel and swapaxes

Now, let's switch the positions of the `Category` and `ShipMode` index levels. Level numbers or level names can be provided as arguments:

```
multi_df.swaplevel(i = 1, j = 0, axis = 0)
```

The following will be the output:

		Sales		Quantity	
		sum	mean	sum	mean
ShipMode	Category				
First Class	Furniture	5.875523e+05	410.588620	5034	3.517820
Same Day	Furniture	1.998643e+05	393.433729	1801	3.545276
Second Class	Furniture	8.175204e+05	415.406714	6891	3.501524
Standard Class	Furniture	2.505937e+06	419.825285	21228	3.556375
First Class	Office Supplies	5.574531e+05	121.238165	15922	3.462810
Same Day	Office Supplies	1.964628e+05	117.291198	5638	3.365970
Second Class	Office Supplies	8.012851e+05	126.966427	21637	3.428458
Standard Class	Office Supplies	2.231869e+06	119.421546	64985	3.477179
First Class	Technology	6.859707e+05	464.749824	5083	3.443767
Same Day	Technology	2.708749e+05	522.924505	1791	3.457529
Second Class	Technology	9.468661e+05	466.436525	7196	3.544828
Standard Class	Technology	2.840846e+06	464.418133	21106	3.450384

Levels swapped

Similarly, such switches can also be executed on the column labels by setting `axis` to 1:

```
multi_df.swaplevel(i = 0, j = 1, axis = 1)
```

The following will be the output:

Category	ShipMode	sum Sales	mean Sales	sum Quantity	mean Quantity
Furniture	First Class	5.875523e+05	410.588620	5034	3.517820
	Same Day	1.998643e+05	393.433729	1801	3.545276
	Second Class	8.175204e+05	415.406714	6891	3.501524
	Standard Class	2.505937e+06	419.825285	21228	3.556375
Office Supplies	First Class	5.574531e+05	121.238165	15922	3.462810
	Same Day	1.964628e+05	117.291198	5638	3.365970
	Second Class	8.012851e+05	126.966427	21637	3.428458
	Standard Class	2.231869e+06	119.421546	64985	3.477179
Technology	First Class	6.859707e+05	464.749824	5083	3.443767
	Same Day	2.708749e+05	522.924505	1791	3.457529
	Second Class	9.468661e+05	466.436525	7196	3.544828
	Standard Class	2.840846e+06	464.418133	21106	3.450384

Levels swapped along axis 1

The `swapaxes` function is functionally similar to the `transpose` function. The following shows the `swapaxes` function in action:

```
multi_df.swapaxes(axis1 = 0, axis2 = 1)
```

The following will be the output:

Category		Furniture				Office Supplies				Technology
	ShipMode	First Class	Same Day	Second Class	Standard Class	First Class	Same Day	Second Class	Standard Class	First Class
Sales	sum	587552.31570	199864.334100	817520.413100	2.505937e+06	557453.082100	196462.756300	801285.122400	2.231869e+06	685970.740400	2
	mean	410.58862	393.433729	415.406714	4.198253e+02	121.238165	117.291198	126.966427	1.194215e+02	464.749824
Quantity	sum	5034.00000	1801.000000	6891.000000	2.122800e+04	15922.000000	5638.000000	21637.000000	6.498500e+04	5083.000000
	mean	3.51782	3.545276	3.501524	3.556375e+00	3.462810	3.365970	3.428458	3.477179e+00	3.443767

Axis swapped

Squeeze

`squeeze` helps to convert a 1D DataFrame to a series. Let's consider a 1D DataFrame:

```
dim1_df = sales_data[["Sales","OrderID"]].set_index("OrderID")
dim1_df
```

The following will be the output:

	Sales
OrderID	
CA-2012-124891	2309.650
IN-2013-77878	3709.395
IN-2013-71249	5175.171
ES-2013-1579342	2892.510
SG-2013-4320	2832.960
IN-2013-42360	2862.675
IN-2011-81826	1822.080
IN-2012-86369	5244.840

Data to squeeze

The type of the preceding object has been deciphered here – it is a DataFrame:

```
type(dim1_df)
```

The following will be the output:

```
pandas.core.frame.DataFrame
```

Object type before squeezing

Now, let's apply the `squeeze` function and find the object type. The required snippet and the output looks as shown following:

```
type(dim1_df.squeeze())
```

```
pandas.core.series.Series
```

Object type after squeezing

As you can see, `squeeze` transforms the DataFrame into a series.

nsmallest and nlargest

The `nsmallest` and `nlargest` functions are extremely useful for returning the n smallest and n largest rows after ordering by the desired column.

In the sample sales data, let's find the 3 smallest records by `Profit`:

```
sales_data.nsmallest(3, "Profit")
```

The following will be the output:

	OrderID	OrderDate	ShipDate	ShipMode	Customer Name	Segment	Country	Region	ProductID	Category	Sub-Category	Sales	Quantity	Discount	Profit
1	CA-2013-108196	26-11-2013	03-12-2013	Standard Class	Cindy Stewart	Consumer	United States	East	TEC-MA-10000418	Technology	Machines	4499.985	5	0.7	-6599.9780
91	TU-2013-9400	26-09-2013	26-09-2013	Same Day	Denise Monton	Corporate	Turkey	EMEA	TEC-MOT-10003050	Technology	Phones	3085.344	12	0.6	-4088.3760
37	US-2014-168116	05-11-2014	05-11-2014	Same Day	Grant Thornton	Corporate	United States	South	TEC-MA-10004125	Technology	Machines	7999.980	4	0.5	-3839.9904

Figure6.73: Result of nsmallest

The ordering can also be done with respect to multiple columns, as shown here:

```
sales_data.nlargest(3, ["Quantity", "Profit"])
```

The following will be the output:

	OrderID	OrderDate	ShipDate	ShipMode	Customer Name	Segment	Country	Region	ProductID	Category	Sub-Category	Sales	Quantity	Discount	Profit
17	ES-2014-1651774	08-09-2014	14-09-2014	Standard Class	Patrick Jones	Corporate	Italy	South	OFF-AP-10004512	Office Supplies	Appliances	7958.58	14	0.0	3979.08
81	MO-2014-2000	28-10-2014	30-10-2014	Second Class	Dave Poirier	Corporate	Morocco	Africa	TEC-CAN-10001437	Technology	Copiers	5301.24	14	0.0	2597.28
334	IN-2014-56206	24-06-2014	28-06-2014	Standard Class	Maria Bertelson	Consumer	Australia	Oceania	FUR-BO-10001471	Furniture	Bookcases	5486.67	14	0.1	2316.51

Result of nlargest

These functions – `nsmallest` and `nlargest` have the `keep` parameter to decide how duplicates are handled. It helps to choose either the first occurrence, the last occurrence, or to retain all duplicates.

Summary

This chapter added to our arsenal of pandas tricks to aggregate, join, and transform data. Here is a quick recap of the chapter:

- `groupby` creates groups of rows – one group for each category in a categorical variable (or a combination of categories across categorical variables).
- Using `groupby`, the same analysis can be performed on different groups efficiently.
- Similarly shaped DataFrames can be concatenated or appended to perform analysis simultaneously for the entire dataset.
- SQL-like joining or merging between DataFrames is also possible.
- Wide data can be made longer, or vice versa, depending on the requirement.
- pandas can handle multi-index data and there are functions to convert multi-index data to single-index data and vice versa.
- Spreadsheet operations such as pivot tables and transposes are possible and provide more flexibility than in spreadsheets.

In the next chapter, we will discuss and elaborate on the methods, syntax, and usage of some of these special data operations in pandas.

7
Special Data Operations in pandas

pandas has an array of special operators for generating, aggregating, transforming, reading, and writing data from and to a variety of data types, such as number, string, date, timestamp, and time series. The basic operators in pandas were introduced in the previous chapter. In this chapter, we will continue that discussion and elaborate on the methods, syntax, and usage of some of these operators.

Reading this chapter will allow you to perform the following tasks with confidence:

- Writing custom functions and applying them on a column or an entire DataFrame
- Understanding the nature of missing values and handling them
- Transforming and performing calculations on series using functions
- Miscellaneous numeric operations on data

Let's delve into it right away. For the most part, we will generate our own data to demonstrate the methods.

The following topics will be covered in this chapter:

- Writing and applying one-liner custom functions
- Handling missing values
- A survey of methods on series
- pandas string methods
- Binary operations on DataFrames and series
- Binning values
- Using mathematical methods on DataFrames

Writing and applying one-liner custom functions

Python provides lambda functions, which are a way to write one-liner custom functions so that we can perform certain tasks on a DataFrame's column(s) or the entire DataFrame. Lambda functions are similar to the traditional functions that are defined using the `def` keyword but are more elegant, are more amenable to apply on DataFrame columns, and have lucid and crisp syntax, much like a list comprehension for implementing for loops on lists. Let's look at how lambda functions are defined and applied.

lambda and apply

In order to see how the `lambda` keyword can be used, we need to create some data. We'll create data containing date columns. Handling date columns is a topic in itself, but we'll get a brief glimpse of this process here.

In the following code, we are creating two date columns:

- **Start Date**: A sequence of 300 consecutive days starting from 2016-01-15
- **End Date**: A sequence of 300 days taken randomly from any day between 2010 and 2025

Some date/time methods have been used to create these dates in the following code block. Please take note of them and ensure that you understand them:

```
### Importing required libraries
import datetime
import pandas as pd
from random import randint

### Creating date sequence of 300 (periods=300) consecutive days (freq='D')
starting from 2016-01-15
D1=pd.date_range('2016-01-15',periods=300,freq='D')

### Creating a date sequence with of 300 days with day (b/w 1-30), month
(b/w 1-12) and year (b/w 2010-2025) chosen at random
date_str=[]
for i in range(300):
    date_str1=str(randint(2010,2025))+'-'+str(randint(1,30))+'-
'+str(randint(3,12))
    date_str.append(date_str1)
D2=date_str
```

```
### Creating a dataframe with two date sequences and call them as Start
Date and End Date
Date_frame=pd.DataFrame({'Start Date':D1,'End Date':D2})
Date_frame['End Date'] = pd.to_datetime(Date_frame['End Date'], format='%Y-
%d-%m')
```

The output DataFrame has two columns, as shown here:

	Start Date	End Date
0	2016-01-15	2022-04-30
1	2016-01-16	2024-04-19
2	2016-01-17	2020-10-29
3	2016-01-18	2024-08-19
4	2016-01-19	2022-10-14

Output DataFrame with **Start Date** and **End Date**

Using this data, we will create some lambda functions to find the following:

- Number of days between today and start date or end date
- Number of days between the start date and end date
- Days in the start date or end date that come before a given date

In the following code block, we have written the lambda functions carry out these tasks:

```
f1=lambda x:x-datetime.datetime.today()
f2=lambda x,y:x-y
f3=lambda x:pd.to_datetime('2017-28-01', format='%Y-%d-%m')>x
```

Note how x and y have been used as placeholder arguments, that is, the parameters of the functions. While applying these functions to a column of data, these placeholders are replaced with the column name.

Lambda just helps to define a function. We need to call these functions with the actual arguments to execute these functions. Let's see how this is done. For example, to execute the functions we defined previously, we can do the following:

```
Date_frame['diff1']=Date_frame['End Date'].apply(f1)
Date_frame['diff2']=f2(Date_frame['Start Date'],Date_frame['End Date'])
Date_frame['Before 28-07-17']=Date_frame['End Date'].apply(f3)
```

The following will be the output:

	Start Date	End Date	diff1	diff2	Before 28-07-17
0	2016-01-15	2022-04-30	1159 days 06:57:55.337646	-2297 days	False
1	2016-01-16	2024-04-19	1879 days 06:57:55.336613	-3016 days	False
2	2016-01-17	2020-10-29	611 days 06:57:55.336613	-1747 days	False
3	2016-01-18	2024-08-19	2001 days 06:57:55.336613	-3136 days	False
4	2016-01-19	2022-10-14	1326 days 06:57:55.336613	-2460 days	False

Output DataFrame with calculated fields on the date columns

It should be noted that these functions can be called like so:

- **Like simple functions**: With a function name and required argument
- **With the apply method**: The DataFrame column name for this to be applied on, followed by `apply`, which takes a function name as an argument

Instead of `apply`, in this case, `map` would also work. Try the following and compare the results of `diff1` and `diff3`. They should be the same:

```
Date_frame['diff3']=Date_frame['End Date'].map(f1)
```

There are three related methods that perform similar kinds of work with subtle differences:

Name	What does it do?
map	Applies a function over a column or a list of columns.
apply	Applies a function over a column, row, or a list of columns or rows.
applymap	Applies a function over the entire DataFrame, that is, each cell. Will work if the function is executable on each column.

Some use cases where these methods are very useful are as follows.

Suppose each row in a dataset represents daily sales of an SKU for a retail company for a year. Each column represents an SKU. We'll call this data `sku_sales`. Let's get started:

1. To find the annual sales of each SKU, we will use the following code:

```
sku_sales.apply(sum,axis=0) # axis=0 represents summing across rows
```

2. To find the daily sales across each SKU for each day, we will use the following code:

```
sku_sales.apply(sum,axis=1) # axis=1 represents summing across columns
```

3. To find the mean daily sales for SKU1 and SKU2, we will use the following code:

```
sku_sales[['SKU1','SKU2']].map(mean)
```

4. To find the mean and standard deviation of daily sales for all SKUs, we will use the following code:

```
sku_sales.applymap(mean)
sku_sales.applymap(sd)
```

Now, you will be able to write and apply one-liner custom Lambda functions. Now, we'll look into how missing values can be handled.

Handling missing values

Missing values and NANs are commonplace occurrences in a dataset and need to be taken care of before data can be put to any use. We will look into various sources of missing values and the different types, as well as how to handle them in the upcoming sections.

Sources of missing values

A missing value can enter a dataset because of or during the following processes.

Data extraction

This entails the data that's available but we missed during its extraction from a source. It deals with engineering tasks such as the following:

- Scraping from a website
- Querying from a database
- Extracting from flat files

There can be many sources of missing values, some of which are as follows:

- Regular expressions resulting in the wrong or non-unique results
- Wrong query
- A different data type storage
- Incomplete download
- Incomplete processing

Data collection

This entails the data points that are not available or are difficult to collect. Suppose you are surveying 100,000 people for the type of electric car they own. In this case, if we encounter someone who doesn't own an electric car, we would have a missing value for that person's car type.

Missing values originating because of data extraction, in theory, can be rectified if we are able to identify the issue that led to the missing value and rerun the extraction process. Missing values originating from data collection issues are difficult to rectify.

How do you know your data has missing values? The easiest way to find this out is to run a summary of the dataset, which gives a count of rows as well. Since the rows containing missing values don't get counted, this count will be lower for columns containing a missing value. Take a look at the following diagram, which shows a summary of the famous `titanic` dataset, for an illustration of this:

	pclass	survived	age	sibsp	parch	fare	body
count	1309.000000	1309.000000	1046.000000	1309.000000	1309.000000	1308.000000	121.000000
mean	2.294882	0.381971	29.881135	0.498854	0.385027	33.295479	160.809917
std	0.837836	0.486055	14.413500	1.041658	0.865560	51.758668	97.696922
min	1.000000	0.000000	0.166700	0.000000	0.000000	0.000000	1.000000
25%	2.000000	0.000000	21.000000	0.000000	0.000000	7.895800	72.000000
50%	3.000000	0.000000	28.000000	0.000000	0.000000	14.454200	155.000000
75%	3.000000	1.000000	39.000000	1.000000	0.000000	31.275000	256.000000
max	3.000000	1.000000	80.000000	8.000000	9.000000	512.329200	328.000000

Data summary table showing the differences in the count of columns, indicating missing values

The **age** and **body** columns have missing values as they have fewer rows than the others.

It is of prime importance to take care of missing values because they propagate the missing values to the results of numeric operations and can lead to incorrect interpretations of data. They don't allow many numeric computations to run. They may also lead to an incorrect hypothesis if only a sample of the data gets used.

There are other ways in which the origin of missing values can be classified. Let's go over them now.

Data missing at random

Here, there is no particular reason why the data may be missing. Taking the previous example of electric cars, a missing car type is the case of data missing at random.

Data not missing at random

In this case, there may be a particular reason why data may be missing. Continuing with the same example, suppose among the people who have cars, we have some license plate numbers missing in a certain pocket where they use a fancy font on their license plate and the OCR software is unable to decipher it properly and returns a missing value. This is a case of data not missing at random.

Different types of missing values

The following are different types of missing values:

- **Not a Number** (NaN): NaN is a placeholder for missing values for any data type. These can be created using `numpy.nan`. NaNs that are created using `numpy.nan` can be assigned to a nullable integer datatype. The missing value of an integer type is saved as a NaN. It is the default identifier of a missing value in Python.
- **NA**: NA comes mostly from R, where NA is an identifier for a missing value.
- **NaT**: This is equivalent to a NaN for timestamp data points.
- **None**: This represents missing values of data types other than numeric.
- **Null**: This originates when a function doesn't return a value or if the value is undefined.
- **Inf**: Inf is **infinity**—a value that is greater than any other value. `inf` is, therefore, smaller than any other value. It is generated by all the calculations, leading to very large or very small values. Often, we need to treat `inf` as a missing value. This can be done by specifying the following options in `pandas`:

      pandas.options.mode.use_inf_as_na = True

A placeholder infinity variable can also be generated for comparison purposes, as shown in the following example:

```
import math
test = math.inf
test>pow(10,10) #Comparing whether Inf is larger than 10 to the power 10
```

It returns `True`.

Miscellaneous analysis of missing values

To get a sense of how mad the missing value problem is, you may want to find out about the following information:

- How many cells in a column have a missing value
- Which cells in a column have a missing value
- How many columns have missing values

These tasks can be performed as follows:

- Finding cells that have missing values:

```
pd.isnull(data['body']) #returns TRUE if a cell has missing values
pd.notnull(data['body']) #returns TRUE if a cell doesn't have
missing values
```

- Finding the number of missing values in a column:

```
pd.isnull(data['body']).values.ravel().sum() #returns the total
number of missing values
pd.nottnull(data['body']).values.ravel().sum()#returns the total
number of non-missing values
```

The third one has been left as an exercise for you.

Strategies for handling missing values

The following are the major strategies for handling missing values.

Deletion

This will delete the entire row or column that contains the missing value.

Deletion leads to data loss and is not recommended unless there is no other way out.

Deletion can be performed as follows:

- Dropping all the rows where all the cells have missing values:

```
data.dropna(axis=0,how='all')# axis=0 means along rows
```

- Dropping all the rows where any of the cells have missing values:

```
data.dropna(axis=0,how='any')
```

Imputation

This replaces the missing value with a number that makes sense.

There are various ways in which imputation can be performed. Some of them are as follows:

- Imputing all the missing values in a dataset with 0:

```
data.fillna(0)
```

- Imputing all the missing values with specified text:

```
data.fillna('text')
```

- Imputing only the missing values in the body column with 0:

```
data['body'].fillna(0)
```

- Imputing with a mean of non-missing values:

```
data['age'].fillna(data['age'].mean())
```

- Imputing with a forward fill – this works especially well for time series data. Here, a missing value is replaced with the value in the previous row (period):

```
data['age'].fillna(method='ffill')
```

The following is the output:

```
1295   21.0   1295   21.0
1296   27.0   1296   27.0
1297   NaN    1297   27.0
1298   36.0   1298   36.0
1299   27.0   1299   27.0
1300   15.0   1300   15.0
1301   45.5   1301   45.5
1302   NaN    1302   45.5
1303   NaN    1303   45.5
1304   14.5   1304   14.5
1305   NaN    1305   14.5
1306   26.5   1306   26.5
1307   27.5   1307   27.0
1308   29.0
1309   NaN
```

Output DataFrame with missing values imputed with the forward fill method

- Imputing with a backward fill – this works especially well for time series data. Here, a missing value is replaced with the value in the previous row (period). You can control the number of rows that get filled after the first NaN using `pad` options. `Pad=1` means only 1 row will be filled forward or backward:

```
data['age'].fillna(method='backfill')
```

The following is the output:

1295	21.0	1295	21.0
1296	27.0	1296	27.0
1297	NaN	1297	36.0
1298	36.0	1298	36.0
1299	27.0	1299	27.0
1300	15.0	1300	15.0
1301	45.5	1301	45.5
1302	NaN	1302	14.5
1303	NaN	1303	14.5
1304	14.5	1304	14.5
1305	NaN	1305	26.5
1306	26.5	1306	26.5
1307	27.0		
1308	29.0		
1309	NaN		

Output DataFrame with missing values imputed with the backward fill method

Interpolation

Interpolation is a technique that uses two endpoints at the extremes of consecutive missing values to create a rough mathematical relationship to fill the missing values. By default, it does a linear interpolation (which assumes a linear relationship between data points), but there are many more methods, such as polynomial, spline, quadratic, and Akima (which assumes a polynomial or piece-wise polynomial relationship).

The `interpolate` method can be applied to a series or all the columns of a DataFrame directly:

```
import numpy as np
import pandas as pd
A=[1,3,np.nan,np.nan,11,np.nan,91,np.nan,52]
pd.Series(A).interpolate()
```

The following is the output:

```
0     1.000000
1     3.000000
2     5.666667
3     8.333333
4    11.000000
5    51.000000
6    91.000000
7    71.500000
8    52.000000
dtype: float64
```

Output DataFrame with missing values filled using simple interpolation

Instead, other methods, such as `spline`, can be used, which assume a piece-wise polynomial relationship:

```
pd.Series(A).interpolate(method='spline',order=2)
```

The following is the output:

```
0     1.000000
1     3.000000
2    -1.362504
3    -4.908131
4    11.000000
5    54.049664
6    91.000000
7    89.193996
8    52.000000
dtype: float64
```

Output DataFrame with missing values filled using spline interpolation

Similarly, polynomial interpolation can be done like so:

```
pd.Series(A).interpolate(method='polynomial',order=2)
```

A different column can be created for each interpolation method in the same DataFrame to compare their results, as shown here:

```
#Needed for generating plot inside Jupyter notebook
%matplotlib inline
#Setting seed for regenerating the same random number
np.random.seed(10)
#Generate Data
A=pd.Series(np.arange(1,100,0.5)**3+np.random.normal(5,7,len(np.arange(
1,100,0.5))))
```

```
#Sample random places to introduce missing values
np.random.seed(5)
NA=set([np.random.randint(1,100) for i in range(25)])
#Introduce missing values
A[NA]=np.nan
#Define the list of interpolation methods
methods=['linear','quadratic','cubic']
#Apply the interpolation methods and create a DataFrame
df = pd.DataFrame({m: A.interpolate(method=m) for m in methods})
#Find the mean of each column (each interpolation method)
df.apply(np.mean,axis=0)
```

The following is the output:

```
linear          250015.013617
quadratic       250012.128002
cubic           250012.165381
dtype: float64
```

Comparing mean values after interpolating using different methods

As we can see, the means are slightly different for each column because separate interpolation methods were used.

You can also check the values where interpolations were made to see how different/similar they are. This can be done as follows:

```
np.random.seed(5)
NA1=[np.random.randint(1,100) for i in range(25)]
df.iloc[NA1,:]
```

KNN

K-nearest neighbors (KNN) is an unsupervised locality-based regression and classification method. It considers each row of data as a point in n-dimensional space and finds k similar (neighboring) points based on their distance (for example, Euclidean for numeric data and Hamming for categorical data). To find the value for that row and that column of data, it takes an average of all its neighboring rows for that column and assigns the average as a value.

To summarize, it can be said that it defines a locality around a point and calculates a local average instead of a global average. This makes sense most of the time and is used instead of the global average because neighborhood behavior is a better approximator of the behavior of a sample point.

Because of this property, KNN can be used for imputing missing values. The intuition is that missing value should have a value similar to its neighboring points. It is a local imputation method, in contrast with the `fillna` method, which is a global method.

`kNeighborsClassifier` or `kNeighborsRegressor` from scikit-learn can be used for KNN and using the results for imputation. The following is an illustrated example where the following occurs, in order:

1. Sample training data is generated.
2. NaNs are introduced in the same data.
3. A KNN model is fit on the sample training data.
4. The fitted model is used to predict/impute the missing values.

This is represented in the following code block:

```
#Creating training dataset
A=np.random.randint(2,size=100)
B=np.random.normal(7,3,100)
C=np.random.normal(11,4,100)
X=(np.vstack((A,B,C))).T

#Creating testing data by replacing column A (outcome variable) with NaNs
X_with_nan = np.copy(X)
X_with_nan[:,0]=np.nan

# Load libraries
import numpy as np
from sklearn.neighbors import KNeighborsClassifier

# Train KNN learner
clf = KNeighborsClassifier(3, weights='uniform')
trained_model = clf.fit(X[:,1:], X[:,0])

#Predicting/Imputing on test dataset
imputed_values = trained_model.predict(X_with_nan[:,1:])
imputed_values
```

You can print A and `imputed_values` to see the difference between them or to assess how accurately the values were imputed. The following screenshot shows the actual values of column A:

```
array([0, 0, 1, 1, 1, 0, 0, 0, 1, 1, 1, 0, 1, 0, 0, 0, 1, 1, 1, 0, 0, 1,
       0, 1, 0, 0, 0, 1, 0, 0, 1, 0, 1, 1, 1, 0, 0, 1, 1, 0, 0, 1, 1, 0,
       0, 1, 1, 0, 0, 0, 1, 0, 1, 0, 0, 0, 1, 0, 0, 1, 0, 1, 1, 1, 0, 0,
       1, 0, 1, 0, 0, 1, 1, 1, 1, 1, 1, 1, 0, 0, 0, 1, 0, 0, 1, 0, 0, 1,
       0, 0, 1, 1, 0, 0, 1, 0, 0, 0, 0, 1])
```

Actual values of column A

The following screenshot shows `imputed_values` of column A:

```
array([0., 0., 1., 0., 1., 1., 1., 1., 1., 1., 1., 1., 0., 1., 1., 0., 1.,
       0., 0., 1., 0., 0., 0., 1., 1., 1., 0., 0., 1., 0., 0., 0., 1., 1.,
       0., 0., 0., 1., 1., 0., 1., 0., 0., 0., 1., 1., 0., 1., 1., 1., 0.,
       1., 0., 1., 0., 0., 1., 0., 0., 1., 1., 0., 0., 1., 0., 1., 1., 0.,
       0., 0., 1., 1., 0., 1., 0., 1., 0., 1., 0., 0., 1., 0., 0., 1., 1.,
       0., 0., 1., 1., 1., 1., 1., 1., 0., 1., 0., 0., 1., 0., 1.])
```

Imputed values of column A

A survey of methods on series

Let's use the following DataFrame to understand some methods and functions that can be used with a series:

```
sample_df = pd.DataFrame([["Pulp Fiction", 62, 46], ["Forrest Gump", 38,
46], ["Matrix", 26, 39], ["It's a Wonderful Life", 6, 0], ["Casablanca", 5,
6]], columns = ["Movie", "Wins", "Nominations"])
sample_df
```

The following is the output:

	Movie	Wins	Nominations
0	Pulp Fiction	62	46
1	Forrest Gump	38	46
2	Matrix	26	39
3	It's a Wonderful Life	6	0
4	Casablanca	5	6

Sample DataFrame—IMDB database

The items() method

The `items()` method provides a means of iteratively accessing each row in a series or DataFrame. It performs a lazy evaluation to store each value in a row, along with the index in the form of a tuple. The results of this lazy evaluation can be obtained through an iterative process such as a `for` loop. Let's apply the `items` method on the `Wins` column of the DataFrame:

```
for item in sample_df["Wins"].items():
print(item)
```

The following is the output:

```
(0, 62)
(1, 38)
(2, 26)
(3, 6)
(4, 5)
```

Looping with the items method

The `iteritems()` method behaves in a similar way to the `items()` method:

```
for item in sample_df["Wins"].iteritems():
print(item)
```

```
(0, 62)
(1, 38)
(2, 26)
(3, 6)
(4, 5)
```

Looping with the iteritems method

The `items` and iteritems methods return a zip type object. We need an iterative process to unzip the object. Applying the `items` or `iteritems` methods on a DataFrame give different results. In this case, each column is stacked within a tuple, along with the column name:

```
for col in sample_df.items():
print(col)
```

The following is the output:

```
('Movie', 0            Pulp Fiction
1               Forrest Gump
2                     Matrix
3      It's a Wonderful Life
4                  Casablanca
Name: Movie, dtype: object)
('Wins', 0    62
1     38
2     26
3      6
4      5
Name: Wins, dtype: int64)
('Nominations', 0     46
1     46
2     39
3      0
4      6
Name: Nominations, dtype: int64)
```

Items method used on a DataFrame

The keys() method

When used with a series, the keys() method returns the row-labels or index of the series and serves the same function it does when accessing the index attribute of a DataFrame or series. The keys() method shows different behaviors when used with a DataFrame and with a series; it returns the column labels when used on a DataFrame and the row index when used with a series:

```
In: sample_df["Wins"].keys()
Out: RangeIndex(start=0, stop=5, step=1)

In: sample_df.keys()
Out: Index(['Movie', 'Wins', 'Nominations'], dtype='object')
```

The pop() method

If you are familiar with lists in Python, the pop() method will ring a bell. The pop() method in series and DataFrames behaves exactly the same as it does with lists. It helps remove entire columns from DataFrames or specific rows from series. Upon being called, the pop() method returns the popped out entity (row or column).

The following snippet demonstrates the use of `pop()` with a series. Let's pop the item with row index 2 from the `"Wins"` column:

```
In: sample_df["Wins"].pop(2)
Out: 26
```

Now, let's print the `Wins` series:

```
0      62
1      38
3       6
4       5
Name: Wins, dtype: int64
```

Output of the pop method

It can be seen that index 2 is no longer present in the series. The same method can be applied to a DataFrame as well. Let's pop the `Nominations` column to understand this:

```
sample_df.pop("Nominations")
```

The following is the output:

```
0      46
1      46
2      39
3       0
4       6
Name: Nominations, dtype: int64
```

Pop applied on the DataFrame

The following command is used to show the DataFrame result after popping:

```
sample_df
```

The following is the output:

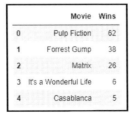

	Movie	Wins
0	Pulp Fiction	62
1	Forrest Gump	38
2	Matrix	26
3	It's a Wonderful Life	6
4	Casablanca	5

DataFrame result after popping

The apply() method

The `apply()` method provides us with a fast and efficient way to apply a function to all the values in a series. The function could be a built-in function such as a NumPy function or a user-defined function.

In the following snippet, `apply()` has been used to find the exponential value of all the rows in the `Wins` series:

```
sample_df["Wins"].apply(np.exp)
```

The following is the output:

```
0     8.438357e+26
1     3.185593e+16
2     1.957296e+11
3     4.034288e+02
4     1.484132e+02
Name: Wins, dtype: float64
```

Apply method on series

You can also define your own function and apply it to a series. Let's demonstrate this with a simple function to divide values by 100:

```
def div_by_100(x):
return x/100

sample_df["Nominations"].apply(div_by_100)
```

The following is the output:

```
0     0.46
1     0.46
2     0.39
3     0.00
4     0.06
Name: Nominations, dtype: float64
```

Apply for user-defined functions

The map() method

The map() method is similar to the apply method as it helps in making elementwise changes that have been defined by functions. However, in addition, the map function also accepts a series or dictionary to define these elementwise changes.

Using the map function, let's change some of the values in the "Wins" column:

```
sample_df["Wins"].map({62 : 60, 38 : 20})
```

The following is the output:

```
0    60.0
1    20.0
2     NaN
3     NaN
4     NaN
Name: Wins, dtype: float64
```

Map method used on a series

Values for which the mapping is not defined are replaced with NAs.

The drop() method

The drop() method is another useful method that removes entire rows or columns from a DataFrame or a series. Indices can be dropped along any axis – row indices can be dropped along axis 0 and column indices can be dropped along axis 1.

Let's drop indices 0 and 2 from the Wins series. The indices to be removed can be defined through a list. The default setting for the axis is 0, and hence no change is needed in this case:

```
sample_df["Wins"].drop([0, 2])
```

The following is the output:

```
1    38
3     6
4     5
Name: Wins, dtype: int64
```

Drop method used on a series

As we can see, the result does not have 0 and 2 and indexes. The following snippet shows the use of the `drop` method to remove columns from DataFrames:

```
sample_df.drop(labels=["Wins", "Nominations"], axis = 1)
```

The following is the output:

Using the drop method on a DataFrame

Indices can also be effectively removed when there is multi-level indexing. The level parameter of drop helps us do this. Consider the following DataFrame with multi-level indexing:

```
                Movie
Wins            Pulp Fiction            62
                Forrest Gump            38
                Matrix                  26
                It's a Wonderful Life    6
                Casablanca               5
Nominations     Pulp Fiction            46
                Forrest Gump            46
                Matrix                  39
                It's a Wonderful Life    0
                Casablanca               6
dtype: int64
```

Multi-level indexed DataFrame

To remove a specific movie from the `Movie` column, the `level` parameter should be set to 1. By default, `level` is set to 0. The following snippet removes the movie `Matrix`:

```
multidf.drop(["Matrix"], level = 1 )
```

The following is the output:

```
                  Movie
Wins          Pulp Fiction            62
              Forrest Gump            38
              It's a Wonderful Life    6
              Casablanca               5
Nominations   Pulp Fiction            46
              Forrest Gump            46
              It's a Wonderful Life    0
              Casablanca               6
dtype: int64
```

Dropping index for a hierarchical index

The equals() method

The `equals()` method checks whether two series or DataFrames are equal in terms of values, datatype, and shape. The column headers could be of different data types. The output is a Boolean. A practical application of this function is shown here. Let's create a new series that we can compare with the existing `sample_df` DataFrame:

```
In: compare_series = pd.Series([62, 38, 26, 6, 5])
In: sample_df["Wins"].equals(compare_series)
Out: True
```

This function can be applied this way to compare two DataFrames or two series within the same DataFrame.

The sample() method

The `sample()` method can be used for the random sampling of a DataFrame or series. The parameters of the `sample` function support sampling across either axis and also sampling with and without replacement. For sampling, either the number of records to be sampled or the fraction of records to be sampled must be specified.

Let's sample three records from the `Movie` series:

```
sample_df["Movie"].sample(3) \
```

The following is the output:

```
1            Forrest Gump
4              Casablanca
3    It's a Wonderful Life
Name: Movie, dtype: object
```

Sample function for series

Now, let's sample 50% of the columns from the DataFrame:

```
sample_df.sample(frac = 0.5, axis = 1)
```

The following is the output:

	Movie	Wins
0	Pulp Fiction	62
1	Forrest Gump	38
2	Matrix	26
3	It's a Wonderful Life	6
4	Casablanca	5

Column sampling with the fraction parameter

The replace parameter can be set to True or False so that we can sample with or without replacement; the default is False. The random state parameter helps in setting the seed of the random number generator and it depends on the Random module of the NumPy package.

The ravel() function

The ravel() function flattens out a series into a one-dimensional array. It is fundamentally similar to the numpy.ravel function. The ravel function cannot be applied on DataFrames:

```
In: sample_df["Wins"].ravel()
Out: array([62, 38, 26, 6, 5], dtype=int64)
```

The value_counts() function

The `value_counts()` function works only on series, and not DataFrames. It counts the number of times each variable occurs and provides a frequency table-like output:

```
pd.Series(["Pandas", "Pandas", "Numpy", "Pandas", "Numpy"]).value_counts()
```

The following is the output:

```
Pandas     3
Numpy      2
dtype: int64
```

Frequency count for categorical series

The `value_counts()` function can also be applied to a numeric column. It results in a count of each time a value occurs:

```
sample_df["Nominations"].value_counts()
```

The following is the output:

```
46     2
39     1
6      1
0      1
Name: Nominations, dtype: int64
```

The value_counts function used on the numeric column

It is more useful to count the occurrence of numeric values within the range of bins. The `bins` parameter of `value_counts` groups data into bins before counting:

```
sample_df["Nominations"].value_counts(bins = 2)
```

The following is the output:

```
(23.0, 46.0]      3
(-0.047, 23.0]    2
Name: Nominations, dtype: int64
```

The value_counts function with binning for the numeric columns

The interpolate() function

The `interpolate()` function provides an efficient way to handle missing data. Through this method, the NaNs can be replaced with a value through linear interpolation or polynomial interpolation, or even simple padding. This function fits the series to a function such as a `spline` or `quadratic` and then computes the possible missing data.

Consider the following series:

```
lin_series = pd.Series([17,19,np.NaN,23,25,np.NaN,29])
```

Since the values are all equally spaced apart, linear interpolation is the most suitable method here. Linear interpolation is the default value of the `method` parameter of the `interpolate` function:

```
lin_series.interpolate()
```

The following is the output:

```
0    17.0
1    19.0
2    21.0
3    23.0
4    25.0
5    27.0
6    29.0
dtype: float64
```

Linear interpolation

The direction in which interpolation should take place can be specified. Let's consider the preceding example and fill in the NaNs through backward padding, as shown here:

```
lin_series.interpolate(method = "pad", limit_direction = "backward")
```

The following is the output:

```
0    17.0
1    19.0
2    19.0
3    23.0
4    25.0
5    25.0
6    29.0
dtype: float64
```

Backward interpolation with padding

The align() function

The `align()` function takes two objects, reindexes both objects based on a `join` condition (inner, outer, and so on), and returns a tuple with both objects:

```
s1 = pd.Series([5,6,7,8,9], index = ["a","b","c","d","e"])
s2 = pd.Series([1,2,3,4,5], index = ["d","b","g","f","a"])
s1.align(s2, join="outer")
```

The following is the output:

```
(a     5.0
 b     6.0
 c     7.0
 d     8.0
 e     9.0
 f     NaN
 g     NaN
 dtype: float64, a    5.0
 b     2.0
 c     NaN
 d     1.0
 e     NaN
 f     4.0
 g     3.0
 dtype: float64)
```

Align with outer join

Since the alignment was based on an outer join, the indexes that were found in both series are found in the output. For an inner join, only the common indexes are returned, such as a, b, and d:

```
s1.align(s2, join="inner")
```

The following is the output:

```
(a     5
 b     6
 d     8
 dtype: int64, a    5
 b     2
 d     1
 dtype: int64)
```

Align with inner join

pandas string methods

This section talks about the pandas string methods. These methods are useful when dealing with messy text data. These methods clean the text data, structure it, segment it, and search important chunks of it. Let's look into these methods and find out what each of them contains.

upper(), lower(), capitalize(), title(), and swapcase()

String methods such as upper(), lower(), capitalize(), title(), and swapcase() help when we wish to convert all the string elements into an entire series. The upper and lower methods convert the entire string into uppercase or lowercase. The following command shows converting a series into uppercase:

```
sample_df["Movie"].str.upper()
```

The following is the output:

```
0              PULP FICTION
1              FORREST GUMP
2                    MATRIX
3     IT'S A WONDERFUL LIFE
4                CASABLANCA
Name: Movie, dtype: object
```

Converting a series into uppercase

The following command shows converting a series into lowercase:

```
sample_df["Movie"].str.lower()
```

The following is the output:

```
0              pulp fiction
1              forrest gump
2                    matrix
3     it's a wonderful life
4                casablanca
Name: Movie, dtype: object
```

Converting a series into lowercase

The `capitalize()` method converts the first letter into uppercase and the rest into lowercase:

```
pd.Series(["elon musk", "tim cook", "larry page", "jeff
bezos"]).str.capitalize()
```

The following is the output:

```
0       Elon musk
1        Tim cook
2      Larry page
3       Jeff bezos
dtype: object
```

Capitalize function for a series

The `title()` method ensures that the first letter of each word of a string is capitalized while the rest are in lowercase:

```
pd.Series(["elon musk", "tim cook", "larry page", "jeff
bezos"]).str.title()
```

```
0       Elon Musk
1        Tim Cook
2      Larry Page
3       Jeff Bezos
dtype: object
```

Title case conversion for a string

The `swapcase()` method switches uppercase to lowercase and vice versa:

```
sample_df["Movie"].str.swapcase()
```

The following is the output:

```
0              pULP fICTION
1             fORREST gUMP
2                   mATRIX
3    iT'S A wONDERFUL lIFE
4               cASABLANCA
Name: Movie, dtype: object
```

The swapcase() function

contains(), find(), and replace()

The `contains()` method returns checks for the presence of a substring or pattern in all the elements of the series and returns a series of Booleans:

```
sample_df["Movie"].str.contains("atr")
```

The following is the output:

```
0     False
1     False
2      True
3     False
4     False
Name: Movie, dtype: bool
```

Contains function for string type series

Since `Matrix` is the only movie that contains the `atr` substring, `True` is returned at index 2. The substring can also be a regex pattern. To use a regex pattern for string matching, the `regex` parameter should be set to `True`. For example, let's identify a string that contains either `atr` or `der`:

```
sample_df["Movie"].str.contains("atr|der", regex = True)
```

The following is the output:

```
0     False
1     False
2      True
3      True
4     False
Name: Movie, dtype: bool
```

Contains function with a regex

As we can see, two matches have been identified. Setting the `case` parameter to `True` ensures case sensitivity when pattern matching is executed:

```
sample_df["Movie"].str.contains("cas", case = True)
```

The following is the output:

```
0    False
1    False
2    False
3    False
4    False
Name: Movie, dtype: bool
```

Handling case sensitivity in the contains function

The `flags` parameter can be used to indicate any regex condition, such as ignoring case:

```
import re
sample_df["Movie"].str.contains("MATrix", flags = re.IGNORECASE,
regex=True)
```

The following is the output:

```
0    False
1    False
2     True
3    False
4    False
Name: Movie, dtype: bool
```

Regex flags for the contains function

Note that the `re` package should be imported before defining any regex flags.

The `find` function returns the lowest index at which the substring could be found. Consider the following series:

```
find_series = pd.Series(["abracadabra", "mad man"])
```

Let's use the `find` function to get the index of the `ra` substring from the previous series:

```
find_series.str.find("ra")
```

The following is the output:

```
0     2
1    -1
dtype: int64
```

Find function for a series

In the first element, `abracadabra`, the first occurrence of `ra` was at index position 2. Hence, 2 is returned. The second element, `mad man`, did not show a string match, and so −1 is returned.

The `find` function has a `start` parameter that can be used to specify the left-most index to begin the search from. Equivalently, there is an `end` parameter to define the right-most index until which search is permissible. `start` is set to 0 and `end` is set to `None` by default:

```
find_series.str.find("a", start = 2)
```

The following is the output:

```
0    3
1    5
dtype: int64
```

The find function with a start limit specified

In the preceding example, we can see that by specifying the starting index, a, index 0 and 1 are ignored.

The `replace` function can be considered as an extension of the `contains` function since most of the parameters are similar. Functionally, `replace` finds a substring within a string in a series and substitutes it with a replacement string. Parameters such as `flags`, `case`, and `regex`, which are found in the `contains` function, are also found here, and they serve the same purpose. Let's replace the letter `I` in the series with the `rep` substring:

```
sample_df["Movie"].str.replace("i","'rep'")
```

The following is the output:

```
0            Pulp F'rep'ct'rep'on
1                   Forrest Gump
2                    Matr'rep'x
3       It's a Wonderful L'rep'fe
4                     Casablanca
Name: Movie, dtype: object
```

The replace function for a series

Note that in cases where there is more than one occurrence of `i`, multiple replacements are made. The number of replacements can be controlled with the n parameter:

```
sample_df["Movie"].str.replace("i","'rep'", n = 1)
```

The following is the output:

```
0                Pulp F'rep'ction
1                 Forrest Gump
2                   Matr'rep'x
3      It's a Wonderful L'rep'fe
4                   Casablanca
Name: Movie, dtype: object
```

The replace function with the number of replacements specified

strip() and split()

The `strip()` function can come in quite handy in data cleaning. It removes trailing whitespaces or any specific pattern of a string from textual content in series. If the substring to be removed is not specified, trailing whitespaces are trimmed by default. The following example demonstrates an application of the `strip` function with stray whitespaces:

```
strip_series = pd.Series(["\tChina", "U.S.A ", "U\nK"])
strip_series
```

The following is the output:

```
0      \tChina
1      U.S.A
2        U\nK
dtype: object
```

Series with stray whitespaces

The following example demonstrates an application of the `strip()` function with trailing whitespaces:

```
strip_series.strip()
```

The following is the output:

```
0      China
1      U.S.A
2       U\nK
dtype: object
```

Stripping trailing whitespaces

This shows that `strip()` only removes trailing whitespaces and not those in the middle. Now, let's use `strip()` to remove a specific string:

```
sample_df["Movie"].str.strip("opnf")
```

The following is the output:

```
0                Pulp Ficti
1               Forrest Gum
2                    Matrix
3        It's a Wonderful Life
4                Casablanca
Name: Movie, dtype: object
```

The strip function for removing string sequences

In the preceding example, the `strip()` function strips out any of the characters of the substring found in the trailing ends of the series elements.

The `split()` function splits a string at specified delimiters. Consider the following series:

```
split_series = pd.Series(["Black, White", "Red, Blue, Green", "Cyan,
Magenta, Yellow"])
split_series
```

The following is the output:

```
0              Black, White
1           Red, Blue, Green
2      Cyan, Magenta, Yellow
dtype: object
```

Sample series for the split function

Each element has two to three items separated by `,`. Let's use this as a delimiter to separate the items stacked together in each row of the series:

```
split_series.str.split(", ")
```

The following is the output:

```
0              [Black, White]
1           [Red, Blue, Green]
2      [Cyan, Magenta, Yellow]
dtype: object
```

Splitting as a list

The result is a list of items in each row. The `expand()` parameter creates a separate column for each item. By default, `expand` is set to `False`, which leads to a list being created in each row:

```
split_series.str.split(", ", expand = True)
```

The following is the output:

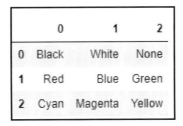

	0	1	2
0	Black	White	None
1	Red	Blue	Green
2	Cyan	Magenta	Yellow

Splitting multiple columns

startswith() and endswith()

While the `contains()` function helps evaluate whether a substring is present in each element of a series, the `startswith()` and `endswith()` functions specifically look for the presence of the substring at the start and the end of strings, respectively:

```
start_series = pd.Series(["strange", "stock", "cost", "past", "state"])
start_series.str.startswith("st")
```

The following is the output:

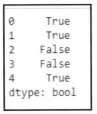

```
0       True
1       True
2      False
3      False
4       True
dtype: bool
```

The startswith function

Similarly, `endswith` can be used as shown here:

```
end_series= pd.Series(["ramen", "program", "cram", "rammed", "grammer"])
end_series.str.endswith("ram")
```

The following is the output:

```
0      False
1       True
2       True
3      False
4      False
dtype: bool
```

The `endswith` function

However, unlike `contains()`, these functions do not accept regular expressions.

The is...() functions

The following table lists a group of functions that help ascertain other properties of the string elements of a series. For example, the `isupper` function returns `True` if all the characters of a string are in uppercase. These functions return a Boolean output corresponding to each row in the series:

Function	Returns true when all characters are...
isalnum()	Alphanumeric
isalpha()	Alphabetic
isdigit()	Digits
isspace()	Whitespace
islower()	Lowercase
isupper()	Uppercase
istitle()	Title case
isnumeric()	Numeric
isdecimal()	Decimal

Some examples of the preceding functions are as follows:

```
pd.Series(["ui26", "ui", "26"]).str.isalpha()
```

The following is the output:

```
0      False
1       True
2      False
dtype: bool
```

The isalpha function

This is a example of the `isalnum` function:

```
pd.Series(["ui26", "ui", "26"]).str.isalnum()
```

The following is the output:

```
0       True
1       True
2       True
dtype: bool
```

The isalnum function

This is an example of the `isnumeric` function:

```
pd.Series(["ui26", "ui", "26"]).str.isnumeric()
```

The following is the output:

```
0      False
1      False
2       True
dtype: bool
```

The isnumeric function

These functions are only applicable to strings and not to other data types. Using these with other data types results in NaN being returned.

The following is an example of the `isdigit()` function:

```
pd.Series(["ui26", "ui", 26]).str.isdigit()
```

The following is the output:

```
0       False
1       False
2         NaN
dtype: object
```

The isdigit function

Binary operations on DataFrames and series

Some binary functions such as, `add`, `sub`, `mul`, `div`, `mod`, and `pow`, perform common arithmetic operations involving two DataFrames or series.

The following example shows the addition of two DataFrames. One of the DataFrames has the shape (2,3) while the other has the shape (1,3). The add function performs an elementwise addition. When a corresponding element is missing in any of the DataFrames, the missing values are filled with NaNs:

```
df_1 = pd.DataFrame([[1,2,3],[4,5,6]])
df_2 = pd.DataFrame([[6,7,8]])
df_1.add(df_2)
```

The following is the output:

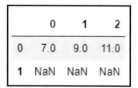

	0	1	2
0	7.0	9.0	11.0
1	NaN	NaN	NaN

Adding two DataFrames elementwise

Instead of using NaNs, we can choose to fill it with any value using the `fill_value` argument. Let's explore this through the `mul` function for multiplication:

```
df_1.mul(df_2, fill_value = 0)
```

The following is the output:

	0	1	2
0	6.0	14.0	24.0
1	0.0	0.0	0.0

The fill_value parameter in binary operators in pandas

The second value that's used for the arithmetic operation doesn't necessarily need be a DataFrame or series; it can also be a scalar, as shown here:

```
df_1.sub(2)
```

The following is the output:

	0	1	2
0	-1	0	1
1	2	3	4

Binary operation with a scalar

In the preceding cases, the two DataFrames were uniformly indexed. Elements are compatible for operations that are across the same index labels:

```
pd.Series([1, 2, 3, 4], index=['a', 'b', 'c', 'd']).pow(pd.Series([4, 3, 2, 1], index=['a', 'b', 'd', 'e']))
```

The following is the output:

```
a       1.0
b       8.0
c       NaN
d      16.0
e       NaN
dtype: float64
```

Binary operations being used on a series with different indexes

For indexes that aren't in both series, `NaN` is returned. Similar behavior will be seen with respect to column labels. Only elements sharing a similar column name can be used together. This is shown in the following code:

```
pd.DataFrame([[27, 33, 44]], columns=["a", "b", "c"]).mod(pd.DataFrame([[7,
6, 2]], columns=["b", "a", "d"])).
```

The following is the output:

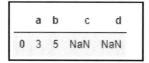

Binary operations used on DataFrames with different columns

Now, consider the following two DataFrames, one of which shows hierarchical indexing:

```
df = pd.DataFrame([[1, 4, 6], [np.NaN, 5, 3], [2, 7, np.NaN], [5, 9, 4],
[1, np.NaN, 11]], columns = ["ColA", "ColB", "ColC"], index = ["a", "b",
"c", "d", "e"])

df
```

The following is the output:

	ColA	ColB	ColC
a	1.0	4.0	6.0
b	NaN	5.0	3.0
c	2.0	7.0	NaN
d	5.0	9.0	4.0
e	1.0	NaN	11.0

Sample DataFrame

The following code block is an example of a multi-indexed DataFrame:

```
df_multi = df.iloc[0:4, :]
df_multi.index = pd.MultiIndex.from_tuples([(1, 'a'), (1, 'b'), (1, 'c'),
(2, 'a')])
df_multi
```

The following is the output:

		ColA	ColB	ColC
1	a	1.0	1.000000	1.0
	b	NaN	1.000000	1.0
	c	1.0	1.000000	NaN
2	a	0.2	0.444444	1.5

Multi-indexed DataFrame

To divide `df` by the elements of `df_multi`, or to perform any of the aforementioned binary operations, the level parameter can be used to specify the `level` of the index that is shared by both DataFrames:

```
df.div(df_multi, level = 1)
```

The following is the output:

		ColA	ColB	ColC
1	a	1.0	1.000000	1.0
	b	NaN	1.000000	1.0
	c	1.0	1.000000	NaN
2	a	0.2	0.444444	1.5

Binary operations used for DataFrames with a hierarchical index

The `lt`, `le`, `gt`, and `ge` functions help with DataFrame comparisons by establishing the truth of *less than, less than or equal to, greater than,* and *greater than or equal to* comparisons. They have the same parameters as the functions we discussed previously and show similar behaviors in all those scenarios. Let's compare `df` and `df_multi`:

```
df.lt(df_multi, level = 1)
```

The following is the output:

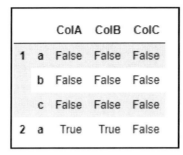

Less than function

The following code block shows the `le` function:

```
df.le(df_multi, level = 1)
```

The following is the output:

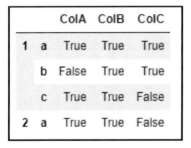

Less than or equal to function

The `round` function rounds decimals to the desired number of places, as specified by the `decimals` parameter:

```
pd.Series([6.78923, 8.02344, 0.1982]).round()
```

The following is the output:

```
0       7.0
1       8.0
2       0.0
dtype: float64
```

The round function

By default, rounding off takes place to make the input a whole number (`decimals = 0`):

```
pd.Series([6.78923, 8.02344, 0.1982]).round(2)
```

The following is the output:

```
0    6.79
1    8.02
2    0.20
dtype: float64
```

The round function with a number of places set

The `combine` function takes two overlapping DataFrames and executes the function defined within them. Let's combine two series and find the maximum of the two. Note that a comparison takes place, with the index as a reference:

```
pd.Series([9, 10, 11]).combine(pd.Series([7, 15, 12]), max)
```

The following is the output:

```
0     9
1    15
2    12
dtype: int64
```

The combine function

Binning values

The pandas `cut()` function bins values in a 1-dimensional array. Consider the following 1-dimensional array with 10 values. Let's group it into three bins:

```
bin_data = np.array([1, 5, 2, 12, 3, 25, 9, 10, 11, 4])
pd.cut(bin_data, bins = 3)
```

The following is the output:

```
[(0.976, 9.0], (0.976, 9.0], (0.976, 9.0], (9.0, 17.0], (0.976, 9.0], (17.0, 25.0], (0.976, 9.0], (9.0, 17.0], (9.0, 17.0], (0.976, 9.0]]
Categories (3, interval[float64]): [(0.976, 9.0] < (9.0, 17.0] < (17.0, 25.0]]
```

pandas cut function with three bins

Each of the 10 elements is mapped to one of the three bins. The cut function maps the items to a bin and provides information about each bin. Instead of specifying the number of bins, the boundaries of the bins could also be provided in a sequence:

```
pd.cut(bin_data, bins = [0.5, 7, 10, 20, 30])
```

The following is the output:

```
[(0.499, 7.0], (0.499, 7.0], (0.499, 7.0], (10.0, 20.0], (0.499, 7.0], (20.0, 30.0], (7.0, 10.0], (7.0, 10.0], (10.0, 20.0],
(0.499, 7.0]]
Categories (4, interval[float64]): [(0.499, 7.0] < (7.0, 10.0] < (10.0, 20.0] < (20.0, 30.0]]
```

pandas cut function with bin values

The intervals for binning can be directly defined using the pandas interval_range function. Consider the following example, demonstrating the creation of a pandas IntervalIndex object:

```
interval = pd.interval_range(start = 0, end = 30, periods = 5)
interval
```

The following is the output:

```
IntervalIndex([(0, 6], (6, 12], (12, 18], (18, 24], (24, 30]]
              closed='right',
              dtype='interval[int64]')
```

pandas IntervalIndex

This interval can be directly passed to the cut function:

```
pd.cut(bin_data, bins = interval)
```

The following is the output:

```
[(0, 6], (0, 6], (0, 6], (6, 12], (0, 6], (24, 30], (6, 12], (6, 12], (6, 12], (0, 6]]
Categories (5, interval[int64]): [(0, 6] < (6, 12] < (12, 18] < (18, 24] < (24, 30]]
```

pandas cut function with the interval index

Setting the right parameter to True includes the right interval in the bin, while setting the right parameter to False excludes it from the bin range. The default setting is True:

```
pd.cut(bin_data, bins = [0.5, 7, 10, 20, 30], right = False)
```

The following is the output:

```
[[0.5, 7.0), [0.5, 7.0), [0.5, 7.0), [10.0, 20.0), [0.5, 7.0), [20.0, 30.0), [7.0, 10.0), [10.0, 20.0), [10.0, 20.0), [0.5, 7.
0)]
Categories (4, interval[float64]): [[0.5, 7.0) < [7.0, 10.0) < [10.0, 20.0) < [20.0, 30.0)]
```

Open right interval

Equivalently, the `include_lowest` parameter decides whether the lowest interval should be included. By default, it is set to `False`:

```
pd.cut(bin_data, bins = [0.5, 7, 10, 20, 30], include_lowest= True)
```

The following is the output:

```
[(0.499, 7.0], (0.499, 7.0], (0.499, 7.0], (10.0, 20.0], (0.499, 7.0], (20.0, 30.0], (7.0, 10.0], (7.0, 10.0], (10.0, 20.0],
(0.499, 7.0]]
Categories (4, interval[float64]): [(0.499, 7.0] < (7.0, 10.0] < (10.0, 20.0] < (20.0, 30.0]]
```

Including the lowest value in the left range

The function returns the bins when `retbins` is set to `True`:

```
pd.cut(bin_data, bins = 5, retbins = True)
```

The following is the output:

```
([[0.976, 5.8], (0.976, 5.8], (0.976, 5.8], (10.6, 15.4], (0.976, 5.8], (20.2, 25.0], (5.8, 10.6], (5.8, 10.6], (10.6, 15.4],
(0.976, 5.8]]
 Categories (5, interval[float64]): [(0.976, 5.8] < (5.8, 10.6] < (10.6, 15.4] < (15.4, 20.2] < (20.2, 25.0]],
 array([ 0.976,   5.8 ,  10.6 ,  15.4 ,  20.2 ,  25.   ]))
```

Returning bins

The second value in the output tuple is an array of the bin values.

The bins can be assigned labels by passing a list of label names to the `labels` parameter:

```
pd.cut(bin_data, bins = 3, labels = ["level1", "level2", "level3"])
```

The following is the output:

```
[level1, level1, level1, level2, level1, level3, level1, level2, level2, level1]
Categories (3, object): [level1 < level2 < level3]
```

Label bins

When the bins that are passed contain duplicates, an error is raised by default. This is because the duplicates parameter is set to `raise` by default. Setting it to `drop` will drop the duplicates:

```
pd.cut(bin_data, bins = [0.5, 7, 10, 30, 30], duplicates = "drop")
```

The following is the output:

```
[(0.5, 7.0], (0.5, 7.0], (0.5, 7.0], (10.0, 30.0], (0.5, 7.0], (10.0, 30.0], (7.0, 10.0], (7.0, 10.0], (10.0, 30.0], (0.5, 7.
0]]
Categories (3, interval[float64]): [(0.5, 7.0] < (7.0, 10.0] < (10.0, 30.0]]
```

Handling duplicates in bins

The precision of digits up to which the bins are created and stored can be set by the `precision` parameter:

```
pd.cut(bin_data, bins = 3, precision = 1)
```

The following is the output:

```
[(1.0, 9.0], (1.0, 9.0], (1.0, 9.0], (9.0, 17.0], (1.0, 9.0], (17.0, 25.0], (1.0, 9.0], (9.0, 17.0], (9.0, 17.0], (1.0, 9.0]]
Categories (3, interval[float64]): [(1.0, 9.0] < (9.0, 17.0] < (17.0, 25.0]]
```

Setting precision in bins

The `qcut` function is similar to the `cut` function, with the exception that bins can be created by specifying the number of quantiles based on which the bins are to be created:

```
pd.qcut(bin_data, q = 5)
```

The following is the output:

```
[(0.999, 2.8], (4.6, 9.4], (0.999, 2.8], (11.2, 25.0], (2.8, 4.6], (11.2, 25.0], (4.6, 9.4], (9.4, 11.2], (9.4, 11.2], (2.8, 4.
6]]
Categories (5, interval[float64]): [(0.999, 2.8] < (2.8, 4.6] < (4.6, 9.4] < (9.4, 11.2] < (11.2, 25.0]]
```

The qcut function

Using mathematical methods on DataFrames

Computations such as sum, mean, and median can be performed with ease on pandas DataFrames using the built-in mathematical methods in the pandas library. Let's make use of a subset of the sales data to explore the mathematical functions and methods in pandas. While applying these mathematical functions, it should be ensured that the selected columns are numeric. The following screenshot shows the data with five rows and three columns, all of which will be used in this section:

	Sales	Quantity	Discount
0	2309.650	7	0.0
1	3709.395	9	0.1
2	5175.171	9	0.1
3	2892.510	5	0.1
4	2832.960	8	0.0

Sample sales data

The abs() function

The abs() function returns the absolute values of records in the DataFrame. For columns with complex values in the form x+yj, the absolute value is computed as $\sqrt{x^2 + y^2}$:

```
abs_df = pd.DataFrame({"Integers": [-1, -2, -3, 0, 2], "Complex": [5+2j,
1+1j, 3+3j, 2+3j, 4+2j]})
abs_df.abs()
```

The following is the output:

	Integers	Complex
0	1.0	5.385165
1	2.0	1.414214
2	3.0	4.242641
3	0.0	3.605551
4	2.0	4.472136

The abs() function

corr() and cov()

The corr() function returns the correlation coefficient of each combination of variables in the DataFrame. If any NAs are present, they are excluded for correlation computation. The corr() function accepts the Pearson, Kendall, and Spearman methods. By default, the Pearson correlation coefficient is calculated:

```
sales_df.corr()
```

The following is the output:

	Sales	Quantity	Discount
Sales	1.000000	0.622575	0.662610
Quantity	0.622575	1.000000	0.054554
Discount	0.662610	0.054554	1.000000

The corr() function

Just like the correlation function, the cov() function returns the covariance matrix:

```
sales_df.cov()
```

The following is the output:

	Sales	Quantity	Discount
Sales	1.253403e+06	1166.3151	40.63161
Quantity	1.166315e+03	2.8000	0.00500
Discount	4.063161e+01	0.0050	0.00300

The cov() function

The min_periods argument in corr() and cov() decides the minimal presence of non-NA values in the DataFrame.

cummax(), cumin(), cumsum(), and cumprod()

The `cummax()`, `cummin()`, `cumsum()`, and `cumprod()` functions compute the maximum, minimum, sum, and product on a cumulative basis, respectively. Let's understand this by applying the `cummax()` function on the sample DataFrame:

```
sales_df.cummax()
```

The following is the output:

	Sales	Quantity	Discount
0	2309.650	7.0	0.0
1	3709.395	9.0	0.1
2	5175.171	9.0	0.1
3	5175.171	9.0	0.1
4	5175.171	9.0	0.1

The cummax() function

The `skipna` parameter in these functions provides control over handling NAs. It is set to `True` by default, and NAs are excluded. Consider the following DataFrame with NAs to understand the function of this parameter:

```
sales_df_na
```

The following is the output:

	Sales	Quantity	Discount
0	2309.650	7.0	0.0
1	3709.395	9.0	NaN
2	5175.171	9.0	0.1
3	2892.510	NaN	0.1
4	2832.960	8.0	0.0

Sample data with NAs

The `cumsum()` method can be applied as shown here:

```
sales_df_na.cumsum()
```

The following is the output:

	Sales	Quantity	Discount
0	2309.650	7.0	0.0
1	6019.045	16.0	NaN
2	11194.216	25.0	0.1
3	14086.726	NaN	0.2
4	16919.686	33.0	0.2

The cumsum() function

We can choose to not ignore NAs while doing a cumulative sum by setting `skipna` to `False`:

```
sales_df_na.cumsum(skipna=False)
```

The following is the output:

	Sales	Quantity	Discount
0	2309.650	7.0	0.0
1	6019.045	16.0	NaN
2	11194.216	25.0	NaN
3	14086.726	NaN	NaN
4	16919.686	NaN	NaN

The cumulative function with skipna

By default, the aggregation is performed across the row axis since the `axis` parameter is set to `0` by default. Using the `axis` parameter, cumulative aggregation can also be performed across columns:

```
sales_df.cumprod(axis = 1)
```

The following is the output:

	Sales	Quantity	Discount
0	2309.650	16167.550	0.0000
1	3709.395	33384.555	3338.4555
2	5175.171	46576.539	4657.6539
3	2892.510	14462.550	1446.2550
4	2832.960	22663.680	0.0000

The cumprod() function

The describe() function

The `describe()` function provides a representation of the distribution of data and computes some useful summary statistics. It serves quite useful for **exploratory data analysis (EDA)** techniques:

```
sales_df.describe()
```

The following is the output:

	Sales	Quantity	Discount
count	5.000000	5.00000	5.000000
mean	3383.937200	7.60000	0.060000
std	1119.554695	1.67332	0.054772
min	2309.650000	5.00000	0.000000
25%	2832.960000	7.00000	0.000000
50%	2892.510000	8.00000	0.100000
75%	3709.395000	9.00000	0.100000
max	5175.171000	9.00000	0.100000

The describe() function

The `describe()` function can be applied to numeric and categorical variables. The `include` and `exclude` parameters of the `describe` function set the data type of the function it should evaluate. By default, `include` is set to `numeric`. Hence, any categorical variables in the Dataframe will be ignored. Let's apply `describe` on the following DataFrame by setting the `include` parameter to the `object` data type:

```
sales_df_full
```

The following is the output:

OrderID	OrderDate	ShipDate	ShipMode	Customer Name	Segment	Country	Region	ProductID	Category	Sub-Category	Sales	Quantity	Discount	Profit
CA-2012-124891	31-07-2012	31-07-2012	Same Day	Rick Hansen	Consumer	United States	East	TEC-AC-10003033	Technology	Accessories	2309.650	7	0.0	762.1845
IN-2013-77878	05-02-2013	07-02-2013	Second Class	Justin Ritter	Corporate	Australia	Oceania	FUR-CH-10003950	Furniture	Chairs	3709.395	9	0.1	-288.7650
IN-2013-71249	17-10-2013	18-10-2013	First Class	Craig Reiter	Consumer	Australia	Oceania	TEC-PH-10004664	Technology	Phones	5175.171	9	0.1	919.9710
ES-2013-1579342	28-01-2013	30-01-2013	First Class	Katherine Murray	Home Office	Germany	Central	TEC-PH-10004583	Technology	Phones	2892.510	5	0.1	-96.5400
SG-2013-4320	05-11-2013	06-11-2013	Same Day	Rick Hansen	Consumer	Senegal	Africa	TEC-SHA-10000501	Technology	Copiers	2832.960	8	0.0	311.5200

Sample data with mixed datatypes

Take a look at the following:

```
sales_df_full.describe(include = np.object)
```

The following is the output:

	OrderID	OrderDate	ShipDate	ShipMode	Customer Name	Segment	Country	Region	ProductID	Category	Sub-Category
count	51290	51290	51290	51290	51290	51290	51290	51290	51290	51290	51290
unique	25035	1430	1464	4	795	3	147	13	10292	3	17
top	CA-2014-100111	18-06-2014	22-11-2014	Standard Class	Muhammed Yedwab	Consumer	United States	Central	OFF-AR-10003651	Office Supplies	Binders
freq	14	135	130	30775	108	26518	9994	11117	35	31273	6152

The describe() function for categorical variables

All the datatypes can be included by setting `include` to `all`. Similarly, the `exclude` parameter can also be used to exclude certain datatypes.

For numeric variables, `describe` evaluates the percentiles at 0.25, 0.5, 0.75, and 1. This can be customized like so:

```
sales_df.describe(percentiles = [0.1, 0.2, 0.3, 0.4, 0.5])
```

The following is the output:

	Sales	Quantity	Discount
count	5.000000	5.00000	5.000000
mean	3383.937200	7.60000	0.060000
std	1119.554695	1.67332	0.054772
min	2309.650000	5.00000	0.000000
10%	2518.974000	5.80000	0.000000
20%	2728.298000	6.60000	0.000000
30%	2844.870000	7.20000	0.020000
40%	2868.690000	7.60000	0.060000
50%	2892.510000	8.00000	0.100000
max	5175.171000	9.00000	0.100000

Custom percentiles in the describe function

The diff() function

The `diff()` function computes the difference between subsequent rows in the same column or subsequent columns in the same row. `diff()` can be evaluated along a row or column by setting the `axis` parameter, which is set to 0 by default. Therefore, computation takes place by row:

```
sales_df.diff()
```

The following is the output:

	Sales	Quantity	Discount
0	NaN	NaN	NaN
1	1399.745	2.0	0.1
2	1465.776	0.0	0.0
3	-2282.661	-4.0	0.0
4	-59.550	3.0	-0.1

The diff() function

The `diff` method can be applied as shown here:

```
sales_df.diff(axis = 1)
```

The following is the output:

	Sales	Quantity	Discount
0	NaN	NaN	-2309.650
1	NaN	NaN	-3709.295
2	NaN	NaN	-5175.071
3	NaN	NaN	-2892.410
4	NaN	NaN	-2832.960

The diff() function applied along axis 1

The `periods()` parameter can be used to find the difference of the nth previous row. A negative value would allow us to find the difference from the nth row that follows:

```
sales_df.diff(periods = 2)
```

The following is the output:

	Sales	Quantity	Discount
0	NaN	NaN	NaN
1	NaN	NaN	NaN
2	2865.521	2.0	0.1
3	-816.885	-4.0	0.0
4	-2342.211	-1.0	-0.1

diff() being used at different periodic intervals

The rank() function

The `rank()` function returns a DataFrame with the rank of each value that was estimated along the specified axis. Ranking takes place in ascending order by default:

```
sales_df.rank()
```

The following is the output:

	Sales	Quantity	Discount
0	1.0	2.0	1.5
1	4.0	4.5	4.0
2	5.0	4.5	4.0
3	3.0	1.0	4.0
4	2.0	3.0	1.5

Ranking function result

The `rank()` method can be applied as shown here:

```
sales_df.rank(ascending = False)
```

The following is the output:

	Sales	Quantity	Discount
0	5.0	4.0	4.5
1	2.0	1.5	2.0
2	1.0	1.5	2.0
3	3.0	5.0	2.0
4	4.0	3.0	4.5

Ranking in descending order

Ranking can also be obtained as a percentage, as shown here:

```
sales_df.rank(pct = True)
```

The following is the output:

	Sales	Quantity	Discount
0	0.2	0.4	0.3
1	0.8	0.9	0.8
2	1.0	0.9	0.8
3	0.6	0.2	0.8
4	0.4	0.6	0.3

Ranking with percentiles

The `method()` argument helps settle ties. By default, the average of the range of ranks that could possibly be occupied by items in a tie is shown in the result. It can also be modified to show the minimum rank, maximum rank, the order in which values appear, or dense ranking:

```
sales_df.rank(method = "min")
```

The following is the output:

	Sales	Quantity	Discount
0	1.0	2.0	1.0
1	4.0	4.0	3.0
2	5.0	4.0	3.0
3	3.0	1.0	3.0
4	2.0	3.0	1.0

Using the ranking method to find the minimum value for a tiebreaker

The quantile() function

The `quantile()` function returns the value for every column for the specified quantiles. It accepts a single quantile value or an array of quantile values:

```
sales_df.quantile(q = [0.1, 0.9])
```

The following is the output:

	Sales	Quantity	Discount
0.1	2518.9740	5.8	0.0
0.9	4588.8606	9.0	0.1

Finding the quantiles for a DataFrame

Quantiles can also be computed for timestamps. We can achieve this by setting the `numeric_only` parameter to `False`:

```
time_col = pd.DataFrame({"time": pd.date_range("2017-01-01",
"2017-12-31")})
time_col.quantile(q = [0.1, 0.5], numeric_only = False)
```

The following is the output:

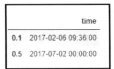

	time
0.1	2017-02-06 09:36:00
0.5	2017-07-02 00:00:00

Quantiles for the datetime value

The round() function

The round() function helps in rounding off decimals. By default, the values are rounded off to a whole number:

```
sales_df.round()
```

The following is the output:

	Sales	Quantity	Discount
0	2310.0	7	0.0
1	3709.0	9	0.0
2	5175.0	9	0.0
3	2893.0	5	0.0
4	2833.0	8	0.0

The round() function's results

The round function can be applied as shown here:

```
sales_df.round(decimals = 10)
```

The following is the output:

	Sales	Quantity	Discount
0	2309.650	7	0.0
1	3709.395	9	0.1
2	5175.171	9	0.1
3	2892.510	5	0.1
4	2832.960	8	0.0

The round() function for decimals = 10

The pct_change() function

The `pct_change()` function works similar to the `diff` function and computes the percentage of the difference between two different values in the DataFrame. Just like in `diff()`, the `periods` parameter provides flexibility so that we can evaluate between different elements that are spaced apart by a few rows:

```
sales_df.pct_change()
```

The following is the output:

	Sales	Quantity	Discount
0	NaN	NaN	NaN
1	0.606042	0.285714	inf
2	0.395152	0.000000	0.000000
3	-0.441079	-0.444444	0.000000
4	-0.020588	0.600000	-1.000000

Percentage change across rows

The `fill_method` parameter allows NAs to be handled by methods such as padding prior to computation. The `limit` parameter helps set a threshold on a permissible number of NAs.

min(), max(), median(), mean(), and mode()

These functions accept a similar set of parameters and compute the aggregates (min, max, median, or mode) for each column or row based on the axis parameter setting:

```
sales_df.min()
```

The following is the output:

```
Sales      2309.65
Quantity      5.00
Discount      0.00
dtype: float64
```

The min () result

The `max` method can be applied as shown here:

```
sales_df.max(axis = 1)
```

The following is the output:

```
0    2309.650
1    3709.395
2    5175.171
3    2892.510
4    2832.960
dtype: float64
```

The `max ()` result

The `skipna` parameter helps us handle NAs. Consider the following DataFrame:

```
sales_df_na
```

The following is the output:

	Sales	Quantity	Discount
0	2309.650	7.0	0.0
1	3709.395	9.0	NaN
2	5175.171	9.0	0.1
3	2892.510	NaN	0.1
4	2832.960	8.0	0.0

DataFrame with NAs

By default, the NAs are skipped during evaluation, as the `skipna` parameter is set to `True`:

```
sales_df_na.median()
```

The following is the output:

```
Sales       2892.51
Quantity       8.50
Discount       0.05
dtype: float64
```

The `median ()` function

By default, NAs are ignored in mean calculations. If `skipna` is set to `False`, the calculation also result to NA if there is a missing value:

```
sales_df_na.median(skipna = False)
```

The following is the output:

```
Sales        2892.51
Quantity         NaN
Discount         NaN
dtype: float64
```

The `median()` function with `skipna`

Consider the following multi indexed DataFrame. Let's compute the mean for it:

```
multileveldf
```

The following is the output:

Category	ShipMode	Sales	Quantity
Furniture	First Class	5.875523e+05	5034
	Same Day	1.998643e+05	1801
	Second Class	8.175204e+05	6891
	Standard Class	2.505937e+06	21228
Office Supplies	First Class	5.574531e+05	15922
	Same Day	1.964628e+05	5638
	Second Class	8.012851e+05	21637
	Standard Class	2.231869e+06	64985
Technology	First Class	6.859707e+05	5083
	Same Day	2.708749e+05	1791
	Second Class	9.468661e+05	7196
	Standard Class	2.840846e+06	21106

Multi indexed DataFrame

The mean of this multi-index dataset can be obtained as shown here:

```
multileveldf.mean()
```

The following is the output:

```
Sales       1.053542e+06
Quantity    1.485933e+04
dtype: float64
```

The mean of the multi indexed DataFrame

The `level` parameter computes the aggregate across any level of index in a multi-indexed DataFrame:

```
multileveldf.mean(level = 0)
```

The following is the output:

Category	Sales	Quantity
Furniture	1.027719e+06	8738.5
Office Supplies	9.467676e+05	27045.5
Technology	1.186139e+06	8794.0

mean () for a specific index level

all() and any()

The `all()` and `any()` functions help us test for the presence of `False` values or zeros in a DataFrame. If all the values along the chosen axis are `True`, then the `all()` function returns `True`. The `any()` function requires at least a single value to be `True` to return `True`. Let's apply `all()` and `any()` on the following DataFrame:

```
all_any = pd.DataFrame({"A": [True, False, False, True, True], "B": [1, 1,
1, 1, 1], "C": [10, 11, 20, 22, 33], "D": ["abc", "xyz", "pqr", "ijk",
"def"], "E": [False, False, False, False, False]})
all_any
```

This results in the following output:

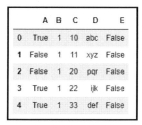

Sample DataFrame

All the values are `True` in columns B, C, and D. Hence, `all()` returns `True` for these columns. Column E, which has no `True` values, returns `False` with `any()`:

```
all_any.all()
```

The following is the output:

```
A      False
B       True
C       True
D       True
E      False
dtype: bool
```

The `all()` result

Similarly, `any()` can be applied as shown here:

```
all_any.any()
```

The following is the output:

```
A       True
B       True
C       True
D       True
E      False
dtype: bool
```

The `any()` result

The `all()` and `any()` functions have the `axis`, `skipna`, and `level` parameters, just like some of the functions we discussed previously. The `bool_only` parameter can be used to include or exclude datatypes other than Booleans:

```
all_any.all(bool_only = True)
```

The following is the output:

```
A     False
E     False
dtype: bool
```

The bool_only parameter

The clip() function

The `clip()` function specifies a lower limit and upper limit. Values in the DataFrame exceeding the upper limit, are reduced to the upper limit and values under the lower limit are raised to this lower limit:

```
sales_df.clip(8, 3000)
```

The following is the output:

	Sales	Quantity	Discount
0	2309.65	8.0	8.0
1	3000.00	9.0	8.0
2	3000.00	9.0	8.0
3	2892.51	8.0	8.0
4	2832.96	8.0	8.0

clip() result

The count() function

The `count()` function helps count the total non-NA values in the DataFrame:

```
sales_df_na
```

The following is the output:

	Sales	Quantity	Discount
0	2309.650	7.0	0.0
1	3709.395	9.0	NaN
2	5175.171	9.0	0.1
3	2892.510	NaN	0.1
4	2832.960	8.0	0.0

DataFrame with NA

The count method can be applied as shown here:

```
sales_df_na.count()
```

The following is the output:

```
Sales       5
Quantity    4
Discount    4
dtype: int64
```

count() result

The `count()` function has the `axis`, `level`, and `numeric_only` parameters, just like several other functions we discussed previously.

Summary

This chapter provided a collection of special methods that show the flexibility and usefulness of pandas. This chapter has been like an illustrated glossary in which each function serves a very unique purpose. Now, you should have an idea of how to create and apply one-liner functions in pandas, and you should understand the concepts of missing values and the methods that take care of them. This is also a compendium of all the miscellaneous methods that can be applied to a series and the numeric methods that can be applied to any kind of Python data structure.

In the next chapter, we will take a look at how we can handle time series data and plot it using `matplotlib`. We will also have a look into the manipulation of time series data by looking at rolling, resampling, shifting, lagging, and time element separation.

8
Time Series and Plotting Using Matplotlib

Time series data is generated by a variety of processes, including the **Internet of Things (IoT)** sensors, machine/server logs, and monthly sales data from **Customer Relationship Management (CRM)** system. Some common characteristics of time series data is that the data points are generated at a fixed frequency and that there is an inherent trend and seasonality associated with the data.

In this chapter, we will take a tour of some topics that are necessary to develop expertise in using pandas. Knowledge of these topics is very useful for the preparation of data as input to programs for data analysis, prediction, or visualization.

The topics that we'll discuss in this chapter are as follows:

- Handling time series data and dates
- Manipulation of time series data—rolling, resampling, shifting, lagging, and time element separation
- Formatting—changing the date format and converting text to a date
- Plotting time series using `matplotlib`

By the end of this chapter, you should be proficient in these critical areas.

Handling time series data

In this section, we show you how to handle time series data. Handling involves reading, creating, resampling, and reindexing timestamp data. These tasks need to be performed on timestamp data to make it usable. We will start by showing you how to create time series data using the data read in from a `csv` file.

Reading in time series data

In this section, we demonstrate the various ways to read in time series data, starting with the simple `read_csv` method:

```
In [7]: ibmData=pd.read_csv('ibm-common-stock-closing-
prices-1959_1960.csv')
    ibmData.head()
Out[7]:    TradeDate  closingPrice
0    1959-06-29    445
1    1959-06-30    448
2    1959-07-01    450
3    1959-07-02    447
4    1959-07-06    451
5 rows 2 columns
```

The source of this information can be found at `http://datamarket.com`.

We would like the `TradeDate` column to be a series of `datetime` values so that we can index it and create a time series:

1. Let's first check the type of values in the `TradeDate` series:

    ```
    In [16]: type(ibmData['TradeDate'])
    Out[16]: pandas.core.series.Series
    In [12]: type(ibmData['TradeDate'][0])
    Out[12]: str
    ```

2. Next, we convert these values to a `Timestamp` type:

    ```
    In [17]: ibmData['TradeDate']=pd.to_datetime(ibmData['TradeDate'])
            type(ibmData['TradeDate'][0])
    Out[17]: pandas.tslib.Timestamp
    ```

3. We can now use the `TradeDate` column as an index:

    ```
    In [113]: #Convert DataFrame to TimeSeries
              #Resampling creates NaN rows for weekend dates,
              hence use dropna
              ibmTS=ibmData.set_index('TradeDate').resample('D'
    ['closingPrice'].dropna()
          ibmTS
      Out[113]: TradeDate
              1959-06-29    445
              1959-06-30    448
              1959-07-01    450
              1959-07-02    447
    ```

```
1959-07-06     451
...
Name: closingPrice, Length: 255
```

In the next section, we will learn how to assign a date column as an index and then perform subsetting based on the index. For this section, we will use the `Object Occupancy` dataset where some room parameters were observed every few minutes for several weeks and the corresponding room occupancy was observed. This dataset is present as three separate files.

Assigning date indexes and subsetting in time series data

Let's read them and concatenate them to make a single file:

```
import pandas as pd
import os os.chdir(' ')
ts1=pd.read_csv('datatraining.txt')
ts2=pd.read_csv('datatest.txt')
ts3=pd.read_csv('datatest2.txt')
ts=pd.concat([ts1,ts2,ts3]
```

Before using the date column as an index, we will convert it to a `datetime` format and drop the actual date column:

```
ts['datetime'] = pd.to_datetime(ts['date'])
ts = ts.set_index('datetime')
ts.drop(['date'], axis=1, inplace=True)
```

Once the new `datetime` column is set to an index, it can be used for subsetting. For example, for filtering all the records for a particular day, we can just enclose the data inside the subsetting (square, `[]`) brackets:

```
ts['2015-02-05']
```

The output is similar to the following screenshot:

datetime	Temperature	Humidity	Light	CO2	HumidityRatio	Occupancy
2015-02-05 00:00:00	21.245000	25.2450	0.0	456.500000	0.003938	0
2015-02-05 00:01:00	21.245000	25.2450	0.0	458.500000	0.003938	0
2015-02-05 00:02:00	21.260000	25.2600	0.0	459.666667	0.003944	0
2015-02-05 00:03:00	21.245000	25.2450	0.0	464.000000	0.003938	0
2015-02-05 00:04:00	21.245000	25.2000	0.0	465.000000	0.003931	0
2015-02-05 00:04:59	21.290000	25.2000	0.0	461.000000	0.003942	0
2015-02-05 00:06:00	21.245000	25.2000	0.0	458.500000	0.003931	0
2015-02-05 00:07:00	21.290000	25.2000	0.0	459.000000	0.003942	0

Filtering all records for a particular day

To filter all the records for a particular hour across all days, the following snippet will do the job:

```
ts[ts.index.hour==4]
```

The following is the output:

datetime	Temperature	Humidity	Light	CO2	HumidityRatio	Occupancy
2015-02-05 04:00:00	21.000000	24.390000	0.0	442.000000	0.003747	0
2015-02-05 04:01:00	21.000000	24.356667	0.0	442.666667	0.003742	0
2015-02-05 04:01:59	21.000000	24.290000	0.0	439.000000	0.003731	0
2015-02-05 04:02:59	20.890000	24.390000	0.0	440.000000	0.003721	0
2015-02-05 04:04:00	20.945000	24.390000	0.0	440.000000	0.003734	0
2015-02-05 04:05:00	21.000000	24.390000	0.0	444.000000	0.003747	0
2015-02-05 04:06:00	20.890000	24.390000	0 0	439.500000	0.003721	0

Filtering all records for a particular hour

We can also filter out all the records between two timestamps by using the following snippet:

```
ts['2015-02-05':'2015-02-06']
```

The following is the output:

	Temperature	Humidity	Light	CO2	HumidityRatio	Occupancy
datetime						
2015-02-05 00:00:00	21.245000	25.2450	0.0	456.500000	0.003938	0
2015-02-05 00:01:00	21.245000	25.2450	0.0	458.500000	0.003938	0
2015-02-05 00:02:00	21.260000	25.2600	0.0	459.666667	0.003944	0
2015-02-05 00:03:00	21.245000	25.2450	0.0	464.000000	0.003938	0
2015-02-05 00:04:00	21.245000	25.2000	0.0	465.000000	0.003931	0
2015-02-05 00:04:59	21.290000	25.2000	0.0	461.000000	0.003942	0

Filtering all records between two timestamps

Plotting the time series data

To better understand the trends and any seasonality present in the data, it can be plotted using a basic plot function. Here, the humidity and CO_2 variables of the dataset have been plotted:

```
ts.plot(y="Humidity",style='.',figsize=(15,1))
ts.plot(y="CO2",style='.',figsize=(15,1))
```

The following is the output:

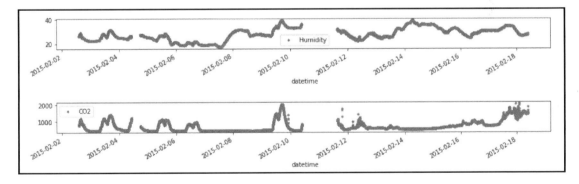

Plotting humidity and CO2 levels across time in the same graph using matplotlib

Resampling and rolling of the time series data

Resampling means changing the frequency of the observed time series. For example, in this dataset, a data point is observed every few seconds. This dataset can be resampled to an hourly frequency where all the data points for an hour will be aggregated using an aggregation function of choice to result in one data point for an hour. It can be done at a daily level as well, where all the data points in a day will be aggregated. Resampling can also be thought of as data smoothing as it smooths or averages out the bumps in data.

In pandas, it is easy to resample time series data as there is a built-in function for that. Let's see how we can use that.

For example, to resample at an hourly level, we write the following code:

```
ts[["Humidity"]].resample("1h").median().plot(figsize=(15,1))
```

The following is the output:

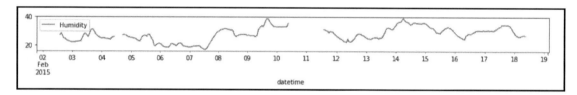

Resampling the data at an hourly level using the median as the aggregate measure

Similarly, to resample at a daily level, we write the following code:

```
ts[["Humidity"]].resample("1d").median().plot(figsize=(15,1))
```

The following is the output:

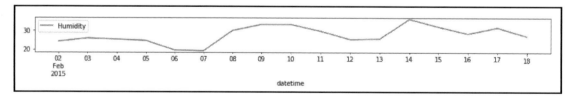

Resampling the data at a daily level using the median as the aggregate measure

Please note how data sampled at an hourly level has more variations than the daily one, which is smoother.

Rolling is also a similar concept for aggregating data points, although it is more flexible. A rolling window, that is, the number of data points that are aggregated can be provided to control the level of aggregation or smoothing.

If you look at the `datetime` column carefully, you can see that a data point has been observed every minute. Hence, 60 such points constitute an hour. Let's see how we can use the rolling method to aggregate the data.

For rolling 60 data points, starting from each data point as one record, we provide 60 as the rolling window, which is shown as follows. This should return a plot similar to the hourly resampling previously obtained:

```
ts[["Humidity"]].rolling(60).median().plot(figsize=(15,1))
```

The following is the output:

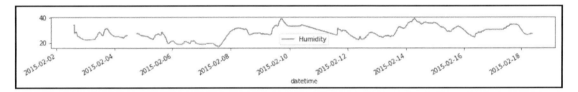

Rolling every consecutive 60 points and aggregating them to give the median as the final value

For rolling at a day level, the rolling window should be *60 x 24*:

```
ts[["Humidity"]].rolling(60*24).median().plot(figsize=(15,1))
```

The following is the output:

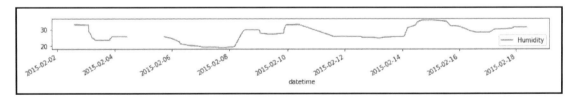

Rolling every consecutive 60*24 points and aggregating them to give their median as the final value; this amounts to finding daily aggregate values for minute-level data

Note that the median has been used for aggregation. You can also use any other function such as mean or sum.

Separating timestamp components

A timestamp object is made of several components, namely, year, month, day, hour, minute, and second. For many time series analyses, it is important to segregate these components and keep them as new columns for later usage.

Since we have made the date column our index, it becomes a lot easier. A separate column for each component can be created as follows:

```
ts['Year']=ts.index.year
ts['Month']=ts.index.month
ts['Day']=ts.index.day
ts['Hour']=ts.index.hour
ts['Minute']=ts.index.minute
ts['Second']=ts.index.second
```

The following is the output:

datetime	Temperature	Humidity	Light	CO2	HumidityRatio	Occupancy	Year	Month	Day	Hour	Minute	Second
2015-02-04 17:51:00	23.18	27.2720	426.0	721.25	0.004793	1	2015	2	4	17	51	0
2015-02-04 17:51:59	23.15	27.2675	429.5	714.00	0.004783	1	2015	2	4	17	51	59
2015-02-04 17:53:00	23.15	27.2450	426.0	713.50	0.004779	1	2015	2	4	17	53	0
2015-02-04 17:54:00	23.15	27.2000	426.0	708.25	0.004772	1	2015	2	4	17	54	0
2015-02-04 17:55:00	23.10	27.2000	426.0	704.50	0.004757	1	2015	2	4	17	55	0

Time series components created as separate columns

DateOffset and TimeDelta objects

A `DateOffset` object represents a change or offset in time. The key features of a `DateOffset` object are as follows:

- This can be added to/subtracted from a `datetime` object to obtain a shifted date.
- This can be multiplied by an integer (positive or negative) so that the increment can be applied multiple times.
- This has the `rollforward` and `rollback` methods to move a date forward to the next offset date or backward to the previous offset date.

Let's create some date objects using the `datetime` method in `pandas`:

```
In [371]: xmasDay=pd.datetime(2014,12,25)
          xmasDay
Out[371]: datetime.datetime(2014, 12, 25, 0, 0)
In [373]: boxingDay=xmasDay+pd.DateOffset(days=1)
          boxingDay
Out[373]: Timestamp('2014-12-26 00:00:00', tz=None)
In [390}: today=pd.datetime.now()
          today
Out[390]: datetime.datetime(2014, 5, 31, 13, 7, 36, 440060)
```

Note that `datetime.datetime` is different from `pd.Timestamp`. The former is a Python class and is inefficient, while the latter is based on the `numpy.datetime64` datatype.

The `pd.DateOffset` object works with `pd.Timestamp`, and adding it to a `datetime.datetime` function casts that object into a `pd.Timestamp` object.

The following illustrates the command for 1 week from today:

```
In [392]: today+pd.DateOffset(weeks=1)
Out[392]: Timestamp('2014-06-07 13:07:36.440060', tz=None)
```

The following illustrates the command for 5 years from today:

```
In [394]: today+2*pd.DateOffset(years=2, months=6)
Out[394]: Timestamp('2019-05-30 13:07:36.440060', tz=None)
```

Here is an example of using the `rollforward` functionality. `QuarterBegin` is a `DateOffset` object that is used to increment a given `datetime` object to the start of the next calendar quarter:

```
In [18]: lastDay=pd.datetime(2013,12,31)
In [24]: from pandas.tseries.offsets import QuarterBegin
         dtoffset=QuarterBegin()
         lastDay+dtoffset
Out[24]: Timestamp('2014-03-01 00:00:00', tz=None)
In [25]: dtoffset.rollforward(lastDay)
Out[25]: Timestamp('2014-03-01 00:00:00', tz=None)
```

Thus, we can see that the next quarter after December 31, 2013 starts on March 1, 2014. `Timedelta` is similar to `DateOffset` but works with `datetime.datetime` objects. The use of these objects is explained with the following command:

```
In [40]: weekDelta=datetime.timedelta(weeks=1)
         weekDelta
Out[40]: datetime.timedelta(7)
In [39]: today=pd.datetime.now()
         today
Out[39]: datetime.datetime (2014, 6, 2, 3, 56, 0, 600309)
In [41]: today+weekDelta
Out[41]: datetime.datetime (2014, 6, 9, 3, 56,0, 600309)
```

We have learned about datatypes, conversions between datatypes, date offsets, separating time components from timestamps, and so on, up to now. Next, we will see how we can apply some mathematical operators such as lagging, shifting, and so on.

Time series-related instance methods

In this section, we explore various methods for time series objects such as shifting, frequency conversion, and resampling.

Shifting/lagging

Sometimes, we may wish to shift the values in a time series backward or forward in time. One possible scenario is when a dataset contains the list of start dates of the new employees in a firm, and the company's HR program wishes to shift these dates forward by one year so that the employees' benefits can be activated. We can do this by using the `shift()` function as follows:

```
In [117]: ibmTS.shift(3)
Out[117]: TradeDate
    1959-06-29    NaN
    1959-06-30    NaN
    1959-07-01    NaN
    1959-07-02    445
    1959-07-06    448
    1959-07-07    450
    1959-07-08    447
    ...
```

This shifts all the calendar days. However, if we wish to shift only business days, we must use the following command:

```
In [119]: ibmTS.shift(3, freq=pd.datetools.bday)
Out[119]: TradeDate
    1959-07-02    445
    1959-07-03    448
    1959-07-06    450
    1959-07-07    447
    1959-07-09    451
```

In the preceding snippet, we have specified the `freq` argument to shift; this tells the function to shift only the business days. The `shift` function has a `freq` argument whose value can be a `DateOffset` class, `TimeDelta`-like object, or an offset alias. Thus, using `ibmTS.shift(3, freq='B')` would also produce the same result.

Frequency conversion

Time series usually comes with a fixed frequency, for example, every microsecond, every second, every minute, and so on. These frequencies can be changed from one to another.

We can use the `asfreq` function to change frequencies, as shown in the following snippet:

```
In [131]: # Frequency conversion using asfreq
          ibmTS.asfreq('BM')
Out[131]: 1959-06-30    448
     1959-07-31    428
     1959-08-31    425
     1959-09-30    411
     1959-10-30    411
     1959-11-30    428
     1959-12-31    439
     1960-01-29    418
     1960-02-29    419
     1960-03-31    445
     1960-04-29    453
     1960-05-31    504
     1960-06-30    522
     Freq: BM, Name: closingPrice, dtype: float64
```

In this case, we just obtain the values corresponding to the last day of the month from the `ibmTS` time series. Here, bm stands for business month end frequency. For a list of all possible frequency aliases, go to `http://pandas.pydata.org/pandas-docs/stable/timeseries.html#offset-aliases`.

If we specify a frequency that is smaller than the granularity of the data, the gaps will be filled in with NaN values:

```
In [132]: ibmTS.asfreq('H')
Out[132]: 1959-06-29 00:00:00    445
     1959-06-29 01:00:00    NaN
     1959-06-29 02:00:00    NaN
     1959-06-29 03:00:00    NaN
     ...
     1960-06-29 23:00:00    NaN
     1960-06-30 00:00:00    522
     Freq: H, Name: closingPrice, Length: 8809
```

We can also apply the `asfreq` method to the `Period` and `PeriodIndex` objects, similar to how we do it for the `datetime` and `Timestamp` objects. `Period` and `PeriodIndex` are introduced later and are used to represent time intervals.

The `asfreq` method accepts a method argument that allows you to forward fill (`ffill`) or back fill the gaps, similar to `fillna`:

```
In [140]: ibmTS.asfreq('H', method='ffill') Out[140]: 1959-06-29
00:00:00 445 1959-06-29 01:00:00 445 1959-06-29 02:00:00 445 1959-06-29
03:00:00 445 ... 1960-06-29 23:00:00 522 1960-06-30 00:00:00 522 Freq: H,
Name: closingPrice, Length: 8809
```

Resampling of data

The `TimeSeries.resample` function enables us to summarize/aggregate more granular data, based on a sampling interval and a sampling function.

Downsampling is a term that originates from digital signal processing and refers to the process of reducing the sampling rate of a signal. In the case of data, we use it to reduce the amount of data that we wish to process.

The opposite process is upsampling, which is used to increase the amount of data to be processed and requires interpolation to obtain the intermediate data points.

 For more information on downsampling and upsampling, refer to *Practical Applications of Upsampling and Downsampling* at `http://bit.ly/1JC95HD` and *Downsampling Time Series for Visual Representation* at `http://bit.ly/1zrExVP`.

Here, we examine some tick data for use in resampling. Before we examine the data, we need to prepare it. In doing so, we will learn some useful techniques for time series data, which are as follows:

- Epoch timestamps
- Time zone handling

Here is an example that uses tick data for the stock prices of Google for Tuesday, May 27, 2014:

```
In [150]: googTickData=pd.read_csv('./GOOG_tickdata_20140527.csv')
In [151]: googTickData.head()
Out[151]: Timestamp    close     high      low       open    volume
      0    1401197402  555.008  556.41  554.35  556.38    81100
      1    1401197460  556.250  556.30  555.25  555.25    18500
      2    1401197526  556.730  556.75  556.05  556.39     9900
      3    1401197582  557.480  557.67  556.73  556.73    14700
      4    1401197642  558.155  558.66  557.48  557.59    15700
5 rows 6 columns
```

The source for the preceding data can be found at
`http://chartapi.finance.yahoo.com/instrument/1.0/GOOG/chartdata;type=quote;rang`
`e=1d/csv`.

As you can see in the preceding code, we have a `Timestamp` column along with the
columns for the closing, high, low, and opening prices, and the volume of trades of the
Google stock.

So, why does the `Timestamp` column seem a bit strange? Well, tick data timestamps are
generally expressed in epoch time (for more information, refer to
`http://en.wikipedia.org/wiki/Unix_epoch`) as a more compact means of storage. We'll
need to convert this into a more human-readable time format, and we can do this as
follows:

```
    In [201]:
googTickData['tstamp']=pd.to_datetime(googTickData['Timestamp'],unit='s',ut
c=True)
    In [209]: googTickData.head()
    Out[209]:
       Timestamp    close    high     low     open    volume tstamp
    0  14011974020 555.008  556.41  554.35  556.38  81100  2014-05-27 13:30:02
    1  1401197460  556.250  556.30  555.25  555.25  18500  2014-05-27 13:31:00
    2  1401197526  556.730  556.75  556.05  556.39   9900  2014-05-27 13:32:06
    3  1401197582  557.480  557.67  556.73  556.73  14700  2014-05-27 13:33:02
    4  1401197642  558.155  558.66  557.48  557.59  15700  2014-05-27 13:34:02
    5 rows 7 columns
```

We would now like to make the `tstamp` column the index and eliminate the epoch
`Timestamp` column:

```
    In [210]: googTickTS=googTickData.set_index('tstamp')
              googTickTS=googTickTS.drop('Timestamp',axis=1)
              googTickTS.head()
    Out[210]:                        close   high    low    open    volume
              tstamp
              2014-05-27 13:30:02    555.008 556.41 554.35 556.38   811000
    2014-05-27 13:31:00    556.250 556.30 555.25 555.25   18500
    2014-05-27 13:32:06    556.730 556.75 556.05 556.39   9900
    2014-05-27 13:33:02    557.480 557.67 556.73 556.73   14700
    2014-05-27 13:34:02    558.155 558.66 557.48 557.59   15700
    5 rows 5 columns
```

Note that the `tstamp` index column has the times in **Universal Time Coordinated** (**UTC**), and we can convert these times to US/Eastern Time using two operators: `tz_localize` and `tz_convert`:

```
    In [211]:
googTickTS.index=googTickTS.index.tz_localize('UTC').tz_convert('US/Eastern')
    In [212]: googTickTS.head()
    Out[212]:                       close    high     low    open    volume
    tstamp
    2014-05-27 09:30:02-04:00      555.008  556.41  554.35  556.38  81100
    2014-05-27 09:31:00-04:00      556.250  556.30  555.25  555.25  18500
    2014-05-27 09:32:06-04:00      556.730  556.75  556.05  556.39   9900
    2014-05-27 09:33:02-04:00      557.480  557.67  556.73  556.73  14700
    2014-05-27 09:34:02-04:00      558.155  558.66  557.48  557.59  15700
    5 rows 5 columns
    In [213]: googTickTS.tail()
    Out[213]:
            close      high     low     open    volume
    tstamp
    2014-05-27 15:56:00-04:00      565.4300  565.48  565.30  565.385   14300
    2014-05-27 15:57:00-04:00      565.3050  565.46  565.20  565.400   14700
    2014-05-27 15:58:00-04:00      565.1101  565.31  565.10  565.310   23200
    2014-05-27 15:59:00-04:00      565.9400  566.00  565.08  565.230   55600
    2014-05-27 16:00:00-04:00      565.9500  565.95  565.95  565.950  126000
    5 rows 5 columns
    In [214]: len(googTickTS)
    Out[214]: 390
```

From the preceding output (**Out[213]**), we can see ticks for every minute of the trading day—from 9:30 a.m., when the stock market opens, to 4:00 p.m., when it closes. This results in 390 rows in the dataset since there are 390 minutes between 9:30 a.m. and 4:00 p.m.

Suppose we want to obtain a snapshot every 5 minutes instead of every minute? We can achieve this using downsampling as follows:

```
    In [216]: googTickTS.resample('5Min').head(6)
    Out[216]:                       close      high      low      open     volume
    tstamp
    2014-05-27 09:30:00-04:00 556.72460 557.15800 555.97200 556.46800 27980
    2014-05-27 09:35:00-04:00 556.93648 557.64800 556.85100 557.34200
24620
    2014-05-27 09:40:00-04:00 556.48600 556.79994 556.27700 556.60678
8620
    2014-05-27 09:45:00-04:00 557.05300 557.27600 556.73800 556.96600
9720
    2014-05-27 09:50:00-04:00  556.66200  556.93596  556.46400  556.80326
```

```
14560
    2014-05-27 09:55:00-04:00  555.96580  556.35400  555.85800  556.23600
12400
    6 rows 5 columns
```

The default function used for resampling is the mean. However, we can also specify other functions, such as the minimum, and we can do this using the how parameter to resample:

```
In [245]: googTickTS.resample('10Min', how=np.min).head(4)
Out[245]:          close    high      low   open   volume
tstamp
2014-05-27 09:30:00-04:00  555.008  556.3000  554.35  555.25  9900
2014-05-27 09:40:00-04:00  556.190  556.5600  556.13  556.35  3500
2014-05-27 09:50:00-04:00  554.770  555.5500  554.77  555.55  3400
2014-05-27 10:00:00-04:00  554.580  554.9847  554.45  554.58  1800
```

Various function names can be passed to the how parameter, such as sum, ohlc, max, min, std, mean, median, first, and last.

The ohlc function returns open-high-low-close values on time series data, which are the first, maximum, minimum, and last values. To specify whether the left or right interval is closed, we can pass the closed parameter as follows:

```
In [254]: pd.set_option('display.precision',5)
googTickTS.resample('5Min', closed='right').tail(3) Out[254]: close high
low open volume tstamp 2014-05-27 15:45:00-04:00 564.3167 564.3733 564.1075
564.1700 12816.6667 2014-05-27 15:50:00-04:00 565.1128 565.1725 565.0090
565.0650 13325.0000 2014-05-27 15:55:00-04:00 565.5158 565.6033 565.3083
565.4158 40933.3333 3 rows 5 columns
```

Thus, in the preceding command, we can see that the last row shows the tick at 15:55 instead of 16:00.

For upsampling, we need to specify a fill method to determine how the gaps should be filled through the fill_method parameter:

```
In [263]: googTickTS[:3].resample('30s', fill_method='ffill')
Out[263]:          close    high     low    open  volume
tstamp
2014-05-27 09:30:00-04:00  555.008  556.41  554.35  556.38  81100
2014-05-27 09:30:30-04:00  555.008  556.41  554.35  556.38  81100
2014-05-27 09:31:00-04:00  556.250  556.30  555.25  555.25  18500
2014-05-27 09:31:30-04:00  556.250  556.30  555.25  555.25  18500
2014-05-27 09:32:00-04:00  556.730  556.75  556.05  556.39  9900
5 rows 5 columns
In [264]: googTickTS[:3].resample('30s', fill_method='bfill')
Out[264]:
```

```
                                 close      high      low  open    volume
tstamp
2014-05-27 09:30:00-04:00        555.008   556.41   554.35  556.38   81100
2014-05-27 09:30:30-04:00        556.250   556.30   555.25  555.25   18500
2014-05-27 09:31:00-04:00        556.250   556.30   555.25  555.25   18500
2014-05-27 09:31:30-04:00        556.730   556.75   556.05  556.39    9900
2014-05-27 09:32:00-04:00        556.730   556.75   556.05  556.39    9900
5 rows 5 columns
```

The `fill_method` parameter currently supports only two methods—`forwardfill` and `backfill`. An interpolation method can also be supported, though, which would be vary.

Aliases for time series frequencies

To specify offsets, a number of aliases are available; some of the most commonly used ones are as follows:

- **B, BM**: This stands for business day, business month. These are the working days of the month, that is, any day that is not a holiday or a weekend.
- **D, W, M, Q, A**: This stands for calendar day, week, month, quarter, and year end.
- **H, T, S, L, U**: This stands for hour, minute, second, millisecond, and microsecond.

These aliases can also be combined. In the following case, we resample every 7 minutes and 30 seconds:

```
In [267]: googTickTS.resample('7T30S').head(5)
Out[267]:
                                 close      high      low     open      volume
tstamp
2014-05-27 09:30:00-04:00       556.8266   557.4362  556.3144  556.8800   28075.0
2014-05-27 09:37:30-04:00       556.5889   556.9342  556.4264  556.7206   11642.9
2014-05-27 09:45:00-04:00       556.9921   557.2185  556.7171  556.9871    9800.0
2014-05-27 09:52:30-04:00       556.1824   556.5375  556.0350  556.3896   14350.0
2014-05-27 10:00:00-04:00       555.2111   555.4368  554.8288  554.9675   12512.5
5 rows x 5 columns
```

Suffixes can be applied to the frequency aliases to specify when in frequency period to start. These are known as anchoring offsets:

- **W – SUN, MON, ... example**: W-TUE indicates a weekly frequency starting on a Tuesday.
- **Q – JAN, FEB, ... DEC example**: Q-MAY indicates a quarterly frequency with the year end in May.
- **A – JAN, FEB, ... DEC example**: A-MAY indicates an annual frequency with the year end in May.

These offsets can be used as arguments for the `date_range` and `bdate_range` functions, as well as constructors for index types such as `PeriodIndex` and `DatetimeIndex`. A comprehensive discussion on this can be found in the pandas documentation at `http://pandas.pydata.org/pandas-docs/stable/timeseries.html#`.

Time series concepts and datatypes

When dealing with time series, there are two main concepts that you have to consider: points in time ranges, and time spans. In pandas, the former is represented by the `Timestamp` datatype, which is equivalent to the Python `datetime.datetime` (`datetime`) datatype and is interchangeable with it. The latter (time span) is represented by the `Period` datatype, which is specific to pandas.

Each of these datatypes has index datatypes associated with them: `DatetimeIndex` for `Timestamp`/`Datetime` and `PeriodIndex` for `Period`. These index datatypes are basically subtypes of `numpy.ndarray` that contain the corresponding `Timestamp` and `Period` datatypes and can be used as indexes for the `Series` and `DataFrame` objects.

Period and PeriodIndex

The `Period` datatype is used to represent a range or span of time. Here are a few examples:

```
# Period representing May 2014
In [287]: pd.Period('2014', freq='A-MAY')
Out[287]: Period('2014', 'A-MAY')
# Period representing specific day – June 11, 2014
In [292]: pd.Period('06/11/2014')
Out[292]: Period('2014-06-11', 'D')
# Period representing 11AM, Nov 11, 1918
In [298]: pd.Period('11/11/1918 11:00',freq='H')
Out[298]: Period('1918-11-11 11:00', 'H')
```

We can add integers to the `Period` datatypes to advance the period by the requisite number of frequency units:

```
In [299]: pd.Period('06/30/2014')+4
Out[299]: Period('2014-07-04', 'D')
In [303]: pd.Period('11/11/1918 11:00',freq='H') - 48
Out[303]: Period('1918-11-09 11:00', 'H')
```

We can also calculate the difference between two the `Period` datatypes and return the number of units of frequency between them:

```
In [304]: pd.Period('2014-04', freq='M')-pd.Period('2013-02', freq='M')
Out[304]: 14
```

PeriodIndex

A `PeriodIndex` function, which is an `index` type for a `Period` object, can be created in two ways:

1. You can do it from a series of Period objects using the `period_range` function to create an analogue of `date_range`:

```
In [305]: perRng=pd.period_range('02/01/2014','02/06/2014',freq='D')
          perRng
Out[305]: <class 'pandas.tseries.period.PeriodIndex'>
          freq: D
          [2014-02-01, ..., 2014-02-06]
          length: 6
In [306]: type(perRng[:2])
Out[306]: pandas.tseries.period.PeriodIndex
In [307]: perRng[:2]
Out[307]: <class 'pandas.tseries.period.PeriodIndex'>
          freq: D
          [2014-02-01, 2014-02-02]
```

As we can confirm from the preceding command, when you pull the covers, a `PeriodIndex` function is really an `ndarray` of `Period` objects.

2. It can also be done through a direct call to the `Period` constructor:

```
In [312]: JulyPeriod=pd.PeriodIndex(['07/01/2014','07/31/2014'],
freq='D')
      JulyPeriod
Out[312]: <class 'pandas.tseries.period.PeriodIndex'>
      freq: D
      [2014-07-01, 2014-07-31]
```

The difference between the two approaches, as can be seen from the preceding output, is that `period_range` fills in the resulting `ndarray`, but the `Period` constructor does not, and you have to specify all the values that should be in the index.

Conversion between time series datatypes

We can convert the `Period` and `PeriodIndex` datatypes to the `Datetime/Timestamp` and `DatetimeIndex` datatypes through the `to_period` and `to_timestamp` functions, as follows:

```
In [339]: worldCupFinal=pd.to_datetime('07/13/2014',
                                        errors='raise')
          worldCupFinal
   Out[339]: Timestamp('2014-07-13 00:00:00')
In [340]: worldCupFinal.to_period('D')
   Out[340]: Period('2014-07-13', 'D')
In [342]: worldCupKickoff=pd.Period('06/12/2014','D')
          worldCupKickoff
Out[342]: Period('2014-06-12', 'D')
In [345]: worldCupKickoff.to_timestamp()
Out[345]: Timestamp('2014-06-12 00:00:00', tz=None)
In [346]: worldCupDays=pd.date_range('06/12/2014',periods=32,
                                      freq='D')
          worldCupDays
Out[346]: <class 'pandas.tseries.index.DatetimeIndex'>
    [2014-06-12, ..., 2014-07-13]
    Length: 32, Freq: D, Timezone: None
In [347]: worldCupDays.to_period()
Out[347]: <class 'pandas.tseries.period.PeriodIndex'>
    freq: D
    [2014-06-12, ..., 2014-07-13]
    length: 32
```

In the preceding examples, note how periods are converted into timestamps and vice versa.

A summary of time series-related objects

There are many time series-related objects in pandas that are used for manipulating, creating, and processing timestamp data. The following table gives a summary of time series-related objects:

Object	Summary
datetime.datetime	This is a standard Python datetime class.
Timestamp	This is a pandas class derived from. datetime.datetime.
DatetimeIndex	This is a pandas class and is implemented as an immutable numpy.ndarray of the Timestamp/datetime object type.
Period	This is a pandas class representing a time period.
PeriodIndex	This is a pandas class and is implemented as an immutable numpy.ndarray of the Period object type.
DateOffset	DataOffset is used to move forward a date by a given number of valid dates (days, weeks, months, and so on).
timedelta	Timedelta calculates the difference in time between two dates.

Interconversions between strings and timestamps

Consider the following DataFrame with a column containing strings representing dates and a column containing numeric values:

```
ts_df = pd.DataFrame({"ts_col": ["2013-01-01", "2015-02-10", "2016-10-24"],
"value": [5, 6, 9]})
ts_df
```

The following is the output:

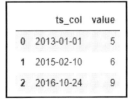

Creating a DataFrame with a date column

The datatype of the time series column can be seen to be an object and not a timestamp. The following code and its output confirms that:

```
ts_df.dtypes
```

The following is the output:

```
ts_col       object
value         int64
dtype: object
```

The `to_datetime` function helps in converting the string to `datetime`:

```
ts_df["ts_col"] = pd.to_datetime(ts_df["ts_col"],
format = "%Y-%m-%d")
    ts_df.dtypes
```

The following is the output:

```
ts_col     datetime64[ns]
value               int64
dtype: object
```

Converting the string format date column to a datetime format

The pandas `to_datetime` function converts a column of strings into `datetime`, given the format of the string. The `infer_datetime_format` argument of this function automatically detects the format and parses the string into `datetime`. The `exact` argument, when set to `False`, looks for the closest matching format and helps to overcome cases where there is not an exact match to the specified format.

The conversion shown can also be done using the `strptime` function from the `datetime` library:

```
import datetime as dt
ts_df["ts_col"] = ts_df["ts_col"].apply(lambda x:
dt.datetime.strptime(x,'%Y-%m-%d'))
```

The conversion from `datetime` to a string is aided by the `strftime` function, which accepts the format for the resulting string:

```
ts_df["ts_col"] = ts_df["ts_col"].dt.strftime("%d/%m/%Y")
ts_df
```

The following is the output:

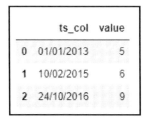

Converting the datetime format date column to a string format

Here, the original `datetime` value was in the `%Y-%m-%d` format. However, the `strftime` function allowed a change in format.

Interconversion between the string and `datetime` can also be achieved through the `astype()` method, as follows:

```
ts_df["ts_col"] = ts_df["ts_col"].astype("datetime64[ns]")
ts_df["ts_col"] = ts_df["ts_col"].astype("object")
```

Data-processing techniques for time series data

This section deals with common data manipulation or feature engineering techniques used with time series data before applying machine learning techniques.

Data transformation

Consider the following pieces of a single dataset:

```
ts_complete_df = pd.read_csv("sensor_df.csv")
```

The following screenshot shows the head of sensor data that contains the time series components of unequal length:

	Timestamp	ID	RSS_anchor2	RSS_anchor3	RSS_anchor4
0	01-01-2012 00:00	1	-0.48	0.28571	0.30
1	01-01-2012 00:10	1	-0.32	0.14286	0.30
2	01-01-2012 00:20	1	-0.28	-0.14286	0.35
3	01-01-2012 00:30	1	-0.20	-0.47619	0.35
4	01-01-2012 00:40	1	-0.20	0.14286	-0.20

Head of sensor data containing time series components of unequal length

The following screenshot shows the tail of sensor data that contains the time series components of unequal length:

	Timestamp	ID	RSS_anchor2	RSS_anchor3	RSS_anchor4
13192	01-01-2012 06:40	314	-0.60000	0.73333	1.00000
13193	01-01-2012 06:50	314	-0.46667	0.73333	1.00000
13194	01-01-2012 07:00	314	-0.42222	0.73333	0.36170
13195	01-01-2012 07:10	314	-0.33333	0.55556	-0.31915
13196	01-01-2012 07:20	314	-0.46667	0.46667	-0.31915

Tail of sensor data containing time series components of unequal length

The dataset here consists of time series data in 10-minute intervals for 314 different devices. All these 314 devices have data captured for different durations. Let's examine the duration for which data has been captured in each device:

```
ts_complete_df.groupby("ID").size().describe()
```

The following is the output:

```
count      314.000000
mean        42.028662
std         16.185303
min         19.000000
25%         26.000000
50%         41.000000
75%         56.000000
max        129.000000
dtype:  float64
```

Summary of sensor data

The lengths of data for each device vary drastically. Several time series problems such as Shapelet transformation and **Long-Short Term Memory** (**LSTM**) require the length of data for each device to be the same. The following code snippet truncates each device to the highest possible length:

```
truncate_df = pd.DataFrame()
min_len = ts_complete_df.groupby("ID").size().min()
for i in range(1,315):
df = ts_complete_df[ts_complete_df["ID"] == i].iloc[0:min_len, :]
truncate_df = truncate_df.append(df)
```

After truncating, the length can be seen to be uniform. It can be checked by running the following:

```
truncate_df.groupby("ID").size().describe()
```

The following is the output:

```
count      314.0
mean        19.0
std          0.0
min         19.0
25%         19.0
50%         19.0
75%         19.0
max         19.0
dtype:  float64
```

Summary of sensor data after all the time series components have been made equal in length

Let's perform feature extraction for the following univariate time series data:

```
ts = pd.read_csv("D:datatest.txt").iloc[:,0:2].set_index("date") ts
```

The following is the output:

	date	Temperature
140	2015-02-02 14:19:00	23.700000
141	2015-02-02 14:19:59	23.718000
142	2015-02-02 14:21:00	23.730000
143	2015-02-02 14:22:00	23.722500
144	2015-02-02 14:23:00	23.754000
145	2015-02-02 14:23:59	23.760000
146	2015-02-02 14:25:00	23.730000
147	2015-02-02 14:25:59	23.754000

Reading the occupancy data and setting the datetime column as an index

Feature extraction is vital for performing machine learning with time series data in order to obtain better performance metrics. Here, let's extract the rolling mean, rolling standard deviation, and gradient for the temperature data:

```
feat_ext = pd.concat([ts.rolling(5).mean(), ts.rolling(5).std(), (ts -
ts.shift(-5))/ts], axis=1).iloc[5:,:]
    feat_ext.columns = ['5_day_mean', '5_day_std', '5_day_gradient']
    feat_ext.head(5)
```

The following is the output:

	5_day_mean	5_day_std	5_day_gradient
date			
2015-02-02 14:23:59	23.7369	0.018962	0.000631
2015-02-02 14:25:00	23.7393	0.016582	0.001264
2015-02-02 14:25:59	23.7441	0.016690	0.002273
2015-02-02 14:26:59	23.7504	0.011696	0.002273
2015-02-02 14:28:00	23.7468	0.013008	0.001517

Feature (5_day_mean, 5_day_std) generation using rolling functions

The first 5 rows with NA values have been dropped in the feature extraction process. Here, the features have been extracted for a rolling window of 5 days. Using a similar method, it is possible to extract hundreds of features from a time series variable.

Plotting using matplotlib

This section provides a brief introduction to plotting in `pandas` using `matplotlib`. The `matplotlib` API is imported using the standard convention, as shown in the following command:

```
In [1]: import matplotlib.pyplot as plt
```

`Series` and `DataFrame` have a plot method, which is simply a wrapper around `plt.plot`. Here, we will examine how we can do a simple plot of a sine and cosine function. Suppose we wished to plot the following functions over the interval pi to pi:

- $f(x) = \cos(x) + \sin(x)$
- $g(x) = \cos(x) - \sin(x)$

This gives the following interval:

```
In [51]: import numpy as np
In [52]: X = np.linspace(-np.pi, np.pi, 256,endpoint=True)
In [54]: f,g = np.cos(X)+np.sin(X), np.sin(X)-np.cos(X)
In [61]: f_ser=pd.Series(f)
         g_ser=pd.Series(g)
In [31]: plotDF=pd.concat([f_ser,g_ser],axis=1)
         plotDF.index=X
         plotDF.columns=['sin(x)+cos(x)','sin(x)-cos(x)']
         plotDF.head()
Out[31]:    sin(x)+cos(x)   sin(x)-cos(x)
-3.141593   -1.000000       1.000000
-3.116953   -1.024334       0.975059
-3.092313   -1.048046       0.949526
-3.067673   -1.071122       0.923417
-3.043033   -1.093547       0.896747
5 rows × 2 columns
```

We can now plot the DataFrame using the `plot()` command and the `plt.show()` command to display it:

```
In [94]: plotDF.plot()
         plt.show()
We can apply a title to the plot as follows:
In [95]: plotDF.columns=['f(x)','g(x)']
         plotDF.plot(title='Plot of f(x)=sin(x)+cos(x), \n
g(x)=sinx(x)-cos(x)')
         plt.show()
```

The following is the output of the preceding command:

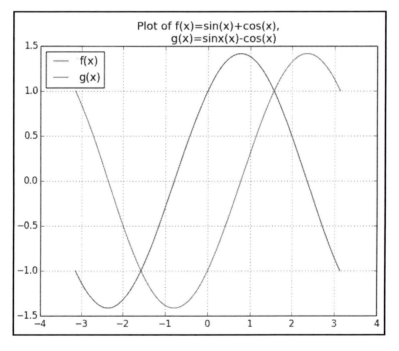

Plotting time series data using matplotlib

We can also plot the two series (functions) separately in different subplots, using the following command:

```
In [96]: plotDF.plot(subplots=True, figsize=(6,6))
         plt.show()
```

The following is the output of the preceding command:

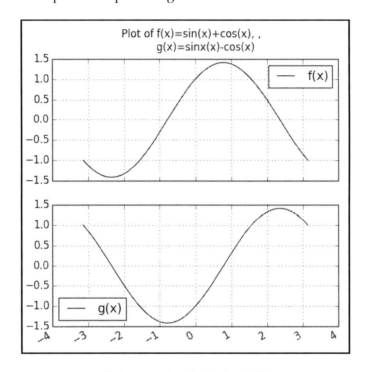

Plotting some more time series data using matplotlib

There is a lot more to using the plotting functionality of `matplotlib` within pandas. For more information, take a look at the documentation at `http://pandas.pydata.org/pandas-docs/dev/visualization.html`.

It is often quite useful to visualize all the variables of a multivariate time series data. Let's plot all the variables of the following data in a single plot. Note that the `date` column is the index here:

date	Temperature	Humidity	Light	CO2	HumidityRatio	Occupancy
2015-02-11 14:48:00	21.760000	31.133333	437.333333	1029.666667	0.005021	1
2015-02-11 14:49:00	21.790000	31.000000	437.333333	1000.000000	0.005009	1
2015-02-11 14:50:00	21.767500	31.122500	434.000000	1003.750000	0.005022	1
2015-02-11 14:51:00	21.767500	31.122500	439.000000	1009.500000	0.005022	1
2015-02-11 14:51:59	21.790000	31.133333	437.333333	1005.666667	0.005030	1
2015-02-11 14:53:00	21.760000	31.260000	437.333333	1014.333333	0.005042	1
2015-02-11 14:54:00	21.790000	31.197500	434.000000	1018.500000	0.005041	1

Occupancy dataset

The subplot feature in matplotlib lets us plot all of the variables at once:

```
axes = plot_ts.plot(figsize=(20,10), title='Timeseries Plot',
subplots=True, layout=(plot_ts.shape[1],1), xticks = plot_ts.index)
    # Get current axis from plot
    ax = plt.gca()
    import matplotlib.dates as mdates
    # Set frequency of xticks
    ax.xaxis.set_major_locator(mdates.DayLocator(interval = 1))
    # Format dates in xticks
    ax.xaxis.set_major_formatter(mdates.DateFormatter('%Y-%m-%d'))
    plt.show()
```

The following is the output:

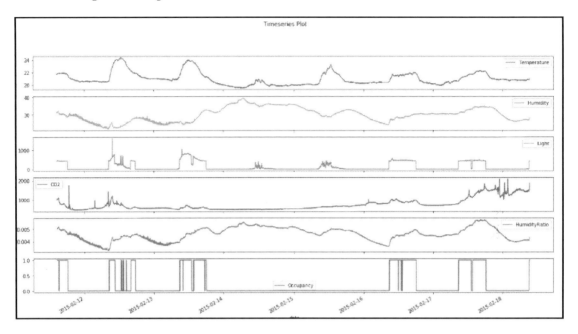

Time series plot for all the variables in the occupancy dataset

Summary

In this chapter, we discussed time series data and the steps you can take to process and manipulate it. A `date` column can be assigned as an index for `Series` or `DataFrame` and can then be used for subsetting them based on the index column. Time series data can be resampled—to either increase or decrease the frequency of the time series. For example, data generated every millisecond can be resampled to capture the data only every second or can be averaged for 1,000 milliseconds for each second. Similarly, data generated every minute can be resampled to have data every second by backfilling or forward filling (filling in the same value as the last or next minute value for all the seconds in that minute).

String to datetime conversion can be done via the `datetime`, `strptime`, and `strftime` packages , and each type of date entry (for example, 22nd July, 7/22/2019, and so on) needs to be decoded differently based on a convention. pandas has the following types of time series objects—`datetime.datetime`, `Timestamp`, `DateIndex`, `Period`, `PeriodIndex`, `timedelta`, and so on. Certain algorithms for time series classification such as shapelets and LSTM require time series components (one separable data entity containing multiple entries of time series data) to be of the same length. This can be done either by truncating all the components to the smallest length or expanding them to the longest length and imputing with zeros or some other value. Matplotlib can be used to plot basic time series data. Shifting, lagging, and rolling functions are used to calculate moving averages, detecting behavioral change at time series component change points.

In the next chapter, we will learn how to use the power of pandas in Jupyter Notebooks to make powerful and interactive reports.

4
Section 4: Going a Step Beyond with pandas

Now that we have seen the basic as well as the advanced functionalities that pandas has to offer when it comes to data manipulation, it's time to go a step beyond and explore the other different possibilities for getting the most out of pandas for effective insight generation.

This section is comprised of the following chapters:

- Chapter 9, *Making Powerful Reports Using pandas in Jupyter*
- Chapter 10, *A Tour of Statistics with pandas and NumPy*
- Chapter 11, *A Brief Tour of Bayesian Statistics and Maximum Likelihood Estimates*
- Chapter 12, *Data Case Studies Using Pandas*
- Chapter 13, *The pandas Library Architecture*
- Chapter 14, *Pandas Compared with Other Tools*
- Chapter 15, *Brief Tour of Machine Learning*

Making Powerful Reports In Jupyter Using pandas

9

pandas and Jupyter Notebook can be used to create nicely formatted output, reports, and/or tutorials that are easy to share with a wide range of audiences. In this chapter, we will look into the application of a range of styles and the formatting options that pandas provides. We will also understand how to create dashboards and reports in Jupyter Notebook.

The following topics will be covered in this chapter:

- pandas styling
- Navigating Jupyter Notebook
- Making reports using Jupyter Notebooks

pandas styling

pandas allow for a wide variety of operations to be performed on DataFrames, making it easier to handle structured data. Another intriguing property of DataFrames is that they allow us to format and style regular rows and columns in tabular data. These styling properties help enhance the readability of tabular data. The `Dataframe.style` method returns a Styler object. Any formatting to be applied before displaying a DataFrame can be applied over this Styler object. Styling can be done either with in-built functions that have predefined rules for formatting or with user-defined rules.

Let's consider the following DataFrames so that we can take a look at pandas' styling properties:

```
df = pd.read_csv("titanic.csv")
df
```

The following screenshot shows the preceding DataFrame loaded into Jupyter Notebook:

	PassengerId	Survived	Pclass	Name	Sex	Age	SibSp	Parch	Ticket	Fare	Cabin	Embarked
0	1	0	3	Braund, Mr. Owen Harris	male	22.0	1	0	A/5 21171	7.2500	NaN	S
1	2	1	1	Cumings, Mrs. John Bradley (Florence Briggs Th...	female	38.0	1	0	PC 17599	71.2833	C85	C
2	3	1	3	Heikkinen, Miss. Laina	female	26.0	0	0	STON/O2. 3101282	7.9250	NaN	S
3	4	1	1	Futrelle, Mrs. Jacques Heath (Lily May Peel)	female	35.0	1	0	113803	53.1000	C123	S
4	5	0	3	Allen, Mr. William Henry	male	35.0	0	0	373450	8.0500	NaN	S
5	6	0	3	Moran, Mr. James	male	NaN	0	0	330877	8.4583	NaN	Q
6	7	0	1	McCarthy, Mr. Timothy J	male	54.0	0	0	17463	51.8625	E46	S
7	8	0	3	Palsson, Master. Gosta Leonard	male	2.0	3	1	349909	21.0750	NaN	S
8	9	1	3	Johnson, Mrs. Oscar W (Elisabeth Vilhelmina Berg)	female	27.0	0	2	347742	11.1333	NaN	S

DataFrame loaded into Jupyter Notebook

Let's see how Jupyter Notebook elements can be styled.

In-built styling options

pandas has predefined formatting rules written and stored as functions that can be readily used.

The `highlight_null` method highlights all NaNs or Null values in the data with a specified color. In the DataFrame under discussion, the Age and Cabin columns have NaNs. Hence, in the following screenshot, the NaNs are flagged in blue in these columns.

The following snippet highlights the NaN values in these columns:

```
df.style.highlight_null(null_color = "blue")
```

This results in the following output:

	PassengerId	Survived	Pclass	Name	Sex	Age	SibSp	Parch	Ticket	Fare	Cabin	Embarked
0	1	0	3	Braund, Mr. Owen Harris	male	22	1	0	A/5 21171	7.25	nan	S
1	2	1	1	Cumings, Mrs. John Bradley (Florence Briggs Thayer)	female	38	1	0	PC 17599	71.2833	C85	C
2	3	1	3	Heikkinen, Miss. Laina	female	26	0	0	STON/O2. 3101282	7.925	nan	S
3	4	1	1	Futrelle, Mrs. Jacques Heath (Lily May Peel)	female	35	1	0	113803	53.1	C123	S
4	5	0	3	Allen, Mr. William Henry	male	35	0	0	373450	8.05	nan	S
5	6	0	3	Moran, Mr. James	male	nan	0	0	330877	8.4583	nan	Q
6	7	0	1	McCarthy, Mr. Timothy J	male	54	0	0	17463	51.8625	E46	S
7	8	0	3	Palsson, Master. Gosta Leonard	male	2	3	1	349909	21.075	nan	S
8	9	1	3	Johnson, Mrs. Oscar W (Elisabeth Vilhelmina Berg)	female	27	0	2	347742	11.1333	nan	S
9	10	1	2	Nasser, Mrs. Nicholas (Adele Achem)	female	14	1	0	237736	30.0708	nan	C

Figure 9.2: Highlighting Nulls and NANs with blue

The `highlight_max` and `highlight_min` methods apply highlighting (with a chosen color) to the maximum or minimum value across either axis. In the following example, the minimum values in each column have been highlighted:

```
df.iloc[0:10, :].style.highlight_max(axis = 0)
```

Please note that only columns with the numeric datatype are subject to highlighting.

The following screenshot highlights the maximum values for each column:

	PassengerId	Survived	Pclass	Name	Sex	Age	SibSp	Parch	Ticket	Fare	Cabin	Embarked
0	1	0	3	Braund, Mr. Owen Harris	male	22	1	0	A/5 21171	7.25	nan	S
1	2	1	1	Cumings, Mrs. John Bradley (Florence Briggs Thayer)	female	38	1	0	PC 17599	71.2833	C85	C
2	3	1	3	Heikkinen, Miss. Laina	female	26	0	0	STON/O2. 3101282	7.925	nan	S
3	4	1	1	Futrelle, Mrs. Jacques Heath (Lily May Peel)	female	35	1	0	113803	53.1	C123	S
4	5	0	3	Allen, Mr. William Henry	male	35	0	0	373450	8.05	nan	S
5	6	0	3	Moran, Mr. James	male	nan	0	0	330877	8.4583	nan	Q
6	7	0	1	McCarthy, Mr. Timothy J	male	54	0	0	17463	51.8625	E46	S
7	8	0	3	Palsson, Master. Gosta Leonard	male	2	3	1	349909	21.075	nan	S
8	9	1	3	Johnson, Mrs. Oscar W (Elisabeth Vilhelmina Berg)	female	27	0	2	347742	11.1333	nan	S
9	10	1	2	Nasser, Mrs. Nicholas (Adele Achem)	female	14	1	0	237736	30.0708	nan	C

Figure 9.3: Highlighting the maximums across rows (among numerical columns) with yellow

In the preceding code, `highlight_max` has been used to highlight the maximum values in each column.

Next, we use the same function to find the maximum for each column, changing the value of the axis parameter while doing so:

```
df.style.highlight_max(axis = 1)
```

The following screenshot shows the highlighted maximum values across columns:

	PassengerId	Survived	Pclass	Name	Sex	Age	SibSp	Parch	Ticket	Fare	Cabin	Embarked
0	1	0	3	Braund, Mr. Owen Harris	male	22	1	0	A/5 21171	7.25	nan	S
1	2	1	1	Cumings, Mrs. John Bradley (Florence Briggs Thayer)	female	38	1	0	PC 17599	71.2833	C85	C
2	3	1	3	Heikkinen, Miss. Laina	female	26	0	0	STON/O2. 3101282	7.925	nan	S
3	4	1	1	Futrelle, Mrs. Jacques Heath (Lily May Peel)	female	35	1	0	113803	53.1	C123	S
4	5	0	3	Allen, Mr. William Henry	male	35	0	0	373450	8.05	nan	S
5	6	0	3	Moran, Mr. James	male	nan	0	0	330877	8.4583	nan	Q
6	7	0	1	McCarthy, Mr. Timothy J	male	54	0	0	17463	51.8625	E46	S
7	8	0	3	Palsson, Master. Gosta Leonard	male	2	3	1	349909	21.075	nan	S
8	9	1	3	Johnson, Mrs. Oscar W (Elisabeth Vilhelmina Berg)	female	27	0	2	347742	11.1333	nan	S
9	10	1	2	Nasser, Mrs. Nicholas (Adele Achem)	female	14	1	0	237736	30.0708	nan	C

Highlighting the maximums across columns (among numerical columns) with yellow

Now, let's use the `highlight_min` function to highlight the minimum values with a custom-defined color. Both `highlight_min` and `highlight_max` have the same syntax and accept the same set of parameters:

	PassengerId	Survived	Pclass	Name	Sex	Age	SibSp	Parch	Ticket	Fare	Cabin	Embarked
0	1	0	3	Braund, Mr. Owen Harris	male	22	1	0	A/5 21171	7.25	nan	S
1	2	1	1	Cumings, Mrs. John Bradley (Florence Briggs Thayer)	female	38	1	0	PC 17599	71.2833	C85	C
2	3	1	3	Heikkinen, Miss. Laina	female	26	0	0	STON/O2. 3101282	7.925	nan	S
3	4	1	1	Futrelle, Mrs. Jacques Heath (Lily May Peel)	female	35	1	0	113803	53.1	C123	S
4	5	0	3	Allen, Mr. William Henry	male	35	0	0	373450	8.05	nan	S
5	6	0	3	Moran, Mr. James	male	nan	0	0	330877	8.4583	nan	Q
6	7	0	1	McCarthy, Mr. Timothy J	male	54	0	0	17463	51.8625	E46	S
7	8	0	3	Palsson, Master. Gosta Leonard	male	2	3	1	349909	21.075	nan	S
8	9	1	3	Johnson, Mrs. Oscar W (Elisabeth Vilhelmina Berg)	female	27	0	2	347742	11.1333	nan	S
9	10	1	2	Nasser, Mrs. Nicholas (Adele Achem)	female	14	1	0	237736	30.0708	nan	C

Highlighting the minimums with green

A background color gradient based on conditional formatting can be applied to columns to give a sense of high, medium, and low values based on color. The backgrounds are colored with different colors based on whether they are high, medium, or low.

The background gradient of the table can be controlled through the `background_gradient()` styling function. Any existing colormaps or user-defined colormaps can be used as a gradient. Parameters such as `low` and `high` help us use part of the colormap's color range. Further, the axis and subset parameters can be set to vary the gradient along a certain axis and subset of columns:

```
df.style.background_gradient(cmap='plasma', low = 0.25, high = 0.5)
```

This results in the following output:

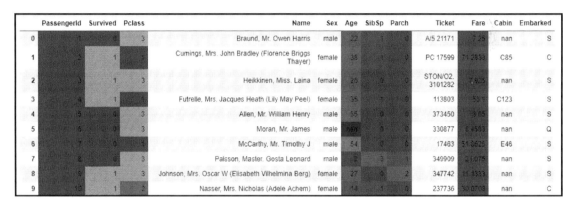

Creating a background color gradient separately for each numerical column based on its high and low values

Styling can also be done independently of values. Let's modify the properties to change the font color, background color, and border color. You can do so by using the following code.

```
df.style.set_properties(**{'background-color': 'teal',
                           'color': 'white',
                           'border-color': 'black'})
```

This results in the following output:

	PassengerId	Survived	Pclass	Name	Sex	Age	SibSp	Parch	Ticket	Fare	Cabin	Embarked
0	1	0	3	Braund, Mr. Owen Harris	male	22	1	0	A/5 21171	7.25	nan	S
1	2	1	1	Cumings, Mrs. John Bradley (Florence Briggs Thayer)	female	38	1	0	PC 17599	71.2833	C85	C
2	3	1	3	Heikkinen, Miss. Laina	female	26	0	0	STON/O2. 3101282	7.925	nan	S
3	4	1	1	Futrelle, Mrs. Jacques Heath (Lily May Peel)	female	35	1	0	113803	53.1	C123	S
4	5	0	3	Allen, Mr. William Henry	male	35	0	0	373450	8.05	nan	S
5	6	0	3	Moran, Mr. James	male	nan	0	0	330877	8.4583	nan	Q
6	7	0	1	McCarthy, Mr. Timothy J	male	54	0	0	17463	51.8625	E46	S
7	8	0	3	Palsson, Master. Gosta Leonard	male	2	3	1	349909	21.075	nan	S
8	9	1	3	Johnson, Mrs. Oscar W (Elisabeth Vilhelmina Berg)	female	27	0	2	347742	11.1333	nan	S
9	10	1	2	Nasser, Mrs. Nicholas (Adele Achem)	female	14	1	0	237736	30.0708	nan	C

Changing the background colour, font color, font type, and font size for an output DataFrame

Styling options also help us control the numerical precision. Consider the following DataFrames:

	0	1	2	3	4
0	-0.993030	0.959721	-0.865392	-1.725737	0.885758
1	1.699628	-0.515173	-1.000088	-0.829903	-0.384537
2	0.749428	0.895125	-2.075737	0.018601	1.275775
3	1.167042	-1.475232	0.729561	0.362731	0.324559
4	0.273424	-0.538150	0.137174	-0.686177	0.453571

DataFrame numbers without precision rounding off

Take a look at the following code, which sets the precision to 2 decimal places or rounds off a number number to 2 decimal places.

```
rand_df.style.set_precision(2)
```

This results in the following output:

	0	1	2	3	4
0	-0.99	0.96	-0.87	-1.7	0.89
1	1.7	-0.52	-1	-0.83	-0.38
2	0.75	0.9	-2.1	0.019	1.3
3	1.2	-1.5	0.73	0.36	0.32
4	0.27	-0.54	0.14	-0.69	0.45

DataFrame numbers with precision rounding off to 2 decimal places

Now, let's set a caption for the preceding DataFrame:

```
rand_df.style.set_precision(2).set_caption("Styling Dataframe : Precision
Control")
```

This results in the following output:

Styling Dataframe : Precision Control

	0	1	2	3	4
0	-0.99	0.96	-0.87	-1.7	0.89
1	1.7	-0.52	-1	-0.83	-0.38
2	0.75	0.9	-2.1	0.019	1.3
3	1.2	-1.5	0.73	0.36	0.32
4	0.27	-0.54	0.14	-0.69	0.45

DataFrame numbers with precision rounding off to 2 decimal places and a table caption

The `set_table_styles` function can also be used to modify the table independently of the data. It accepts a list of `table_styles`. Each `table_style` should be a dictionary consisting of a selector and a property. `table_styles` can be used to define custom action-based styles. For example, the following style gives the selected cell the `lawngreen` background color:

```
df.style.set_table_styles([{'selector': 'tr:hover','props': [('background-
color', 'lawngreen')]}])
```

This results in the following output:

	PassengerId	Survived	Pclass	Name	Sex	Age	SibSp	Parch	Ticket	Fare	Cabin	Embarked
0	1	0	3	Braund, Mr. Owen Harris	male	22	1	0	A/5 21171	7.25	nan	S
1	2	1	1	Cumings, Mrs. John Bradley (Florence Briggs Thayer)	female	38	1	0	PC 17599	71.2833	C85	C
2	3	1	3	Heikkinen, Miss. Laina	female	26	0	0	STON/O2. 3101282	7.925	nan	S
3	4	1	1	Futrelle, Mrs. Jacques Heath (Lily May Peel)	female	35	1	0	113803	53.1	C123	S
4	5	0	3	Allen, Mr. William Henry	male	35	0	0	373450	8.05	nan	S
5	6	0	3	Moran, Mr. James	male	nan	0	0	330877	8.4583	nan	Q
6	7	0	1	McCarthy, Mr. Timothy J	male	54	0	0	17463	51.8625	E46	S
7	8	0	3	Palsson, Master. Gosta Leonard	male	2	3	1	349909	21.075	nan	S
8	9	1	3	Johnson, Mrs. Oscar W (Elisabeth Vilhelmina Berg)	female	27	0	2	347742	11.1333	nan	S
9	10	1	2	Nasser, Mrs. Nicholas (Adele Achem)	female	14	1	0	237736	30.0708	nan	C

table_style output showing a lawngreen background color for the selected cell

The `hide_index` and `hide_columns` styling options allow us to hide either the index or specified columns when they're displayed. In the following code, we have hidden the default index column:

```
df.style.hide_index()
```

The following screenshot shows the output DataFrame, without its index:

PassengerId	Survived	Pclass	Name	Sex	Age	SibSp	Parch	Ticket	Fare	Cabin	Embarked
1	0	3	Braund, Mr. Owen Harris	male	22	1	0	A/5 21171	7.25	nan	S
2	1	1	Cumings, Mrs. John Bradley (Florence Briggs Thayer)	female	38	1	0	PC 17599	71.2833	C85	C
3	1	3	Heikkinen, Miss. Laina	female	26	0	0	STON/O2. 3101282	7.925	nan	S
4	1	1	Futrelle, Mrs. Jacques Heath (Lily May Peel)	female	35	1	0	113803	53.1	C123	S
5	0	3	Allen, Mr. William Henry	male	35	0	0	373450	8.05	nan	S
6	0	3	Moran, Mr. James	male	nan	0	0	330877	8.4583	nan	Q
7	0	1	McCarthy, Mr. Timothy J	male	54	0	0	17463	51.8625	E46	S
8	0	3	Palsson, Master. Gosta Leonard	male	2	3	1	349909	21.075	nan	S
9	1	3	Johnson, Mrs. Oscar W (Elisabeth Vilhelmina Berg)	female	27	0	2	347742	11.1333	nan	S
10	1	2	Nasser, Mrs. Nicholas (Adele Achem)	female	14	1	0	237736	30.0708	nan	C

Hiding the Index column from an output DataFrame

Now, let's use the `hide_columns` option to hide the `"Name"`, `"Sex"`, `"Ticket"`, and `"Cabin"` columns:

```
df.style.hide_columns(["Name", "Sex", "Ticket", "Cabin"])
```

The following screenshot displays the columns that are shown after hiding a few columns from a DataFrame:

	PassengerId	Survived	Pclass	Age	SibSp	Parch	Fare	Embarked
0	1	0	3	22	1	0	7.25	S
1	2	1	1	38	1	0	71.2833	C
2	3	1	3	26	0	0	7.925	S
3	4	1	1	35	1	0	53.1	S
4	5	0	3	35	0	0	8.05	S
5	6	0	3	nan	0	0	8.4583	Q
6	7	0	1	54	0	0	51.8625	S
7	8	0	3	2	3	1	21.075	S
8	9	1	3	27	0	2	11.1333	S
9	10	1	2	14	1	0	30.0708	C
10	11	1	3	4	1	1	16.7	S

Hiding a number of columns from an output DataFrame

User-defined styling options

Apart from the in-built functions, pandas provides us with the option to write our own functions to be used for styling. Let's write a function to change the background color of negative values to red:

```
def color_negative(val):
    color = 'red' if val < 0 else 'green'
    return 'background-color: %s' % color
```

Such functions can be applied as a styling option through the apply() and applymap methods of pandas. The applymap method applies the function elementwise. The apply() method can be used to apply styles either row-wise or column-wise by setting the axis parameter to 1 or 0. Setting the axis to None applies the function table-wise. Here, our intended operation is elementwise. Let's use applymap:

```
rand_df.style.applymap(color_negative)
```

This results in the following output:

	0	1	2	3	4
0	-0.99303	0.959721	-0.865392	-1.72574	0.885758
1	1.69963	-0.515173	-1.00009	-0.829903	-0.384537
2	0.749428	0.895125	-2.07574	0.0186005	1.27577
3	1.16704	-1.47523	0.729561	0.362731	0.324559
4	0.273424	-0.53815	0.137174	-0.686177	0.453571

Customized conditional formatting based on user-defined styling options for all the columns

The `apply()` and `applymap` methods also allow us to style a slice of the data. The columns to be styled can be passed through the subset parameter as a list. Let's try to apply the styling to columns 1 and 3:

```
rand_df.style.applymap(color_negative, subset = [1, 3])
```

This results in the following output:

	0	1	2	3	4
0	-0.99303	0.959721	-0.865392	-1.72574	0.885758
1	1.69963	-0.515173	-1.00009	-0.829903	-0.384537
2	0.749428	0.895125	-2.07574	0.0186005	1.27577
3	1.16704	-1.47523	0.729561	0.362731	0.324559
4	0.273424	-0.53815	0.137174	-0.686177	0.453571

Customized conditional formatting based on user-defined styling options for a subset of columns

This can also be done by passing a suitable label-based indexer. In the following, the styling has been done for columns 1 and 4 on rows 0, 1, and 2:

```
rand_df.style.applymap(color_negative, subset=pd.IndexSlice[0:2, [1, 4]])
```

This results in the following output:

	0	1	2	3	4
0	-0.99303	0.959721	-0.865392	-1.72574	0.885758
1	1.69963	-0.515173	-1.00009	-0.829903	-0.384537
2	0.749428	0.895125	-2.07574	0.0186005	1.27577
3	1.16704	-1.47523	0.729561	0.362731	0.324559
4	0.273424	-0.53815	0.137174	-0.686177	0.453571

Customized conditional formatting based on user-defined styling options for a subset of rows and columns

The `format()` function allows the string to be formatted as specified. The following code shows formatting being applied to display restricted digits:

```
rand_df.style.format("{:.2f}")
```

This results in the following output:

	0	1	2	3	4
0	-0.99	0.96	-0.87	-1.73	0.89
1	1.70	-0.52	-1.00	-0.83	-0.38
2	0.75	0.90	-2.08	0.02	1.28
3	1.17	-1.48	0.73	0.36	0.32
4	0.27	-0.54	0.14	-0.69	0.45

Figure 9.17: Applying the same 2-decimal-place digit formatting on all the columns

Separate formats can be applied to different columns, as shown here:

```
rand_df.style.format({0: "{:.3%}", 3: '{:.2f}'})
```

This results in the following output:

	0	1	2	3	4
0	-99.303%	0.959721	-0.865392	-1.73	0.885758
1	169.963%	-0.515173	-1.00009	-0.83	-0.384537
2	74.943%	0.895125	-2.07574	0.02	1.27577
3	116.704%	-1.47523	0.729561	0.36	0.324559
4	27.342%	-0.53815	0.137174	-0.69	0.453571

Figure 9.18: Applying different formatting to different columns via a styling dictionary with column indices as keys and formatting options as values

The `lambda` function can be used to apply formatting conditions across multiple columns:

```
rand_df.style.format(lambda x: "±{:.2f}".format(abs(x)))
```

This results in the following output:

	0	1	2	3	4
0	±0.99	±0.96	±0.87	±1.73	±0.89
1	±1.70	±0.52	±1.00	±0.83	±0.38
2	±0.75	±0.90	±2.08	±0.02	±1.28
3	±1.17	±1.48	±0.73	±0.36	±0.32
4	±0.27	±0.54	±0.14	±0.69	±0.45

Figure 9.19: Applying lambda functions to style several columns at once

Navigating Jupyter Notebook

Jupyter Notebook, known as **IPython Notebook** previously, is a wonderful tool for reporting. It allows us to integrate regular code with rich styling, formatting, markdown, and special text such as equation plots and live coding. This section will help you understand the essence of a Jupyter Notebook.

Jupyter Notebook can be launched through Anaconda Navigator or from the Terminal using the Jupyter Notebook command. It opens in the browser. The following window opens on startup:

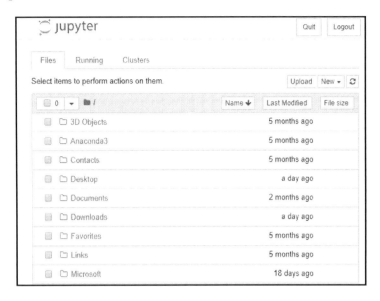

Figure 9.20: Startup screen once a Jupyter Notebook loads up

A Jupyter Notebook can be created in any of the folders in the directory. The **New** option creates a new notebook, folder, or Terminal. The most interesting feature of this option is that it allows us to shift between multiple Conda environments with ease. For example, both Python 2 and Python 3 environments can be accessed through Jupyter, if installed already. Any notebooks in other directories can be transferred to the current working directory of Jupyter Notebook through the **Upload** option.

A notebook consists of a menu bar, a toolbar, and a cell area. A single notebook can comprise of multiple cells:

Figure 9.21: Menu bar and toolbar in Jupyter Notebook

Exploring the menu bar of Jupyter Notebook

The menu bar provides options that allow us to control the kernel and notebook area. The **File** menu helps create new notebooks, open saved notebooks, save checkpoints in the notebook, and revert to a previously saved stable version of a checkpoint. The **Edit** menu consists of a range of actions to be performed on entire cells: copying cells, deleting cells, splitting or merging cells, and moving cells up and down. The **View** menu can be used to toggle headers, line numbers, and the toolbar, and edit metadata, attachments, and tags. Cells can be inserted above or below existing cells from the **Insert** menu. The **Cell** menu allows us to run either a single cell or multiple cells together. The Kernel state can be modified through the **Kernel** menu. This includes clearing output, restarting the kernel, interrupting the kernel, and shutting down the kernel. Jupyter notebook allows us to create and use widgets. The **Widget** menu helps us save, clear, download widget states, and embed widgets in HTML content. The **Help** menu offers quick references and shortcuts.

Edit mode and command mode

A Jupyter Notebook can either be in edit mode or command mode. When in edit mode, the contents of a cell can be changed; the cell gets highlighted in green, as shown in the following screenshot:

Edit mode of a cell in Jupyter Notebook

You will then notice a pencil icon appear in the top right corner:

Edit mode of a cell in Jupyter Notebooks

Edit mode can be entered by clicking on a cell or by pressing *Enter* on the keyboard.

The *Esc* key helps us switch from edit mode to command mode. This can also be done by clicking anywhere outside a cell. A gray boundary around the cell with a blue margin on the left indicates command mode:

Command mode for a cell in Jupyter Notebooks

Command mode allows us to edit the entire notebook, while edit mode serves more like a text editor. The *Enter* key helps us enter edit mode when we're in command mode. Several keyboard shortcuts are available in edit mode and command mode. Command mode is mapped to a higher number of shortcuts than edit mode:

Keyboard shortcuts

Command Mode (press `Esc` to enable)   Edit Shortcuts

`F` : find and replace	`Shift-Down` : extend selected cells below
`Ctrl-Shift-F` : open the command palette	`Shift-J` : extend selected cells below
`Ctrl-Shift-P` : open the command palette	`A` : insert cell above
`Enter` : enter edit mode	`B` : insert cell below
`P` : open the command palette	`X` : cut selected cells
`Shift-Enter` : run cell, select below	`C` : copy selected cells
`Ctrl-Enter` : run selected cells	`Shift-V` : paste cells above
`Alt-Enter` : run cell and insert below	`V` : paste cells below
`Y` : change cell to code	`Z` : undo cell deletion
`M` : change cell to markdown	`D` , `D` : delete selected cells
`R` : change cell to raw	`Shift-M` : merge selected cells, or current
`1` : change cell to heading 1	cell with cell below if only one
`2` : change cell to heading 2	cell is selected
`3` : change cell to heading 3	`Ctrl-S` : Save and Checkpoint
`4` : change cell to heading 4	`S` : Save and Checkpoint
`5` : change cell to heading 5	`L` : toggle line numbers

Keyboard shortcuts in Command mode

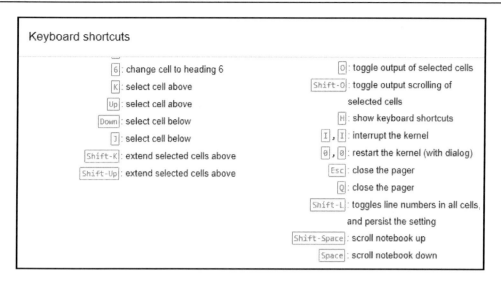

Keyboard shortcuts in Command mode – 2

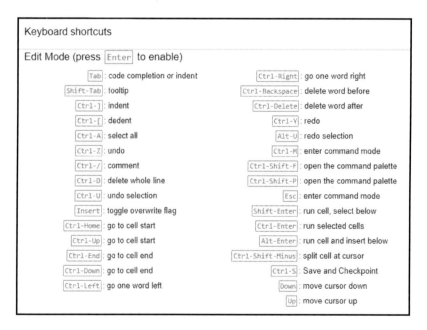

Keyboard shortcuts in Edit mode

The keyboard shortcuts in the preceding screenshots help us navigate Jupyter Notebook.

Mouse navigation

The most basic action that is involved when navigating via the mouse is clicking a cell to select and edit it. Further navigation via the mouse is aided by the toolbar options. The different options that are available in the toolbar are as follows:

- 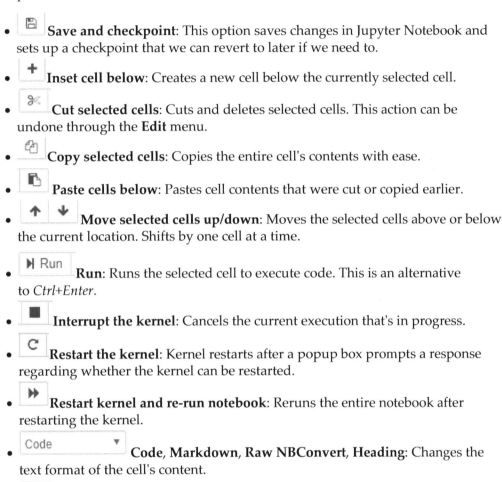 **Save and checkpoint**: This option saves changes in Jupyter Notebook and sets up a checkpoint that we can revert to later if we need to.

- **Inset cell below**: Creates a new cell below the currently selected cell.

- **Cut selected cells**: Cuts and deletes selected cells. This action can be undone through the **Edit** menu.

- **Copy selected cells**: Copies the entire cell's contents with ease.

- **Paste cells below**: Pastes cell contents that were cut or copied earlier.

- **Move selected cells up/down**: Moves the selected cells above or below the current location. Shifts by one cell at a time.

- **Run**: Runs the selected cell to execute code. This is an alternative to *Ctrl+Enter*.

- **Interrupt the kernel**: Cancels the current execution that's in progress.

- **Restart the kernel**: Kernel restarts after a popup box prompts a response regarding whether the kernel can be restarted.

- **Restart kernel and re-run notebook**: Reruns the entire notebook after restarting the kernel.

- **Code, Markdown, Raw NBConvert, Heading**: Changes the text format of the cell's content.

- **Open command palette**: Displays the shortcut options that are available.

Jupyter Notebook Dashboard

Jupyter offers an interactive reporting ability through Jupyter Dashboard. It allows the creation of widgets to make visualizations more interactive. The dashboard experience transforms code-laden notebooks into an application with a user-friendly interface.

Ipywidgets

Widgets are an integral part of the Jupyter Dashboard. The following section explores `Ipywidgets` in greater detail. First, the widgets should be imported from the `Ipywidgets` library:

```
from ipywidgets import widgets
```

The following screenshot shows how a widget for text input is created:

```
text = widgets.Text()
display(text)
```

Widget to get a text input

Now, let's print the value that was entered in the widget:

```
text = widgets.Text()
display(text)

def text_handler(sender):
    print(text.value)

text.on_submit(text_handler)
```

my test text

```
my test text
```

Figure 9.39: Widget to get a text input with printed output

Using similar methods, other widgets can be created. The following screenshot shows a **Button** widget:

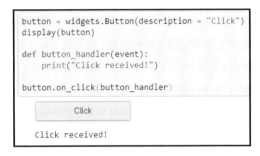

```
button = widgets.Button(description = "Click")
display(button)

def button_handler(event):
    print("Click received!")

button.on_click(button_handler)
```

```
        Click
    Click received!
```

Creating a Click button widget

Any widget has two parts: the UI and the event handler. The event handler is usually a Python script that instructs us about the response we should provide to the user input. In the preceding examples, the event handler printed a message based on the user's input.

Unlike the default widgets, `interact` is a special kind that chooses the form of the widget based on the user input. In the following screenshot, a single value was provided to the function by the widget. The interactive widget decided to create a slider input:

```
def int_func(val):
    print(val)

interact(int_func, val = 10)
            val  ━━━━━○━━━━━     10
    10
```

Creating a value slider widget

Now, let's change the input to Boolean, that is, True. The widget becomes a checkbox:

```
def int_func(val):
    print(val)

interact(int_func, val = True)
```
☑ val

True

Creating a Boolean selector widget

Interactive visualizations

The widgets in the preceding example were simple and delivered a `print` command. Instead of the `print` command, the response could be harnessed through a visualization.

The following is an example where two inputs from two different slider inputs are used to control the axes and inputs to a line plot:

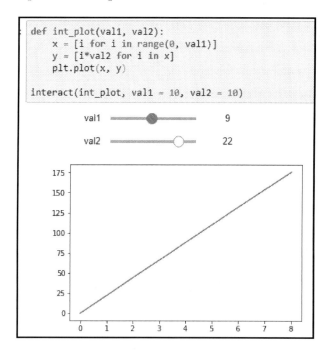

```
def int_plot(val1, val2):
    x = [i for i in range(0, val1)]
    y = [i*val2 for i in x]
    plt.plot(x, y)

interact(int_plot, val1 = 10, val2 = 10)
```

Two slider inputs with a plot reflecting the changes in values

The following is an example of an interactive visualization with a Seaborn plot, where the user can alter the legends and variables that color the plot:

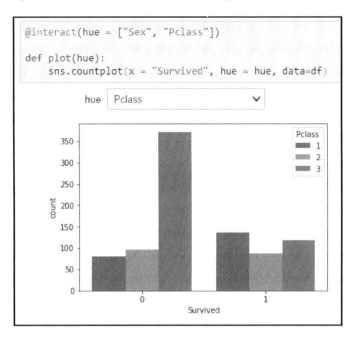

Drop-down selector widget for choosing the coloring variable

Writing mathematical equations in Jupyter Notebook

Jupyter Notebook is a comprehensive tool for making powerful reports and tutorials involving complex mathematical expressions and algorithms. This is because Jupyter Notebook provides powerful typesetting features for text formatting and mathematical equation typing. Jupyter Notebook cells with these features are called Markdown cells, as opposed to Code cells, where code is written and executed. Typesetting in Jupyter Notebook is derived from the versatile JavaScript library called **MathJax** used for typing scientific equations in web products. It also supports LaTex syntaxes, in fact, most syntax we are going to discuss.

In this section, we are going to discuss how to write these equations and format text. We will start with a quick walkthrough regarding how to write mathematical equations.

Some high-level guidelines to keep in mind while writing equations in Jupyter Notebook are as follows:

- Select the cell type as **Markdown**, as shown in the following screenshot. It is `Code` by default for a new cell.
- Enclose the equation between $$.
- Keywords and symbols such as frac (fractions), times (multiplication), leq (less than or equal to), alpha, beta, and others are preceded by a backward slash, \.
- Note that double-clicking on a rendered Markdown cell takes it back to the LaTex/MathJax code snippet:

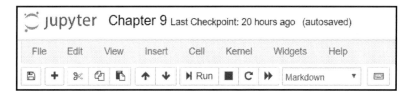

Selecting the cell type as Markdown

With these instructions in mind, let's start learning how to write equations. This section has been written in a cookbook format where we will see the LaTex/MathJax snippet source followed by the output equation.

Simple mathematical operations such as addition, multiplication, division, and so on can be written as follows. \times and \over are the keywords for the multiplication and division operators. Note how equations begin and end with $$:

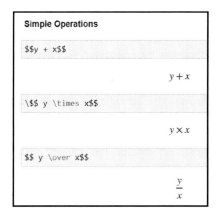

LaTex snippet and output equations for simple mathematical operations

Power and exponential operations can be written as follows. ^ is the power or exponential symbol in LaTex syntax:

Powers

```
$$ x^2 + x^3 + 2x $$
```

$$x^2 + x^3 + 2x$$

```
$$ e^{2+3y^2+5y}$$
```

$$e^{2+3y^2+5y}$$

```
$$ e^{1 \over 2y + 3y^2} $$
```

$$e^{\frac{1}{2y+3y^2}}$$

LaTex snippet and output equations for power and exponential operations

Often, mathematical equations involve complex fractions. These can be written as follows. The \frac keyword gives us more flexibility when it comes to writing complex fractions:

Fractions

```
$$(y^3 + y )/ x^2$$
```

$$(y^3 + y)/x^2$$

```
$$ \frac {x^2 + 3}  {x^3 + x^2 + 4}$$
```

$$\frac{x^2 + 3}{x^3 + x^2 + 4}$$

LaTex snippet and output equations for fraction operations

Now, let's look at how inequalities can be written. The keywords to note here are `\geq` and `\leq`, which stand for greater than or equal to and less than or equal to, respectively:

LaTex snippet and output equations for inequalities

Greek letters and symbols are heavily used in mathematical equations and expressions. Here, we have provided a glossary of symbols and the instructions we can use to write them. Notice how superscripts can be written by preceding them with _, that is, an underscore:

LaTex snippet and output equations for symbols and indices

Roots and logs are important components of mathematical equations. Let's look at how we can write them. \sqrt is the main keyword for roots and provides two parameters—the root type, that is, 2nd root, 3rd root, or 4th root, and the expression or the number on which the root is to be applied. For log, the base is preceded by _, that is, an underscore:

Roots and Logs

```
$$ D = \frac {\sqrt{b^2-4ac}} {2a} $$
```

$$D = \frac{\sqrt{b^2 - 4ac}}{2a}$$

```
$$ y = \frac {\sqrt[3]{x} + 5} {\sqrt[4]{x} + 3} $$
```

$$y = \frac{\sqrt[3]{x} + 5}{\sqrt[4]{x} + 3}$$

```
$$log_{10} 100 $$
```

$$log_{10} 100$$

```
$$log_{e} \theta^2 $$
```

$$log_e \theta^2$$

LaTex snippet and output equations for roots and logs

Often, we have to deal with summations and products across elements of data vectors. Let's look at how to write these. \sum and \prod are the main keywords and have a \limit attribute which takes inputs for the lower and upper bounds for the summation or product:

Algebraic Sum and Products

```
$$ Error = \sum \limits_{i=1}^{n} {(y_i - yhat_i)}^2 $$
```

$$Error = \sum\limits_{i=1}^{n} (y_i - yhat_i)^2$$

```
$$ L = \prod \limits_{i=1}^{n} {\frac {e^\lambda * \lambda^i} {i!}} $$
```

$$L = \prod\limits_{i=1}^{n} \frac{e^\lambda * \lambda^i}{i!}$$

```
$$ \sum \limits_{i=1}^{m} \sum \limits_{j=i}^{n} {(a_{ij} + b_{ij})} $$
```

$$\sum\limits_{i=1}^{m} \sum\limits_{j=i}^{n} (a_{ij} + b_{ij})$$

LaTex snippet and output equations for summations and products

Combinations and statistics have their own set of symbols. Let's look at how to write them. \choose is the keyword for combinations:

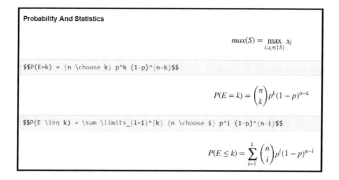

Probability And Statistics

$$max(S) = \max_{i: x_i \in \{S\}} x_i$$

$$P(E=k) = {n \choose k} p^k (1-p)^{n-k}$$

$$P(E = k) = \binom{n}{k} p^k (1-p)^{n-k}$$

$$P(E \leq k) = \sum \limits_{i=1}^{k} {n \choose i} p^i (1-p)^{n-i}$$

$$P(E \leq k) = \sum_{i=1}^{k} \binom{n}{i} p^i (1-p)^{n-i}$$

LaTex snippet and output equations for probability and statistics

Calculus is a vast field and is the source of many mathematical expressions and equations for many data science algorithms. \lim is the keyword we use to write limit expressions and supplies the \limits and \to parameter keywords to provide a variable tending to a value. The \partial keyword is used to write partial derivatives, while the \frac keyword is used to write normal derivatives. \int is used for writing integrals. It comes with the \limits parameter, which provides the lower and upper bounds of the integer:

$$ \lim \limits_{x \to 0} {\sin(x) \over x} = 1 $$

$$\lim_{x \to 0} \frac{\sin(x)}{x} = 1$$

$$ \int \limits_2^\infty e^x \, dx $$

$$\int_2^\infty e^x \, dx$$

$$ \frac {dZ} {dx}$$

$$\frac{dZ}{dx}$$

$$ \frac {d^2Z} {dx^2}$$

$$\frac{d^2Z}{dx^2}$$

$$ \frac {\partial Z} {\partial x}$$

$$\frac{\partial Z}{\partial x}$$

LaTex snippet and output equations for calculus

Linear algebra is used extensively in data science algorithms and we deal with a lot of matrices in linear algebra. Let's look at how we can write matrices. \matrix is the main keyword we use to write a matrix. Elements are written row-wise; those in the same row are separated by &, while a new row is marked by a line break symbol, that is, //:

Matrix

`$$ \begin{matrix} a & b \\ c & d \end{matrix} $$`

$$\begin{matrix} a & b \\ c & d \end{matrix}$$

`$$ A = \begin{bmatrix} X_{11} & X_{12} & X_{13} \\ X_{21} & X_{22} & X_{23} \\ X_{21} & X_{22} & X_{23} \end{bmatrix} $$`

$$A = \begin{bmatrix} X_{11} & X_{12} & X_{13} \\ X_{21} & X_{22} & X_{23} \\ X_{21} & X_{22} & X_{23} \end{bmatrix}$$

`$$ \begin{bmatrix} a & b \\ c & d \end{bmatrix}^T $$`

$$\begin{bmatrix} a & b \\ c & d \end{bmatrix}^T$$

LaTex snippet and output equations for matrices

It is also common to encounter functions that have different definitions across a different range of variable(s). Let's learn how to write these function definitions. The following is a high-level overview of the keywords and elements that are needed to write such definitions.

The following are the new formatting options that are used in multi-period functions:

- **Large Curly Bracket**: Uses the \left and \right keywords to denote the and the end respectively of an equation.
- **Equation Array Alignment**: begin{}, end{}.
- **Line Breaker**: Uses the \ symbol to take the text to the next line.
- **Text Alignment Box**: Uses \mbox{text} to align text.

They can be used as follows:

Multi-Period Functions

```
$$f(x) = \left\{\begin{array}{ll} ax & \mbox{if } x \leq 0 \\ x & \mbox{if } x > 0 \end{array} \right. $$
```

$$f(x) = \begin{cases} ax & \text{if } x \leq 0 \\ x & \text{if } x > 0 \end{cases}$$

```
$$ \begin{align}
\dot{x} & = \sigma(y-x) \\
\dot{y} & = \rho x - y - xz \\
\dot{z} & = -\beta z + xy
\end{align} $$
```

$$\dot{x} = \sigma(y - x)$$
$$\dot{y} = \rho x - y - xz$$
$$\dot{z} = -\beta z + xy$$

```
$$f(x) = \left\{\begin{array}{ll} -x & \mbox{if } x \leq -5 \\ -5 & \mbox{if } -5 < x \leq 5 \\ x & \mbox{if} x \geq 5 \end{array} \right. $$
```

$$f(x) = \begin{cases} -x & \text{if } x \leq -5 \\ -5 & \text{if } -5 < x \leq 5 \\ x & \text{if} x \geq 5 \end{cases}$$

LaTex snippet and output equations for multi-period functions

Formatting text in Jupyter Notebook

Markdown cells come with a lot of options for formatting text. In this section, we will go through these options one by one.

Headers

Text can be specified as a header by preceding any text with # in a markdown cell. One # means Header 1, two # means Header 2, and so on. This shown in the following screenshot. We follow the same format as the LaTex snippet source, followed by the output formatted text:

LaTex snippet and output formatted text for headers

Bold and italics

To format text as bold, enclose it within `**`, for example, `**<text>**`.

To format text as italics, enclose it within `*`, for example, `*<text>*`:

LaTex snippet and output formatted text for bold and italics formatting

Alignment

Text can be centrally aligned by using an HTML-like `<center>` tag, as follows:

```
<center> **Bold** *Italic* </center>

                                              Bold Italic
```

LaTex snippet and output formatted text for alignment

Font color

The font color for text can be specified as follows. It has to be written inside another HTML-like `<font>` tag:

LaTex snippet and output formatted text for font color

Bulleted lists

Bullet lists can be created by preceding a list item by an asterisk, *, and a space. The list can be nested as well, as shown in the following screenshot:

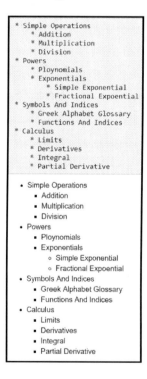

LaTex snippet and output formatted text for bulleted lists

Tables

Tables can be created by using a combination of |, spaces, ---, and :. They are as follows:

- |: Used as a column separator.
- **Spaces**: For padding and aligning columns and rows.
- ---: For creating a solid horizontal line.
- :: For text alignment in a cell. If it appears at the beginning, then the text is left-aligned:

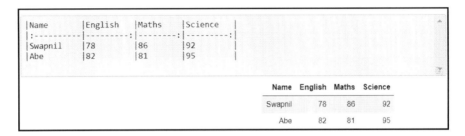

LaTex snippet and output formatted text for tables

Tables

Horizontal lines are used to separate sections from one another. *** results in a normal horizontal line while − − − provides a solid horizontal line:

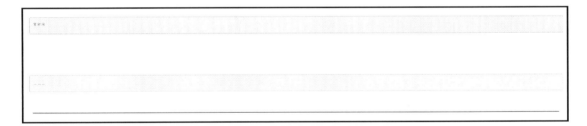

LaTex snippet and output formatted text for tables

HTML

Markdown cells can be used to render code as well, as shown in the following screenshot:

```
<dl>
  <dt>Definition list</dt>
  <dd>Is something people use sometimes.</dd>

  <dt>Markdown in HTML</dt>
  <dd>Does *not* work **very** well. Use HTML <em>tags</em>.</dd>
</dl>
```

Definition list
Is something people use sometimes.
Markdown in HTML
Does *not* work **very** well. Use HTML *tags*.

LaTex snippet and output formatted text for HTML

Citation

Quotes and excerpts need to be cited in reports on many occasions. This is done by starting each line of the text with >. This results in indented text and a citation at the end:

```
> Look again at that dot. That's here. That's home. That's us. On it everyone you love, everyone you know, everyone you
> ever heard of, every human being who ever was, lived out their lives. The aggregate of our joy and suffering, thousands
> of confident religions, ideologies, and economic doctrines, every hunter and forager, every hero and coward, every creator
> and destroyer of civilization, every king and peasant, every young couple in love, every mother and father, hopeful child,
> inventor and explorer, every teacher of morals, every corrupt politician, every "superstar," every "supreme leader," every
> saint and sinner in the history of our species lived there--on a mote of dust suspended in a sunbeam.

> The Earth is a very small stage in a vast cosmic arena. Think of the rivers of blood spilled by all those generals and
emperors
> so that, in glory and triumph, they could become the momentary masters of a fraction of a dot. Think of the endless cruelties
> visited by the inhabitants of one corner of this pixel on the scarcely distinguishable inhabitants of some other corner, how
> frequent their misunderstandings, how eager they are to kill one another, how fervent their hatreds.

<cite> Carl Sagan, Pale Blue Dot, 1994 </cite>
```

> Look again at that dot. That's here. That's home. That's us. On it everyone you love, everyone you know, everyone you ever heard of, every human being who ever was, lived out their lives. The aggregate of our joy and suffering, thousands of confident religions, ideologies, and economic doctrines, every hunter and forager, every hero and coward, every creator and destroyer of civilization, every king and peasant, every young couple in love, every mother and father, hopeful child, inventor and explorer, every teacher of morals, every corrupt politician, every "superstar," every "supreme leader," every saint and sinner in the history of our species lived there--on a mote of dust suspended in a sunbeam.

> The Earth is a very small stage in a vast cosmic arena. Think of the rivers of blood spilled by all those generals and emperors so that, in glory and triumph, they could become the momentary masters of a fraction of a dot. Think of the endless cruelties visited by the inhabitants of one corner of this pixel on the scarcely distinguishable inhabitants of some other corner, how frequent their misunderstandings, how eager they are to kill one another, how fervent their hatreds.

Carl Sagan, Pale Blue Dot, 1994

LaTex snippet and output formatted text for citation and indented text

Miscellaneous operations in Jupyter Notebook

Apart from text formatting and equations, some miscellaneous operations such as loading an image, writing a cell to a Python file, and other are needed to make effective reports. In this section, we will look at these operations and learn how to use them.

Loading an image

Most popular image formats, such as `.viz`, `.jpg`, `.png`, `.gif`, and so on, can be loaded into Jupyter Notebooks to better illustrate reports. A `.gif` can even be loaded and shown as an animation.

These image files need to be kept in the current working directory. The current working directory can be found by running `os.getcwd( )` in a code block in the notebook. Images to be loaded should be kept in this directory. The working directory can be changed by using `os.chdir` (the directory path). Note that these commands assume that `import os` has already been run. The following code is used to show a `.jpg` image, as well as its output:

LaTex snippet and output .jpg image

The following code is used to show a `.gif` image, as well as its output:

LaTex snippet and output .gif image

Hyperlinks

Hyperlinking is frequently used to navigate users to relevant resources such as input data, algorithm explanations, further readings, videos, and more. The syntax to do this is quite simple:

```
![Text to appear](URL to navigate to)
```

This results in the following output:

```
#### Get [Facebook Live Sellers in Thailand Data Set ](http://archive.ics.uci.edu/ml/datasets/Facebook+Live+Sellers+in+Thailand) here.

Get Facebook Live Sellers in Thailand Data Set here.

#### Get [Metro Interstate Traffic Volume Data Set ](http://archive.ics.uci.edu/ml/datasets/Metro+Interstate+Traffic+Volume) here.

Get Metro Interstate Traffic Volume Data Set here.
```

LaTex snippet and output hyperlinks

Writing to a Python file

The contents of a code cell(s) can be written to a Python file. This is quite helpful while taking code from prototyping in Jupyter Notebook to production environments in Python files. These files are written to the current working directory:

```
%%file input_cumsum.py
input_num=[]
i=0
while len(input_num) < 5:
    a = int(input('Please enter a number'))
    input_num.append(a)

tot=0
for item in input_num:
    tot += item
print(tot)

Overwriting input_cumsum.py
```

Figure 9.69: LaTex snippet for writing a code cell to a Python file

Running a Python file

External Python files can be run directly from within Jupyter Notebooks. This can be used to load functions and classes that have been saved in Python files so that they can be used later in the notebook. They can also be used to run Python files without having to use the command prompt and so that we can see the output quickly. Again, these Python files need to be present in the current working directory:

```
%run input_cumsum.py

Please enter a number2
Please enter a number3
Please enter a number4
Please enter a number5
Please enter a number6
20
```

LaTex snippet and output after running a Python file from a cell in Jupyter Notebook

Loading a Python file

The contents of a Python file can be loaded into a notebook cell. This is done to edit, modify, and test code from the interactive notebook environment:

```
%load input_cumsum.py

# %load input_cumsum.py
input_num=[]
i=0
while len(input_num) < 5:
    a = int(input('Please enter a number'))
    input_num.append(a)

tot=0
for item in input_num:
    tot += item
print(tot)
```

LaTex snippet and output after loading a Python file from a cell in Jupyter Notebook

Internal Links

Internal (hyper)links can be created to navigate to different sections of a notebook from a context summary index. Clicking on the items in the index takes you to a specific section once the internal linking has been done.

Making internal links work in a Jupyter Notebook consists of two steps:

1. Create an ID or identifier for a section:

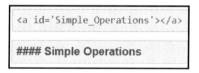

```
<a id='Simple_Operations'></a>

#### Simple Operations
```

LaTex snippet to create an ID identifier for a section

The ID for a section is provided in the <a> tag. In this case, Simple_Operations is the ID for the Simple Operations section. This ID would be used to refer to this section in the second step while creating the link.

On running the two preceding cells, the following is provided as output. The first cell containing the ID definition becomes invisible. Make sure this cell has been run before clicking on the hyperlink. If it has not been run, the link will not work. Another important point to note is that this ID definition needs to happen just before we create the section header:

```
Simple Operations
```

Output of the LaTex snippet creating an ID identifier for a section

2. Use this ID to create an internal link.

The syntax for creating an internal link is as follows:

```
[Text to Appear](#Section ID)
```

For example, for the **Simple Operations** section, we need to do the following:

```
* [Simple Operations](#Simple_Operations)
```
• Simple Operations

LaTex snippet and output after creating an internal link

Note how **Simple Operations** now appears as a hyperlink. Clicking on this would take the user to the **Simple Operations** section.

Similarly, we can define section IDs for all the other sections:

```
<a id='Simple_Operations'></a>
<a id='Powers'></a>
<a id='Fractions'></a>
<a id='Inequalities'></a>
<a id='Symbols_Indices'></a>
<a id='Roots_Logs'></a>
<a id='Sum_Products'></a>
<a id='Prob_Stats'></a>
<a id='Calculus'></a>
<a id='Matrix'></a>
<a id='MPFunctions'></a>
```

LaTex snippet for different section IDs

Please note that the section ID definition should happen immediately before the section header markdown cell to mark the section ID definition cell as the beginning of that section. This has been shown as the bulk definition, just for illustration purposes:

```
#### Content
* [Simple Operations](#Simple_Operations) <br>
* [Powers](#Powers) <br>
* [Fractions](#Fractions) <br>
* [Inequalities](#Inequalities) <br>
* [Symbols And Indices](#Symbols_Indices) <br>
* [Roots And Logs](#Roots_Logs) <br>
* [Sums And Products](#Sum_Products) <br>
* [Probability And Statistics](#Prob_Stats) <br>
* [Calculus](#Calculus) <br>
* [Special Functions](#MPFunctions) <br>
```

LaTex snippet for different internal links referring to section IDs

Notice how the `<br>` tag has been used at the end of each line. This tag denotes a line break and takes the text that appears after it to the next line:

Content

- Simple Operations
- Powers
- Fractions
- Inequalities
- Symbols And Indices
- Roots And Logs
- Sums And Products
- Probability And Statistics
- Calculus
- Special Functions

LaTex output for different internal links referring to section IDs

Sharing Jupyter Notebook reports

Once reports have been created, they need to shared to their audience for consumption. There are several options for sharing these reports. Let's take a look at these options now.

Using NbViewer

NbViewer is an online viewer for `ipynb` files. The following steps need to be followed if we wish to use this option to share Jupyter Notebook reports:

1. Save the report as an `ipynb` file.
2. Upload the `ipynb` file to GitHub and get the URL for this file.
3. Paste the URL from *Step 2* into NbViewer. NbViewer can be accessed from `www.nbviewer.jupyter.org`.
4. Use this GitHub URL where we shared the Notebook that we used in this chapter: `https://github.com/ashishbt08b004/Experiments/blob/master/writing_equations_in_jupyter.ipynb`.

Using the browser

Reports can also be saved as HTML files. These HTML files can be viewed directly in any normal browser by double-clicking them and choosing a browser as the default program for HTML files. One such example file can be obtained at this link. `https://github.com/ashishbt08b004/Experiments/blob/master/writing_equations_in_jupyter.html`.

Using Jupyter Hub

Jupyter Hub is a Python program that can be used to deploy and share Jupyter Notebook reports to multiple users. It can be thought of as a multi-user version of the normal Jupyter Notebook and is accessible through URLs; it is frequently used by companies, research groups, and course instructors to share their experiments and knowledge with a large group in an interactive environment.

This works on Linux machines and is mostly deployed on a machine with huge computing power. This can be either a cloud or on-premise machine.

Four subsystems make up JupyterHub:

- A **Hub** (tornado process), which is the heart of JupyterHub.
- A **configurable http proxy** (node-http-proxy) that receives requests from the client's browser.

- Multiple **single-user Jupyter notebook servers** (Python/IPython/tornado) that are monitored by spawners.
- An **authentication class** that manages how users can access the system:

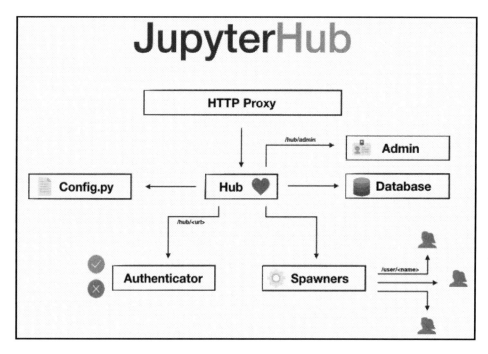

Jupyter Hub architecture

There are a few prerequisites for installing Jupyter Hub:

- A Linux machine (cloud or on-premise)
- Python 3.5+
- Nodejs/npm
- TLS certificate and the key for HTTPS communication
- Domain name for the machine/server

Jupyter Hub gives a server-client kind of multi-user environment where data and `ipynb` files can be shared with multiple users. It provides multiple robust features for security and login authentication.

The following guides can be followed for the installation and deployment of a notebook report for multiple users: `https://tljh.jupyter.org/en/latest/`.

Summary

This chapter focused on three main themes: styling and result formatting options in pandas, creating interactive dashboards in Jupyter Notebook, and exploring formatting and typesetting options in Jupyter Notebook to create powerful reports.

Output formatting such as conditional formatting, bold and italics output, highlighting certain sections, and so on can be done by styling options in pandas. Basic interactive dashboards can be created in Jupyter Notebook. LaTex, and MathJax and provide powerful typesetting and markdown options for writing equations and formatting text. Reports can be shared as `ipynb` files on GitHub, and can be viewed in an online viewer called **NbViewer**. Jupyter Hub is the multi-user server-based deployment method.

In the next chapter, we will look at how pandas can be used to perform statistical calculations using packages; we will also perform calculations from scratch.

A Tour of Statistics with pandas and NumPy

10

In this chapter, we'll take a brief tour of classical statistics (also called the frequentist approach) and show you how we can use pandas together with the `numpy` and `stats` packages, such as `scipy.stats` and `statsmodels`, to conduct statistical analysis. We will also learn how to write the calculations behind these statistics from scratch in Python. This chapter and the following ones are not intended to be primers on statistics; they just serve as an illustration of using pandas along with the `stats` and `numpy` packages. In the next chapter, we will examine an alternative approach to the classical view—that is, **Bayesian statistics**.

In this chapter, we will cover the following topics:

- Descriptive statistics versus inferential statistics
- Measures of central tendency and variability
- Hypothesis testing – the null and alternative hypotheses
- The z-test
- The t-test
- The chi-square test
- Analysis of variance (ANOVA) test
- Confidence intervals
- Correlation and linear regression

Descriptive statistics versus inferential statistics

In descriptive or summary statistics, we attempt to describe the features of a collection of data in a quantitative way. This is different from inferential or inductive statistics because its aim is to summarize a sample rather than use the data to infer or draw conclusions about the population from which the sample is drawn.

Measures of central tendency and variability

Some of the measures that are used in descriptive statistics include the measures of central tendency and measures of variability.

A measure of central tendency is a single value that attempts to describe a dataset by specifying a central position within the data. The three most common measures of central tendency are the **mean**, **median**, and **mode**.

A measure of variability is used to describe the variability in a dataset. Measures of variability include variance and standard deviation.

Measures of central tendency

Let's take a look at the measures of central tendency, along with illustrations of them, in the following subsections.

The mean

The mean or sample is the most popular measure of central tendency. It is equal to the sum of all the values in the dataset, divided by the number of values in the dataset. Thus, in a dataset of n values, the mean is calculated as follows:

$$\bar{x} = \frac{x_1 + x_2 + x_3 + ... + x_n}{n} = \frac{1}{n}\sum_{i=1}^{n} x_i$$

We use $\bar{x}$ if the data values are from a sample and $\mathbf{\mu}$ if the data values are from a population.

The sample mean and population mean are different. The sample mean is what is known as an unbiased estimator of the true population mean. By repeatedly randomly sampling the population to calculate the sample mean, we can obtain a mean of sample means. We can then invoke the law of large numbers and the **central limit theorem** (**CLT**) and denote the mean of the sample means as an estimate of the true population mean.

The population mean is also referred to as the expected value of the population.

The mean, as a calculated value, is often not one of the values observed in the dataset. The main drawback of using the mean is that it is very susceptible to outlier values, or if the dataset is very skewed.

The median

The median is the data value that divides the set of sorted data values into two halves. It has exactly half of the population to its left and the other half to its right. In the case when the number of values in the dataset is even, the median is the average of the two middle values. It is less affected by outliers and skewed data.

The mode

The mode is the most frequently occurring value in the dataset. It is more commonly used for categorical data so that we can find out which category is the most common. One downside to using the mode is that it is not unique. A distribution with two modes is described as bimodal, while one with many modes is described as multimodal. The following code is an illustration of a bimodal distribution with modes at two and seven, since they both occur four times in the dataset:

```
In [4]: import matplotlib.pyplot as plt
        %matplotlib inline
In [5]: plt.hist([7,0,1,2,3,7,1,2,3,4,2,7,6,5,2,1,6,8,9,7])
        plt.xlabel('x')
        plt.ylabel('Count')
        plt.title('Bimodal distribution')
        plt.show()
```

The generated bimodal distribution appears as follows:

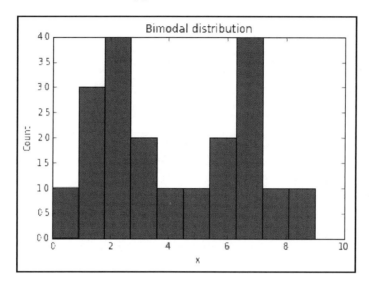

Computing the measures of central tendency of a dataset in Python

To illustrate this, let's consider the following dataset, which consists of marks that were obtained by 15 pupils for a test scored out of 20:

```
In [18]: grades = [10, 10, 14, 18, 18, 5, 10, 8, 1, 12, 14, 12, 13, 1, 18]
```

The mean, median, and mode can be obtained as follows:

```
In [29]: %precision 3  # Set output precision to 3 decimal places
Out[29]:u'%.3f'
In [30]: import numpy as np
         np.mean(grades)
Out[30]: 10.933
In [35]: %precision
         np.median(grades)
Out[35]: 12.0
In [24]: from scipy import stats
         stats.mode(grades)
Out[24]: (array([ 10.]), array([ 3.]))
In [39]: import matplotlib.pyplot as plt
In [40]: plt.hist(grades)
         plt.title('Histogram of grades')
```

```
plt.xlabel('Grade')
plt.ylabel('Frequency')
plt.show()
```

The following is the output of the preceding code:

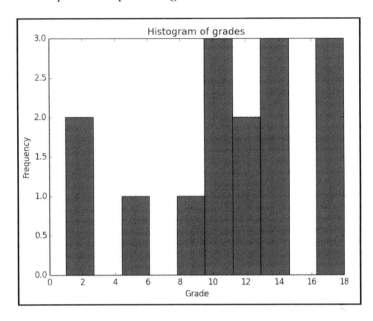

To illustrate how the skewness of data or an outlier value can drastically affect the usefulness of the mean as a measure of central tendency, consider the following dataset, which shows the wages (in thousands of dollars) of the staff at a factory:

```
In [45]: %precision 2
         salaries = [17, 23, 14, 16, 19, 22, 15, 18, 18, 93, 95]
In [46]: np.mean(salaries)
Out[46]: 31.82
```

Based on the mean value, we may make the assumption that the data is centered around the mean value of 31.82. However, we would be wrong. To explain why, let's display an empirical distribution of the data using a bar plot:

```
In [59]: fig = plt.figure()
         ax = fig.add_subplot(111)
         ind = np.arange(len(salaries))
         width = 0.2
         plt.hist(salaries, bins=xrange(min(salaries),
         max(salaries)).__len__())
         ax.set_xlabel('Salary')
         ax.set_ylabel('# of employees')
         ax.set_title('Bar chart of salaries')
         plt.show()
```

The following is the output of the preceding code:

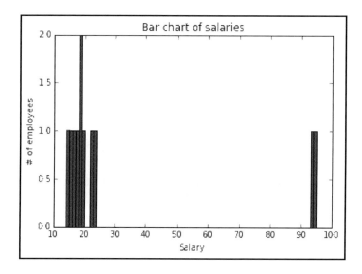

From the preceding bar plot, we can see that most of the salaries are far below 30K and that no one is close to the mean of 32K. Now, if we take a look at the median, we will see that it is a better measure of central tendency in this case:

```
In [47]: np.median(salaries)
Out[47]: 18.00
```

We can also take a look at a histogram of the data:

```
In [56]: plt.hist(salaries, bins=len(salaries))
         plt.title('Histogram of salaries')
         plt.xlabel('Salary')
         plt.ylabel('Frequency')
         plt.show()
```

The following is the output of the preceding code:

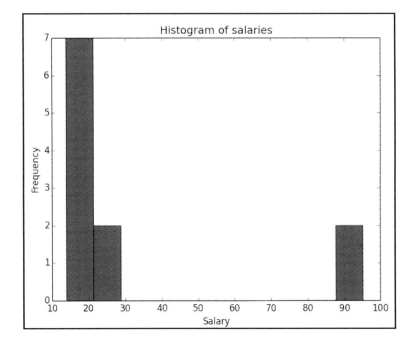

The histogram is actually a better representation of the data as bar plots are generally used to represent categorical data, while histograms are preferred for quantitative data, which is the case for the salaries data. For more information on when to use histograms versus bar plots, refer to http://onforb.es/1Dru2gv.

If the distribution is symmetrical and unimodal (that is, has only one mode), the three measures—mean, median, and mode—will be equal. This is not the case if the distribution is skewed. In that case, the mean and median will differ from each other. With a negatively skewed distribution, the mean will be lower than the median and vice versa for a positively skewed distribution:

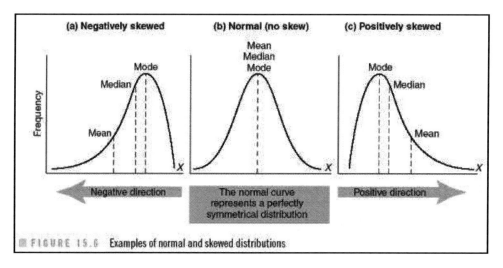

FIGURE 15.6   Examples of normal and skewed distributions

Diagram sourced from http://www.southalabama.edu/coe/bset/johnson/lectures/lec15_files/iage014.jpg.

Measures of variability, dispersion, or spread

Another characteristic of distribution that we measure in descriptive statistics is variability.

Variability specifies how much the data points are different from each other or dispersed. Measures of variability are important because they provide an insight into the nature of the data that is not provided by the measures of central tendency.

As an example, suppose we conduct a study to examine how effective a pre-K education program is in lifting test scores of economically disadvantaged children. We can measure the effectiveness not only in terms of the average value of the test scores of the entire sample, but also in terms of the dispersion of the scores. Is it useful for some students and not so much for others? The variability of the data may help us identify some steps to be taken to improve the usefulness of the program.

Range

The simplest measure of dispersion is the range. The range is the difference between the lowest and highest scores in a dataset. This is the simplest measure of spread, and can be calculated as follows:

$$Range = highest\ value - lowest\ value$$

Quartile

A more significant measure of dispersion is the quartile and related interquartile ranges. It also stands for *quarterly percentile*, which means that it is the value on the measurement scale below which 25, 50, 75, and 100 percent of the scores in the sorted dataset fall. The quartiles are three points that split the dataset into four groups, with each one containing one-fourth of the data. To illustrate this, suppose we have a dataset of 20 test scores that are ranked, as follows:

```
In [27]: import random
         random.seed(100)
         testScores = [random.randint(0,100) for p in
                       xrange(0,20)]
         testScores
Out[27]: [14, 45, 77, 71, 73, 43, 80, 53, 8, 46, 4, 94, 95, 33, 31, 77,
20, 18, 19, 35]
In [28]: #data needs to be sorted for quartiles
         sortedScores = np.sort(testScores)
In [30]: rankedScores = {i+1: sortedScores[i] for i in
                         xrange(len(sortedScores))}
In [31]: rankedScores
Out[31]:
{1: 4,
 2: 8,
 3: 14,
 4: 18,
 5: 19,
 6: 20,
 7: 31,
 8: 33,
 9: 35,
 10: 43,
 11: 45,
 12: 46,
 13: 53,
 14: 71,
 15: 73,
```

```
16: 77,
17: 77,
18: 80,
19: 94,
20: 95}
```

The first quartile (Q1) lies between the fifth and sixth score, the second quartile (Q2) lies between the tenth and eleventh score, and the third quartile (Q3) lies between the fifteenth and sixteenth score. Thus, we get the following results by using linear interpolation and calculating the midpoint:

```
Q1 = (19+20)/2 = 19.5
Q2 = (43 + 45)/2 = 44
Q3 = (73 + 77)/2 = 75
```

To see this in IPython, we can use the `scipy.stats` or `numpy.percentile` packages:

```
In [38]: from scipy.stats.mstats import mquantiles
         mquantiles(sortedScores)
Out[38]: array([ 19.45,   44.  ,   75.2 ])
In [40]: [np.percentile(sortedScores, perc) for perc in [25,50,75]]
Out[40]: [19.75, 44.0, 74.0]
```

The reason why the values don't match exactly with our previous calculations is due to the different interpolation methods. The interquartile range is the first quartile subtracted from the third quartile (*Q3 - Q1*). It represents the middle 50 in a dataset.

For more information on statistical measures, refer to `https://statistics.laerd.com/statistical-guides/measures-central-tendency-mean-mode-median.php`.
For more details on the `scipy.stats` and `numpy.percentile` functions, see the documents at `http://docs.scipy.org/doc/scipy/reference/generated/scipy.stats.mstats.mquantiles.html` and `http://docs.scipy.org/doc/numpy-dev/reference/generated/numpy.percentile.html`.

Deviation and variance

A fundamental idea in the discussion of variability is the concept of deviation. Simply put, a deviation measure tells us how far away a given value is from the mean of the distribution—that is, $x - \bar{x}$.

To find the deviation of a set of values, we define the variance as the sum of the squared deviations and normalize it by dividing it by the size of the dataset. This is referred to as the variance. We need to use the sum of the squared deviations. By taking the sum of the deviations around the mean results in 0, since the negative and positive deviations cancel each other out. The sum of the squared deviations is defined as follows:

$$SS = \sum_{i=1}^{N} (X - \bar{X})^2$$

The preceding expression is equivalent to the following:

$$SS = \sum_{i=1}^{N} X^2 - \frac{(\sum_{i=1}^{N} X)^2}{N}$$

Formally, the variance is defined as follows:

- For sample variance, use the following formula:

$$s^2 = \frac{SS}{N-1} = \frac{1}{N-1} \sum_{i=1}^{N} (X - \bar{X})^2$$

- For population variance, use the following formula:

$$\sigma^2 = \frac{SS}{N} = \frac{1}{N} \sum_{i=1}^{N} (X - \mu)^2$$

The reason why the denominator is *N-1* for the sample variance instead of *N* is that, for sample variance, we want to use an unbiased estimator. For more details on this, take a look at http://en.wikipedia.org/wiki/Bias_of_an_estimator.

The values of this measure are in squared units. This emphasizes the fact that what we have calculated as the variance is the squared deviation. Therefore, to obtain the deviation in the same units as the original points of the dataset, we must take the square root, and this gives us what we call the standard deviation. Thus, the standard deviation of a sample is given by using the following formula:

$$s = \sqrt{\frac{SS}{N-1}} = \sqrt{\frac{\sum (X - \bar{X})^2}{N-1}}$$

However, for a population, the standard deviation is given by the following formula:

$$\sigma = \sqrt{\frac{SS}{N}} = \sqrt{\frac{\Sigma(X - \mu)^2}{N}}$$

Hypothesis testing – the null and alternative hypotheses

In the preceding section, we had a brief discussion of what is referred to as descriptive statistics. In this section, we will discuss what is known as inferential statistics, whereby we try to use characteristics of the sample dataset to draw conclusions about the wider population as a whole.

One of the most important methods in inferential statistics is hypothesis testing. In hypothesis testing, we try to determine whether a certain hypothesis or research question is true to a certain degree. One example of a hypothesis would be this: eating spinach improves long-term memory.

In order to investigate this statement using hypothesis testing, we can select a group of people as subjects for our study and divide them into two groups, or samples. The first group will be the experimental group, and it will eat spinach over a predefined period of time. The second group, which does not receive spinach, will be the control group. Over selected periods of time, the memory of The individuals in the two groups will be measured and tallied.

Our goal at the end of our experiment will be to be able to make a statement such as "Eating spinach results in an improvement in long-term memory, which is not due to chance". This is also known as significance.

In the preceding scenario, the collection of subjects in the study is referred to as the sample, and the general set of people about whom we would like to draw conclusions is the population.

The ultimate goal of our study will be to determine whether any effects that we observed in the sample can be generalized to the population as a whole. In order to carry out hypothesis testing, we need to come up with what's known as the null and alternative hypotheses.

The null and alternative hypotheses

By referring to the preceding spinach example, the null hypothesis would be "Eating spinach has no effect on long-term memory performance".

The null hypothesis is just that—it nullifies what we're trying to *prove* by running our experiment. It does so by asserting that a statistical metric (to be explained later) is zero.

The alternative hypothesis is what we hope to support. It is the opposite of the null hypothesis and we assume it to be true until the data provides sufficient evidence that indicates otherwise. Thus, our alternative hypothesis, in this case, is "Eating spinach results in an improvement in long-term memory".

Symbolically, the null hypothesis is referred to as *H0* and the alternative hypothesis is referred to as *H1*. You may wish to restate the preceding null and alternative hypotheses as something more concrete and measurable for our study. For example, we could recast *H0* as follows:

"The mean memory score for a sample of 1,000 subjects who ate 40 grams of spinach daily for a period of 90 days would not differ from the control group of 1,000 subjects who consume no spinach within the same time period."

In conducting our experiment/study, we focus on trying to prove or disprove the null hypothesis. This is because we can calculate the probability that our results are due to chance. However, there is no easy way to calculate the probability of the alternative hypothesis since any improvement in long-term memory could be due to factors other than just eating spinach.

We test out the null hypothesis by assuming that it is true and calculate the probability of the results we gather arising by chance alone. We set a threshold level—alpha (*a*)—for which we can reject the null hypothesis if the calculated probability is smaller or accept it if it is greater. Rejecting the null hypothesis is tantamount to accepting the alternative hypothesis and vice versa.

The alpha and p-values

In order to conduct an experiment to support or disprove our null hypothesis, we need to come up with an approach that will allow us to make the decision in a concrete and measurable way. To do this test of significance, we have to consider two numbers—the p-value of the test statistic and the threshold level of significance, which is also known as **alpha**.

The p-value is the probability that the result we observe by assuming that the null hypothesis is true occurred by chance alone.

The p-value can also be thought of as the probability of obtaining a test statistic as extreme as or more extreme than the obtained test statistic, given that the null hypothesis is true.

The alpha value is the threshold value against which we compare p-values. This gives us a cut-off point at which we can accept or reject the null hypothesis. It is a measure of how extreme the results we observe must be in order to reject the null hypothesis of our experiment. The most commonly used values of alpha are 0.05 or 0.01.

In general, the rule is as follows:

- If the p-value is less than or equal to alpha (p< .05), then we reject the null hypothesis and state that the result is statistically significant.
- If the p-value is greater than alpha (p > .05), then we have failed to reject the null hypothesis, and we say that the result is not statistically significant.

In other words, the rule is as follows:

- If the test statistic value is greater than or smaller than the two critical test statistic values (for two-tailed tests), then we reject the null hypothesis and state that the (alternative) result is statistically significant.
- If the test statistic value lies within the two critical test statistic values, then we have failed to reject the null hypothesis, and we say that the (alternative) result is not statistically significant.

The seemingly arbitrary values of alpha in usage is one of the shortcomings of the frequentist methodology, and there are many questions concerning this approach. An article in the *Nature* journal highlights some of these problems; you can find it at: http://www.nature.com/news/scientific-method-statistical-errors-1.14700.

For more details on this topic, please refer to the following links:

http://statistics.about.com/od/Inferential-Statistics/a/What-Is-The-Difference-Between-Alpha-And-P-Values.htm

http://courses.washington.edu/p209s07/lecturenotes/Week%205_Monday%20overheads.pdf

Type I and Type II errors

There are two types of errors:

- **Type I Error**: In this type of error, we reject *H0* when, in fact, *H0* is true. An example of this would be a jury convicting an innocent person for a crime that the person did not commit.
- **Type II Error**: In this type of error, we fail to reject *H0* when, in fact, *H1* is true. This is equivalent to a guilty person escaping conviction.

Here's a table showing null hypothesis conditions leading to an error:

	Accept	Reject
True	No Error	Type 1 Error False Positive
False	Type 2 Error False Negative	No Error

Statistical hypothesis tests

A statistical hypothesis test is a method that we use to make a decision. We do this using data from a statistical study or experiment. In statistics, a result is termed statistically significant if it is unlikely to have occurred only by chance based on a predetermined threshold probability or significance level. There are two classes of statistical tests: 1-tailed and 2-tailed tests.

In a 2-tailed test, we allot half of our alpha to testing the statistical significance in one direction and the other half to testing the statistical significance in the other direction.

In a 1-tailed test, the test is performed in one direction only.

For more details on this topic, please refer to
`http://www.ats.ucla.edu/stat/mult_pkg/faq/general/tail_tests.htm`
.

Background

To apply statistical inference, it is important to understand the concept of what is known as a sampling distribution. A sampling distribution is the set of all possible values of a statistic, along with their probabilities, assuming that we sample at random from a population where the null hypothesis holds true.

A more simplistic definition is this: a sampling distribution is the set of values that the statistic can assume (distribution) if we were to repeatedly draw samples from the population, along with their associated probabilities.

The value of a statistic is a random sample from the statistic's sampling distribution. The sampling distribution of the mean is calculated by obtaining many samples of various sizes and taking their mean.

The central limit theorem states that the sampling distribution is normally distributed if the original or raw-score population is normally distributed, or if the sample size is large enough. Conventionally, statisticians define large enough sample sizes as N ≥ 30—that is, a sample size of 30 or more. This is still a topic of debate, though.

For more details on this topic, refer to
`http://stattrek.com/sampling/sampling-distribution.aspx`.

The standard deviation of the sampling distribution is often referred to as the standard error of the mean, or just the standard error.

The z-test

The z-test is appropriate under the following conditions:

- The study involves a single sample mean and the parameters μ and σ of the null hypothesis population are known
- The sampling distribution of the mean is normally distributed
- The size of the sample is $N \geq 30$

We use the z-test when the mean of the population is *known*. In the z-test, we ask the question of whether the population mean, μ, is different from a hypothesized value. The null hypothesis in the case of the z-test is as follows:

$$H_0 : \mu = \mu_o$$

Here, μ is the population mean and μ_0 is the hypothesized value.

The alternative hypothesis, H_α, can be one of the following:

$$H_\alpha : \mu < \mu_0$$

$$H_\alpha : \mu > \mu_0$$

$$H_\alpha : \mu \neq \mu_0$$

The first two are 1-tailed tests, while the last one is a 2-tailed test. In concrete terms, to test μ, we calculate the test statistic:

$$z = \frac{X - \mu_0}{\sigma_{\bar{x}}}$$

Here, $\sigma_{\bar{x}}$ is the true standard deviation of the sampling distribution of $\bar{X}$. If H_0 is true, the z-test statistics will have the standard normal distribution.

Let's go through a quick illustration of the z-test.

Suppose we have a fictional company, Intelligenza, that claims that they have come up with a radical new method for improved memory retention and study. They claim that their technique can improve grades over traditional study techniques. Suppose the improvement in grades is 40 percent with a standard deviation of 10 percent compared with results obtained using traditional study techniques.

A random test was run on 100 students using the Intelligenza method, and this resulted in a mean improvement of 44 percent. Does Intelligenza's claim hold true?

The null hypothesis for this study states that there is no improvement in grades using Intelligenza's method over traditional study techniques. The alternative hypothesis is that there is an improvement in using Intelligenza's method over traditional study techniques.

The null hypothesis is given by the following equation:

$$H_0 : \mu = \mu_o$$

The alternative hypothesis is given by the following equation:

$$H_\alpha : \mu > \mu_0$$

$$\text{std error} = 10/\text{sqrt}(100) = 1$$

$$z = (43.75-40)/(10/10) = 3.75 \text{ std errors}$$

Remember that if the null hypothesis is true, then the test statistic, z, will have a standard normal distribution that would look like this:

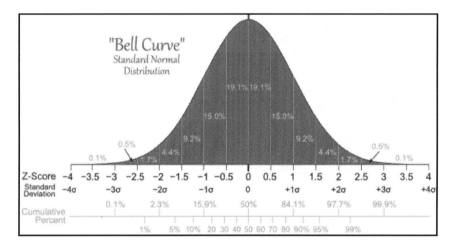

Diagram sourced from http://mathisfun.com/data/images/normal-distrubution-large.gif.

This value of z would be a random sample from the standard normal distribution, which is the distribution of z if the null hypothesis is true.

The observed value of z=43.75 corresponds to an extreme outlier p-value on the standard normal distribution curve, which is much less than 0.1 percent.

The p-value is the area under the curve to the right of the value of *3.75* on the preceding normal distribution curve.

This suggests that it would be highly unlikely for us to obtain the observed value of the test statistic if we were sampling from a standard normal distribution.

We can look up the actual p-value using Python by using the `scipy.stats` package, as follows:

```
In [104]: 1 - stats.norm.cdf(3.75)
Out[104]: 8.841728520081471e-05
```

Therefore, $P(z \geq 3.75 = 8.8e\text{-}05)$—that is, if the test statistic was normally distributed, then the probability of obtaining the observed value is *8.8e-05*, which is close to zero. So it would be almost impossible to obtain the value that we observed if the null hypothesis was actually true.

In more formal terms, we would normally define a threshold or alpha value and reject the null hypothesis if the p-value was $\leq \alpha$ or fail to reject it otherwise.

The typical values for α are 0.05 or 0.01. The following list explains the different values of alpha:

- *p-value <0.01*: There is strong evidence against *H0*
- *0.01 < p-value < 0.05*: There is strong evidence against *H0*
- *0.05 < p-value < 0.1*: There is weak evidence against *H0*
- *p-value > 0.1*: There is little or no evidence against *H0*

Therefore, in this case, we would reject the null hypothesis and give credence to Intelligenza's claim and state that their claim is highly significant. The evidence against the null hypothesis, in this case, is significant. There are two methods that we use to determine whether to reject the null hypothesis:

- The p-value approach
- The rejection region approach

The approach that we used in the preceding example was the latter one.

The smaller the p-value, the less likely it is that the null hypothesis is true. In the rejection region approach, we have the following rule:

If $|Z_{exp}| > |Z_{cri}|$, reject the null hypothesis; otherwise, retain it.

The t-test

The z-test is useful when the standard deviation of the population is known. However, in most real-world cases, this is an unknown quantity. For these cases, we turn to the t-test of significance.

For the t-test, given that the standard deviation of the population is unknown, we replace it with the standard deviation, *s*, of the sample. The standard error of the mean is now as follows:

$$S\bar{X} = \frac{S}{\sqrt{N}}$$

The standard deviation of the sample, *s*, is calculated as follows:

$$S = \sqrt{\frac{\Sigma(X - \bar{X})^2}{N - 1}}$$

The denominator is *N-1* and not *N*. This value is known as the number of degrees of freedom. We will now state (without an explanation) that, by the CLT, the t-distribution approximates the normal, Guassian, or z-distribution as *N*, and so *N-1* increases—that is, with increasing **degrees of freedom (df)**. When *df* = ∞, the t-distribution is identical to the normal or z-distribution. This is intuitive since, as *df* increases, the sample size increases and *s* approaches σ, which is the true standard deviation of the population. There are an infinite number of t-distributions, each corresponding to a different value of *df*.

This can be seen in the following diagram:

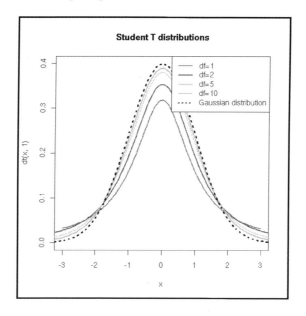

Diagram sourced from http://zoonek2.free.fr/UNIX/48_R/g593.png

A more detailed technical explanation on the relationship between t-distribution, z-distribution, and the degrees of freedom can be found at `http://en.wikipedia.org/wiki/Student's_t-distribution`.

Types of t-tests

There are various types of t-tests. The following are the most common one. They typically formulate a null hypothesis that makes a claim about the mean of a distribution:

- **One-sample independent t-test**: This is used to compare the mean of a sample with that of a known population mean or known value. Let's assume that we're health researchers in Australia who are concerned with the health of the aboriginal population and wish to ascertain whether babies born to low-income aboriginal mothers have lower birth weight than normal.

  An example of a null hypothesis test for a one-sample t-test would be this: the mean birth weight for our sample of 150 deliveries of full-term, live babies from low-income aboriginal mothers is no different from the mean birth weight of babies in the general Australian population—that is, 3,367 grams.

  The reference for this information can be found at `http://www.healthinfonet.ecu.edu.au/health-facts/overviews/births-and-pregnancy-outcome`.

- **Independent samples t-tests**: This is used to compare means from independent samples with each other. An example of an independent sample t-test would be a comparison of the fuel economy of automatic transmission versus manual transmission vehicles. This is what our real-world example will focus on.

  The null hypothesis for the t-test would be this: there is no difference between the average fuel efficiency of cars with manual and automatic transmissions in terms of their average combined city/highway mileage.

- **Paired samples t-test**: In a paired/dependent samples t-test, we take each data point in one sample and pair it with a data point in the other sample in a meaningful way. One way to do this would be to measure against the same sample at different points in time. An example of this would be to examine the efficacy of a slimming diet by comparing the weight of a sample of participants before and after the diet.

The null hypothesis, in this case, would be this: there is no difference between the mean weights of participants before and after going on the slimming diet, or more succinctly, the mean difference between paired observations is zero.

This information can be found at `http://en.wikiversity.org/wiki/T-test`.

A t-test example

In simplified terms, to do **Null Hypothesis Significance Testing (NHST)**, we need to do the following:

1. Formulate our null hypothesis. The null hypothesis is our model of the system, assuming that the effect we wish to verify was actually due to chance.
2. Calculate our p-value.
3. Compare the calculated p-value with that of our alpha, or threshold value, and decide whether to reject or accept the null hypothesis. If the p-value is low enough (lower than the alpha), we will draw the conclusion that the null hypothesis is likely to be false.

For our real-world illustration, we want to investigate whether manual transmission vehicles are more fuel efficient than automatic transmission vehicles. In order to do this, we will make use of the Fuel Economy data that was published by the US government for 2014 at `http://www.fueleconomy.gov`:

```
In [53]: import pandas as pd
import numpy as np
feRawData = pd.read_csv('2014_FEGuide.csv')

In [54]: feRawData.columns[:20]
Out[54]: Index([u'Model Year', u'Mfr Name', u'Division', u'Carline',
u'Verify Mfr Cd', u'Index (Model Type Index)', u'Eng Displ', u'# Cyl',
u'Trans as listed in FE Guide (derived from col AA thru AF)', u'City FE
(Guide) - Conventional Fuel', u'Hwy FE (Guide) - Conventional Fuel', u'Comb
FE (Guide) - Conventional Fuel', u'City Unadj FE - Conventional Fuel',
u'Hwy Unadj FE - Conventional Fuel', u'Comb Unadj FE - Conventional Fuel',
u'City Unrd Adj FE - Conventional Fuel', u'Hwy Unrd Adj FE - Conventional
Fuel', u'Comb Unrd Adj FE - Conventional Fuel', u'Guzzler? ', u'Air Aspir
Method'], dtype='object')
In [51]: feRawData = feRawData.rename(columns={'Trans as listed in FE Guide
(derived from col AA thru AF)' :'TransmissionType', 'Comb FE (Guide) -
Conventional Fuel' : 'CombinedFuelEcon'})
    In [57]: transType=feRawData['TransmissionType']
             transType.head()
    Out[57]: 0       Auto(AM7)
```

```
1       Manual(M6)
2        Auto(AM7)
3       Manual(M6)
4       Auto(AM-S7)
Name: TransmissionType, dtype: object
```

Now, we wish to modify the preceding series so that the values just contain the Auto and Manual strings. We can do this as follows:

```
In [58]: transTypeSeries = transType.str.split('(').str.get(0)
         transTypeSeries.head()
Out[58]: 0        Auto
         1       Manual
         2        Auto
         3       Manual
         4        Auto
Name: TransmissionType, dtype: object
```

Now, let's create a final modified DataFrame from Series that consists of the transmission type and the combined fuel economy figures:

```
In [61]:
feData=pd.DataFrame([transTypeSeries,feRawData['CombinedFuelEcon']]).T
         feData.head()
Out[61]:     TransmissionType      CombinedFuelEcon
         0   Auto                  16
         1   Manual                15
         2   Auto                  16
         3   Manual                15
         4   Auto                  17
         5 rows × 2 columns
```

We can now separate the data for vehicles with automatic transmission from those with manual transmission, as follows:

```
In [62]: feData_auto=feData[feData['TransmissionType']=='Auto']
         feData_manual=feData[feData['TransmissionType']=='Manual']
In [63]: feData_auto.head()
Out[63]:     TransmissionType      CombinedFuelEcon
         0   Auto                  16
         2   Auto                  16
         4   Auto                  17
         6   Auto                  16
         8   Auto                  17
         5 rows × 2 columns
```

This shows that there were 987 vehicles with automatic transmission versus 211 with manual transmission:

```
In [64]: len(feData_auto)
Out[64]: 987
In [65]: len(feData_manual)
Out[65]: 211
In [87]: np.mean(feData_auto['CombinedFuelEcon'])
Out[87]: 22.173252279635257
In [88]: np.mean(feData_manual['CombinedFuelEcon'])
Out[88]: 25.061611374407583
In [84]: import scipy.stats as stats
         stats.ttest_ind(feData_auto['CombinedFuelEcon'].tolist(),
                         feData_manual['CombinedFuelEcon'].tolist())
Out[84]: (array(-6.5520663209014325), 8.4124843426100211e-11)
In [86]: stats.ttest_ind(feData_auto['CombinedFuelEcon'].tolist(),
                         feData_manual['CombinedFuelEcon'].tolist(),
                         equal_var=False)
Out[86]: (array(-6.949372262516113), 1.9954143680382091e-11)
```

chi-square test

In this section, we will learn how to implement a chi-square test from scratch in Python and run it on an example dataset.

A chi-square test is conducted to determine the statistical significance of a causal relationship of two categorical variables with each other.

For example, in the following dataset, a chi-square test can be used to determine whether color preferences affect a personality type (introvert and extrovert) or not, and vice versa:

	Red	Yellow	Green	Blue
Introvert	20	6	30	44
Extrovert	180	34	50	36

The two hypotheses for chi-square tests are as follows:

- **H0**: Color preferences are not associated with a personality type
- **Ha**: Color preferences are associated with a personality type

To calculate the chi-square statistic, we assume that the null hypothesis is true. If there is no relationship between the two variables, we could just take the contribution (proportion) of that column as the total and multiply that with the row total for that cell; that would give us the expected cell. In other words, the absence of a specific relationship implies a simple proportional relationship and distribution. Therefore, we calculate the expected number in each subcategory (assuming the null hypothesis is true) as follows:

Expected Frequency = (Row Total X Column Total)/ Total:

	Red	Yellow	Green	Blue
Introvert	50	10	20	20
Extrovert	150	30	60	60

Once the expected frequency has been calculated, the ratio of the square of the difference between the expected and observed frequency, divided by the expected frequency, is calculated:

Chi_Square_Stat =Sum((Expected Frequency-Observed Frequency)**2/Expected Frequency)

These statistics follow a chi-square distribution with a parameter called the **degree of freedom (DOF)**. The degree of freedom is given by the following equation:

DOF = (Number of Rows -1)*(Number of Column-1)

There is a different distribution for each degree of freedom. This is shown in the following diagram:

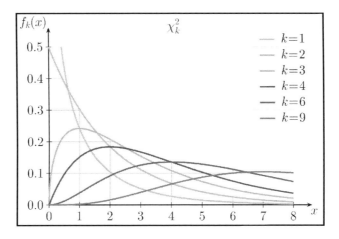

Chi-square distributions at different degrees of freedoms

Like any other test we've looked at, we need to decide a significance level and find the p-value associated with the chi-square statistics for that degree of freedom.

If the p-value is less than the alpha value, the null hypothesis can be rejected.

This whole calculation can be done by writing some Python code. The following two functions calculate the chi-square statistic and the degrees of freedom:

```
#Function to calculate the chi-square statistic
def chi_sq_stat(data_ob):
    col_tot=data_ob.sum(axis=0)
    row_tot=data_ob.sum(axis=1)
    tot=col_tot.sum(axis=0)
    row_tot.shape=(2,1)
    data_ex=(col_tot/tot)*row_tot
    num,den=(data_ob-data_ex)**2,data_ex
    chi=num/den
    return chi.sum()

#Function to calculate the degrees of freedom
def degree_of_freedom(data_ob):
    dof=(data_ob.shape[0]-1)*(data_ex.shape[1]-1)
    return dof

# Calculting these for the observed data
data_ob=np.array([[(20,6,30,44),(180,34,50,36)]])
chi_sq_stat(data_ob)
degree_of_freedom(data_ob)
```

The chi-square statistic is 71.99, while the degrees of freedom is 3. The p-values can be calculated using the table found here: `https://people.smp.uq.edu.au/YoniNazarathy/stat_models_B_course_spring_07/distributions/chisqtab.pdf`.

From the tables, the p-value for 71.99 is very close to 0. Even if we choose alpha to be a small number, such as 0.01, the p-value is still smaller. With this, we can say that the null hypothesis can be rejected with a good degree of statistical confidence.

ANOVA test

Now let's talk about another popular hypothesis test, called ANOVA. It is used to test whether similar data points coming from different groups or under a different set of experiments are statistically similar to each other or different—for example, the average height of different sections of a class in a school or the peptide length of a certain protein found in humans across different ethnicities.

ANOVA calculates two metrics to conduct this test:

- Variance among different groups
- Variance within each group

Based on these metrics, a statistic is calculated with variance among different groups as a numerator. If it is a statistically large enough number, it means that the variance among different groups is larger than the variance within the group, implying that the data points coming from the different groups are different.

Let's look at how variance among different groups and variance within each group can be calculated. Suppose we have k groups that data points are coming from:

The data points from group 1 are $X_{11}, X_{12}, ..., X_{1n}$.

The data points from group 2 are $X_{21}, X_{22}, ..., X_{2n}$.

This means that the data points from group k are $X_{k1}, X_{k2}, ..., X_{kn}$.

Let's use the following abbreviations and symbols to describe some features of this data:

- Variance among different groups is represented by SSAG
- Variance within each group is represented by SSWG
- Number of elements in group k is represented by n_k
- Mean of data points in a group is represented by μ_k
- Mean of all data points across groups is represented by μ
- Number of groups is represented by k

Let's define the two hypotheses for our statistical test:

- **Ho:** $\mu_1 = \mu_2 = ... = \mu_k$
- **Ho:** $\mu_1 \mathrel{!=} \mu_2 \mathrel{!=} ..... = \mu_k$

In other words, the null hypothesis states that the mean of the data points across all the groups is the same, while the alternative hypothesis says that the mean of at least one group is different from the others.

This leads to the following equations:

$$SSAG = (\Sigma\, n_k * (X_k - \mu)**2) / k\text{-}1$$

$$SSWG = (\Sigma\Sigma(X_{ki}\text{-}\mu_k)**2) / n*k\text{-}k\text{-}1$$

In SSAG, the summation is over all the groups.

In SSWG, the first summation is across the data points from a particular group and the second summation is across the groups.

The denominators in both cases denote the degree of freedom. For SSAG, we are dealing with k groups and the last value can be derived from the other *k-1* values. Therefore, DOF is *k-1*. For SSWG, there are *n*k* data points, but the k-1 mean values are restricted (or fixed) by those choices, and so the DOF is *n*k-k-1*.

Once these numbers have been calculated, the test statistic is calculated as follows:

Test Statistic = SSAG/SSWG

This ratio of SSAG and SSWG follows a new distribution called F-distribution, and so the statistic is called an F statistic. It is defined by the two different degrees of freedom, and there is a separate distribution for each combination, as shown in the following graph:

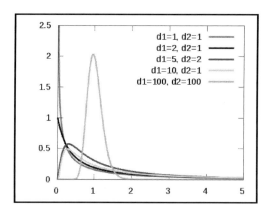

F-distribution based on the two DOFs, d1 =k-1 and d2=n*k-k-1

Like any of the other tests we've looked at, we need to decide a significance level and need to find the p-value associated with the F statistics for those degrees of freedom. If the p-value is less than the alpha value, the null hypothesis can be rejected. This whole calculation can be done by writing some Python code.

Let's have a look at some example data and see how ANOVA can be applied:

```
import pandas as pd
data=pd.read_csv('ANOVA.csv')
data.head()
```

This results in the following output:

	OD	Lot	Run
0	1.053	1	1
1	1.708	1	1
2	0.977	1	1
3	0.881	1	2
4	0.788	1	2

Head of the OD data by Lot and Run

We are interested in finding out whether the mean OD is the same for different lots and runs. We will apply ANOVA for that purpose, but before that, we can draw a boxplot to get an intuitive sense of the differences in the distributions for different lots and runs:

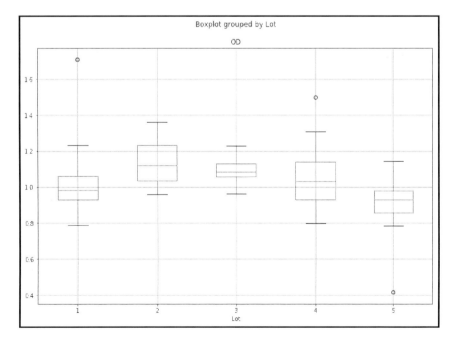

Boxplot of OD by Lot

Similarly, a boxplot of OD grouped by Run can also be plotted:

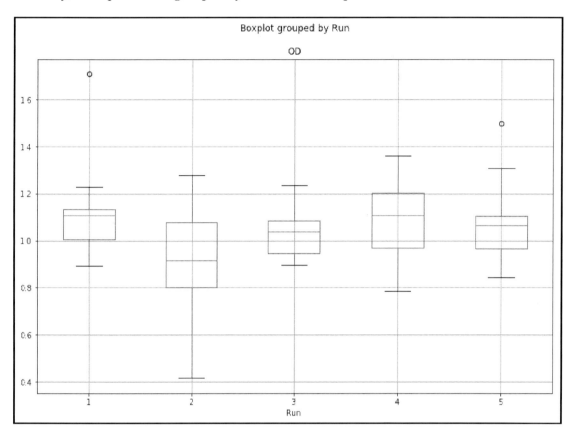

Boxplot of OD by Run

Now, let's write the Python code to perform the calculations:

```
# Calculating SSAG
group_mean=data.groupby('Lot').mean()
group_mean=np.array(group_mean['OD'])
tot_mean=np.array(data['OD'].mean())
group_count=data.groupby('Lot').count()
group_count=np.array(group_count['OD'])
fac1=(group_mean-tot_mean)**2
fac2=fac1*group_count
DF1=(data['Lot'].unique()).size-1
SSAG=(fac2.sum())/DF1
SSAG
```

```
#Calculating SSWG
group_var=[]
for i in range((data['Lot'].unique()).size):
    lot_data=np.array(data[data['Lot']==i+1]['OD'])
    lot_data_mean=lot_data.mean()
    group_var_int=((lot_data-lot_data_mean)**2).sum()
    group_var.append(group_var_int)
group_var_sum=(np.array(group_var)).sum()
DF2=data.shape[0]-(data['Lot'].unique()).size-1
SSAW=group_var_sum/DF2
SSAW

F=SSAG/SSAW
F
```

The value of the F statistic comes out to be 3.84, while the degrees of freedom are 4 and 69, respectively.

At a significance level—that is, alpha—of 0.05, the critical value of the F statistic lies between 2.44 and 2.52 (from the F-distribution table found at: `http://socr.ucla.edu/ Applets.dir/F_Table.html`).

Since the value of the F statistic (3.84) is larger than the critical value of 2.52, the F statistic lies in the rejection region, and so the null hypothesis can be rejected. Therefore, it can be concluded that the mean OD values are different for different lot groups. At a significance level of 0.001, the F statistic becomes smaller than the critical value, and so the null hypothesis can't be rejected. We would have to accept that the OD means from the different groups are statistically the same. The same test can be performed for different run groups. This has been left as an exercise for you to practice with.

Confidence intervals

In this section, we will address the issue of confidence intervals. A confidence interval allows us to make a probabilistic estimate of the value of the mean of a population's given sample data.

This estimate, called an interval estimate, consists of a range of values (intervals) that act as good estimates of the unknown population parameter.

The confidence interval is bounded by confidence limits. A 95 percent confidence interval is defined as an interval in which the interval contains the population mean with a 95 percent probability. So how do we construct a confidence interval?

Suppose we have a 2-tailed t-test and we want to construct a 95 percent confidence interval. In this case, we want the sample t-value, H_0, corresponding to the mean to satisfy the following inequality:

$$-t_{0.025} \leqslant t_{samp} \leqslant t_{0.025}$$

Given that $t_{samp} = \dfrac{X_{samp} - \mu}{s_X}$, we can substitute this in the preceding inequality relation to obtain the following equation:

$$X_{samp} - s_X t_{0.025} \leqslant \mu \leqslant X_{samp} + s_X t_{0.025}$$

The $[X_{samp} - s_X t_{0.025} \leqslant \mu \leqslant X_{samp} + s_X t_{0.025}]$ interval is our 95 percent confidence interval.

Generalizing any confidence interval for any percentage, y, can be expressed as $[X_{samp} - s_X t_{cri} \leqslant \mu \leqslant X_{samp} + s_X t_{cri}]$, where t_{cri} is the t-tailed value of t—that is, $t_{\gamma/2}$ correlation to the desired confidence interval for y.

We will now take the opportunity to illustrate how we can calculate the confidence interval using a dataset from the popular statistical environment known as R. The `stats` models' module provides access to the datasets that are available in the core datasets package of R through the `get_rdataset` function.

An illustrative example

We will consider the dataset known as faithful, which consists of data that was obtained by observing the eruptions of the Old Faithful geyser in the Yellowstone National Park in the US. The two variables in the dataset are eruptions, which are the length of time the geyser erupts, and waiting, which is the time until the next eruption. There were 272 observations:

```
In [46]: import statsmodels.api as sma
         faithful=sma.datasets.get_rdataset("faithful")
         faithful
Out[46]: <class 'statsmodels.datasets.utils.Dataset'>
In [48]: faithfulDf=faithful.data
         faithfulDf.head()
Out[48]:    eruptions   waiting
         0    3.600       79
         1    1.800       54
         2    3.333       74
         3    2.283       62
```

```
        4   4.533            85
5 rows × 2 columns
In [50]: len(faithfulDf)
Out[50]: 272
```

Let's calculate a 95 percent confidence interval for the mean waiting time of the geyser. To do this, we must obtain the sample mean and standard deviation of the data:

```
In [80]: mean,std=(np.mean(faithfulDf['waiting']),
                    np.std(faithfulDf['waiting']))
```

Now, we'll make use of the `scipy.stats` package to calculate the confidence interval:

```
In [81]: from scipy import stats
     N=len(faithfulDf['waiting'])
       ci=stats.norm.interval(0.95,loc=mean,scale=std/np.sqrt(N))
In [82]: ci
Out[82]: (69.28440107709261, 72.509716569966201)
```

Thus, we can state with 95 percent confidence that the [69.28, 72.51] interval contains the actual mean waiting time of the geyser.

> This information can be found
> at `http://statsmodels.sourceforge.net/devel/datasets/index.html`
> and
> `http://docs.scipy.org/doc/scipy-0.14.0/reference/generated/scipy`
> `.stats.norm.html`.

Correlation and linear regression

One of the most common tasks in statistics when determining the relationship between two variables is whether there is dependence between them. Correlation is the general term we use in statistics for variables that express dependence with each other.

We can then use this relationship to try and predict the value of one set of variables from the other. This is known as regression.

Correlation

The statistical dependence that's expressed in a correlation relationship does not imply a causal relationship between the two variables; the famous line regarding this is *correlation does not imply causation*. Thus, the correlation between two variables or datasets implies just a casual rather than a causal relationship or dependence. For example, there is a correlation between the amount of ice cream purchased on a given day and the weather.

 For more information on correlation and dependency, refer to
http://en.wikipedia.org/wiki/Correlation_and_dependence.

The correlation measure, known as the correlation coefficient, is a number that describes the size and direction of the relationship between the two variables. It can vary from -1 to +1 in direction and 0 to 1 in magnitude. The direction of the relationship is expressed through the sign, with a + sign expressing a positive correlation and a - sign expressing a negative correlation. The higher the magnitude, the greater the correlation, with a 1 being termed as the perfect correlation.

The most popular and widely used correlation coefficient is the Pearson product-moment correlation coefficient, known as r. It measures the linear correlation or dependence between two x and y variables and takes values between -1 and +1.

The sample correlation coefficient, r, is defined as follows:

$$r = \frac{\sum_{i=1}^{N}(X_i - \bar{X})(Y_i - \bar{Y})}{\sqrt{\sum_{i=1}^{N}(X_i - \bar{X})^2 \sum_{i=1}^{N}(Y_i - \bar{Y})^2}}$$

This can also be written as follows:

$$r = \frac{N \sum X_i Y_i - \sum X_i \sum Y_i}{\sqrt{N \sum X_i^2 - (\sum X_i)^2} \sqrt{N \sum Y_i^2 - (\sum Y_i)^2}}$$

Here, we have omitted the summation limits.

Linear regression

As we mentioned previously, regression focuses on using the relationship between two variables for prediction. In order to make predictions using linear regression, the best-fitting straight line must be computed.

If all the points (values for the variables) lie on a straight line, then the relationship is deemed perfect. This rarely happens in practice and the points do not all fit neatly on a straight line. Because of this, the relationship is imperfect. In some cases, a linear relationship only occurs among log-transformed variables. This is a log-log model. An example of such a relationship would be a power law distribution in physics, where one variable varies as a power of another.

Thus, an expression such as this results in the linear relationship.

 For more information, refer to http://en.wikipedia.org/wiki/Power_law.

To construct the best-fit line, the method of least squares is used. In this method, the best-fit line is the optimal line that is constructed between the points for which the sum of the squared distance from each point to the line is the minimum. This is deemed to be the best linear approximation of the relationship between the variables we are trying to model using linear regression. The best-fit line in this case is called the least squares regression line.

More formally, the least squares regression line is the line that has the minimum possible value for the sum of squares of the vertical distance from the data points to the line. These vertical distances are also known as residuals.

Thus, by constructing the least squares regression line, we're trying to minimize the following expression:

$$\sum_{i=1}^{N}(Y_i - Y)^2$$

An illustrative example

We will now illustrate all the preceding points with an example. Suppose we're doing a study in which we would like to illustrate the effect of temperature on how often crickets chirp. The data for this example was obtained from the book *The Song of Insects*, by George W Pierce, which was written in 1948. George Pierce measured the frequency of chirps made by a ground cricket at various temperatures.

We want to investigate the frequency of cricket chirps and the temperature, as we suspect that there is a relationship between them. The data consists of 16 data points, and we will read it into a DataFrame.

The data is sourced from http://college.cengage.com/mathematics/brase/understandable_statistics/7e/ students/datasets/slr/frames/slr02.html. Let's take a look at it:

```
In [38]: import pandas as pd
         import numpy as np
         chirpDf= pd.read_csv('cricket_chirp_temperature.csv')
In [39]: chirpDf
Out[39]:chirpFrequency   temperature
0          20.000000        88.599998
1          16.000000        71.599998
2          19.799999        93.300003
3          18.400000        84.300003
4          17.100000        80.599998
5          15.500000        75.199997
6          14.700000        69.699997
7          17.100000        82.000000
8          15.400000        69.400002
9          16.200001        83.300003
10         15.000000        79.599998
11         17.200001        82.599998
12         16.000000        80.599998
13         17.000000        83.500000
14         14.400000        76.300003
15 rows × 2 columns
```

First, let's make a scatter plot of the data, along with a regression line, or line of best fit:

```
In [29]: plt.scatter(chirpDf.temperature,chirpDf.chirpFrequency,
             marker='o',edgecolor='b',facecolor='none',alpha=0.5)
         plt.xlabel('Temperature')
         plt.ylabel('Chirp Frequency')
         slope, intercept =
np.polyfit(chirpDf.temperature,chirpDf.chirpFrequency,1)
         plt.plot(chirpDf.temperature,chirpDf.temperature*slope +
intercept,'r')
         plt.show()
```

As you can see from the following diagram, there seems to be a linear relationship between temperature and the chirp frequency:

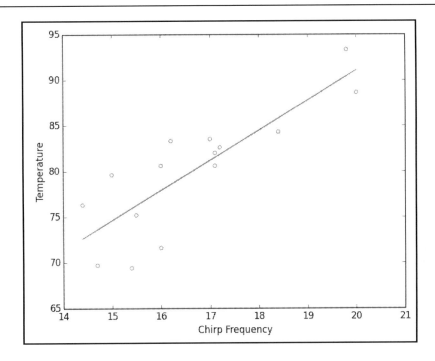

We can now proceed to investigate further by using the `statsmodels.ols` (ordinary least squares) method:

```
[37]: chirpDf= pd.read_csv('cricket_chirp_temperature.csv')
      chirpDf=np.round(chirpDf,2)
      result=sm.ols('temperature ~ chirpFrequency',chirpDf).fit()
      result.summary()
Out[37]: OLS Regression Results
```

Dep. Variable: temperature	R-squared:	0.697

Model: OLS   Adj. R-squared: 0.674
Method: Least Squares   F-statistic: 29.97
Date: Wed, 27 Aug 2014   Prob (F-statistic):   0.000107
Time: 23:28:14   Log-Likelihood: -40.348
No. Observations: 15   AIC: 84.70
Df Residuals: 13   BIC: 86.11
Df Model: 1

	coef	std err	t	P>|t|	[95.0% Conf. Int.]
Intercept	25.2323	10.060	2.508	0.026	3.499 46.966
chirpFrequency	3.2911	0.601	5.475	0.000	1.992 4.590

Omnibus: 1.003   Durbin-Watson: 1.818
Prob(Omnibus): 0.606   Jarque-Bera (JB):   0.874
Skew: -0.391 Prob(JB):   0.646
Kurtosis: 2.114   Cond. No.   171.

We will ignore most of the preceding results, except for the R-squared, Intercept, and chirpFrequency values.

From the preceding result, we can conclude that the slope of the regression line is 3.29 and that the intercept on the temperature axis is 25.23. Thus, the regression line equation looks like temperature = 25.23 + 3.29 * chirpFrequency.

This means that as the chirp frequency increases by 1, the temperature increases by about 3.29 degrees Fahrenheit. However, note that the intercept value is not really meaningful as it is outside the bounds of the data. We can also only make predictions for values within the bounds of the data. For example, we cannot predict what chirpFrequency is at 32 degrees Fahrenheit as it is outside the bounds of the data; moreover, at 32 degrees Fahrenheit, the crickets would have frozen to death. The value of R—that is, the correlation coefficient—is given as follows:

```
In [38]: R=np.sqrt(result.rsquared)
         R
Out[38]: 0.83514378678237422
```

Thus, our correlation coefficient is R = 0.835. This would indicate that about 84 percent of the chirp frequency can be explained by the changes in temperature.

 The book containing this data, *The Song of Insects,* can be found at http://www.hup.harvard.edu/catalog.php?isbn=9780674420663.

For a more in-depth treatment of single and multivariable regression, refer to the following websites:

- **Regression (Part I)**: http://bit.ly/1Eq5kSx
- **Regression (Part II)**: http://bit.ly/1OmuFTV

Summary

In this chapter, we took a brief tour of the classical or frequentist approach to statistics and saw how to combine pandas with the `numpy` and `stats` packages—`scipy.stats` and `statsmodels`—to calculate, interpret, and make inferences from statistical data.

In the next chapter, we will examine an alternative approach to statistics called the Bayesian approach. For a deeper look at the statistics topics that we touched on, take a look at *Understanding Statistics in the Behavioral Sciences*, which can be found at `http://www.amazon.com/Understanding-Statistics-Behavioral-Sciences-Robert/dp/04` `95596523`.

11

A Brief Tour of Bayesian Statistics and Maximum Likelihood Estimates

In this chapter, we take a brief tour of an alternative approach to statistical inference called **Bayesian statistics**. It is not intended to be a full primer, but will simply serve as an introduction to the Bayesian approach. We will also explore the associated Python-related libraries and learn how to use `pandas` and `matplotlib` to help with the data analysis. The various topics that will be discussed are as follows:

- Introduction to Bayesian statistics
- The mathematical framework for Bayesian statistics
- Probability distributions
- Bayesian versus frequentist statistics
- Introduction to PyMC and Monte Carlo simulations
- Bayesian analysis example – switchpoint detection

Introduction to Bayesian statistics

The field of Bayesian statistics is built on the work of Reverend Thomas Bayes, an 18th-century statistician, philosopher, and Presbyterian minister. His famous Bayes' theorem, which forms the theoretical underpinnings of Bayesian statistics, was published posthumously in 1763 as a solution to the problem of *inverse probability*. For more details on this topic, refer to `http://en.wikipedia.org/wiki/Thomas_Bayes`.

Inverse probability problems were all the rage in the early 18th century, and were often formulated as follows.

Suppose you play a game with a friend. There are 10 green balls and 7 red balls in bag 1 and 4 green balls and 7 red balls in bag 2. Your friend tosses a coin (without telling you the result), picks a ball from one of the bags at random, and shows it to you. The ball is red. What is the probability that the ball was drawn from bag 1?

These problems were called inverse probability problems because we are trying to estimate the probability of an event that has already occurred (which bag the ball was drawn from) in light of the subsequent result (the ball is red):

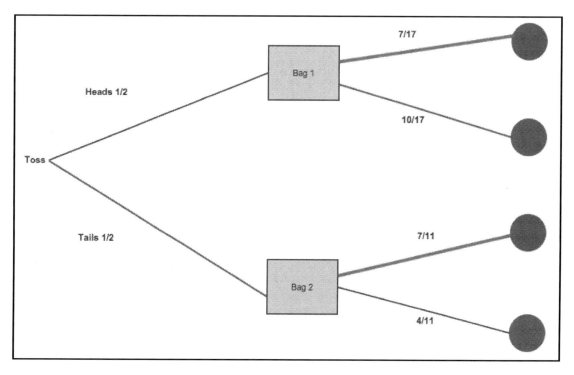

Bayesian balls illustration

Let's quickly illustrate how one would go about solving the inverse probability problem illustrated earlier. We want to calculate the probability that the ball was drawn from bag 1, given that it is red. This can be denoted as *P(Bag 1 | Red Ball)*.

Let's start by calculating the probability of selecting a red ball. This can be calculated by following the two paths in red, as shown in the preceding figure. Therefore, we have the following:

$$P(Red\ Ball) = \tfrac{1}{2} * \tfrac{7}{17} + \tfrac{1}{2} * \tfrac{7}{11} = 0.524$$

Now, the probability of choosing a red ball from bag 1 is shown by only taking the upper path and is calculated as follows:

$$P(Red\ Ball\ from\ Bag\ 1) = \frac{1}{2} * \frac{7}{17} = \frac{7}{34} = 0.206$$

The probability of choosing a red ball from bag 2 is calculated as follows:

$$P(Red\ Ball\ from\ Bag\ 2) = \frac{1}{2} * \frac{7}{11} = \frac{7}{22} = 0.318$$

Note that this probability can also be written as follows:

$$P(RedBall, Bag1) = P(RedBall|Bag1) * P(Bag1)$$

We can see that *P(Bag 1)=1/2*, and the final branch of the tree is only traversed if the ball is firstly in bag 1 and is a red ball. Therefore, we'll get the following outcome:

$$P(Bag\ 1\ |\ Red\ Ball) = \frac{P(Red\ Ball, Bag\ 1)}{P(Red\ Ball)}$$

$$= \frac{P(Red\ Ball, Bag\ 1)\ *\ P(Bag\ 1)}{P(Red\ Ball)}$$

$$= \frac{0.206}{0.524} = 0.393$$

The mathematical framework for Bayesian statistics

Bayesian methods are an alternative way of making a statistical inference. We will first look at Bayes' theorem, the fundamental equation from which all Bayesian inference is derived.

A few definitions regarding probability are in order before we begin:

- *A,B*: These are events that can occur with a certain probability.
- *P(A)* and *P(B)*: This is the probability of the occurrence of a particular event.
- *P(A|B)*: This is the probability of A happening, given that B has occurred. This is known as a **conditional probability**.
- *P(AB) = P(A and B)*: This is the probability of A and B occurring together.

We begin with the following basic assumption:

$$P(AB) = P(B) * P(A|B)$$

The preceding equation shows the relation of the joint probability of $P(AB)$ to the conditional probability $P(A|B)$ and what is known as the marginal probability, $P(B)$. If we rewrite the equation, we have the following expression for conditional probability:

$$P(A|B) = P(AB)/P(B)$$

This is somewhat intuitive—the probability of A given B is obtained by dividing the probability of both A and B occurring by the probability that B occurred. The idea is that B is given, so we divide by its probability. A more rigorous treatment of this equation can be found at http://bit.ly/1bCYXRd, which is titled *Probability: Joint, Marginal and Conditional Probabilities*.

Similarly, by symmetry we have $P(AB) = P(BA) = P(A) * P(B|A)$. Thus, we have $P(A) * P(B|A) = P(B) * P(A|B)$. By dividing the expression by $P(B)$ on both sides and assuming $P(B)!=0$, we obtain the following:

$$P(A|B) = P(A) * \frac{P(B|A)}{P(B)}$$

The preceding equation is referred to as **Bayes' theorem**, the bedrock of all Bayesian statistical inference. In order to link Bayes' theorem to inferential statistics, we will recast the equation as what is called the **diachronic interpretation**, as follows:

$$P(H|D) = P(H) * \frac{P(D|H)}{P(B)}$$

Here, **H** represents a hypothesis and **D** represents an event that has already occurred that we are using in our statistical study, and is also referred to as data.

The expression (**H**) is the probability of our hypothesis before we observe the data. This is known as the **prior probability**. The use of prior probability is often touted as an advantage by Bayesian statisticians since prior knowledge of previous results can be used as input for the current model, resulting in increased accuracy. For more information on this, refer to http://www.bayesian-inference.com/advantagesbayesian.

P(D) is the probability of obtaining the data that we observe regardless of the hypothesis. This is called the **normalizing constant**. The normalizing constant doesn't always need to be calculated, especially in many popular algorithms, such as **Markov Chain Monte Carlo (MCMC)**, which we will examine later in this chapter.

P(H|D) is the probability that the hypothesis is true, given the data that we observe. This is called the **posterior**.

P(D|H) is the probability of obtaining the data, considering our hypothesis. This is called the **likelihood**.

Thus, Bayesian statistics amounts to applying Bayes' rule to solve problems in inferential statistics with *H* representing our hypothesis and *D* the data.

A Bayesian statistical model is cast in terms of parameters, and the uncertainty in these parameters is represented by probability distributions. This is different from the frequentist approach where the values are regarded as deterministic. An alternative representation is as follows:

$$P(\Theta/x)$$

Here, *Θ* is our unknown data and *x* is our observed data.

In Bayesian statistics, we make assumptions about the prior data and use the likelihood to update the posterior probability using Bayes' rule. As an illustration, let's consider the following problem. Here is a classic case of what is commonly known as the **urn problem**:

- Two urns contain colored balls
- Urn 1 contains 50 red and 50 blue balls
- Urn 2 contains 30 red and 70 blue balls
- One of the two urns is randomly chosen (50 percent probability) and then a ball is drawn at random from one of the two urns

If a red ball is drawn, what is the probability that it came from urn 1? We want *P(H|D)*—that is *P(ball came from Urn 1 | Red ball is drawn)*.

Here, *H* denotes that the ball is drawn from urn 1, and *D* denotes that the drawn ball is red:

$$P(H) = P(ball\ is\ drawn\ from\ Urn\ 1) = 0.5$$

We know that $P(H|D) = P(H) * P(D|H)/P(D)$, $P(D|H) = 0.5$, $P(D) = (50 + 30)/(100 + 100) = 0.4$. This can also be phrased as follows:

$$P(D) = P(H)\,P(D|H) + P(\bar{H})\,P(D|\bar{H}) = 0.5*0.5 + 0.5*0.3 = 0.25 + 0.15 = 0.4$$

Therefore, we conclude that $P(H|D) = 0.5 * 0.5/0.4 = 0.25/0.4 = 0.625$.

Bayes' theory and odds

Bayes' theorem can sometimes be represented in a more natural and convenient form by using an alternative formulation of probability called *odds*. Odds are generally expressed in terms of ratios and are commonly used. A 3-to-1 odds (written often as 3:1) of a horse winning a race represents the fact that there is a 75 percent probability that the horse will win.

Given a probability p, the odds can be calculated as odds = *p:(1 - p)*, which in the case of *p=0.75* becomes 0.75:0.25, which is 3:1.

Using odds, we can rewrite Bayes' theorem as follows:

$$o(A|D) = o(A)\,P(D|A)/P(D|B)$$

Applications of Bayesian statistics

Bayesian statistics can be applied to many problems that we encounter in classical statistics, such as the following:

- Parameter estimation
- Prediction
- Hypothesis testing
- Linear regression

There are many compelling reasons for studying Bayesian statistics, such as using prior information to better inform a current model. The Bayesian approach works with probability distributions rather than point estimates, thus producing more realistic predictions. Bayesian inference bases a hypothesis on the available data—*P(hypothesis|data)*. The frequentist approach tries to fit the data based on a hypothesis. It can be argued that the Bayesian approach is the more logical and empirical one as it tries to base its belief on the facts rather than the other way round. For more information on this, refer to
http://www.bayesian-inference.com/advantagesbayesian.

Probability distributions

In this section, we will briefly examine the properties of various probability distributions. Many of these distributions are used for Bayesian analysis, and so a brief synopsis is needed before we can proceed. We will also illustrate how to generate and display these distributions using `matplotlib`. In order to avoid repeating the `import` statements for every code snippet in each section, we will be presenting the following standard set of Python code imports that need to be run before any of the code snippets mentioned in the following command. You only need to run these imports once per session. The imports are as follows:

```
import pandas as pd
import numpy as np
from matplotlib import pyplot as plt
from matplotlib import colors
import matplotlib.pyplot as plt
import matplotlib
%matplotlib inline
```

Fitting a distribution

One of the steps that we have to take in a Bayesian analysis is to fit our data to a probability distribution. Selecting the correct distribution can be something of an art, and often requires statistical knowledge and experience, but we can follow a few guidelines to help us along the way. These guidelines are as follows:

- Determine whether the data is discrete or continuous
- Examine the skewness/symmetry of the data, and if skewed, determine the direction
- Determine the lower and upper limits, if there are any
- Determine the likelihood of observing extreme values in the distribution

A statistical trial is a repeatable experiment with a set of well-defined outcomes that is known as the sample space. A Bernoulli trial is a yes/no experiment where the random X variable is assigned the value of 1 in the case of a yes and 0 in the case of a no. The event of tossing a coin and seeing whether it lands heads up is an example of a Bernoulli trial.

There are two classes of probability distributions: discrete and continuous. In the following sections, we will discuss the differences between these two classes of distributions and learn about the main distributions.

Discrete probability distributions

In this scenario, the variable can take only certain distinct values, such as integers. An example of a discrete random variable is the number of heads obtained when we flip a coin five times: the possible values are {0,1,2,3,4,5}—we cannot obtain 3.82 heads, for example. The range of values that the random variable can take is specified by what is known as a **probability mass function (PMF)**.

Discrete uniform distribution

The discrete uniform distribution is a distribution that models an event with a finite set of possible outcomes where each outcome is equally likely to be observed. For *n* outcomes, each has a probability of occurrence of *1/n*.

An example of this is throwing a fair die. The probability of any of the six outcomes is *1/6*. The PMF is given by *1/n*, and the expected value and variance are given by *(max + min)/2* and *(n^2-1)/12* respectively:

```
from matplotlib import pyplot as plt
import matplotlib.pyplot as plt
X=range(0,11)
Y=[1/6.0 if x in range(1,7) else 0.0 for x in X]
plt.plot(X,Y,'go-', linewidth=0, drawstyle='steps-pre',
    label="p(x)=1/6")
plt.legend(loc="upper left")
plt.vlines(range(1,7),0,max(Y), linestyle='-')
plt.xlabel('x')
plt.ylabel('p(x)')
plt.ylim(0,0.5)
plt.xlim(0,10)
plt.title('Discrete uniform probability distribution with
        p=1/6')
plt.show()
```

The following is the output:

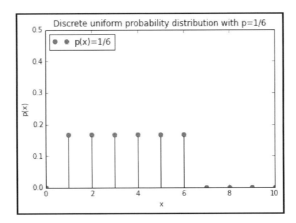

Discrete uniform distribution

The Bernoulli distribution

The Bernoulli distribution measures the probability of success in a trial, for example, the probability that a coin toss turns up a head or a tail. This can be represented by a random X variable that takes a value of 1 if the coin turns up as heads and 0 if it is tails. The probability of it turning up heads or tails is denoted by p and $q=1-p$ respectively.

This can be represented by the following PMF:

$$f(k) = \begin{cases} 1-p, & k=0 \\ p, & k=1 \end{cases}$$

The expected value and variance are given by the following formula:

$$E(X) = p$$

$$Var(X) = p(1-p)$$

For more information, go to http://en.wikipedia.org/wiki/Bernoulli_distribution.

We will now plot the Bernoulli distribution using matplotlib and scipy.stats as follows:

```
In [20]:import matplotlib
        from scipy.stats import bernoulli
        a = np.arange(2)
```

```
colors = matplotlib.rcParams['axes.color_cycle']
plt.figure(figsize=(12,8))
for i, p in enumerate([0.0, 0.2, 0.5, 0.75, 1.0]):
    ax = plt.subplot(1, 5, i+1)
    plt.bar(a, bernoulli.pmf(a, p), label=p, color=colors[i],
alpha=0.5)
    ax.xaxis.set_ticks(a)
    plt.legend(loc=0)
        if i == 0:
            plt.ylabel("PDF at $k$")
    plt.suptitle("Bernoulli probability for various values of $p$")
```

The following is the output:

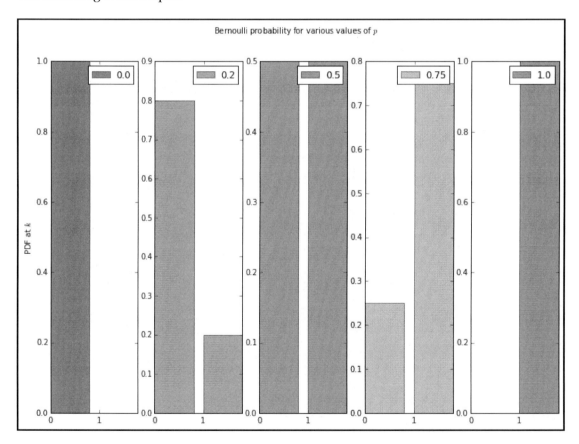

Bernoulli distribution output

The binomial distribution

The binomial distribution is used to represent the number of successes in *n*-independent Bernoulli trials, which can be expressed as the following:

$$Y = X_1 + X_2 + \dots + X_n$$

Using the coin toss example, this distribution models the chance of getting X heads over *n* trials. For 100 tosses, the binomial distribution models the likelihood of getting 0 heads (extremely unlikely) to 50 heads (highest likelihood) to 100 heads (also extremely unlikely). This ends up making the binomial distribution symmetrical when the odds are perfectly even and skewed when the odds are far less even. The PMF is given by the following expression:

$$f(k) = \binom{n}{k} p^k q^{n-k}, 0 \leqslant k \leqslant n$$

The expectation and variance are given respectively by the following expressions:

$$E(X) = np$$

$$Var(X) = np(1 - p)$$

This is shown using the following code block:

```
from scipy.stats import binom
clrs = ['blue','green','red','cyan','magenta']
plt.figure(figsize=(12,6))
k = np.arange(0, 22)
for p, color in zip([0.001, 0.1, 0.3, 0.6, 0.999], clrs):
    rv = binom(20, p)
    plt.plot(k, rv.pmf(k), lw=2, color=color, label="$p$=" +
str(round(p,1)))
        plt.legend()
plt.title("Binomial distribution PMF")
plt.tight_layout()
plt.ylabel("PDF at $k$")
plt.xlabel("$k$")
```

The following is the output:

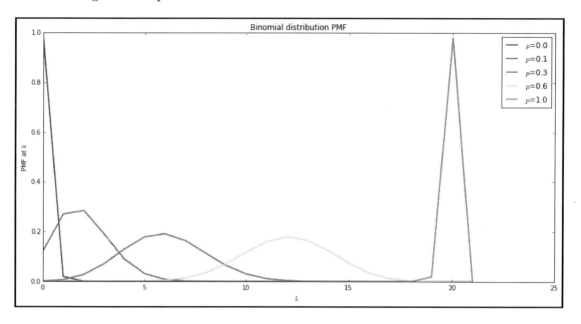

Binomial distribution

The Poisson distribution

The Poisson distribution models the probability of a number of events within a given time interval, assuming that these events occur with a known average rate and successive events occur independently of the time that has passed since the previous event.

A concrete example of a process that can be modeled by a Poisson distribution would be if an individual received an average of, say, 23 emails per day. If we assume that the arrival times for the emails are independent of each other, then the total number of emails an individual receives each day can be modeled by a Poisson distribution.

Another example could be the number of trains that stop at a particular station each hour. The PMF for a Poisson distribution is given by the following expression:

$$f(k) = \frac{\lambda^k e^{-\lambda}}{k!}$$

Here, λ is the rate parameter, which, represents the expected number of events/arrivals that occur per unit time, and k is the random variable that represents the number of events/arrivals.

The expectation and variance are given respectively by the following expressions:

$$E(X) = \lambda$$

$$Var(X) = \lambda$$

For more information, refer to http://en.wikipedia.org/wiki/Poisson_process.

The PMF is plotted using matplotlib for various values as follows:

```
In [11]: %matplotlib inline
    import numpy as np
    import matplotlib
    import matplotlib.pyplot as plt
    from scipy.stats import poisson
    colors = matplotlib.rcParams['axes.color_cycle']
    k=np.arange(15)
    plt.figure(figsize=(12,8))
    for i, lambda_ in enumerate([1,2,4,6]):
        plt.plot(k, poisson.pmf(k, lambda_), '-o',
        label="$\lambda$=" + str(lambda_), color=colors[i])
        plt.legend()
    plt.title("Possion distribution PMF for various $\lambda$")
    plt.ylabel("PMF at $k$")
    plt.xlabel("$k$")
    plt.show()
```

The following is the output:

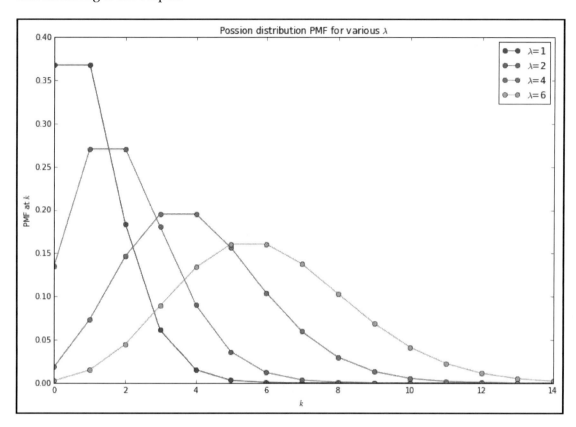

Poisson distribution

The geometric distribution

The geometric distribution is used for independent Bernoulli trials and measures the number of trials (X) that are needed to get one success. It can also represent the number of failures (Y = X-1) before the first success.

The PMF is expressed as follows:

$$f(k) = p(1-p)^{k-1}$$

The preceding expression makes sense because $f(k) = P(X = k)$, and if it takes k trials to get one success (p), then this means that we must have had k-1 failures, which are equal to $(1-p)$.

The expectation and variance are given as follows:

$$E(X) = 1/p$$

$$Var(X) = (1 - p)/p2$$

The following command explains the preceding formula clearly:

```
In [12]: from scipy.stats import geom
         p_vals=[0.01,0.2,0.5,0.8,0.9]
    x = np.arange(geom.ppf(0.01,p),geom.ppf(0.99,p))
         colors = matplotlib.rcParams['axes.color_cycle']
         for p,color in zip(p_vals,colors):
            x = np.arange(geom.ppf(0.01,p),geom.ppf(0.99,p))
               plt.plot(x,geom.pmf(x,p),'-o',ms=8,label='$p$=' + str(p))
          plt.legend(loc='best')
         plt.ylim(-0.5,1.5)
         plt.xlim(0,7.5)
         plt.ylabel("Pmf at $k$")
         plt.xlabel("$k$")
         plt.title("Geometric distribution PMF")
```

The following is the output:

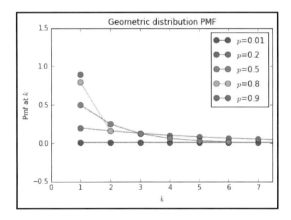

Geometric distribution

The negative binomial distribution

The negative binomial distribution is used for independent Bernoulli trials and measures the number of tries ($X=k$) that are needed before a specified number of successes (r) occur. An example would be the number of coin tosses it would take to obtain five heads. The PMF is given as follows:

$$P(X = k) = f(k) = \binom{k-1}{r-1} p^r (1-p)^{k-r}$$

The expectation and variance are given respectively by the following expressions:

$$E(X) = \frac{pr}{1-p}$$

$$Var(X) = \frac{pr}{(1-p)^2}$$

We can see that the negative binomial is a generalization of the geometric distribution, with the geometric distribution being a special case of the negative binomial, where $r=1$.

The code and plot are shown as follows:

```
In [189]: from scipy.stats import nbinom
       from matplotlib import colors
    clrs = matplotlib.rcParams['axes.color_cycle']
    x = np.arange(0,11)
    n_vals = [0.1,1,3,6]
    p=0.5
           for n, clr in zip(n_vals, clrs):
               rv = nbinom(n,p)
               plt.plot(x,rv.pmf(x), label="$n$=" + str(n), color=clr)
               plt.legend()
           plt.title("Negative Binomial Distribution PMF")
           plt.ylabel("PMF at $x$")
           plt.xlabel("$x$")
```

The following is the output:

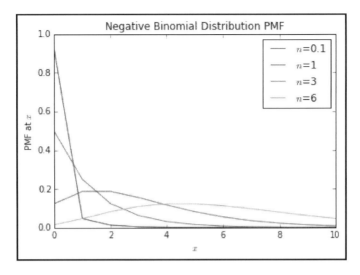

Negative binomial distribution

Continuous probability distributions

In a continuous probability distribution, the variable can take on any real number. It is not limited to a finite set of values, as it is in a discrete probability distribution; for example, the average weight of a healthy newborn baby can range from approximately 6–9 lbs (its weight can be 7.3 lbs, for example). A continuous probability distribution is characterized by a **probability density function (PDF)**.

The sum of all the probabilities that the random variable can assume is 1. Thus, the area under the graph of the probability density function adds up to 1.

The continuous uniform distribution

The uniform distribution models a random variable, *X*, that can take any value within the range *[a, b]* with equal probability.

The PDF is given by $f(x) = \dfrac{1}{b-a}$ for $a \leq x \leq b$, and 0 otherwise.

The expectation and variance are given respectively by the following expressions:

$$E(x) = (a+b)/2$$

$$Var(x) = (b-a)2/12$$

A continuous uniform probability distribution is generated and plotted for various sample sizes in the following code:

```
In [11]: np.random.seed(100)   # seed the random number generator
                               # so plots are reproducible
         subplots = [111,211,311]
         ctr = 0
         fig, ax = plt.subplots(len(subplots), figsize=(10,12))
         nsteps=10
         for i in range(0,3):
           cud = np.random.uniform(0,1,nsteps) # generate distrib
           count, bins, ignored = ax[ctr].hist(cud,15,normed=True)
           ax[ctr].plot(bins,np.ones_like(bins),linewidth=2, color='r')
           ax[ctr].set_title('sample size=%s' % nsteps)
           ctr += 1
           nsteps *= 100
         fig.subplots_adjust(hspace=0.4)
         plt.suptitle("Continuous Uniform probability distributions for
various sample sizes" , fontsize=14)
```

The following is the output:

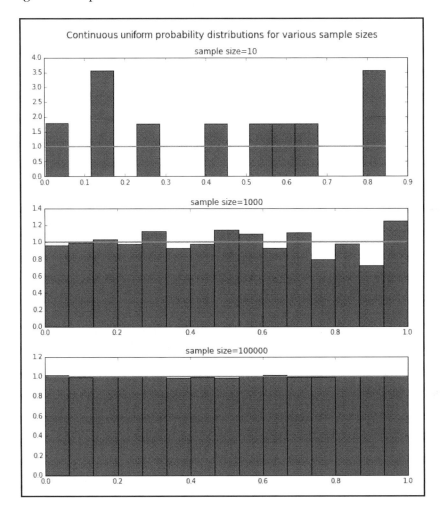

Continuous uniform distribution

The exponential distribution

The exponential distribution models the waiting time between two events in a Poisson process. A Poisson process is a process that follows a Poisson distribution in which events occur unpredictably with a known average rate. The exponential distribution can be described as the *continuous limit* of the geometric distribution, and is also Markovian (memoryless).

A memoryless random variable exhibits the property that its future state depends only on relevant information about the current time and not the information from further in the past. An example of modeling a Markovian/memoryless random variable is modeling short-term stock price behavior based on the idea that it follows a random walk. This leads to what is called the efficient market hypothesis in finance. For more information, refer to http://en.wikipedia.org/wiki/Random_walk_hypothesis.

The PDF of the exponential distribution is given by $f(x) = \lambda e^{-\lambda x}$. The expectation and variance are given respectively by the following expressions:

$$E(X) = 1/\lambda$$

$$Var(X) = 1/\lambda^2$$

For reference, refer to the link at http://en.wikipedia.org/wiki/Exponential_distribution.

The plot of the distribution and code is given as follows:

```
In [15]: import scipy.stats
         clrs = colors.cnames
          x = np.linspace(0,4, 100)
        expo = scipy.stats.expon
       lambda_ = [0.5, 1, 2, 5]
      plt.figure(figsize=(12,4))
      for l,c in zip(lambda_,clrs):
          plt.plot(x, expo.pdf(x, scale=1./l), lw=2,
                   color=c, label = "$\lambda = %.1f$"%l)
         plt.legend()
         plt.ylabel("PDF at $x$")
      plt.xlabel("$x$")
      plt.title("Pdf of an Exponential random variable for various
$\lambda$");
```

The following is the output:

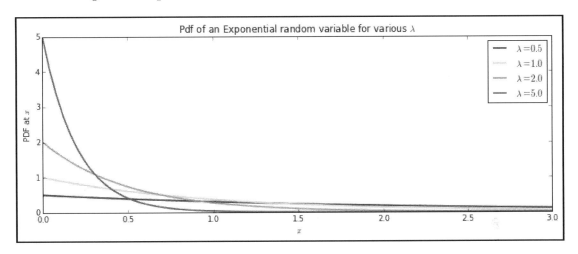

Exponential distribution

The normal distribution

The most important distribution in statistics is arguably the normal/Gaussian distribution. It models the probability distribution around a central value with no left or right bias. There are many examples of phenomena that follow the normal distribution, such as the following:

- The birth weights of babies
- Measurement errors
- Blood pressure
- Test scores

The normal distribution's importance is underlined by the central limit theorem, which states that the mean of many random variables drawn independently from the same distribution is approximately normal, regardless of the form of the original distribution. Its expected value and variance are given as follows:

$$E(X) = \mu$$

$$Var(X) = \sigma^2$$

The PDF of the normal distribution is given by the following expression:

$$f(x) = \frac{1}{\sqrt{2\pi\sigma^2}} \, exp(\frac{-(x-\mu)^2}{2\sigma^2})$$

The following code and plot explain the formula:

```
In [54]: import matplotlib
    from scipy.stats import norm
      X = 2.5
   dx = 0.1
   R = np.arange(-X,X+dx,dx)
   L = list()
   sdL = (0.5,1,2,3)
   for sd in sdL:
        f = norm.pdf
        L.append([f(x,loc=0,scale=sd) for x in R])
   colors = matplotlib.rcParams['axes.color_cycle']
   for sd,c,P in zip(sdL,colors,L):
        plt.plot(R,P,zorder=1,lw=1.5,color=c,
                 label="$\sigma$=" + str(sd))
        plt.legend()
   ax = plt.axes()
   ax.set_xlim(-2.1,2.1)
   ax.set_ylim(0,1.0)
   plt.title("Normal distribution Pdf")
   plt.ylabel("PDF at $\mu$=0, $\sigma$")
```

The following is the output:

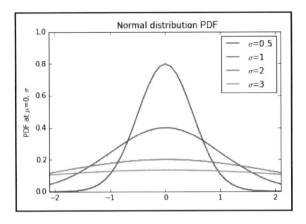

Normal distribution

A reference for the Python code to the plot the distributions can be found at http://bit.ly/1E17nYx.

The normal distribution can also be regarded as the continuous limit of the binomial distribution, and other distributions as $n \to \infty$. We can see this in the following code and plot:

```
In [18]:from scipy.stats import binom
     from matplotlib import colors
   cols = colors.cnames
   n_values = [1, 5,10, 30, 100]
   subplots = [111+100*x for x in range(0,len(n_values))]
   ctr = 0
   fig, ax = plt.subplots(len(subplots), figsize=(6,12))
   k = np.arange(0, 200)
   p=0.5
   for n, color in zip(n_values, cols):
         k=np.arange(0,n+1)
         rv = binom(n, p)
         ax[ctr].plot(k, rv.pmf(k), lw=2, color=color)
         ax[ctr].set_title("$n$=" + str(n))
         ctr += 1
   fig.subplots_adjust(hspace=0.5)
   plt.suptitle("Binomial distribution PMF (p=0.5) for various values of
 n", fontsize=14)
```

The following is the output:

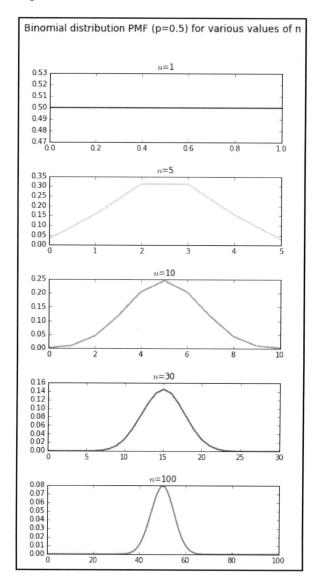

As *n* increases, the binomial distribution approaches the normal distribution. In fact, this is clearly seen in the preceding plots for *n>=30*.

Bayesian statistics versus frequentist statistics

In statistics today, there are two schools of thought as to how we interpret data and make statistical inferences. The classical and more dominant approach to date has been what is termed the frequentist approach (refer to `Chapter 7`, *A Tour of Statistics – The Classical Approach*). We are looking at the Bayesian approach in this chapter.

What is probability?

At the heart of the debate between the Bayesian and frequentist worldview is the question of how we define probability.

In the frequentist worldview, probability is a notion that is derived from the frequencies of repeated events—for example, when we define the probability of getting heads when a fair coin is tossed as being equal to half. This is because when we repeatedly toss a fair coin, the number of heads divided by the total number of coin tosses approaches 0.5 when the number of coin tosses is sufficiently large.

The Bayesian worldview is different, and the notion of probability is that it is related to one's degree of belief in the event happening. Thus, for a Bayesian statistician, having a belief that the probability of a fair die turning up five is *1/6* relates to our belief in the chances of that event occurring.

How the model is defined

From the model definition point of view, frequentists analyze how data and calculated metrics vary by making use of repeated experiments while keeping the model parameters fixed. Bayesians, on the other hand, utilize fixed experimental data, but vary their degrees of belief in the model parameters. This is explained as follows:

- **Frequentists**: If the models are fixed, data varies.
- **Bayesians**: If the data is fixed, models vary.

The frequentist approach is to use what is known as the maximum likelihood method to estimate model parameters. It involves generating data from a set of independent and identically distributed observations and fitting the observed data to the model. The value of the model parameter that best fits the data is the **maximum likelihood estimator** (**MLE**), which can sometimes be a function of the observed data.

Bayesianism approaches the problem differently from a probabilistic framework. A probability distribution is used to describe the uncertainty in the values. Bayesian practitioners estimate probabilities using observed data. In order to compute these probabilities, they make use of a single estimator, which is the Bayes formula. This produces a distribution rather than just a point estimate, as in the case of the frequentist approach.

Confidence (frequentist) versus credible (Bayesian) intervals

Let's compare what is meant by a 95 percent confidence interval (a term used by frequentists) with a 95 percent credible interval (a term used by Bayesian practitioners).

In a frequentist framework, a 95 percent confidence interval means that if you repeat your experiment an infinite number of times, generating intervals in the process, 95 percent of these intervals would contain the parameter we're trying to estimate, which is often referred to as θ. In this case, the interval is the random variable and not the parameter estimate, θ, which is fixed in the frequentist worldview.

In the case of the Bayesian credible interval, we have an interpretation that is more in line with the conventional interpretation ascribed to that of a frequentist confidence interval. Thus, we conclude that $Pr(a(Y) < \theta < b(Y)|\theta) = 0.95$. In this case, we can properly conclude that there is a 95 percent chance that θ lies within the interval.

For more information, refer to *Frequentism and Bayesianism: What's the Big Deal?* (Jake VanderPlas, *SciPy, 2014)* at `https://www.youtube.com/watch?v=KhAUfqhLakw`.

Conducting Bayesian statistical analysis

Conducting a Bayesian statistical analysis involves the following steps:

1. **Specifying a probability model**: In this step, we fully describe the model using a probability distribution. Based on the distribution of a sample that we have taken, we try to fit a model to it and attempt to assign probabilities to unknown parameters.

2. **Calculating a posterior distribution**: The posterior distribution is a distribution that we calculate in light of observed data. In this case, we will directly apply Bayes' formula. It will be specified as a function of the probability model that we specified in the previous step.

3. **Checking our model**: This is a necessary step where we review our model and its outputs before we make inferences. Bayesian inference methods use probability distributions to assign probabilities to possible outcomes.

Monte Carlo estimation of the likelihood function and PyMC

Bayesian statistics isn't just another method. It is an entirely different paradigm for practicing statistics. It uses probability models for making inferences, given the data that has been collected. This can be expressed in a fundamental expression as $P(H|D)$.

Here, H is our hypothesis, that is, the thing we're trying to prove, and D is our data or observations.

As a reminder of our previous discussion, the diachronic form of Bayes' theorem is as follows:

$$P(H|D) = P(H) * \frac{P(D|H)}{P(D)}$$

Here, *P(H)* is an unconditional prior probability that represents what we know before we conduct our trial. *P(D|H)* is our likelihood function, or probability of obtaining the data we observe, given that our hypothesis is true.

P(D) is the probability of the data, also known as the normalizing constant. This can be obtained by integrating the numerator over H.

The likelihood function is the most important piece of our Bayesian calculation and encapsulates all the information about the unknowns in the data. It has some semblance to a reverse probability mass function.

One argument against adopting a Bayesian approach is that the calculation of the prior can be subjective. There are many arguments in favor of this approach, one being that external prior information can be included, as mentioned previously.

The likelihood value represents an unknown integral, which in simple cases can be obtained by analytic integration.

Monte Carlo (**MC**) integration is needed for more complicated use cases involving higher-dimensional integrals and can be used to compute the likelihood function.

MC integration can be computed through a variety of sampling methods, such as uniform sampling, stratified sampling, and importance sampling. In Monte Carlo integration, we can approximate the integral as follows:

$$p\,g = \int g\,dP$$

The following is the finite sum:

$$P_n\,g = \frac{1}{n}\sum_{i=1}^{n} g(X_i)$$

Here, x is a sample vector from g. The proof that this estimate is a good one can be obtained from the law of large numbers and by making sure that the simulation error is small.

When conducting Bayesian analysis in Python, we will need a module that will enable us to calculate the likelihood function using the Monte Carlo method. The `PyMC` library fulfills that need. It provides a Monte Carlo method known commonly as MCMC. We will not delve further into the technical details of MCMC, but the interested reader can find out more about MCMC implementation in `PyMC` from the following sources:

- *Monte Carlo Integration in Bayesian Estimation*: `http://bit.ly/1bMALeu`
- *Markov Chain Monte Carlo Maximum Likelihood*: `http://bit.ly/1KBP8hH`
- *Bayesian Statistical Analysis Using Python–Part 1, SciPy 2014, Chris Fonnesbeck*: `http://www.youtube.com/watch?v=vOBB_ycQ0RA`

MCMC is not a universal panacea; there are some drawbacks to the approach, and one of them is the slow convergence of the algorithm.

Bayesian analysis example – switchpoint detection

Here, we will try to use Bayesian inference and model an interesting dataset. The dataset in question consists of the author's **Facebook (FB)** post history over time. We have scrubbed the FB history data and saved the dates in the `fb_post_dates.txt` file. Here is what the data in the file looks like:

```
head -2 ../fb_post_dates.txt
Tuesday, September 30, 2014 | 2:43am EDT
Tuesday, September 30, 2014 | 2:22am EDT
```

Thus, we see a datetime series, representing the date and time at which the author posted on FB. First, we read the file into DataFrame, separating the timestamp into `Date` and `Time` columns:

```
In [91]: filePath="./data/fb_post_dates.txt"
         fbdata_df=pd.read_csv(filePath,  sep='|', parse_dates=[0],
header=None,names=['Date','Time'])
```

Next, we inspect the data as follows:

```
In [92]: fbdata_df.head()   #inspect the data
Out[92]:    Date          Time
0   2014-09-30    2:43am EDT
1   2014-09-30    2:22am EDT
2   2014-09-30    2:06am EDT
3   2014-09-30    1:07am EDT
4   2014-09-28    9:16pm EDT
```

Now, we index the data by `Date`, creating a `DatetimeIndex` so that we can run resample on it to count by month, as follows:

```
In [115]: fbdata_df_ind=fbdata_df.set_index('Date')
          fbdata_df_ind.head(5)
Out[115]:
          Date          Time
          2014-09-30    2:43am EDT
          2014-09-30    2:22am EDT
          2014-09-30    2:06am EDT
          2014-09-30    1:07am EDT
          2014-09-28    9:16pm EDT
```

We then display information about the index as follows:

```
In [116]: fbdata_df_ind.index
Out[116]: <class 'pandas.tseries.index.DatetimeIndex'>
          [2014-09-30, ..., 2007-04-16]
          Length: 7713, Freq: None, Timezone: None
```

Next, we obtain a count of posts by month using resample:

```
In [99]: fb_mth_count_=fbdata_df_ind.resample('M', how='count')
         fb_mth_count_.rename(columns={'Time':'Count'},
                                inplace=True)    # Rename
         fb_mth_count_.head()
Out[99]:            Count
         Date
         2007-04-30  1
         2007-05-31  0
         2007-06-30  5
         2007-07-31  50
         2007-08-31  24
```

The `Date` format is shown as the last day of the month. Now, we create a scatter plot of FB post counts from 2007–2015, and we make the size of the dots proportional to the values in `matplotlib`:

```
In [108]: %matplotlib inline
          import datetime as dt
#Obtain the count data from the DataFrame as a dictionary
          year_month_count=fb_bymth_count.to_dict()['Count']
          size=len(year_month_count.keys())
#get dates as list of strings
          xdates=[dt.datetime.strptime(str(yyyymm),'%Y%m')
                    for yyyymm in year_month_count.keys()]
          counts=year_month_count.values()
          plt.scatter(xdates,counts,s=counts)
         plt.xlabel('Year')
          plt.ylabel('Number of Facebook posts')
          plt.show()
```

The following is the output:

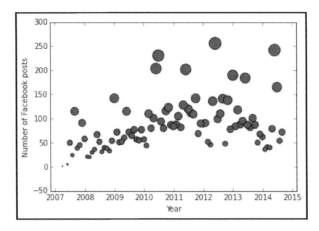

The question we would like to investigate is whether there was a change in behavior at some point over the time period. Specifically, we want to identify whether there was a specific period at which the mean number of FB posts changed. This is often referred to as the switchpoint or changepoint in a time series.

We can make use of the Poisson distribution to model this. You might recall that the Poisson distribution can be used to model time series count data. (Refer to `http://bit.ly/1JniIqy` for more about this.)

If we represent our monthly FB post count by C_i, we can represent our model as follows:

$$(Ci|s, e, l) \sim Poisson(ri)$$

The r_i parameter is the rate parameter of the Poisson distribution, but we don't know what its value is. If we examine the scatter plot of the FB time series count data, we can see that there was a jump in the number of posts sometime around mid to late 2010, perhaps coinciding with the start of the 2010 World Cup in South Africa, which the author attended.

The s parameter is the switchpoint, which is when the rate parameter changes, while e and l are the values of the r_i parameter before and after the switchpoint respectively. This can be represented as follows:

$$r = \begin{cases} e & if\ i < s \\ l & if\ i \geqslant s \end{cases}$$

Note that the variables specified here—*C, s, e, r* and *l*—are all Bayesian random variables. For Bayesian random variables that represent one's beliefs about their values, we need to model them using a probability distribution. We would like to infer the values of *e* and *l*, which are unknown. In PyMC, we can represent random variables using the stochastic and deterministic classes. We note that the exponential distribution is the amount of time between Poisson events. Therefore, in the case of *e* and *l*, we choose the exponential distribution to model them since they can be any positive number:

$$e \sim Exp(r)$$

$$l \sim Exp(r)$$

In the case of *s*, we will choose to model it using the uniform distribution, which reflects our belief that it is equally likely that the switchpoint can occur on any day within the entire time period. This means that we have the following:

$$s \sim Discreet\ Uniform(t0, tf)$$

Here, t_0, t_f corresponds to the lower and upper boundaries of the year, *i*. Let's now use PyMC to represent the model that we developed earlier. We will now use PyMC to see whether we can detect a switchpoint in the FB post data. In addition to the scatter plot, we can also display the data in a bar chart. To do that, we first need to obtain a count of FB posts ordered by month in a list:

```
In [69]: fb_activity_data = [year_month_count[k] for k in
                            sorted(year_month_count.keys())]
         fb_activity_data[:5]
Out[70]: [1, 0, 5, 50, 24]
In [71]: fb_post_count=len(fb_activity_data)
```

We render the bar plot using matplotlib:

```
In [72]: from IPython.core.pylabtools import figsize
         import matplotlib.pyplot as plt
           figsize(8, 5)
         plt.bar(np.arange(fb_post_count),
          fb_activity_data, color="#49a178")
         plt.xlabel("Time (months)")
         plt.ylabel("Number of FB posts")
         plt.title("Monthly Facebook posts over time")
         plt.xlim(0,fb_post_count);
```

The following is the output:

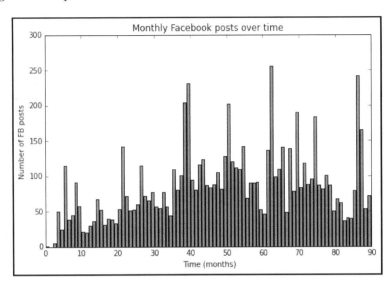

Looking at the preceding bar chart, can we conclude that there was a change in FB frequency posting behavior over time? We can use PyMC on the model that we have developed to help us find out the change as follows:

```
In [88]: # Define data and stochastics
         import pymc as pm
         switchpoint = pm.DiscreteUniform('switchpoint',
                                          lower=0,
                              upper=len(fb_activity_data)-1,
                                doc='Switchpoint[month]')
         avg = np.mean(fb_activity_data)
         early_mean = pm.Exponential('early_mean', beta=1./avg)
         late_mean = pm.Exponential('late_mean', beta=1./avg)
         late_mean
Out[88]:<pymc.distributions.Exponential 'late_mean' at 0x10ee56d50>
```

Here, we define a method for the rate parameter, *r*, and we model the count data using a Poisson distribution as discussed previously:

```
In [89]: @pm.deterministic(plot=False)
         def rate(s=switchpoint, e=early_mean, l=late_mean):
             ''' Concatenate Poisson means '''
             out = np.zeros(len(fb_activity_data))
             out[:s] = e
             out[s:] = l
             return out
```

```
                    fb_activity = pm.Poisson('fb_activity', mu=rate,
                            value=fb_activity_data, observed=True)
                    fb_activity
```
Out[89]: <pymc.distributions.Poisson 'fb_activity' at 0x10ed1ee50>

In the preceding code snippet, `@pm.deterministic` is a decorator that denotes that the rate function is deterministic, meaning that its values are entirely determined by other variables—in this case, *e*, *s*, and *l*. The decorator is necessary to tell `PyMC` to convert the rate function into a deterministic object. If we do not specify the decorator, an error occurs. For more information about Python decorators, refer to `http://bit.ly/1zj8U0o`.

For more information, refer to the following web pages:

- `http://en.wikipedia.org/wiki/Poisson_process`
- `http://pymc-devs.github.io/pymc/tutorial.html`
- `https://github.com/CamDavidsonPilon/Probabilistic-Programming-and-Baye sian-Methods-for-Hackers`

We will now create a model with the FB count data (`fb_activity`) and the *e*, *s*, *l* (`early_mean`, `late_mean`, and `rate` respectively) parameters.

Next, using `PyMC`, we create an `MCMC` object that enables us to fit our data using MCMC methods. We then call sample on the resulting `MCMC` object to do the fitting:

```
In [94]: fb_activity_model=pm.Model([fb_activity,early_mean,
                            late_mean,rate])
In [95]: from pymc import MCMC
         fbM=MCMC(fb_activity_model)
In [96]: fbM.sample(iter=40000,burn=1000, thin=20)
         [----------------100%-----------------] 40000 of 40000
         complete in 11.0 sec
```

Fitting the model using MCMC involves using Markov Chain Monte Carlo methods to generate a probability distribution for the posterior, *P(s,e,l | D)*. It uses the Monte Carlo process to repeatedly simulate sampling of the data and does this until the algorithm seems to converge to a steady state, based on multiple criteria. This is a Markov process because successive samples are dependent only on the previous sample. For further information on Markov chain convergence, refer to `http://bit.ly/1IETkhC`.

The generated samples are referred to as **traces**. We can view what the marginal posterior distribution of the parameters looks like by looking at a histogram of its trace:

```
In [97]: from pylab import hist,show
          %matplotlib inline
         hist(fbM.trace('late_mean')[:])
Out[97]: (array([  15.,   61.,  214.,  421.,  517.,  426.,  202.,
                   70.,   21.,    3.]),
          array([ 102.29451192,  103.25158404,  104.20865616,
                  105.16572829,  106.12280041,  107.07987253,
                  108.03694465,  108.99401677,  109.95108889,
                  110.90816101,  111.86523313]),
          <a list of 10 Patch objects>)
```

The following is the output:

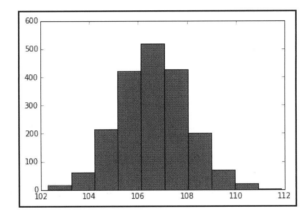

Next, we find the early mean:

```
In [98]:plt.hist(fbM.trace('early_mean')[:])
Out[98]: (array([  20.,  105.,  330.,  489.,  470.,  314.,  147.,
                   60.,    3.,   12.]),
          array([ 49.19781192,  50.07760882,  50.95740571,
                  51.83720261,  52.71699951,  53.59679641,
                  54.47659331,  55.35639021,  56.2361871 ,
                  57.115984  ,  57.9957809 ]),
          <a list of 10 Patch objects>)
```

The following is the output:

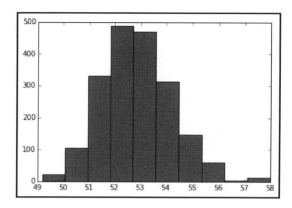

Here, we see what the switchpoint looks like in terms of the number of months:

```
In [99]: fbM.trace('switchpoint')[:]
Out[99]: array([38, 38, 38, ..., 35, 35, 35])
In [150]: plt.hist(fbM.trace('switchpoint')[:])
Out[150]: (array([ 1899.,      0.,      0.,      0.,      0.,      0.,
              0., 0., 0.,     51.]),
          array([ 35. ,   35.3,   35.6,   35.9,   36.2,   36.5,   36.8,
              37.1,   37.4,   37.7,   38. ]),
          <a list of 10 Patch objects>)
```

The following is the output:

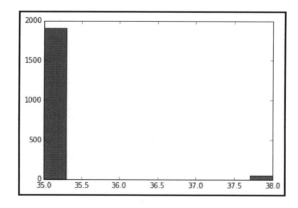

Histogram of the switchpoint for the number of months

We can see that the switchpoint is in the neighborhood of the months 35–38. Here, we use `matplotlib` to display the marginal posterior distributions of *e*, *s*, and *l* in a single diagram:

```
In [141]: early_mean_samples=fbM.trace('early_mean')[:]
          late_mean_samples=fbM.trace('late_mean')[:]
          switchpoint_samples=fbM.trace('switchpoint')[:]
In [142]: from IPython.core.pylabtools import figsize
        figsize(12.5, 10)
      # histogram of the samples:
      fig = plt.figure()
      fig.subplots_adjust(bottom=-0.05)
      n_mths=len(fb_activity_data)
      ax = plt.subplot(311)
      ax.set_autoscaley_on(False)
       plt.hist(early_mean_samples, histtype='stepfilled',
              bins=30, alpha=0.85, label="posterior of $e$",
              color="turquoise", normed=True)
      plt.legend(loc="upper left")
      plt.title(r"""Posterior distributions of the variables
              $e, l, s$""",fontsize=16)
      plt.xlim([40, 120])
       plt.ylim([0, 0.6])
      plt.xlabel("$e$ value",fontsize=14)
       ax = plt.subplot(312)
      ax.set_autoscaley_on(False)
      plt.hist(late_mean_samples, histtype='stepfilled',
              bins=30, alpha=0.85, label="posterior of $l$",
              color="purple", normed=True)
      plt.legend(loc="upper left")
      plt.xlim([40, 120])
       plt.ylim([0, 0.6])
      plt.xlabel("$l$ value",fontsize=14)
      plt.subplot(313)
      w = 1.0 / switchpoint_samples.shape[0] *
          np.ones_like(switchpoint_samples)
      plt.hist(switchpoint_samples, bins=range(0,n_mths), alpha=1,
              label=r"posterior of $s$", color="green",
              weights=w, rwidth=2.)
      plt.xlim([20, n_mths - 20])
      plt.xlabel(r"$s$ (in days)",fontsize=14)
      plt.ylabel("probability")
      plt.legend(loc="upper left")
       plt.show()
```

The following is the output:

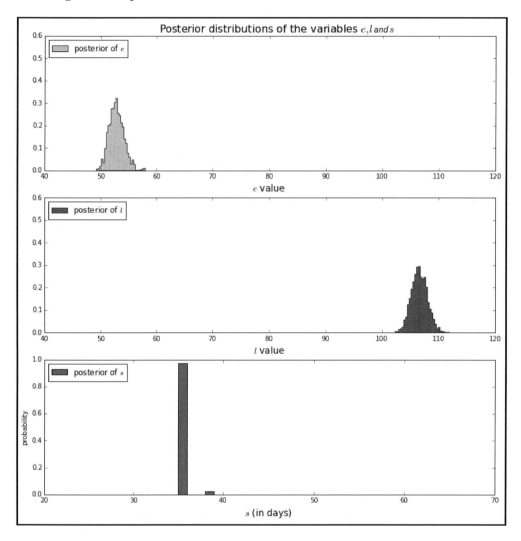

Marginal posterior distributions

PyMC also has plotting functionality as it uses `matplotlib`. In the following plots, we display a time series plot, an **autocorrelation plot (acorr)**, and a histogram of the samples drawn for the early mean, late mean, and switchpoint. The histogram is useful for visualizing the posterior distribution. The autocorrelation plot shows whether values in the previous period are strongly related to values in the current period:

```
In [100]: from pymc.Matplot import plot
          plot(fbM)
      Plotting late_mean
      Plotting switchpoint
      Plotting early_mean
```

The following is the late mean plot:

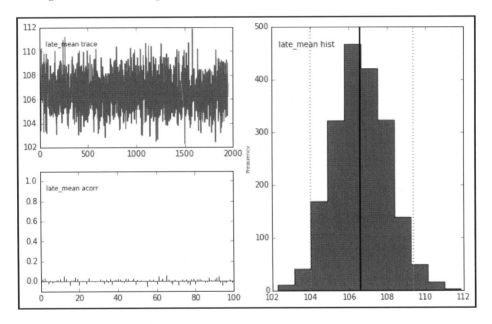

Graph for pymc_comprehensive_late_mean

Here, we display the switchpoint plot:

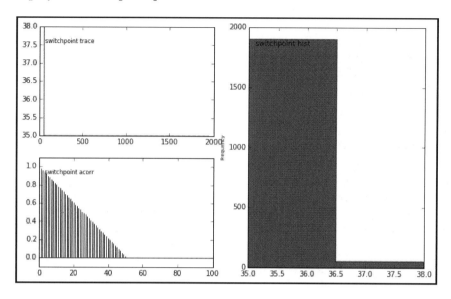

PyMC comprehensive switchpoint

Here, we display the early mean plot:

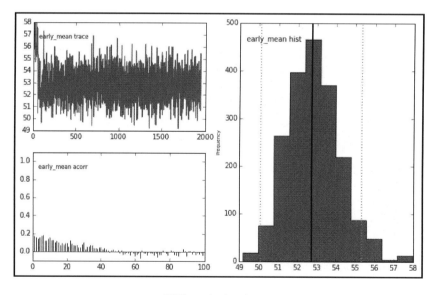

PyMC comprehensive early mean

From the output of `PyMC`, we can conclude that the switchpoint is around 35–38 months from the start of the time series. This corresponds to some time between March and July 2010. The author can testify that this was a banner year for him with respect to the use of FB since it was the year of the FIFA World Cup finals that were held in South Africa, which he attended.

Maximum likelihood estimate

Maximum likelihood estimate (**MLE**) is a method that is used to estimate the probability distribution parameters of a population from the available sample data. MLE methods can also be considered as a Bayesian alternative.

Probability distribution gives the probability of observing a data point given distribution parameters such as mean, standard deviation, and degree of freedom.

The probability of data point given distribution parameters is expressed as $\text{Prob}(X|\mu,\alpha)$ ------1.

MLE deals with the inverse problem. It is used to find the most likely values of distribution parameters given the set of data points. For that purpose, another statistic called likelihood is defined. The likelihood is defined as the probability of observing the distribution parameters given the data points.

The probability of observing the distribution parameters given the data point is expressed as $L(\mu,\alpha|X)$----2.

The quantities in equations 1 and 2 are the same probabilities, just stated differently. Therefore, we can write the following:

$$L(\mu, \alpha|X) = Prob(X|\mu, \alpha)$$

To understand this concept better, have a look at the following graph:

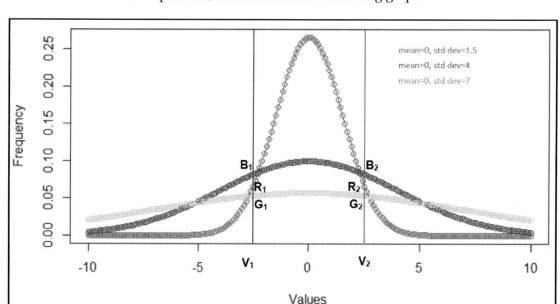

MLE estimation illustration for normal distribution with two data points

The graph shows three normal distributions with different means and standard deviations. The two vertical lines represent values V_1=-2.5 and V_2=2.5.

Suppose that we represent the probability that a data point V_1=-2.5 belongs to the red (mean=0, std dev=1.5) distribution by $P(red | V_1$=-2.5). Similarly, the probability that a data point V_1=-2.5 belongs to the blue (mean=0, std dev=4) distribution is $P(blue | V_1$=-2.5).

Now, looking at the graph shown here, we can state the following:

$$P(red|V_1 = -2.5) = V_1 R_1$$

$$P(blue|V_1 = -2.5) = V_1 B_1$$

$$P(green|V_1 = -2.5) = V_1 G_1$$

If we had to make a decision based on only available datapoints, then we would decide that V_1=2.5 belongs to the blue distribution as $V_1 B_1 > V_1 R_1 > V_1 G_1$, and we choose the distribution with the largest probability of that data point belonging to that distribution.

But what if we have one more data point, or many more? For this situation, let's add another data point called V_2 to our dataset. The individual probabilities for V_2 are as follows:

$$P(red|V_2 = 2.5) = V_2 R_2$$

$$P(blue|V_2 = 2.5) = V_2 B_2$$

$$P(green|V_2 = 2.5) = V_2 G_2$$

Since there are two points now, we can't base our decisions on individual probabilities and would have to calculate joint probabilities. If we assume that the event of one data point occurring is independent of the event of another data point occurring, then the joint probabilities are given by the individual probabilities.

Suppose the joint probability that the two points belong to the red distribution given the two data points is denoted by *P(red|V₁=-2.5, V₂=2.5)*. Then the following will be true:

$$P(red|V_1 = -2.5, V_2 = 2.5) = V_1 R_1 * V_2 R_2$$

$$P(blue|V_1 = -2.5, V_2 = 2.5) = V_1 B_1 * V_2 B_2$$

$$P(green|V_1 = -2.5, V_2 = 2.5) = V_1 G_1 * V_2 G_2$$

We should choose the distribution that has the maximum joint probability. In this case, the blue would have the highest joint probability, as we can conclude by looking at the graph.

As the number of points in the dataset increase, it no longer remains feasible to draw inferences about the maximum joint probability by looking at charts like the preceding charts. We need to resort to algebraic and calculus methods to find the parameters (defining the distribution) to find the distribution that maximises the joint probability of the dataset to belong to that distribution.

If we assume that the individual data points are independent of each other, then the likelihood or probability of observing distribution parameters given all the data points is given by the following formula:

$$L(\mu, \alpha | X_1, X_2, X_3, \ldots, X_n) = L(\mu, \alpha | X_1) * L(\mu, \alpha | X_2) * L(\mu, \alpha | X_3) * \ldots \ldots \ldots L(\mu, \alpha | X_n)$$

In the MLE calculations, we try to find the values of μ, α that maximize $L(\mu,\alpha \mid X_1, X_2, X_3, ..., X_n)$. In that endeavor, taking the log of both sides helps a lot. It doesn't change the objective function as the log is a monotonically increasing function that makes the calculations a lot easier. The log of the likelihood is often called the log-likelihood and is calculated as follows:

$$log(L(\mu, \alpha|X_1, X_2, X_3, ..., X_n)) = log(L(\mu, \alpha|X_1)) + log(L(\mu, \alpha|X_2)) + log(L(\mu, \alpha|X_3)) + ... log(L(\mu, \alpha|X_n))$$

To find the maxima of the log-likelihood function, $log(L(\mu,\alpha \mid X_1, X_2, X_3, ..., X_n))$, we can do the following:

- Take the first derivative of $log(L(\mu,\alpha \mid X_1, X_2, X_3, ..., X_n))$, function w.r.t μ,α and equate it to 0
- Take the second derivative of $log(L(\mu,\alpha \mid X_1, X_2, X_3, ..., X_n))$, function w.r.t μ,α and confirm that it is negative

MLE calculation examples

We will now look at two MLE calculation examples.

Uniform distribution

Suppose we have a probability distribution of X that means the following is true:

$$Pr(X=x) = 1/b\text{-}a \text{ for all } a<X<b$$

$$Pr(X=x) = 0 \text{ for all other } X$$

Here, *a* and *b* are parameters of uniform distribution.

Since the probability is the same (or uniform) for all the values, it is called a uniform distribution.

Suppose there are n data points in a dataset that is hypothesized to follow a uniform distribution. Based on these points, we aim to find the values of a and b to define the distribution to which these data points most likely belong. For this, we can use the maximum likelihood estimate method:

$$Pr(a, b | x_1, x_2, x_3, \ldots, x_n) = [1/(b-a)] * [1/(b-a)] * [1/(b-a)] * \ldots \ldots * [1/(b-a)] = [1/(b-a)]^n$$

$$Pr(a, b | x_1, x_2, x_3, \ldots, x_n) = L(a, b | x_1, x_2, x_3, \ldots, x_n) = [1/(b-a)]^n = (b-a)^{-n}$$

$$log(L(a, b | x_1, x_2, x_3, \ldots, x_n)) = -n^* log(b-a)$$

We have to find the a, b that maximises $log(L(a,b | x_1, x_2, x_3, \ldots, x_n))$.

For this, we would differentiate $log(L(a,b | x_1, x_2, x_3, \ldots, x_n))$ with respect to $b-a$.

This gives $-n/(b-a)$, which is always less than zero, indicating that $log(L(a,b | x_1, x_2, x_3, \ldots, x_n))$ is a monotonically decreasing function and its value would decrease as $(b-a)$ increased. Therefore, a large $b-a$ would maximize the probability.

Keeping that in mind, we get $b=max(X)$, $a = min(X)$.

Poisson distribution

The Poisson distribution has been explained in an earlier section of this chapter. In a nutshell, the Poisson distribution is a binomial distribution with an infinitely large number of samples, so large that the discrete nature of the binomial distribution gives way to the Poisson distribution. The Poisson distribution also deals with the probability of the occurrence of events. But rather than thinking in terms of the probability of the occurrence of the event in each trial, we think in terms of time intervals and ask ourselves how many times the event of interest would occur in that time interval. The parameter also moves from the probability of success for each trial to the number of successes in a given time interval.

Here's a summary:

- **Binomial**: Probability of a number of successes in a given number of trials given a probability of success for each trial
- **Poisson**: Probability of a number of successes in a given interval of time given the arrival or success rate—that is, the average number of successes in a given time interval

The Poisson probability distribution is expressed by the following:

$$Pr(X = x | \lambda) = \lambda x * e - \lambda / x!$$

Here, λ is the arrival or success rate.

This expression gives the probability of observing x successes in the given time interval (the same interval in which the arrival rate is defined).

We are interested in the MLE estimation of λ given a set of datasets that are supposed to be following a Poisson distribution:

$$L(\lambda | x) = \lambda x * e - \lambda / x!$$

$$f(x) = \frac{\lambda^x e^{-\lambda}}{x!} \; ; \text{ where x =0,1,2,...}$$

The likelihood function is:

$$L(\lambda) = \prod_{i=1}^{n} \frac{\lambda^{x_i} e^{-\lambda}}{x_i!} = e^{-\lambda n} \frac{\lambda^{\sum_{i=1}^{n} x_i}}{\prod_{i=1}^{n} x_i}$$

The log-likelihood is:

$$lnL(\lambda) = -\lambda n + \sum_{i=1}^{n} x i . ln(\lambda) - ln(\prod_{i=1}^{n} x i)$$

Setting its derivative with respect to λ to zero, we have:

$$\frac{d}{d\lambda} lnL(\lambda) = -n + \sum_{i=1}^{n} x i . \frac{1}{\lambda} = 0$$

Maths of the MLE calculation for a Poisson distribution

Note how taking the log eases the calculation algebraically. It introduces some numerical challenges though—for example, making sure that the likelihood is never 0, as log cannot be defined as 0. Numerical methods also result in an invalid value if the log-likelihood is infinitely small.

The MLE finds that the estimate of the arrival rate is equal to the mean of the dataset—that is, the number of observed arrivals in the given time interval in the past. The preceding calculation can be done using NumPy and other supporting packages in Python.

There are several steps that we need to take to perform this calculation in Python:

1. Write a function to calculate the Poisson probability for each point:

```
import numpy as np
import math as mh
np.seterr(divide='ignore', invalid='ignore') #ignore division by
zero and invalid numbers
def poissonpdf(x,lbd):
    val = (np.power(lbd,x)*np.exp(-lbd))/(mh.factorial(x))
    return val
```

2. Write a function to calculate the log-likelihood over the data given a value for the arrival rate:

```
def loglikelihood(data,lbd):
    lkhd=1
    for i in range(len(data)):
        lkhd=lkhd*poissonpdf(data[i],lbd)
    if lkhd!=0:
        val=np.log(lkhd)
    else:
        val=0
    return val
```

3. Write a function to calculate the derivative of the log-likelihood for the arrival rate λ:

```
def diffllhd(data,lbd):
    diff = -len(data) + sum(data)/lbd
    return diff
```

4. Generate test data with 100 data points—a random number of arrivals/unit time between 3 and 12:

```
data=[randint(3, 12) for p in range(100)]
```

5. Calculate the log-likelihood for different values of arrival rates (1 to 9) and plot them to find the arrival rate that maximizes:

```
y=[loglikelihood(data,i) for i in range(1,10)]
y=[num for num in y if num ]
x=[i for i in range(1,10) if loglikelihood(data,i)]
plt.plot(x,y)
plt.axvline(x=6,color='k')
plt.title('Log-Likelihoods for different lambdas')
plt.xlabel('Log Likelihood')
plt.ylabel('Lambda')
```

From this, we get the following plot, which shows that the maximum value of the log-likelihood on the test data is obtained when the arrival rate is 6/unit time:

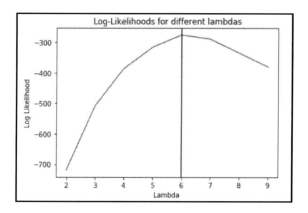

Log-likelihood values at different values of lambda (that is, arrival rate)

6. Use the Newton–Raphson method to find the global maximum of the log-likelihood:

```
def newtonRaphson(data,lbd):
    h = loglikelihood(data,lbd) / diffllhd(data,lbd)
    while abs(h) >= 0.0001:
        if diffllhd!=0:
            h = loglikelihood(data,lbd) / diffllhd(data,lbd)

            # x(i+1) = x(i) - f(x) / f'(x)
            lbd = lbd - h
        else:
            lbd=lbd
    return lbd
```

 Note: The `lbd` parameter in the function definition is the initial value to start the search with.

The Newton–Raphson method is a popular computation method used to find the roots of complex equations. It is an iterative process that finds different values of independent variables until the dependent variable reaches 0. More information can be found at `http://www.math.ubc.ca/~anstee/math104/newtonmethod.pdf`.

The results are greatly affected by the initial value of the parameter that is provided to start the search. The iterative search can go in very different directions if the start values are different, so be careful while using it.

The concept of MLE can be extended to perform distribution-based regression. Suppose that we hypothesize that the arrival rate is a function of one or several parameters. Then the lambda would be defined by a function of the parameters:

$$\Lambda = w0 + c * w1 + d * w2$$

In this case, the arrival rate would be calculated as follows:

1. Use the value of the arrival rate from the previous equation in the log-likelihood calculation.
2. Find the partial derivative of the log-likelihood with regard to w_0, w_1, and w_2.
3. Equate all the partial derivates to 0 and find the optimum values of w_0, w_1, and w_2.
4. Find the optimum value of the arrival rate based on these parameters.

To use the MLE calculations, do the following:

1. Find population parameters, such as the mean, std dev, arrival rate, and density, from the sample parameters.
2. Fit the distribution-based regression on data where simple linear regression wouldn't work, such as the parameter-based arrival rate example discussed previously, or logistic regression weights.

Its usage in fitting the regression model brings it into the same league of optimization methods such as OLS, gradient descent, Adam optimization, RMSprop, and other methods.

References

For a more in-depth look at other Bayesian statistics topics that we touched upon, please take a look at the following references:

- *Probabilistic Programming and Bayesian Methods for Hackers:* `https://github.com/CamDavidsonPilon/Probabilistic-Programming-and-Bayesian-Methods-for-Hackers`
- *Bayesian Data Analysis, Third Edition, Andrew Gelman:* `http://www.amazon.com/Bayesian-Analysis-Chapman-Statistical-Science/dp/1439840954`
- *The Bayesian Choice, Christian P Robert* (this is more theoretical): `http://www.springer.com/us/book/9780387952314`
- *PyMC documentation:* `http://pymc-devs.github.io/pymc/index.html`

Summary

In this chapter, we undertook a whirlwind tour of one of the hottest trends in statistics and data analysis in the past few years—the Bayesian approach to statistical inference. We covered a lot of ground here.

We examined what the Bayesian approach to statistics entails and discussed the various reasons why the Bayesian view is a compelling one, such as the fact that it values facts over belief. We explained the key statistical distributions and showed how we can use the various statistical packages to generate and plot them in `matplotlib`.

We tackled a rather difficult topic without too much oversimplification and demonstrated how we can use the `PyMC` package and Monte Carlo simulation methods to showcase the power of Bayesian statistics to formulate models, perform trend analysis, and make inferences on a real-world dataset (Facebook user posts). The concept of maximum likelihood estimation was also introduced and explained with several examples. It is a popular method for estimating distribution parameters and fitting a probability distribution to a given dataset.

In the next chapter, we will discuss how we can solve real-life data case studies using pandas.

12
Data Case Studies Using pandas

So far, we have covered the extensive functionalities of pandas. We'll try to implement these functionalities in some case studies. These case studies will give us an overview of the use of each functionality and help us determine the pivotal points in handling a DataFrame. Moreover, the step-by-step approach of the case studies helps us to deepen our understanding of the pandas functions. This chapter is equipped with practical examples along with code snippets to ensure that, by the end, you understand the pandas approach to solving the DataFrame problems.

We will cover the following case studies:

- End-to-end exploratory data analysis
- Web scraping with Python
- Data validation

End-to-end exploratory data analysis

Exploratory data analysis refers to the critical process of understanding the quirks of data—the outliers, the columns containing the most relevant information, and determining the relationship between the variables using statistics and graphical representations.

Let's consider the following DataFrame to perform exploratory data analysis:

```
df = pd.read_csv("data.csv")
df
```

The following screenshot shows the DataFrame loaded in Jupyter Notebook:

	zip	state_name	soldBy	customerID	officeID	active_status	days_old	services_completed	services_due	completion_percentage	...	age_median	race_white
0	75087	Texas	23335	477991	9	1	925	12	11.80	1.0169	...	39.0	87.71
1	76002	Texas	2895	485475	9	0	931	9	11.87	0.7582	...	30.0	42.06
2	75068	Texas	3161	485476	9	1	930	12	11.86	1.0118	...	31.0	70.89
3	76013	Texas	3351	485479	9	1	931	13	11.87	1.0952	...	38.0	74.66
4	76002	Texas	2895	485481	9	0	931	2	11.87	0.1685	...	30.0	42.06
5	75068	Texas	2589	485483	9	1	931	12	11.87	1.0110	...	31.0	70.89
6	75052	Texas	3240	485485	9	0	931	4	11.87	0.3370	...	32.0	45.15
7	75052	Texas	3364	485493	9	0	931	2	11.87	0.1685	...	32.0	45.15
8	75040	Texas	3147	485499	9	0	930	10	11.86	0.8432	...	34.0	54.24
9	76248	Texas	2624	485501	9	0	1000	1	12.63	0.0792	...	39.0	87.86
10	76018	Texas	2783	485502	9	1	930	12	11.86	1.0118	...	31.0	43.74

DataFrame loaded in Jupyter Notebook

Data overview

The preceding DataFrame is the customer data of an automobile servicing firm. They basically provide services to their clients on a periodic basis. Each row in the DataFrame corresponds to a unique customer. Hence, it is customer-level data. Here is an observation from the data:

```
data.shape

(27002, 26)
```

The shape of the DataFrame

We can observe that the data contains 27,002 records and 26 characteristics.

Before we start exploratory data analysis on any data, it is advised to know as much about the data as possible—the column names and their corresponding data types, whether they contain null values or not (and if so, how many), and so on. The following screenshot shows some of the basic information about the DataFrame obtained using the `info` function in pandas:

```
data.info()
<class 'pandas.core.frame.DataFrame'>
RangeIndex: 27002 entries, 0 to 27001
Data columns (total 26 columns):
zip                         27002 non-null int64
state_name                  26826 non-null object
soldBy                      27002 non-null int64
customerID                  27002 non-null int64
officeID                    27002 non-null int64
active_status               27002 non-null int64
days_old                    27002 non-null int64
services_completed          27002 non-null int64
services_due                27002 non-null float64
completion_percentage       27002 non-null float64
balance                     27002 non-null int64
difference                  27002 non-null float64
avg_contract_value          27002 non-null int64
distance_in_miles           27002 non-null float64
population_current          26826 non-null float64
gender_male                 26826 non-null float64
age_median                  26826 non-null float64
race_white                  26826 non-null float64
crime_overall               26826 non-null float64
households_total            26826 non-null float64
households_value            26826 non-null float64
households_yearbuilt        26826 non-null float64
households_occupancy_owned  26826 non-null float64
income_average              26826 non-null float64
income_median               26826 non-null float64
costs_overall               26826 non-null float64
dtypes: float64(16), int64(9), object(1)
memory usage: 5.4+ MB
```

Basic information about the DataFrame

Using the `info()` function, we can see that the data only has float and integer values. Also, none of the columns has null/missing values.

The `describe()` function in pandas is used to obtain various summary statistics of all the numeric columns. This function returns the count, mean, standard deviation, minimum and maximum values, and the quantiles of all the numeric columns. The following table shows the description of the data obtained using the `describe` function:

```
data.describe()
```

	zip	soldBy	customerID	officeID	active_status	days_old	services_completed	services_due	completion_percentage	balance
count	27002.000000	27002.000000	2.700200e+04	27002.0	27002.000000	27002.000000	27002.000000	27002.000000	27002.000000	27002.000000
mean	75440.877565	12705.785127	8.836255e+05	9.0	0.614695	484.007555	5.210318	6.970409	0.780082	4.848011
std	638.398164	6092.947358	1.882196e+05	0.0	0.486676	267.792526	2.824159	2.934738	0.269748	23.916224
min	17169.000000	2294.000000	4.779910e+05	9.0	0.000000	154.000000	1.000000	3.350000	0.079000	0.000000
25%	75052.000000	9220.000000	7.438540e+05	9.0	0.000000	233.000000	3.000000	4.220000	0.633700	0.000000
50%	75080.000000	11079.000000	9.007320e+05	9.0	1.000000	535.000000	4.000000	7.530000	0.868500	0.000000
75%	76051.000000	18387.000000	1.038871e+06	9.0	1.000000	619.000000	7.000000	8.450000	0.985200	0.000000
max	85075.000000	26483.000000	1.194463e+06	9.0	1.000000	1004.000000	14.000000	12.670000	1.327400	344.000000

8 rows × 25 columns

Describing the Data

Feature selection

If you a have dataset with many variables, a good way to check correlations among columns is by visualizing the correlation matrix as a heatmap. We can identify and remove those that are highly correlated, thereby simplifying our analysis. The visualization can be achieved using the `seaborn` library in Python:

```python
import seaborn as sns
import numpy as np

corr = data.corr()

mask = np.zeros_like(corr, dtype=np.bool)
mask[np.triu_indices_from(mask)] = True

# Set up the matplotlib figure
f, ax = plt.subplots(figsize=(11, 9))

# Generate a custom diverging colormap
cmap = sns.diverging_palette(220, 10, as_cmap=True)

# Draw the heatmap with the mask and correct aspect ratio
sns.heatmap(corr, mask=mask, cmap=cmap, vmax=.3, center=0,
            square=True, linewidths=.5, cbar_kws={"shrink": .5})
```

The following will be the output:

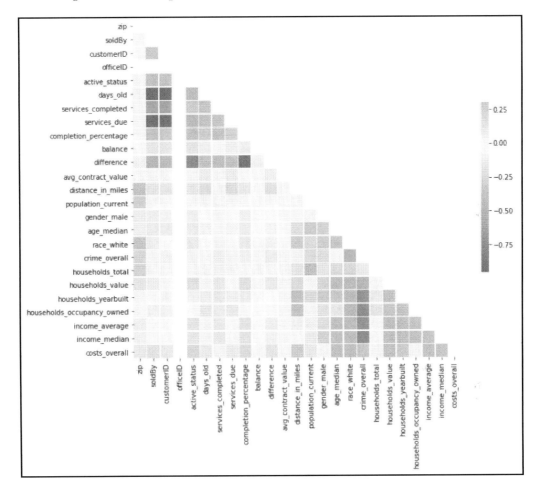

Correlation heatmap of the DataFrame

We can observe the following in the preceding heatmap:

- `soldBy` and `days_old` are highly negatively correlated
- `age_median` and `income_median` are positively correlated

Similarly, we can derive the correlation between different sets of variables. Hence, based on the correlation results, we can minimize the number of independent features by selecting only the important features.

Feature extraction

Apart from selecting the useful features, we also need to extract significant variables from the existing ones. This method is called **feature extraction**. In the current example, a new feature called `new_tenure` has been extracted from the existing variables. This variable gives us the amount of time that a customer has stayed with the firm:

```
data['new_tenure']=data['active_status']*data['days_old']+(1-
data['active_status'])*data['days_active_tenure']
```

The following DataFrame shows the newly extracted variables:

```
In [83]:  data['new_tenure']=data['active_status']*data['days_old']+(1-data['active_status'])*data['days_active_tenure']
          data
```

households_total	households_value	households_yearbuilt	households_occupancy_owned	income_average	income_median	costs_overall	days_active_tenure	new_tenure
10167.0	211811.0	1992.0	78.30	95842.0	85905.0	110.0	1003.75	925.00
9486.0	152379.0	2000.0	88.67	87789.0	81405.0	85.0	730.00	730.00
12156.0	165760.0	2001.0	82.74	84248.0	79003.0	96.0	1003.75	930.00
13284.0	150257.0	1975.0	52.39	69718.0	56926.0	110.0	1095.00	931.00
9486.0	152379.0	2000.0	88.67	87789.0	81405.0	85.0	146.00	146.00
12156.0	165760.0	2001.0	82.74	84248.0	79003.0	96.0	1003.75	931.00
28100.0	145167.0	1991.0	73.04	81585.0	71136.0	88.0	292.00	292.00
28100.0	145167.0	1991.0	73.04	81585.0	71136.0	88.0	146.00	146.00
18792.0	118569.0	1977.0	73.86	67810.0	59509.0	82.0	821.25	821.25
12176.0	270683.0	1996.0	81.56	129637.0	115106.0	114.0	73.00	73.00
8775.0	126099.0	1991.0	78.11	77820.0	69036.0	87.0	1003.75	930.00

The DataFrame with the newly extracted variables

Data aggregation

As mentioned earlier, the data presented is customer-level data. It would be more feasible and easy to perform analysis on aggregated data, which in this case is a region. To start with, we need to understand how the customers are spread across each region. Hence, we are going to use the `groupby` function to find the number of customers in each zip code. The snippet and its output are shown in the following code:

```
data.groupby('zip')['zip'].count().nlargest(10)
```

The following is the output:

```
data.groupby('zip')['zip'].count().nlargest(10)

zip
75070    1117
76179     898
75056     822
75068     755
76244     690
75002     688
75007     629
75071     588
75028     583
76021     550
Name: zip, dtype: int64
```

Aggregating the data based on zip codes

This gives the first 10 zip codes that have the maximum number of customers.

Therefore, we can convert our client-level data into zip-level data using aggregation. After grouping the values, we also have to make sure that we remove the NAs. The following code can be used to perform aggregation on the entire DataFrame:

```
data_mod=data.groupby('zip')
data_clean=pd.DataFrame()
for name,data_group in data_mod:
    data_group1=data_group.fillna(method='ffill')
    data_clean=pd.concat([data_clean,data_group1],axis=0)

data_clean.dropna(axis=0, how='any')
```

The following screenshot is the aggregated DataFrame after removing the NAs:

```
data_mod=data.groupby('zip')
data_clean=pd.DataFrame()

for name,data_group in data_mod:
    data_group1=data_group.fillna(method='ffill')
    data_clean=pd.concat([data_clean,data_group1],axis=0)

data_clean
```

	zip	soldBy	customerID	officeID	active_status	days_old	services_completed	services_due	completion_percentage	balance	...
15001	17169	17505	933063	9	1	287	5	4.81	1.0395	0	...
4708	55056	8147	705852	9	0	689	3	9.22	0.3254	0	...
20659	57067	18251	1049709	9	1	229	4	4.18	0.9569	0	...
19996	57072	19218	1035218	9	1	234	4	4.23	0.9456	0	...
20565	57077	18251	1048073	9	1	230	4	4.19	0.9547	0	...
16533	67040	20113	960705	9	1	262	5	4.54	1.1013	0	...
22386	67210	20113	1087904	9	1	213	4	4.00	1.0000	0	...
16042	70535	17506	949426	9	1	268	5	4.60	1.0870	0	...
5421	70563	8090	708097	9	1	661	9	8.91	1.0101	0	...
6530	70570	9224	739666	9	0	622	5	8.48	0.5896	0	...
6777	70570	9224	745899	9	0	618	6	8.44	0.7109	0	...

Aggregated DataFrame after removing the NAs

`data_clean` will become the cleaned version of our sample DataFrame, which will be passed to a model for further analysis.

Web scraping with Python

Web scraping deals with extracting large amounts of data from websites in either structured or unstructured forms. For example, a website might have some data already present in an HTML table element or as a CSV file. This is an example of structured data on website. But, in most cases, the required information would be scattered across the content of the web page. Web scraping helps collect these data and store it in a structured form. There are different ways to scrape websites such as online services, APIs, or writing your own code.

Here are some important notes about web scraping:

- Read through the website's terms and conditions to understand how you can legally use the data. Most sites prohibit you from using the data for commercial purposes.
- Make sure you are not downloading data at a rapid rate because this may break the website. You may potentially be blocked from the site as well.

Web scraping using pandas

Python provides different libraries for scraping:

- pandas
- BeautifulSoup
- Scrapy

In this section, we'll see how to scrape data by leveraging the power of pandas and BeautifulSoup. To start with, pandas is sufficient to extract structured data from a website without the help of BeautifulSoup. In the earlier sections, we learned about loading data from different formats (.csv, .xlsx, and .xls) in Python. Similar to these, pandas has a separate function for loading tabular data from an HTML file. To read an HTML file, a pandas DataFrame looks for a tag. That tag is called a <td> </td> tag. This tag is used to define a table in HTML.

pandas uses read_html() to read the HTML document. This function loads all the structured data from the URL into the Python environment. So, whenever you pass an HTML to pandas and expect it to output a nice-looking DataFrame, make sure the HTML page has a table in it.

We can try this function on a sample URL (`https://www.bseindia.com/static/members/TFEquity.aspx`):

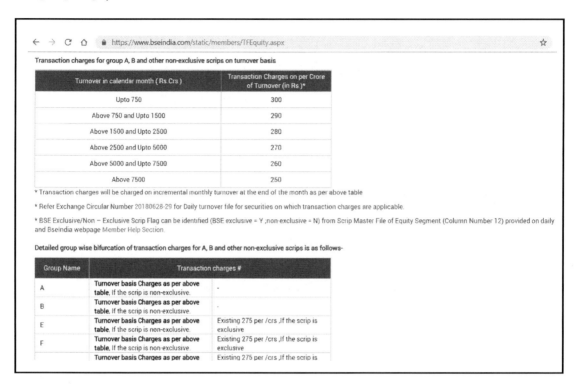

Sample web page

The preceding web page contains multiple tables. Using pandas, we can extract all the tables, which will be stored inside a list:

```
df = pd.read_html('https://www.bseindia.com/static/members/TFEquity.aspx')
df
```

```
[                                                    0
 0  Turnover in calendar month ( Rs.Crs )  Transac...,
                              Unnamed: 0  \
 0  Turnover in calendar month ( Rs.Crs )
 1                             Upto 750
 2               Above 750 and Upto 1500
 3              Above 1500 and Upto 2500
 4              Above 2500 and Upto 5000
 5              Above 5000 and Upto 7500
 6                            Above 7500

                                        Unnamed: 1
 0  Transaction Charges on per Crore of Turnover (...
 1                                             300
 2                                             290
 3                                             280
 4                                             270
 5                                             260
 6                                             250  ,
```

List containing multiple DataFrames

In the following screenshot, the second table from the web page is being extracted:

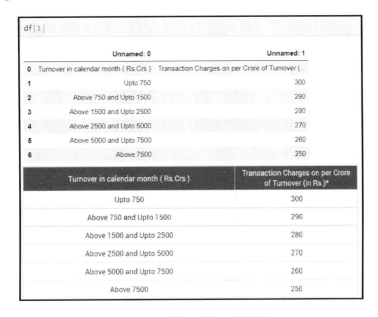

Comparison of the web page and the pandas DataFrame

After cleaning, the extracted DataFrame is an exact replica of what is available on the website:

```
data = df[1]
data.columns = data.iloc[0,:]
data = data.iloc[1:,:]
```

	Turnover in calendar month (Rs.Crs)	Transaction Charges on per Crore of Turnover (in Rs.)*
1	Upto 750	300
2	Above 750 and Upto 1500	290
3	Above 1500 and Upto 2500	280
4	Above 2500 and Upto 5000	270
5	Above 5000 and Upto 7500	260
6	Above 7500	250

DataFrame after cleaning

With proper indexing, all the tables from a web page can be extracted using the `read_html` function.

Web scraping using BeautifulSoup

BeautifulSoup is a Python library (`https://www.crummy.com/software/BeautifulSoup/`) for pulling data out of HTML and XML files. It provides ways of navigating, accessing, searching, and modifying the HTML content of a web page. It is important to understand the basics of HTML in order to successfully scrape a web page. To parse the content, the first thing that we need to do is to figure out where we can locate the links to the files we want to download inside the multiple levels of HTML tags. Simply put, there is a lot of code on a web page, and we want to find the relevant pieces of code that contains our data.

On the website, right-click and click on **Inspect**. This allows you to see the raw code behind the site. Once you've clicked on **Inspect**, you should see the following console pop up:

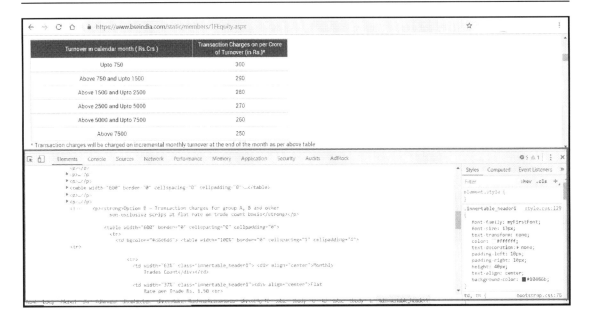

Inspect menu of a browser

Notice that the table that we are referring to is wrapped in a tag called **table**. Each row will be present between `<tr>` tags. Similarly, each cell will be present between `<td>` tags. Understanding these basic differences makes it easier to extract the data.

We start by importing the following libraries:

```
import requests
from bs4 import BeautifulSoup
import pandas as pd
```

Importing libraries

Next, we request the URL with the `requests` library. If the access was successful, you should see the following output:

```
import requests
from bs4 import BeautifulSoup
import pandas as pd

url = 'https://www.bseindia.com/static/members/TFEquity.aspx'
html = requests.get(url)
html

<Response [200]>
```

Successful response from a website

We then parse `html` with `BeautifulSoup` so that we can work with a nicer, nested `BeautifulSoup` data structure. With a little knowledge of HTML tags, the parsed content can be easily converted into a DataFrame using a `for` loop and a pandas DataFrame. The biggest advantage of using BeautifulSoup is that it can even extract data from unstructured sources that can be molded into a table by the supported libraries, whereas the `read_html` function of pandas will only work with structured sources. Hence, based on the requirement, we have used `BeautifulSoup`:

```python
soup = BeautifulSoup(html.content, 'html.parser')

content = soup.find('table',class_='mGrid').findAll('tr',class_='TTRow')
for row in content:
    cells = row.findAll('td')
    B= []
    for i in range(0,5):
        B.append(cells[i].text.replace('\n',''))
    rows.append(B)

df = pd.DataFrame(rows)
```

	Turnover in calendar month (Rs.Crs)	Transaction Charges on per Crore of Turnover (in Rs.)*
1	Upto 750	300
2	Above 750 and Upto 1500	290
3	Above 1500 and Upto 2500	280
4	Above 2500 and Upto 5000	270
5	Above 5000 and Upto 7500	260
6	Above 7500	250

Extracted DataFrame using BeautifulSoup

Data validation

Data validation is the process of examining the quality of data to ensure it is both correct and useful for performing analysis. It uses routines, often called **validation rules**, that check for the genuineness of the data that is input to the models. In the age of big data, where vast caches of information are generated by computers and other forms of technology that contribute to the quantity of data being produced, it would be incompetent to use such data if it lacks quality, highlighting the importance of data validation.

In this case study, we are going to consider two DataFrames:

- Test DataFrame (from a flat file)
- Validation DataFrame (from MongoDB)

Validation routines are performed on the test DataFrame, keeping its counterpart as the reference.

Data overview

The datasets considered here are part of the **Learning Management System (LMS)** data. They project information pertaining to student enrolment, tracking, reporting, and delivery of educational courses. Let's load the test DataFrame from the flat file:

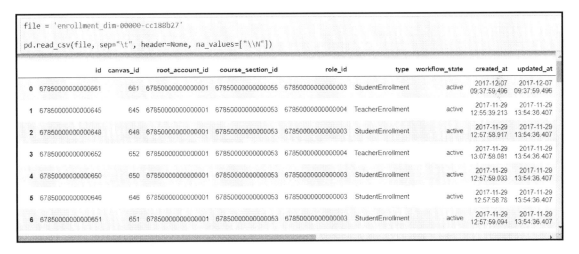

Loading test DataFrame from flat file

The `pymongo` library is used to connect MongoDB to Python. Generally, MongoDB listens on port `27017`:

```python
import pymongo

def connect_mongo(host, port, username, password, db):

    if username and password:
        mongo_uri = 'mongodb://%s:%s@%s:%s/%s' % (username, password, host, port, db)
        conn = pymongo.MongoClient(mongo_uri)
    else:
        conn = pymongo.MongoClient(host, port)

    return conn
```

MongoDB connection from Python

We can see the connection parameters in the following screenshot. Since the database is installed locally, we are connecting to it via localhost. The name of the loaded database is `lms_db`:

```
def read_mongo(db, collection, query={} , no_id=True):

    # Make a query to the specific DB and Collection
    cursor = db[collection].find(query)

    # Expand the cursor and construct the DataFrame
    df =  pd.DataFrame(list(cursor))

    # Delete the _id
    if no_id:
        del df['_id']

    return df

db = connect_mongo(host='localhost', port=27017, username='xxxx', password='yyyyy', db='lms_db')
collection = 'enrollment_dim'

read_mongo(db, collection, query={} , no_id=True)
```

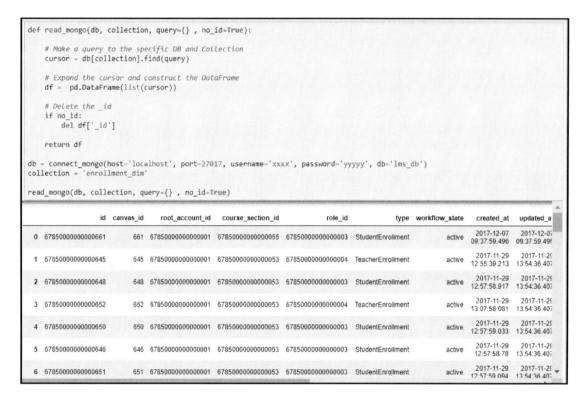

	id	canvas_id	root_account_id	course_section_id	role_id	type	workflow_state	created_at	updated_a
0	6785000000000661	661	67850000000000001	67850000000000055	67850000000000003	StudentEnrollment	active	2017-12-07 09:37:59.496	2017-12-07 09:37:59.49
1	6785000000000645	645	67850000000000001	67850000000000053	67850000000000004	TeacherEnrollment	active	2017-11-29 12:55:39.213	2017-11-29 13:54:36.407
2	6785000000000648	648	67850000000000001	67850000000000053	67850000000000003	StudentEnrollment	active	2017-11-29 12:57:58.917	2017-11-29 13:54:36.407
3	6785000000000652	652	67850000000000001	67850000000000053	67850000000000004	TeacherEnrollment	active	2017-11-29 13:07:58.081	2017-11-29 13:54:36.407
4	6785000000000650	650	67850000000000001	67850000000000053	67850000000000003	StudentEnrollment	active	2017-11-29 12:57:59.033	2017-11-29 13:54:36.407
5	6785000000000646	646	67850000000000001	67850000000000053	67850000000000003	StudentEnrollment	active	2017-11-29 12:57:58.78	2017-11-29 13:54:36.407
6	6785000000000651	651	67850000000000001	67850000000000053	67850000000000003	StudentEnrollment	active	2017-11-29 12:57:59.094	2017-11-29 13:54:36.407

Reading data from MongoDB

Structured databases versus unstructured databases

Since MongoDB falls under the category of unstructured databases, the terminology used widely differs from its structured counterparts, such as MySQL and PostgreSQL. The following table presents various SQL terminology and concepts and the corresponding MongoDB terminology and concepts:

SQL terms/concepts	MongoDB terms/concepts
database	Database (https://docs.mongodb.com/manual/reference/glossary/#term-database)

table	Collection (`https://docs.mongodb.com/manual/reference/glossary/#term-collection`)
row	Document or BSON document
column	Field (`https://docs.mongodb.com/manual/reference/glossary/#term-field`)
index	Index (`https://docs.mongodb.com/manual/reference/glossary/#term-index`)
table joins	`$lookup`, **embedded documents** (`https://docs.mongodb.com/manual/reference/operator/aggregation/lookup/#pipe._S_lookup`)
primary key	Primary key (`https://docs.mongodb.com/manual/reference/glossary/#term-primary-key`)
Specify any unique column or column combination as primary key.	In MongoDB, the primary key is automatically set to the `_id` field. (`https://docs.mongodb.com/manual/reference/glossary/#term-id`)
aggregation (example group by)	Aggregation pipeline
transactions	Transactions (`https://docs.mongodb.com/manual/core/transactions/`)

Comparative view of SQL MongoDB terminologies

Validating data types

A data type is a property of a variable that Python uses to understand how to store and manipulate data. For instance, a program needs to understand that variables storing 5 and 10 are numeric to be able to add them and get 15, or that the variables storing cat and hat are strings so that they could be concatenated (added) together to get cathat. Hence it becomes a preliminary and cardinal property of any pandas DataFrame.

A user-defined comparison function can be used to validate the data types of the test DataFrame:

```
#Test 1 - Validating the Datatypes

comparison = lambda x,y: x==y

File1 = pd.read_csv("enrollment_dim-00000-cc188b27", sep="\t", na_values=["\\N"]) # Reading Flat File

File2 = read_mongo(db, collection, query={} , no_id=True) # Reading Data from MongoDB

comp_count = comparison(File1.dtypes,File2.dtypes)

if comp_count[comp_count==False].count() == 0:
    print 'Datatypes Match!'

else:
    print "Datatypes don't Match"
    print 'Checking columns that don\'t Match'
    comp_cols = comp_count[comp_count==False].count()
    print('Number of Columns that don\'t Match are ' + repr(comp_count[comp_count==False].count()))
    print('Columns with different datatypes are ' + repr(comp_count[comp_count==False].index))
Datatypes Match!
```

Validating data types of test DataFrame

`File1` and `File2` correspond to the test and validation datasets respectively. It is evident from the output that all the data types of the test DataFrame match those of the validation DataFrame. If there is a mismatch, the output will display the number of columns that are inconsistent.

Validating dimensions

A DataFrame is a two-dimensional data structure where data is presented in a tabular manner, much like a relational database table, in rows and columns. One of the basic methods to check whether the test and validation datasets are matching is to equate the number of rows and columns. If the shapes of the DataFrames do not match, it becomes clearly evident that the test DataFrame is different from the validation one. The following is a screenshot that shows how to validate dimensions:

```
#Test 2 - Validating Dimensions

if comparison(file1.shape,file2.shape) == True:
    print 'Number of rows and columns Match!'

else:
    print 'Number of rows and columns doesn\'t Match'

    if comparison(file1.shape[0],file2.shape[0]):
        print 'Number of Rows Match!'
        the_file.write('Number of Rows Match!')

    else:
        print 'Number of Rows don\'t Match'
        print 'Checking the number of missing values'

        if comparison(file2.isnull().sum().sum(),file1.isnull().sum().sum()) == True:
            print 'The number of missing values Match'
            the_file.write('-The number of missing values Match\n\n')

        else:
            print 'The number of missing values doesn\'t Match'
            file1_NA = file1[file1.isnull().any(axis=1)]
            file2_NA = file2[file2.isnull().any(axis=1)]
            print('-The rows with missing values in file 1 are ' + repr(file1_NA.index))
            print('-The rows with missing values in file 2 are ' + repr(file2_NA.index))

    if comparison(file1.shape[1],file2.shape[1]):
        print 'Number of Columns Match!'
    else:
        print 'Number of Columns don\'t Match'

Number of rows and columns Match!
```

Validating dimensions

Validating individual entries

Once the first two test cases are satisfied, it becomes highly important to scan individual entries to find spurious data. The validation process in the preceding figure describes the difference between a value obtained from a data collection process and the true value. As the amount of data increases, validating entries becomes difficult. This effect can be diminished by efficiently utilizing pandas. In the following example, individual entries have been scanned using both looping (the brute force method) and pandas indexing.

Using pandas indexing

The following screenshot shows how to validate cells using pandas:

```
#Test3 - Validating Individual Entries

spurious = list((file1.loc[~file1.set_index(list(file1.columns)).index.isin(file2.set_index(list(file2.columns)).index)]).index)

if spurious == []:
    print("All the Rows of the Flat file are matching with Mongo Documents")
else:
    for i in spurious:
        print("Row "+ str(i)+" of Flat file does not match with any of the Mongo Document")
```
```
All the Rows of the Flat file are matching with Mongo Documents
```

Validating cells using pandas indexing

Using loops

The following screenshot shows how to validate cells by using loops:

```
#Test3 - Validating Individual Entries - Bruteforce Method

cell_count = []
cell_index = []
col_names = []

for i in range(len(file1.columns)):
    col_nam = file1.columns[i]
    col_names.append(col_nam)
    cell_comp = comparison(file1.ix[:,i],file2.ix[:,i])
    cell_cot = cell_comp[cell_comp==False].count()
    cell_count.append(cell_cot)
    cell_ind = cell_comp[cell_comp==False].index
    cell_index.append(cell_ind)
for j in range(len(cell_count)):
    if cell_count[j] == 0:
        print('All the cells in column \"%s\" Match!'% col_names[j])

    else:
        print('All the cells in column \"%s\" doesn\'t Match'% col_names[j])
All the Rows of the Flat file are matching with Mongo Documents
```

Validating cells using loops

The results were highly encouraging when we used pandas indexing. It took only 0.53 seconds to validate a DataFrame with 200,000 rows and 15 columns, whereas the same validation routine took more than 7 minutes to complete using loops. Therefore it is always recommended to leverage the power of pandas and avoid iterative programming.

Summary

pandas is useful for a lot of ancillary data activities, such as exploratory data analysis, validating the sanctity (such as the data type or count) of data between two data sources, and structuring and shaping data obtained from another source, such as scraping a website or a database. In this chapter, we dealt with some case studies on these topics. A data scientist performs these activities on a day-to-day basis, and this chapter should give a flavor of what it is like to perform them on a real dataset.

In the next chapter, we will discuss the architecture and code structure of the pandas library. This will help us develop an exhaustive understanding of the functionalities of the library and enable us to do better troubleshooting.

13
The pandas Library Architecture

In this chapter, we examine the various libraries that are available to pandas users. This chapter is intended to be a short guide to help the user to navigate and find their way around the various modules and libraries that pandas provides. It gives a breakdown of how the library code is organized, and it gives a brief description of the various modules. It will be most valuable to users who are interested in seeing the inner workings of pandas , as well as to those who wish to make contributions to the code base. We will also briefly demonstrate how you can improve performance using Python extensions. The various topics that will be discussed are as follows:

- Introduction to the pandas library hierarchy
- Description of pandas modules and files
- Improving performance using Python extensions

Understanding the pandas file hierarchy

Generally, upon installation, pandas is installed as a Python module in a standard location for third-party Python modules. In the following table, you will see the standard installation location for Unix/ macOS and the Windows platform:

Platform	Standard installation location	Example
Unix/macOS	`prefix/lib/pythonX.Y/site-packages`	`/usr/local/lib/python2.7/site-packages`
Windows	`prefix\Lib\site-packages`	`C:\Python27\Lib\site-packages`

If Python installation was done with Anaconda, then the pandas module can be found in the Anaconda directory, within a similar file path: `Anaconda3\pkgs\pandas-0.23.4-py37h830ac7b_0\Lib\site-packages\pandas`.

Now that we have had a look at the module on third-party Python modules, we will understand the file hierarchy. There are eight types of file in the installed Pandas library. The installed files follow a specific hierarchy, which is described here:

- `pandas/core`: This contains files for fundamental data structures, such as Series/DataFrames and related functionalities.
- `pandas/src`: This contains Cython and C code for implementing fundamental algorithms.
- `pandas/io`: This contains input/output tools for handling different file formats, such as flat files, Excel, HDF5, and SQL.
- `pandas/tools`: This contains auxiliary data algorithms, merge and join routines, concatenation, pivot tables, and more. This module primarily serves data-manipulation operations.
- `pandas/sparse`: This contains sparse versions of data structures, such as series, DataFrame, Panels, and more.
- `pandas/stats`: This contains linear and panel regression, moving window regression, and several other statistical functions. This should be replaced by functionality in statsmodels.
- `pandas/util`: This contains utilities and development and testing tools.
- `pandas/rpy`: This contains the RPy2 interface for connecting to R, thereby widening the scope of analytical operations on data.

For more information, see: `http://pandas.pydata.org/developers.html`.

Description of pandas modules and files

In this section, we provide brief descriptions of the various sub-modules and files that make up the pandas library.

pandas/core

The module contains the core submodules of pandas. They are discussed as follows:

- `api.py`: This imports some key modules and warnings for later use, such as indexing, `groupby`, and reshaping functions.
- `apply.py`: This module contains classes that help to apply a function to a DataFrame or series.

- `arrays`: This isolates pandas' exposure to `numpy`—that is, all direct `numpy` usage. The `base.py` submodule of array handles all array-oriented operations, such as the `ndarray` value, shape, and `ndim`, while the `categorical.py` submodule caters specifically for categorical values.

- `base.py`: This defines fundamental classes such as `StringMixin` and `PandasObject`, which is the base class for various pandas objects, such as `Period`, `PandasSQLTable`, `sparse.array.SparseArray/SparseList`, `internals.Block`, `internals.BlockManager`, `generic.NDFrame`, `groupby.GroupBy`, `base.FrozenList`, `base.FrozenNDArray`, `io.sql.PandasSQL`, `io.sql.PandasSQLTable`, `tseries.period.Period`, `FrozenList`, `FrozenNDArray`: `IndexOpsMixin`, and `DatetimeIndexOpsMixin`.

- `common.py`: This defines common utility methods for handling data structures. For example, the `isnull` object detects missing values.

- `config.py`: This is the module for handling package-wide configurable objects. It defines the following classes: `OptionError`, `DictWrapper`, `CallableDynamicDoc`, `option_context`, and `config_init`.

- `datetools.py`: This is a collection of functions that deal with dates in Python. It also utilizes some functions from the `tseries` module of pandas.

- `frame.py`: This defines the pandas DataFrame class and its various methods. DataFrame inherits from NDFrame (see the following). It borrows functions from several submodules under the `pandas-core` module to define the functional aspects of a DataFrame.

- `generic.py`: This defines the generic NDFrame base class, which is a base class for pandas DataFrame, series, and panel classes. NDFrame is derived from `PandasObject`, which is defined in `base.py`. An NDFrame can be regarded as an N-dimensional version of a pandas DataFrame. For more information on this, go to `http://nullege.com/codes/search/pandas.core.generic.NDFrame`.

- `categorical.py`: This defines categorical, which is a class that derives from `PandasObject` and represents categorical variables 'a' la R/S-plus. (We will expand your knowledge on this a bit more later).

- `groupby.py`: This defines various classes that enable the `groupby` functionality:
    - **Splitter classes**: This includes `DataSplitter`, `ArraySplitter`, `SeriesSplitter`, `FrameSplitter`, and `NDFrameSplitter`.
    - **Grouper/grouping classes**: This includes `Grouper`, `GroupBy`, `BaseGrouper`, `BinGrouper`, `Grouping`, `SeriesGroupBy`, and `NDFrameGroupBy`.

- `ops.py`: This defines an internal API for arithmetic operations on `PandasObjects`. It defines functions that add arithmetic methods to objects. It defines a `_create_methods` metamethod, which is used to create other methods using arithmetic, comparison, and Boolean method constructors. The `add_methods` method takes a list of new methods, adds them to the existing list of methods, and binds them to their appropriate classes. The `add_special_arithmetic_methods`, `add_flex_arithmetic_methods`, `call _create_methods`, and `add_methods` are used to add arithmetic methods to a class.

   It defines the `_TimeOp` class, which is a wrapper for datetime-related arithmetic operations. It contains wrapper functions for arithmetic, comparison, and Boolean operations on series, DataFrame, and panel functions: `_arith_method_SERIES(..)`, `_comp_method_SERIES(..)`, `_bool_method_SERIES(..)`, `_flex_method_SERIES(..)`, `_arith_method_FRAME(..)`, `_comp_method_FRAME(..)`, `_flex_comp_method_FRAME(..)`, `_arith_method_PANEL(..)`, and `_comp_method_PANEL(..)`.

- `index.py`: This defines the index class and its related functionality. Index is used by all pandas objects—series, DataFrame, and panel—to store axis labels. Underneath it is an immutable array that provides an ordered set that can be sliced.
- `indexing.py`: This module contains a series of functions and classes that make multi-indexing easier.
- `missing.py`: This defines techniques such as masking and interpolation to handle missing data.
- `internals.py`: This defines multiple object classes. These are listed as follows:
    - `Block`: This is a homogeneously typed N-dimensional `numpy.ndarray` object with additional functionality for pandass—for example, it uses `__slots__` to restrict the attributes of the object to `ndim`, `values`, and `_mgr_locs`. It acts as the base class for other Block subclasses.
    - `NumericBlock`: This is the base class for blocks with the numeric type.
    - `FloatOrComplexBlock`: This is the base class for `FloatBlock` and `ComplexBlock` that inherits from `NumericBlock`

- **ComplexBlock**: This is the class that handles the Block objects with the complex type.
- **FloatBlock**: This is the class that handles the Block objects with the float type.
- **IntBlock**: This is the class that handles the Block objects with the integer type.
- **TimeDeltaBlock**, **BoolBlock**, and **DatetimeBlock**: These are the block classes for timedelta, Boolean, and datetime.
- **ObjectBlock**: This is the class that handles block objects for user-defined objects.
- **SparseBlock**: This is the class that handles sparse arrays of the same type.
- **BlockManager**: This is the class that manages a set of block objects. It is not a public API class.
- **SingleBlockManager**: This is the class that manages a single block.
- **JoinUnit**: This is the utility class for block objects.

- **nanops.py**: This submodule has a set of classes and functionalities for exclusively handling NaN values.
- **ops.py**: This defines arithmetic operations for pandas objects. It is not a public API.
- **panel.py**, **panel4d.py**, and **panelnd.py**: These provide the functionality for the pandas panel object.
- **resample.py**: This defines a custom groupby class for time-interval grouping and aggregation.
- **series.py**: This defines the pandas Series class and the various methods that Series inherits from NDFrame and IndexOpsMixin to accommodate 1-dimensional data structures and 1-dimensional time series data.
- **sorting.py**: This defines all necessary utilities for sorting.
- **sparse.py**: This defines the import for handling sparse data structures. Sparse data structures are compressed in that data points matching NaN or missing values are omitted. For more information on this, go to http://pandas.pydata.org/pandas-docs/stable/sparse.html.
- **strings.py**: These have various functions, such as str_replace, str_contains, and str_cat, for handling strings manipulations.
- **window.py**: This helps in the windowing of data structures and computing aggregates in a rolling window.

The following diagram gives an overview of the structure of the Pandas core:

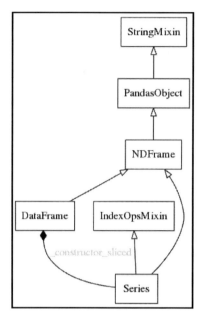

Now, let's move on to the next submodule.

pandas/io

This module contains various modules for data I/O. These are as follows:

- `api.py`: This defines various imports for the data I/O API.
- `common.py`: This defines the common functionality for the I/O API.
- `clipboards.py`: This contains cross-platform clipboard methods to enable the copy and paste functions from the keyboard. The pandas I/O API includes functions such as `pandas.read_clipboard()` and `pandas.to_clipboard(..)`.

- `date_converters.py`: This defines date conversion functions.
- `excel.py`: This module parses and converts Excel data. This defines the `ExcelFile` and `ExcelWriter` classes.
- `feather_format.py`: This module reads and writes data in Feather format.
- `gbq.py` : This is the module for Google's BigQuery.
- `html.py`: This is the module for dealing with HTML I/O.

- `json.py`: This is the module for dealing with JSON I/O in pandas. This defines the `Writer`, `SeriesWriter`, `FrameWriter`, `Parser`, `SeriesParser`, and `FrameParser` classes.
- `msgpack`: This module reads and writes data to `msgpack` format.
- `packer.py`: This is an `msgpack` serializer support for reading and writing pandas data structures to disk.
- `parquet.py`: This module reads and writes data in Parquet format.
- `parsers.py`: This is the module that defines various functions and classes that are used in parsing and processing files to create pandas DataFrames. All of the three `read_*` functions discussed in the following list have multiple configurable options for reading. For more details, see `http://bit.ly/1EKDYbP`:
    - `read_csv(..)`: This defines the `pandas.read_csv()` function that is used to read the contents of a CSV file into a DataFrame.
    - `read_table(..)`: This reads a tab-separated table file into a DataFrame.
    - `read_fwf(..)`: This reads a fixed-width format file into a DataFrame.
    - `TextFileReader`: This is the class that is used for reading text files.
    - `ParserBase`: This is the base class for parser objects.
    - `CParserWrapper`, `PythonParser`: These are the parser for C and Python respectively. They both inherit from `ParserBase`.
    - `FixedWidthReader`: This is the class for reading fixed-width data. A fixed-width data file contains fields in specific positions within the file.
    - `FixedWithFieldParser`: This is the class for parsing fixed-width fields that have been inherited from `PythonParser`.
- `pickle.py`: This provides methods for pickling (serializing) pandas objects. These are as follows:
    - `to_pickle(..)`: This serializes an object to file.
    - `read_pickle(..)`: This reads serialized objects from a file into a pandas object. It should only be used with trusted sources.
- `pytables.py`: This is an interface for PyTables module for reading and writing pandas data structures to files on disk.

- `sql.py`: This is a collection of classes and functions that enable the retrieval of data from relational databases that attempts to be database-agnostic. These classes and functions are as follows:
  - `PandasSQL`: This is the base class for interfacing pandas with SQL. It provides dummy `read_sql` and `to_sql` methods that must be implemented by subclasses.
  - `PandasSQLAlchemy`: This is the subclass of `PandasSQL` that enables conversions between DataFrame and SQL databases using SQLAlchemy.
  - `PandasSQLTable`: This maps pandas tables (DataFrame) to SQL tables.
  - `pandasSQL_builder(..)`: This returns the correct PandasSQL subclass based on the provided parameters.
  - `PandasSQLTableLegacy`: This class is the legacy support version of `PandasSQLTable`.
  - `PandasSQLLegacy`: This class is the legacy support version of `PandasSQLTable`.
  - `get_schema(..)`: This gets the SQL database table schema for a given frame.
  - `read_sql_table(..)`: This reads an SQL database table into a DataFrame.
  - `read_sql_query(..)`: This reads an SQL query into a DataFrame.
  - `read_sql(..)`: This reads an SQL query/table into a DataFrame.
- `stata.py`: This contains tools for processing Stata files into pandas DataFrames.
- `sas`: This module contains submodules that help to read data from SAS outputs.
- `S3.py`: This module provides remote connectivity to S3 buckets.

pandas/tools

The details of the module are as follows:

- `plotting.py`: This serves as a wrapper for the plotting module and has been deprecated in the recent version.
- `merge.py`: This provides functions for combining series, DataFrame, and panel objects, such as `merge(..)` and `concat(..)`, and has been deprecated in the recent version.

pandas/util

This `pandas/util` is the module that provides utility functionalities. The details of this module are as follows:

- `testing.py`: This provides the `assertion`, `debug`, `unit test`, and other classes/functions for use in testing. It contains many special assert functions that make it easier to check whether series, DataFrame, or panel objects are equivalent. Some of these functions include `assert_equal(..)`, `assert_series_equal(..)`, `assert_frame_equal(..)`, and `assert_panelnd_equal(..)`. The `pandas.util.testing` module is especially useful to the contributors of the pandas code base. It defines a `util.TestCase` class. It also provides utilities for handling locales, console debugging, file cleanup, comparators, and so on for testing by potential code base contributors.
- `doctools.py`: This submodule has the `TablePlotter` class, which helps to define a layout for DataFrames.
- `validators.py`: This submodule helps to validate arguments passed to functions. For instance, it helps to evaluate the argument length, the default values, and argument values.
- `print_versions.py`: This defines the `get_sys_info()` function, which returns a dictionary of systems information and the `show_versions(..)` function, which displays the versions of available Python libraries.
- `misc.py`: This defines a couple of miscellaneous utilities.
- `decorators.py`: This defines some decorator functions and classes.
- The substitution and appender classes are decorators that perform substitution and appending on function docstrings. For more information on Python decorators, go to `http://www.artima.com/weblogs/viewpost.jsp?thread=240808`.
- `test_decorators.py`: This submodule provides decorators to test objects.

pandas/tests

This `pandas/tests` is the module that provides many tests for various objects in pandas. The names of the specific library files are fairly self-explanatory, and I will not go into further details here; instead, I invite the reader to explore.

pandas/compat

Functionalities related to compatibility are explained as follows:

- `chainmap.py` and `chainmap_impl.py`: These provide a `ChainMap` class that can group multiple `dicts` or mappings to produce a single view that can be updated.
- `pickle_compat.py`: This provides functionality for pickling pandas objects in versions that are earlier than 0.12.

pandas/computation

This `pandas/computation` is the module that provides functionality for computation and is discussed as follows:

- `expressions.py`: This provides fast expression evaluation through `numexpr`. The `numexpr` function is used to accelerate certain numerical operations. It uses multiple cores as well as smart chunking and caching speedups. It defines the `evaluate(..)` and `where(..)` methods. This module has been deprecated in the most recent version of pandas; the alternative usage will be through `pandas.get_option`.
- For more information on `numexpr`, go to `https://code.google.com/p/numexpr/`. For information on the usage of this module, go to `http://pandas.pydata.org/pandas-docs/version/0.15.0/computation.html`.

pandas/plotting

The `pandas/plotting` is the module that takes care of all of the plotting functionalities pandas offers:

- `compat.py`: This module checks for version compatibility.
- `converter.py`: This module helps process datetime values for plotting. It helps to execute functions such as autoscaling of time series axes and formatting ticks for datetime axes.
- `core.py`: This defines classes that help in creating plots, such as bar plots, scatter plots, hex bin plots, and box plots.

- `misc.py`: This provides a set of plotting functions that take a series or DataFrame as an argument. This module contains the following submodules for performing miscellaneous tasks, such as plotting scatter matries and Andrews curve:
    - `scatter_matrix(..)`: This draws a matrix of scatter plots.
    - `andrews_curves(..)`: This plots multivariate data as curves that are created using samples as coefficients for a Fourier series.
    - `parallel_coordinates(..)`: This is a plotting technique that allows you to see clusters in data and visually estimate statistics.
    - `lag_plot(..)`: This is used to check whether a dataset or a time series is random.
    - `autocorrelation_plot(..)`: This is used for checking randomness in a time series.
    - `bootstrap_plot(..)`: This plot is used to determine the uncertainty of a statistical measure, such as mean or median, in a visual manner
    - `radviz(..)`: This plot is used to visualize multivariate data.
- `style.py`: This provides a set of styling options for the plot.
- `timeseries.py`: This defines auxiliary classes for time series plots.
- `tools.py`: This contains some helper functions that create a table layout from DataFrames and series.

pandas/tseries

This section deals with the `pandas/tseries` module, which gives pandas its functionality to work with time series data:

- `api.py`: This is a set of convenience imports.
- `converter.py`: This defines a set of classes that are used to format and convert.
- `datetime`: Upon importing pandas, this registers a set of unit converters with `matplotlib`. This is done via the `register()` function, as follows:

```
In [1]: import matplotlib.units as munits
In [2]: munits.registry
Out[2]: {}
In [3]: import pandas
In [4]: munits.registry
Out[4]:
{pandas.tslib.Timestamp: <pandas.tseries.converter.DatetimeConverter
instance at 0x7fbbc4db17e8>,
```

```
pandas.tseries.period.Period: <pandas.tseries.converter.PeriodConverter
instance at 0x7fbbc4dc25f0>,
datetime.date: <pandas.tseries.converter.DatetimeConverter instance at
0x7fbbc4dc2fc8>,
datetime.datetime: <pandas.tseries.converter.DatetimeConverter instance at
0x7fbbc4dc2a70>,
datetime.time: <pandas.tseries.converter.TimeConverter instance at
0x7fbbc4d61e18>}
```

- `Converter`: This class includes `TimeConverter`, `PeriodConverter`, and `DateTimeConverter`.
- `Formatters`: This class includes `TimeFormatter`, `PandasAutoDateFormatter`, and `TimeSeries_DateFormatter`.
- `Locators`: This class includes `PandasAutoDateLocator`, `MilliSecondLocator`, and `TimeSeries_DateLocator`.

> The `Formatter` and `Locator` classes are used for handling ticks in `matplotlib` plotting.

- `frequencies.py`: This defines the code for specifying frequencies—daily, weekly, quarterly, monthly, annual, and so on—of time series objects. This submodule depends on the `dtypes` submodule of the pandas/core module.
- `holiday.py`: This defines functions and classes for handling holidays—`Holiday`, `AbstractHolidayCalendar`, and `USFederalHolidayCalendar` are among the classes defined.
- `offsets.py`: This defines various classes, including offsets that deal with time-related periods. These classes are explained as follows:
    - `DateOffset`: This is an interface for classes that provide the time period functionality, such as `Week`, `WeekOfMonth`, `LastWeekOfMonth`, `QuarterOffset`, `YearOffset`, `Easter`, `FY5253`, and `FY5253Quarter`.
    - `BusinessMixin`: This is the mixin class for business objects to provide functionality with time-related classes. This is inherited by the `BusinessDay` class. The `BusinessDay` subclass is derived from `BusinessMixin` and `SingleConstructorOffset`, and provides an offset on business days.
    - `MonthOffset`: This is the interface for classes that provide the functionality for month time periods, such as `MonthEnd`, `MonthBegin`, `BusinessMonthEnd`, and `BusinessMonthBegin`.

- `MonthEnd` and `MonthBegin`: These provide a date offset of one month at the end or the beginning.
- `BusinessMonthEnd` and `BusinessMonthBegin`: These provide a date offset of one month at the end or the beginning of a business day calendar.
- `YearOffset`: This offset is subclassed by classes that provide year-period functionality—`YearEnd`, `YearBegin`, `BYearEnd`, and `BYearBegin`.
- `YearEnd` and `YearBegin`: These provide a date offset of one year at the end or the beginning.
- `BYearEnd` and `BYearBegin`: These provide a date offset of one year at the end or the beginning of a business day calendar.
- `Week`: This provides an offset of one week.
- `WeekDay`: This provides mapping from a weekday (for example, Tue) to any day of the week (for example, =2).
- `WeekOfMonth` and `LastWeekOfMonth`: This describes dates in a week of the month.
- `QuarterOffset`: This is subclassed by classes that provide quarterly period functionality—`QuarterEnd`, `QuarterrBegin`, `BQuarterEnd`, and `BQuarterBegin`.
- `QuarterEnd`, `QuarterrBegin`, `BQuarterEnd`, and `BQuarterBegin`: These are the same as for `Year*` classes, except the period is a quarter instead of a year.
- `FY5253` and `FY5253Quarter`: These classes describe a 52- and 53-week fiscal year respectively. This is also known as a 4-4-5 calendar.
- `Easter`: This is `DateOffset` for the Easter holiday.
- `Tick`: This is the base class for the time unit classes, such as `Day`, `Hour`, `Minute`, `Second`, `Milli`, `Micro`, and `Nano`.
- `plotting.py`: This imports the `tsplot(..)` submodule from the `pandas-plotting` module.

Next, we will see how we can improve the performance of Python codes using Python extensions.

Improving performance using Python extensions

One of the gripes of Python and pandas users is that the ease of use and expressiveness of the language and module comes with a significant downside—the performance. This happens especially when it comes to numeric computing.

According to programming benchmark standards, Python is often slower than compiled languages, such as C/C++, for many algorithms or data structure operations. An example of this would be binary-tree operations. In one simulation experiment, Python3 ran 104 times slower than the fastest C++ implementation of an *n*-body simulation calculation.

So, how can we solve this legitimate, yet vexing problem? We can mitigate this slowness in Python while maintaining the things that we like—clarity and productivity. This can be done by writing the parts of our code that are performance-sensitive-for example, numeric processing, algorithms in C/C++-and having them called by our Python code by writing a Python extension module. For more details, go to
http://docs.python.org/2/extending/extending.html.

Python extension modules enable us to make calls out to user-defined C/C++ code or library functions from Python, which enables us to boost our code performance and benefit from the ease of using Python.

To help us to understand what a Python extension module is, let's consider what happens in Python when a module has been imported. An import statement *imports* a module, but what does this really mean? There are three possibilities, which are as follows:

- Some Python extension modules are linked to the interpreter when it is built.
- An import causes Python to load a `.pyc` file into memory. The `.pyc` files contain Python `bytecode`, as shown in the following code snippet:

```
In [3]: import pandas
             pandas.__file__
Out[3]: '/usr/lib/python2.7/site-packages/pandas/__init__.pyc'
```

- The import statement causes a Python extension module to be loaded into memory. The `.so` (shared object) file is comprised of machine code, as shown in the following code snippet:

```
In [4]: import math
        math.__file__
Out[4]: '/usr/lib/python2.7/lib-dynload/math.so'
```

We will focus on the third possibility as this is the most common. Even though we are dealing with a binary-shared object compiled from C, we can import it as a Python module. This shows the power of Python extensions—applications can import modules from Python machine code or machine code and the interface is the same. Cython and SWIG are the two most popular methods of writing extensions in C and C++. In writing an extension, we wrap up C/C++ machine code and turn it into Python extension modules that behave like pure Python code. In this brief discussion, we will only focus on Cython, as it was designed specifically for Python.

Cython is a superset of Python that was designed to significantly improve Python's performance by allowing us to call externally compiled code in C/C++, as well as declare types on variables.

The Cython command generates an optimized C/C++ source file from a Cython source file and compiles this optimized C/C++ source into a Python extension module. It offers built-in support for NumPy and combines C's performance with Python's usability.

We will give a quick demonstration of how we can use Cython to significantly speed up our code. Let's define a simple Fibonacci function:

```
In [17]: def fibonacci(n):
             a,b=1,1
             for i in range(n):
                 a,b=a+b,a
             return a
In [18]: fibonacci(100)
Out[18]: 927372692193078999176L
In [19]: %timeit fibonacci(100)
         100000 loops, best of 3: 18.2 µs per loop
```

Using the `timeit` module, we see that it takes 18.2 µs per loop.

Let's now rewrite the function in Cython, specifying types for the variables by going through the following steps:

1. First, we import the Cython magic function to iPython as follows:

```
In [22]: %load_ext cythonmagic
```

2. Next, we rewrite our function in Cython, specifying types for our variables:

```
In [24]: %%cython
         def cfibonacci(int n):
             cdef int i, a,b
             for i in range(n):
                 a,b=a+b,a
             return a
```

3. Let's time our new Cython function:

```
In [25]: %timeit cfibonacci(100)
         1000000 loops, best of 3: 321 ns per loop
In [26]: 18.2/0.321
Out[26]: 56.69781931464174
```

4. We can see that the Cython version is 57 times faster than the pure Python version!

For more information on writing Python extensions using Cython/SWIG or other options, please refer to the following sources:

- Pandas documentation, entitled *Enhancing Performance*, at `http://pandas.pydata.org/pandas-docs/stable/enhancingperf.html`
- ScipPy lecture notes, entitled *Interfacing with C*, at `https://scipy-lectures.github.io/advanced/interfacing_with_c/interfacing_with_c.html`
- Cython documentation at `http://docs.cython.org/index.html`
- SWIG documentation at `http://www.swig.org/Doc2.0/SWIGDocumentation.html`

Summary

To summarize this chapter, we took a tour of the library hierarchy of pandas in an attempt to illustrate the internal guts of the library. This understanding will be useful for building custom modules from pandas code or improving the functionalities of pandas as an open source contributor. We also touched on the benefits of speeding up our code performance by using a Python extension module.

In the next chapter, we will see how pandas compares to other data analysis tools in terms of various analysis operations.

14
pandas Compared with Other Tools

This chapter focuses on comparing pandas with R, the statistical package on which much of the pandas functionality is modeled, and other tools such as SQL and SAS, with which it has a significant degree of overlap. It is intended as a guide for R, SQL, and SAS users who wish to use pandas, and for users who wish to replicate functionality that they have seen in their code in pandas. It focuses on a number of key features available to R, SQL, and SAS users, and demonstrates how to achieve similar functionality in pandas by using some illustrative examples. This chapter assumes that you have the R statistical package installed. If not, it can be downloaded and installed from here: `http://www.r-project.org/`.

By the end of the chapter, data analysis users should have a good grasp of the data analysis capabilities of these tools as compared to pandas, enabling them to transition to, or use, pandas should they need to. The various factors where the tools have been compared include the following:

- Data types and the pandas equivalents
- Slicing and selection
- Arithmetic operations on data type columns
- Aggregation and GroupBy
- Matching
- Split-apply-combine
- Melting and reshaping
- Factors and categorical data

Comparison with R

R is the tool on which pandas is loosely designed. Many of the functionalities are very similar in terms of syntax, usage, and output. Differences occur mainly in some of the data types, which can be the matrix in R versus arrays in pandas, an aggregation framework, such as the `aggregate` function in R and the `GroupBy` operation in pandas, and subtle differences in the syntaxes of similarly named functions, such as `melt` and `cut`.

Data types in R

R has five primitive or atomic types:

- Character
- Numeric
- Integer
- Complex
- Logical/Boolean

It also has the following more complex container types:

- **Vector**: This is similar to `numpy.array`. It can only contain objects of the same type.
- **List**: This is a heterogeneous container. Its equivalent in pandas would be a series.
- **DataFrame**: This is a heterogeneous two-dimensional container, equivalent to a pandas DataFrame.
- **Matrix**: This is a homogeneous two-dimensional version of a vector. It is similar to a `numpy.array`.

For this chapter, we will focus on list and DataFrame, which have the following equivalents in pandas: series and DataFrame.

For more information on R data types, refer to the following document at `http://www.statmethods.net/input/datatypes.html`.
For NumPy data types, refer to the following documents at `http://docs.scipy.org/doc/numpy/reference/generated/numpy.array.html` and `http://docs.scipy.org/doc/numpy/reference/generated/numpy.matrix.html`.

R lists

R lists can be created explicitly as a list declaration, shown as follows:

```
>h_lst<- list(23,'donkey',5.6,1+4i,TRUE)
>h_lst
[[1]]
[1] 23

[[2]]
[1] "donkey"

[[3]]
[1] 5.6

[[4]]
[1] 1+4i

[[5]]
[1] TRUE

>typeof(h_lst)
[1] "list"
```

The following code block includes its series equivalent in pandas, with the creation of a list followed by the creation of a series therefrom:

```
In [8]: h_list=[23, 'donkey', 5.6,1+4j, True]
In [9]: import pandas as pd
        h_ser=pd.Series(h_list)
In [10]: h_ser
Out[10]: 0          23
         1      donkey
         2         5.6
         3       (1+4j)
         4        True
dtype: object
```

Array indexing starts at 0 in pandas, unlike R, where it starts at 1. The following is an example:

```
In [11]: type(h_ser)
Out[11]: pandas.core.series.Series
```

R DataFrames

We can construct an R DataFrame as follows by calling the `data.frame()` constructor and then displaying it as follows:

```
>stocks_table<- data.frame(Symbol=c('GOOG','AMZN','FB','AAPL',
                                     'TWTR','NFLX','LINKD'),
                    Price=c(518.7,307.82,74.9,109.7,37.1,
                                          334.48,219.9),
        MarketCap=c(352.8,142.29,216.98,643.55,23.54,20.15,27.31))

>stocks_table
Symbol  PriceMarketCap
1    GOOG 518.70      352.80
2    AMZN 307.82      142.29
3      FB  74.90      216.98
4    AAPL 109.70      643.55
5    TWTR  37.10       23.54
6    NFLX 334.48       20.15
7   LINKD 219.90       27.31
```

In the following code block, we construct a pandas DataFrame and then display it:

```
In [29]: stocks_df=pd.DataFrame({'Symbol':['GOOG','AMZN','FB','AAPL',
                                           'TWTR','NFLX','LNKD'],
                        'Price':[518.7,307.82,74.9,109.7,37.1,
          334.48,219.9],
    'MarketCap($B)' : [352.8,142.29,216.98,643.55,
                                           23.54,20.15,27.31]
                                })
stocks_df=stocks_df.reindex_axis(sorted(stocks_df.columns,reverse=True),axi
s=1)
stocks_df
Out[29]:
Symbol  PriceMarketCap($B)
0       GOOG    518.70  352.80
1       AMZN    307.82  142.29
2       FB       74.90  216.98
3       AAPL    109.70  643.55
4       TWTR     37.10   23.54
5       NFLX    334.48   20.15
6       LNKD219.90   27.31
```

Slicing and selection

In R, we slice objects in the following three ways:

- [: This always returns an object of the same type as the original and can be used to select more than one element.
- [[: This is used to extract elements of a list or DataFrame, and can only be used to extract a single element. The nature of the returned element will not necessarily be a list or DataFrame.
- $: This is used to extract elements of a list or DataFrame by name and is similar to [[.

Here are some slicing examples in R and their equivalents in pandas:

Comparing R-matrix and NumPy array

Let's look at creation and selection in R:

```
>r_mat<- matrix(2:13,4,3)
>r_mat
       [,1] [,2] [,3]
[1,]    2    6   10
[2,]    3    7   11
[3,]    4    8   12
[4,]    5    9   13
```

To select the first row, we write the following:

```
>r_mat[1,]
[1]   2   6 10
```

To select the second column, we use the following command:

```
>r_mat[,2]
[1] 6 7 8 9
```

Let's now look at NumPy array creation and selection:

```
In [60]: a=np.array(range(2,6))
         b=np.array(range(6,10))
         c=np.array(range(10,14))
In [66]: np_ar=np.column_stack([a,b,c])
np_ar
Out[66]: array([[ 2,   6,  10],
       [ 3,   7,  11],
```

```
[ 4,    8,  12],
[ 5,    9,  13]])
```

To select the first row, we use the following command:

```
In [79]: np_ar[0,]
Out[79]: array([ 2,   6,  10])
```

 Indexing is different in R and pandas/NumPy.
In R, indexing starts at 1, while in pandas/NumPy, it starts at 0. Hence, we
have to subtract 1 from all indexes when making the translation from R to
pandas/NumPy.

To select the second column, we use the following command:

```
In [81]: np_ar[:,1]
Out[81]: array([6, 7, 8, 9])
```

Another option is to transpose the array first and then select the column, as follows:

```
In [80]: np_ar.T[1,]
Out[80]: array([6, 7, 8, 9])
```

Comparing R lists and pandas series

List creation and selection in R is as follows:

```
>cal_lst<- list(weekdays=1:8, mth='jan')
>cal_lst
$weekdays
[1] 1 2 3 4 5 6 7 8

$mth
[1] "jan"

>cal_lst[1]
$weekdays
[1] 1 2 3 4 5 6 7 8

>cal_lst[[1]]
[1] 1 2 3 4 5 6 7 8

>cal_lst[2]
$mth
[1] "jan"
```

Series creation and selection in pandas is effected as follows:

```
In [92]: cal_df= pd.Series({'weekdays':range(1,8), 'mth':'jan'})
In [93]: cal_df
Out[93]: mthjan
weekdays      [1, 2, 3, 4, 5, 6, 7]
dtype: object

In [97]: cal_df[0]
Out[97]: 'jan'

In [95]: cal_df[1]
Out[95]: [1, 2, 3, 4, 5, 6, 7]

In [96]: cal_df[[1]]
Out[96]: weekdays      [1, 2, 3, 4, 5, 6, 7]
dtype: object
```

Here, we see a difference between an R-list and a pandas series from the perspective of the `[]` and `[[]]` operators. We can see the difference by considering the second item, which is a character string.

In the case of R, the `[]` operator produces a container type, that is, a list containing the string, while the `[[]]` operator produces an atomic type, in this case, a character, as follows:

```
>typeof(cal_lst[2])
[1] "list"
>typeof(cal_lst[[2]])
[1] "character"
```

In the case of pandas, the opposite is true: `[]` produces the atomic type, while `[[]]` results in a complex type, that is, a series, as follows:

```
In [99]: type(cal_df[0])
Out[99]: str

In [101]: type(cal_df[[0]])
Out[101]: pandas.core.series.Series
```

In both R and pandas, the column name can be specified in order to an element.

Specifying a column name in R

In R, this can be done with the column name preceded by the $ operator as follows:

```
>cal_lst$mth
[1] "jan"
> cal_lst$'mth'
[1] "jan"
```

Specifying a column name in pandas

In pandas, we subset elements in the usual way with the column name in square brackets:

```
In [111]: cal_df['mth']
Out[111]: 'jan'
```

One area where R and pandas differ is in the subsetting of nested elements. For example, to obtain day 4 from weekdays, we have to use the [[ ]] operator in R:

```
>cal_lst[[1]][[4]]
[1] 4
>cal_lst[[c(1,4)]]
[1] 4
```

However, in the case of pandas, we can just use a double []:

```
In [132]: cal_df[1][3]
Out[132]: 4
```

R DataFrames versus pandas DataFrames

Selecting data in R DataFrames and pandas DataFrames follows a similar script. The following section explains how we perform multi-column selects from both.

Multi-column selection in R

In R, we specify the multiple columns to select by stating them in a vector within square brackets:

```
>stocks_table[c('Symbol','Price')]
Symbol  Price
1    GOOG 518.70
2    AMZN 307.82
3     FB   74.90
```

```
4    AAPL 109.70
5    TWTR  37.10
6    NFLX 334.48
7   LINKD 219.90
>stocks_table[,c('Symbol','Price')]
Symbol  Price
1    GOOG 518.70
2    AMZN 307.82
3      FB  74.90
4    AAPL 109.70
5    TWTR  37.10
6    NFLX 334.48
7   LINKD 219.90
```

Multi-column selection in pandas

In pandas, we subset elements in the usual way with the column names in square brackets:

```
In [140]: stocks_df[['Symbol','Price']]
Out[140]:Symbol Price
0       GOOG    518.70
1       AMZN    307.82
2       FB       74.90
3       AAPL    109.70
4       TWTR     37.10
5       NFLX    334.48
6       LNKD    219.90
In [145]: stocks_df.loc[:,['Symbol','Price']]
Out[145]: Symbol   Price
0       GOOG    518.70
1       AMZN    307.82
2       FB       74.90
3       AAPL    109.70
4       TWTR     37.10
5       NFLX    334.48
6       LNKD    219.90
```

Arithmetic operations on columns

In R and pandas, we can apply arithmetic operations in data columns in a similar manner. Hence, we can perform arithmetic operations such as addition or subtraction on elements in corresponding positions in two or more DataFrames.

Here, we construct a DataFrame in R with columns labeled x and y, and subtract column y from column x:

```
>norm_df<- data.frame(x=rnorm(7,0,1), y=rnorm(7,0,1))
>norm_df$x - norm_df$y
 [1] -1.3870730  2.4681458 -4.6991395  0.2978311 -0.8492245  1.5851009
-1.4620324
```

The with operator in R also has the same effect as arithmetic operations:

```
>with(norm_df,x-y)
 [1] -1.3870730  2.4681458 -4.6991395  0.2978311 -0.8492245  1.5851009
-1.4620324
```

In pandas, the same arithmetic operations can be performed on columns and the equivalent operator is eval:

```
In [10]: import pandas as pd
         import numpy as np
      df = pd.DataFrame({'x': np.random.normal(0,1,size=7), 'y':
np.random.normal(0,1,size=7)})
In [11]: df.x-df.y
Out[11]: 0    -0.107313
         1     0.617513
         2    -1.517827
         3     0.565804
         4    -1.630534
         5     0.101900
         6     0.775186
dtype: float64
In [12]: df.eval('x-y')
Out[12]: 0    -0.107313
         1     0.617513
         2    -1.517827
         3     0.565804
         4    -1.630534
         5     0.101900
         6     0.775186
dtype: float64
```

Aggregation and GroupBy

Sometimes, we wish to split data into subsets and apply a function such as the mean, max, or min to each subset. In R, we can do this through the aggregate or tapply functions.

Here, we have a dataset of statistics on the top five strikers of the four clubs that made it to the semi-final of the European Champions League Football tournament in 2014. We will use it to illustrate aggregation in R and its equivalent GroupBy functionality in pandas.

Aggregation in R

In R, aggregation is effected using the following command:

```
> goal_stats=read.csv('champ_league_stats_semifinalists.csv')
> goal_stats
           Club                  Player Goals GamesPlayed
1  Atletico Madrid          Diego Costa     8           9
2  Atletico Madrid            ArdaTuran     4           9
3  Atletico Madrid           RaúlGarcía     4          12
4  Atletico Madrid          AdriánLópez     2           9
5  Atletico Madrid          Diego Godín     2          10
6      Real Madrid    Cristiano Ronaldo    17          11
7      Real Madrid          Gareth Bale     6          12
8      Real Madrid        Karim Benzema     5          11
9      Real Madrid                 Isco     3          12
10     Real Madrid       Ángel Di María     3          11
11   Bayern Munich        Thomas Müller     5          12
12   Bayern Munich          ArjenRobben     4          10
13   Bayern Munich          Mario Götze     3          11
14   Bayern Munich Bastian Schweinsteiger    3           8
15   Bayern Munich       Mario Mandzukić     3          10
16         Chelsea       Fernando Torres     4           9
17         Chelsea             Demba Ba     3           6
18         Chelsea         Samuel Eto'o     3           9
19         Chelsea          Eden Hazard     2           9
20         Chelsea              Ramires     2          10
```

We now compute the goals-per-game ratio for each striker, so as to measure their deadliness in front of goal:

```
> goal_stats$GoalsPerGame<- goal_stats$Goals/goal_stats$GamesPlayed
> goal_stats
           Club    Player       Goals GamesPlayedGoalsPerGame
1  Atletico Madrid Diego Costa     8           9     0.8888889
2  Atletico Madrid ArdaTuran       4           9     0.4444444
3  Atletico Madrid RaúlGarcía      4          12     0.3333333
4  Atletico Madrid AdriánLópez     2           9     0.2222222
5  Atletico Madrid Diego Godín     2          10     0.2000000
6  Real Madrid    Cristiano Ronaldo 17         11     1.5454545
7  Real Madrid    Gareth Bale       6          12     0.5000000
8  Real Madrid    Karim Benzema     5          11     0.4545455
```

```
 9 Real Madrid        Isco          3        12      0.2500000
10 Real Madrid  Ángel Di María      3        11      0.2727273
11 Bayern Munich Thomas Müller      5        12      0.4166667
12 Bayern Munich ArjenRobben        4        10      0.4000000
13 Bayern Munich MarioGötze         3        11      0.2727273
14 Bayern Munich Bastian Schweinsteiger 3     8      0.3750000
15 Bayern Munich MarioMandzukić     3        10      0.3000000
16 Chelsea       Fernando Torres    4         9      0.4444444
17 Chelsea          Demba Ba        3         6      0.5000000
18 Chelsea       Samuel Eto'o       3         9      0.3333333
19 Chelsea        Eden Hazard       2         9      0.2222222
20 Chelsea           Ramires        2        10      0.2000000
```

Suppose that we wanted to know the highest goals-per-game ratio for each team. We would calculate this as follows:

```
>aggregate(x=goal_stats[,c('GoalsPerGame')],
by=list(goal_stats$Club),FUN=max)
          Group.1          x
1 Atletico Madrid 0.8888889
2    Bayern Munich 0.4166667
3          Chelsea 0.5000000
4      Real Madrid 1.5454545
```

The `tapply` function is used to apply a function to a subset of an array or vector that is defined by one or more columns. The `tapply` function can also be used as follows:

```
>tapply(goal_stats$GoalsPerGame,goal_stats$Club,max)
Atletico Madrid   Bayern Munich        Chelsea     Real Madrid
      0.8888889       0.4166667      0.5000000       1.5454545
```

The pandas GroupBy operator

In pandas, we can achieve the same result by using the `GroupBy` function:

```
In [6]: import pandas as pd
importnumpy as np
In [7]:
goal_stats_df=pd.read_csv('champ_league_stats_semifinalists.csv')
    In [27]: goal_stats_df['GoalsPerGame']=
goal_stats_df['Goals']/goal_stats_df['GamesPlayed']
    In [27]: goal_stats_df['GoalsPerGame']=
goal_stats_df['Goals']/goal_stats_df['GamesPlayed']
    In [28]: goal_stats_df
Out[28]: Club             Player      Goals GamesPlayedGoalsPerGame
0        Atletico Madrid Diego Costa  8      9           0.888889
1        Atletico Madrid ArdaTuran    4      9           0.444444
```

2	Atletico Madrid	RaúlGarcía	4	12	0.333333
3	Atletico Madrid	AdriánLópez	2	9	0.222222
4	Atletico Madrid	Diego Godín	2	10	0.200000
5	Real Madrid	Cristiano Ronaldo	17	11	1.545455
6	Real Madrid	Gareth Bale	6	12	0.500000
7	Real Madrid	Karim Benzema	5	11	0.454545
8	Real Madrid	Isco	3	12	0.250000
9	Real Madrid	Ángel Di María	3	11	0.272727
10	Bayern Munich	Thomas Müller	5	12	0.416667
11	Bayern Munich	ArjenRobben	4	10	0.400000
12	Bayern Munich	Mario Götze	3	11	0.272727
13	Bayern Munich	BastianSchweinsteiger	3	8	0.375000
14	Bayern Munich	MarioMandzukić	3	10	0.300000
15	Chelsea	Fernando Torres	4	9	0.444444
16	Chelsea	Demba Ba	3	6	0.500000
17	Chelsea	Samuel Eto'o	3	9	0.333333
18	Chelsea	Eden Hazard	2	9	0.222222
19	Chelsea	Ramires	2	10	0.200000

```
In [30]: grouped = goal_stats_df.groupby('Club')
In [17]: grouped['GoalsPerGame'].aggregate(np.max)
Out[17]: Club
         Atletico Madrid    0.888889
         Bayern Munich      0.416667
         Chelsea            0.500000
         Real Madrid        1.545455
         Name: GoalsPerGame, dtype: float64
In [22]: grouped['GoalsPerGame'].apply(np.max)
Out[22]: Club
         Atletico Madrid    0.888889
         Bayern Munich      0.416667
         Chelsea            0.500000
         Real Madrid        1.545455
         Name: GoalsPerGame, dtype: float64
```

Comparing matching operators in R and pandas

Here, we demonstrate the equivalence of matching operators between R (`%in%`) and pandas (`isin()`). In both cases, a logical vector or series (pandas) is produced, which indicates the position at which a match was found.

R %in% operator

Here, we demonstrate the use of the `%in%` operator in R:

```
>stock_symbols=stocks_table$Symbol
>stock_symbols
[1] GOOG  AMZN  FB  AAPL  TWTR  NFLX  LINKD
Levels: AAPL AMZN FB GOOG LINKD NFLX TWTR
>stock_symbols %in% c('GOOG','NFLX')
[1]  TRUE FALSE FALSE FALSE FALSE  TRUE FALSE
```

Pandas isin() function

Here is an example of using the pandas `isin()` function:

```
In [11]: stock_symbols=stocks_df.Symbol
stock_symbols
Out[11]: 0      GOOG
         1      AMZN
         2        FB
         3      AAPL
         4      TWTR
         5      NFLX
         6      LNKD
         Name: Symbol, dtype: object
In [10]: stock_symbols.isin(['GOOG','NFLX'])
Out[10]: 0       True
         1      False
         2      False
         3      False
         4      False
         5       True
         6      False
         Name: Symbol, dtype: bool
```

Logical subsetting

In R, as well as in pandas, there is more than one way to perform logical subsetting. Suppose that we wished to display all players with the average goals-per-game ratio of greater than or equal to 0.5; that is, on average, they score at least one goal every two games.

Logical subsetting in R

Here's how we can do this in R:

- Using a logical slice:

```
>goal_stats[goal_stats$GoalsPerGame>=0.5,]
      Club            Player       Goals GamesPlayedGoalsPerGame
1  Atletico Madrid Diego Costa       8            9    0.8888889
6  Real Madrid Cristiano Ronaldo    17           11    1.5454545
7  Real Madrid        Gareth Bale    6           12    0.5000000
17 Chelsea            Demba Ba      3            6    0.5000000
```

- Using the `subset()` function:

```
>subset(goal_stats,GoalsPerGame>=0.5)
      Club            Player       Goals GamesPlayedGoalsPerGame
1  Atletico Madrid Diego Costa       8            9    0.8888889
6  Real Madrid Cristiano Ronaldo    17           11    1.5454545
7  Real Madrid        Gareth Bale    6           12    0.5000000
17 Chelsea            Demba Ba      3            6    0.5000000
```

Logical subsetting in pandas

In pandas, we do similar:

- Logical slicing:

```
In [33]: goal_stats_df[goal_stats_df['GoalsPerGame']>=0.5]
Out[33]:        Club          Player         Goals
GamesPlayedGoalsPerGame
0     Atletico Madrid Diego Costa       8      9        0.888889
5     Real Madrid   Cristiano Ronaldo 17      11        1.545455
6     Real Madrid       Gareth Bale    6      12        0.500000
16    Chelsea           Demba Ba       3      6         0.500000
```

- `DataFrame.query()` operator:

```
In [36]:  goal_stats_df.query('GoalsPerGame>= 0.5')
Out[36]:
Club              Player     Goals GamesPlayedGoalsPerGame
0     Atletico Madrid Diego Costa    8     9          0.888889
5     Real Madrid   Cristiano Ronaldo 17   11          1.545455
6     Real Madrid       Gareth Bale   6    12          0.500000
16    Chelsea           Demba Ba      3    6           0.500000
```

Split-apply-combine

R has a library called `plyr` for a split-apply-combine data analysis. The `plyr` library has a function called `ddply`, which can be used to apply a function to a subset of a DataFrame, and then combine the results into another DataFrame.

 For more information on `ddply`, you can refer to the following link:
`http://www.inside-r.org/packages/cran/plyr/docs/ddply`.

To illustrate, let's consider a subset of a recently created dataset in R, which contains data on flights departing NYC in 2013:
`http://cran.r-project.org/web/packages/nycflights13/index.html`.

Implementation in R

Here, we install the package in R and instantiate the library:

```
>install.packages('nycflights13')
...
>library('nycflights13')
>dim(flights)
[1] 336776     16
>head(flights,3)
year month day dep_timedep_delayarr_timearr_delay carrier tailnum
flight
  1 2013    1   1     517          2      830        11       UA   N14228
1545
  2 2013    1   1     533          4      850        20       UA   N24211
1714
  3 2013    1   1     542          2      923        33       AA   N619AA
1141

  origindestair_time distance hour minute
  1    EWR  IAH      227      1400   5     17
  2    LGA  IAH      227      1416   5     33
  3    JFK  MIA      160      1089   5     42
>
flights.data=na.omit(flights[,c('year','month','dep_delay','arr_delay','dis
tance')])
  >flights.sample<-
flights.data[sample(1:nrow(flights.data),100,replace=FALSE),]
  >head(flights.sample,5)
  year month dep_delayarr_delay distance
  155501 2013    3        2         5        184
```

```
2410   2013      1        0        4       762
64158  2013     11       -7      -27       509
221447 2013      5       -5      -12       184
281887 2013      8       -1      -10       937
```

The `ddply` function enables us to summarize the departure delays (mean and standard deviation) by year and month:

```
>ddply(flights.sample,.(year,month),summarize,
mean_dep_delay=round(mean(dep_delay),2),
s_dep_delay=round(sd(dep_delay),2))
   year month mean_dep_delaysd_dep_delay
1  2013     1        -0.20         2.28
2  2013     2        23.85        61.63
3  2013     3        10.00        34.72
4  2013     4         0.88        12.56
5  2013     5         8.56        32.42
6  2013     6        58.14       145.78
7  2013     7        25.29        58.88
8  2013     8        25.86        59.38
9  2013     9        -0.38        10.25
10 2013    10         9.31        15.27
11 2013    11        -1.09         7.73
12 2013    12         0.00         8.58
```

Let's save the `flights.sample` dataset to a CSV file so that we can use the data to show us how to do the same thing in pandas:

```
>write.csv(flights.sample,file='nycflights13_sample.csv',
quote=FALSE,row.names=FALSE)
```

Implementation in pandas

In order to do the same thing in pandas, we read the CSV file saved in the preceding section:

```
In [40]: flights_sample=pd.read_csv('nycflights13_sample.csv')
In [41]: flights_sample.head()
Out[41]: year    month   dep_delayarr_delay      distance
0        2013    3       2       5       184
1        2013    1       0       4       762
2        2013    11      -7      -27     509
3        2013    5       -5      -12     184
4        2013    8       -1      -10     937
```

We achieve the same effect as `ddply` by making use of the `GroupBy()` operator, as shown in the following code and output:

```
In [44]: pd.set_option('precision',3)
In [45]: grouped = flights_sample_df.groupby(['year','month'])
In [48]: grouped['dep_delay'].agg([np.mean, np.std])
Out[48]:            mean     std
year      month
2013      1       -0.20    2.28
          2       23.85    61.63
          3       10.00    34.72
          4        0.88    12.56
          5        8.56    32.42
          6       58.14    145.78
          7       25.29    58.88
          8       25.86    59.38
          9       -0.38    10.25
          10       9.31    15.27
          11      -1.09    7.73
          12       0.00    8.58
```

Reshaping using melt

The `melt` function converts data in a wide format to a single column consisting of unique ID-variable combinations.

R melt function

Here, we demonstrate the use of the `melt()` function in R. It produces long-format data in which the rows are unique variable-value combinations:

```
>sample4=head(flights.sample,4)[c('year','month','dep_delay','arr_delay')]
> sample4
year month dep_delayarr_delay
155501 2013     3         2           5
2410   2013     1         0           4
64158  2013     11       -7          -27
221447 2013     5        -5          -12
>melt(sample4,id=c('year','month'))
year month  variable value
1 2013      3 dep_delay     2
2 2013      1 dep_delay     0
3 2013     11 dep_delay    -7
4 2013      5 dep_delay    -5
```

```
5 2013     3 arr_delay    5
6 2013     1 arr_delay    4
7 2013    11 arr_delay  -27
8 2013     5 arr_delay  -12
>
```

For more information, you can refer to the following link:
`http://www.statmethods.net/management/reshape.html`.

The pandas melt function

In pandas, the `melt` function is similar:

```
In [55]: sample_4_df=flights_sample_df[['year','month','dep_delay', \
'arr_delay']].head(4)
In [56]: sample_4_df
Out[56]: year    month dep_delayarr_delay
0        2013    3     2         5
1        2013    1     0         4
2        2013    11    -7        -27
3        2013    5     -5        -12
In [59]: pd.melt(sample_4_df,id_vars=['year','month'])
Out[59]: year    month    variable      value
0        2013    3        dep_delay     2
1        2013    1        dep_delay     0
2        2013    11       dep_delay     -7
3        2013    5        dep_delay     -5
4        2013    3        arr_delay     5
5        2013    1        arr_delay     4
6        2013    11       arr_delay     -27
7        2013    5        arr_delay     -12
```

The reference source for this information is as follows:
`http://pandas.pydata.org/pandas-docs/stable/reshaping.html#resha`
`ping-by-melt`.

Categorical data

R refers to categorical variables as factors, and the cut () function enables us to break a continuous numerical variable into ranges and treat the ranges as factors or categorical variables, or to classify a categorical variable into a larger bin.

R example using cut()

The following code block shows an example in R:

```
clinical.trial<- data.frame(patient = 1:1000,
age = rnorm(1000, mean = 50, sd = 5),
year.enroll = sample(paste("19", 80:99, sep = ""),
                            1000, replace = TRUE))
>clinical.trial<- data.frame(patient = 1:1000,
+                                age = rnorm(1000, mean = 50, sd = 5),
+                                year.enroll = sample(paste("19", 80:99,
sep = ""),
+                                1000, replace = TRUE))
>summary(clinical.trial)
patient              age           year.enroll
  Min.   :    1.0   Min.   :31.14   1995   : 61
  1st Qu.: 250.8   1st Qu.:46.77   1989   : 60
 Median : 500.5   Median :50.14   1985   : 57
  Mean   : 500.5   Mean   :50.14   1988   : 57
  3rd Qu.: 750.2   3rd Qu.:53.50   1990   : 56
  Max.   :1000.0   Max.   :70.15   1991   : 55
                                   (Other):654
>ctcut<- cut(clinical.trial$age, breaks = 5)> table(ctcut)
ctcut
(31.1,38.9] (38.9,46.7]  (46.7,54.6]  (54.6,62.4]  (62.4,70.2]
          15         232          558          186            9
```

The pandas solution

The following code block contains the equivalent of the earlier explained cut () function in pandas (only applies to version 0.15+):

```
In [79]: pd.set_option('precision',4)
clinical_trial=pd.DataFrame({'patient':range(1,1001),
                                        'age'  :
np.random.normal(50,5,size=1000),
                   'year_enroll': [str(x) for x in
np.random.choice(range(1980,2000),size=1000,replace=True)]})
    In [80]: clinical_trial.describe()
```

```
Out[80]:           age        patient
count     1000.000   1000.000
mean        50.089    500.500
std          4.909    288.819
min         29.944      1.000
            25%        46.572    250.750
            50%        50.314    500.500
            75%        53.320    750.250
max         63.458   1000.000
In [81]: clinical_trial.describe(include=['O'])
Out[81]:          year_enroll
count    1000
unique     20
top      1992
freq       62
In [82]: clinical_trial.year_enroll.value_counts()[:6]
Out[82]: 1992       62
         1985       61
         1986       59
         1994       59
         1983       58
         1991       58
dtype: int64
In [83]: ctcut=pd.cut(clinical_trial['age'], 5)
In [84]: ctcut.head()
Out[84]: 0     (43.349, 50.052]
         1     (50.052, 56.755]
         2     (50.052, 56.755]
         3     (43.349, 50.052]
         4     (50.052, 56.755]
         Name: age, dtype: category
         Categories (5, object): [(29.91, 36.646] < (36.646, 43.349] <
(43.349, 50.052] < (50.052, 56.755] < (56.755, 63.458]]
In [85]: ctcut.value_counts().sort_index()
Out[85]: (29.91, 36.646]          3
            (36.646, 43.349]         82
         (43.349, 50.052]     396
         (50.052, 56.755]     434
         (56.755, 63.458]      85
dtype: int64
```

The comparison in the previous sections can be summarized by the following table:

R	pandas	Comments
Vectors	Homogeneous Lists /Array	Hold values of only same type
Lists	Heterogeneous Lists	Can hold values of different types
DataFrames	DataFrames	Tabular structures in both.
Matrix	Numpy Array	Indexing of elements starts from 1 in R and 0 in Python.
Selection & Indexing	Selection & Indexing	[], [[]], $ in R. .loc, .iloc,[], [:] in pandas.
Lists	Series	Both uniform and 1-dimensional. List of lists possible. Series of lists possible.
Multi-column selections	Multi-column selections	Very similar in both. By specifying names explicitly. .loc can also be used in pandas.
Column Operations	Column Operations	Very similar in both. Just column seelction is little different. $ is used in R while [] in pandas.
Aggregate Function	GroupBy operator	Serve similar functions. GroupBy is more flexible and objects can be reused.
%in%	isin()	Matching operator serve the same function, just the keyword and syntax is different.
Logical Subsetting	Logical Subsetting	Very similar. Just column selection syntax is different.
ddply	GroupBy	For splitting DataFrame, performing an operation and combining the result.
melt	melt	Used for exapnding the number of rows in a DataFrame. Exactly the same even in syntax.
cut	cut	Used for binning a numeric variable. Syntax is slightly different. Supported in pandas v0.15 onwards.

Comparison of data structures and operations in R and pandas

Comparison with SQL

Pandas is similar to SQL in many ways in the sense that it is used for data selection, data filtering, data aggregation, data generation, and data modification. SQL does to the database tables what pandas does to the DataFrames. In this section, we will compare the features in SQL with their equivalents in pandas.

SELECT

SELECT is used to select or subset data in certain columns of the tables. Suppose you have a table/DataFrame called `DallasData`. This data would be attached in your book packet or could be accessed from the cloud drive of the book. To select five rows from the three given columns, you write the following

SQL

In SQL, you can use the following command:

```
select state_name,active_status,services_due from DallasData LIMIT 5;
```

pandas

In pandas, you can use the following command:

```
DallasData[['state_name','active_status','services_due']].head(5)
```

The following is the output to the preceding commands:

	state_name	active_status	services_due
0	Texas	1	11.80
1	Texas	0	11.87
2	Texas	1	11.86
3	Texas	1	11.87
4	Texas	0	11.87

Output of select on DallasData

Where

The `Where` statement is used in SQL to apply filter conditions to filter rows based on certain criteria. The equivalent in pandas is condition-based logical subsetting.

Suppose we want to find out the rows where `active_status ==1`. This can be done in the two tools in the following manner.

SQL

In SQL, you can use the following command:

```
select * from DallasData where active_status ==1 LIMIT 5;
```

pandas

In pandas, you can use the following command:

```
DallasData[DallasData['active_status']==1].head(5);
```

The following is the output to the preceding commands:

	zip	state_name	soldBy	customerID	officeID	active_status	days_old	services_completed	services_due	completion_percentage	...	age_median
0	75087	Texas	23335	477991	9	1	925	12	11.80	1.0169	...	39.0
2	75068	Texas	3161	485476	9	1	930	12	11.86	1.0118	...	31.0
3	76013	Texas	3351	485479	9	1	931	13	11.87	1.0952	...	38.0
5	75068	Texas	2589	485483	9	1	931	12	11.87	1.0110	...	31.0
10	76018	Texas	2783	485502	9	1	930	12	11.86	1.0118	...	31.0

DallasData after filtering only active customers

Suppose we want to find out the rows where the customers are active (`active_status==1`) and have completed fewer than nine services (`services_completed<9`). This can be done in the two tools in the following manner.

SQL

In SQL, you can use the following command:

```
select * from DallasData where active_status ==1 AND services_completed <9
LIMIT 5;
```

pandas

In pandas, you can use the following command:

```
DallasData[(DallasData['active_status']==1) &
(DallasData['services_completed'] <9)].head(5)
```

The following is the output to the preceding commands:

	zip	state_name	soldBy	customerID	officeID	active_status	days_old	services_completed	services_due	completion_percentage	...	age_median
359	75070	Texas	18519	494940	9	1	920	8	11.75	0.6809	...	34.0
1799	75126	Texas	2587	551553	9	1	871	8	11.21	0.7136	...	32.0
1872	75126	Texas	5101	551681	9	1	852	8	11.00	0.7273	...	32.0
2373	75007	Texas	2994	584138	9	1	980	8	12.41	0.6446	...	38.0
4413	76063	Texas	2736	698044	9	1	937	8	11.93	0.6706	...	35.0

DallasData after filtering customers who are active and have completed more than nine services

Suppose we want to find out the rows where the customers are active (active_status ==1), but only find the customer ID, zip code, and seller ID for those rows. This can be done in the two tools in the following manner.

SQL

In SQL, you can use the following command:

```
select customerID,zip,soldBy from DallasData where active_status ==1 LIMIT
5;
```

pandas

In pandas, you can use the following command:

```
DallasData[DallasData['active_status']==1][['customerID','zip','soldBy']].h
ead(5)
```

The following is the output to the preceding commands:

	customerID	zip	soldBy
0	477991	75087	23335
2	485476	75068	3161
3	485479	76013	3351
5	485483	75068	2589
10	485502	76018	2783

DallasData after filtering only active customers and selecting only particular columns

group by

The group by statement is used to aggregate data and find the aggregated values of numerical columns. The keyword for performing this operation is the same, but the syntax is a little different. Let's look at a few examples.

Suppose we are looking to find the numbers of active and inactive customers in the dataset. This can be done as follows in the two tools.

SQL

In SQL, you can use the following command:

```
select active_status, count(*) as number from DallasData group by
active_status;
```

pandas

In pandas, you can use the following command:

```
DallasData.groupby('active_status').size();
```

The following is the output to the preceding commands:

```
active_status
0      10404
1      16598
dtype: int64
```

Count of active and inactive customers using groupby in Python

Different aggregation operations can be applied to two different columns simultaneously while aggregating. The following example shows how to do that.

SQL

In SQL, you can use the following command:

```
select active_status, sum(services_complted), mean(age_median) from
DallasData group by active_status;
```

pandas

In pandas, you can use the following command:

```
DallasData.groupby('active_status').agg({'services_completed':np.sum,'age_m
edian':np.mean})
```

	services_completed	age_median
active_status		
0	45275	34.812856
1	95414	35.467690

Sum of services completed and the mean customer age grouped by active and inactive customers using groupby in Python

Aggregating by more than one column or multi-index aggregation is also possible. Suppose we want zip code-wise details of active and inactive customers.

SQL

In SQL, you can use the following command:

```
select active_status, sum(services_complted), mean(days_old) from
DallasData group by active_status,zip;
```

pandas

In pandas, you can use the following command:

```
DallasData.groupby(['active_status','zip']).agg({'services_completed':np.su
m,'days_old':np.mean}).head(5)
```

The following is the output to the preceding commands:

active_status	zip	services_completed	days_old
0	55056	3	689.0
	70570	11	620.0
	70614	3	555.0
	72609	3	604.0
	72626	4	678.0

Multi-indexed grouping by customer active status and zip code using groupby in Python

update

The update statements in SQL are used to filter data rows based on certain conditions and to update or modify certain values in those rows. In pandas, there is no particular keyword or function for doing this; instead, it is done by means of a direct assignment. Let's look at a few examples.

Suppose it was established that the data administrator had made a mistake in data collection. Due to this error, the data points where the age was actually 45 were randomly assigned a value greater than 35. To rectify this, we will update all such rows (**age>35**) to 45.

SQL

In SQL, you can use the following command:

```
update DallasData set age_median=45 where age_median>35
```

pandas

In pandas, you can use the following command:

```
DallasData[DallasData['age_median']>35]=45
```

The following two screenshots show the data before and after performing the update:

	zip	state_name	soldBy	customerID	officeID	active_status	days_old	services_completed	services_due	completion_percentage	...	age_median
0	75087	Texas	23335	477991	9	1	925	12	11.80	1.0169	...	39.0
3	76013	Texas	3351	485479	9	1	931	13	11.87	1.0952	...	38.0
9	76248	Texas	2624	485501	9	0	1000	1	12.63	0.0792	...	39.0
18	75044	Texas	3147	485518	9	1	927	10	11.83	0.8453	...	39.0
38	76248	Texas	2624	485581	9	1	999	12	12.61	0.9516	...	39.0

	zip	state_name	soldBy	customerID	officeID	active_status	days_old	services_completed	services_due	completion_percentage	...	age_median
1159	76034	Texas	2918	518920	9	0	906	9	11.59	0.7765	...	45.0
1464	76034	Texas	3240	535186	9	1	898	12	11.51	1.0426	...	45.0
1479	76034	Texas	2624	535228	9	1	897	12	11.50	1.0435	...	45.0
1664	76034	Texas	2624	551284	9	1	888	12	11.40	1.0526	...	45.0
1700	76034	Texas	2624	551355	9	1	884	11	11.35	0.9692	...	45.0

Before and after updating all ages greater than 35 to 45

delete

The `delete` statements in SQL are used to delete data rows based on certain conditions from the database tables. In pandas, we don't delete rows; we just deselect them. Let's look at a few examples.

Suppose we want to look at those customers who are in the system for at least 500 days (`days_old>500`).

SQL

In SQL, you can use the following command:

```
delete DallasData where days_old<500
```

pandas

In pandas, you can use the following command:

```
DallasData1 = DallasData[DallasData['days_old']>500]
```

Run the following command to check whether it did the intended operation.

```
DallasData1[DallasData1['days_old']<400]
```

This should return 0 rows if the delete action was performed correctly.

JOIN

The `join` statements are used to merge different tables in a database and extract important information spread across a variety of tables. In pandas, the merge operator does the same job. The only difference is that the syntax is a little different.

Let's create two datasets for illustrating different joins and their syntaxes in SQL and pandas:

```
df1 = pd.DataFrame({'key': ['IN', 'SA', 'SL',
'NZ'],'Result':['W','L','L','W']})
df2 = pd.DataFrame({'key': ['IN', 'SA', 'SA',
'WI'],'Score':[200,325,178,391]})
```

The following is the output to the preceding command:

	key	Result
0	IN	W
1	SA	L
2	SL	L
3	NZ	W

	key	Score
0	IN	200
1	SA	325
2	SA	178
3	WI	391

Two dummy datasets

Suppose we want to do an inner join between the two. This can be done in the two tools as shown preceding.

SQL

In SQL, you can use the following command:

```
SELECT * FROM df1 INNER JOIN df2 ON df1.key = df2.key;
```

pandas

In pandas, you can use the following command:

```
pd.merge(df1,df2,on='key')
```

The following is the output to the preceding commands:

	key	Result	Score
0	IN	W	200
1	SA	L	325
2	SA	L	178

Output of the inner join of the two DataFrames

As expected of an inner join, only the key values present in both the tables appear in the merged dataset.

Suppose we want to implement a left join between the two. This can be done in the two tools as shown here:

SQL

In SQL, you can use the following command:

```
SELECT * FROM df1 LEFT JOIN df2 ON df1.key = df2.key;
```

pandas

In pandas, you can use the following command:

```
pd.merge(df1,df2,on='key',how='left')
```

The following is the output to the preceding commands:

	key	Result	Score
0	IN	W	200.0
1	SA	L	325.0
2	SA	L	178.0
3	SL	L	NaN
4	NZ	W	NaN

Output of the left join between the two tables

As expected of a left join, it retrieves all the unique values of the key present in the left-hand table (df1, in this case), as well as the corresponding values in the right-hand table. For the key values in the left-hand table for which it doesn't find a match in the right-hand table, it returns NaN.

Suppose we want to implement a right join between the two. This can be done in the two tools as shown here:

SQL

In SQL, you can use the following command:

```
SELECT * FROM df1 RIGHT JOIN df2 ON df1.key = df2.key;
```

pandas

In pandas, you can use the following command:

```
pd.merge(df1,df2,on='key',how='right')
```

The following is the output to the preceding commands:

	key	Result	Score
0	IN	W	200
1	SA	L	325
2	SA	L	178
3	WI	NaN	391

Output of the right join between the two tables

As expected of a right join, it retrieves all the unique values of the key present in the right-hand table (`df2`, in this case), as well as the corresponding values in the left-hand table. For the key values in the right-hand table for which it doesn't find a match in the left-hand table, it returns NaN.

Comparison with SAS

SAS is the analytics sledgehammer of yesteryear. It was the market leader in analytics solutions before R and Python, the poster boys of the open source movement, dethroned it from its *numero uno* position. Nevertheless, many enterprises still trust it with all their analytics requirements, despite the unreasonably high costs.

In this section, we will keep all the comparisons to a tabular format. The SAS and pandas equivalents are summarized in the following table:

Pandas	SAS
DataFrame	dataset
column	variable
row	observation
groupby	BY-group
NaN	.

Now, let's see how we can perform the basic data operations in pandas and SAS:

Task	Pandas	SAS
Creating a dataset	`pd.DataFrame({'odds': [1, 3, 5, 7, 9], 'evens': [2, 4, 6, 8, 10]})`	```data df; input x y; datalines; 1 2 3 4 5 6 7 8 9 10; run;```
Reading a dataset	`pd.read_csv('DallasData.csv')`	```proc import datafile='DallasData.csv' dbms=csv out=tips replace; getnames=yes; run;```
Exporting a dataset	`DallasData.to_csv('dallas.csv')`	```proc export data=DallasData outfile='dallas.csv' dbms=csv; run;```

Column operations	`DallasData['days_old_year'] = DallasData['days_old']/365`	```data DallasData;` ` set DallasData;` ` days_old_year =` `days_old / 365;` `run;```
Filtering	`DallasData[DallasData['days_old']>800].head()`	```data tips;` ` set DallasData;` ` if days_old > 800;` `run;```
If-else	`DallasData['income_class'] =` `np.where(DallasData['income_average'] < 40000, 'low', 'high')`	```data DallasData;` ` set dallas;` ` format income_average` `$5.;` ` if days_old < 40000` `then bucket = 'low';` ` else bucket = 'high';` `run;```
Column selection	`DallasData[['zip','customerID','days_old','services_due']].head()`	```data dallas;` ` set DallasData;` ` keep zip CustomerID` `days_old services_due;` `run;```
Sort	`dallas =` `DallasData.sort_values(['days_old','services_completed'])`	```proc sort` `data=DallasData;` ` by days_old` `services_completed;` `run;```
String length	`DallasData['state_name'].str.len().head()`	```data _null_;` `set DallasData;` `put (LENGTHN(state_name));` `put (LENGTHC(state_name));` `run;```
Groupby aggregation	`dallas_grouped = DallasData.groupby(['zip',` `'customerID'])['days_old', 'services_completed'].sum()`	```proc summary` `data=DallasData nway;` ` class zip customerID;` ` var days_old` `services_completed;` ` output` `out=dallas_summed sum=;` `run;```
Join	`df1 = pd.DataFrame({'key': ['A', 'B', 'C', 'D'], 'value':` `np.random.randn(4)})` `df2 = pd.DataFrame({'key': ['B', 'D', 'D', 'E'],'value':` `np.random.randn(4)})` `inner_join = df1.merge(df2, on=['key'], how='inner')` `left_join = df1.merge(df2, on=['key'], how='left')` `right_join = df1.merge(df2, on=['key'], how='right')`	```proc sort data=df1;` ` by key;` `run;` `proc sort data=df2;` ` by key;` `run;` `data left_join inner_join` `right_join outer_join;` ` merge df1(in=a)` `df2(in=b);` ` if a and b then` `output inner_join;` ` if a then output` `left_join;` ` if b then output` `right_join;` ` if a or b then output` `outer_join;` `run;```

Summary

In this chapter, we attempted to compare key features in R and SQL with their pandas equivalents in order to achieve the following objectives:

- To assist R, SQL, and SAS users who may wish to replicate the same functionality in pandas
- To assist any users who on reading some R, SQL, and SAS code, may wish to rewrite the code in pandas

In the next chapter, we will conclude the book by providing a brief introduction to the `scikit-learn` library for performing machine learning, and we will demonstrate how pandas fits in that framework. Reference documentation for this chapter can be found here: `http://pandas.pydata.org/pandas-docs/stable/comparison_with_r.html`.

15
A Brief Tour of Machine Learning

This chapter will take you on a whirlwind tour of machine learning, focusing on using the `pandas` library as a tool to preprocess the data used by machine learning programs. It will also introduce you to the `scikit-learn` library, which is the most popular machine learning toolkit in Python.

In this chapter, we will illustrate machine learning techniques by applying them to a well-known problem about classifying which passengers survived the Titanic disaster at the turn of the last century. The various topics addressed in this chapter include the following:

- The role of pandas in machine learning
- Installing `scikit-learn`
- Introduction to machine learning concepts
- Applying machine learning—Kaggle Titanic competition
- Data analysis and preprocessing using pandas
- A naïve approach to the Titanic problem
- The `scikit-learn` ML classifier interface
- Supervised learning algorithms
- Unsupervised learning algorithms

The role of pandas in machine learning

The library we will be considering for machine learning is called `scikit-learn`. The `scikit-learn` Python library is an extensive library of machine learning algorithms that can be used to create adaptive programs that learn from data inputs.

However, before this data can be used by `scikit-learn`, it must undergo some preprocessing. This is where pandas comes in. pandas can be used to preprocess and filter data before passing it to the algorithm implemented in `scikit-learn`.

In the coming sections, we will see how `scikit-learn` can be used for machine learning. So, as the first step, we will learn how to install it on our machines.

Installation of scikit-learn

As was mentioned in Chapter 2, *Installation of Python and pandas from Third-Party Vendors*, the easiest way to install pandas and its accompanying libraries is to use a third-party distribution such as Anaconda and be done with it. Installing `scikit-learn` should be no different. I will briefly highlight the steps for installation on various platforms and third-party distributions, starting with Anaconda. The `scikit-learn` library requires the following libraries:

- Python 2.6.x or higher
- NumPy 1.6.1 or higher
- SciPy 0.9 or higher

Assuming that you have already installed pandas as described in Chapter 2, *Installation of pandas and Supporting Software*, these dependencies should already be in place. The various options to install `scikit-learn` on different platforms are discussed in the following sections.

Installing via Anaconda

You can install `scikit-learn` on Anaconda by running the `conda` Python package manager:

```
conda install scikit-learn
```

Installing on Unix (Linux/macOS)

For Unix, it is best to install from the source (C compiler is required). Assuming that pandas and NumPy are already installed and the required dependent libraries are already in place, you can install `scikit-learn` via Git by running the following commands:

```
git clone https://github.com/scikit-learn/scikit-learn.git cd scikit-learn
python setup.py install
```

The pandas library can also be installed on Unix by using `pip` from `PyPi`:

```
pip install pandas
```

Installing on Windows

To install on Windows, you can open a console and run the following:

```
pip install -U scikit-learn
```

For more in-depth information on installation, you can take a look at the official `scikit-learn` documentation at `http://scikit-learn.org/stable/install.html`. You can also take a look at the README file for the `scikit-learn` Git repository at `https://github.com/scikit-learn/scikit-learn/blob/master/README.rst`.

Introduction to machine learning

Machine learning is the art of creating software programs that learn from data. More formally, it can be defined as the practice of building adaptive programs that use tunable parameters to improve predictive performance. It is a sub-field of artificial intelligence.

We can separate machine learning programs based on the type of problems they are trying to solve. These problems are appropriately called learning problems. The two categories of these problems, broadly speaking, are referred to as supervised and unsupervised learning problems. Furthermore, there are some hybrid problems that have aspects that involve both categories—supervised and unsupervised.

The input to a learning problem consists of a dataset of n rows. Each row represents a sample and may involve one or more fields referred to as attributes or features. A dataset can be canonically described as consisting of n samples, each consisting of n features.

Supervised versus unsupervised learning

For supervised learning problems, the input to a learning problem is a dataset consisting of *labeled* data. By this, we mean that we have outputs whose values are known. The learning program is fed with input samples and their corresponding outputs and its goal is to decipher the relationship between them. Such input is known as labeled data. Supervised learning problems include the following:

- **Classification**: The learned attribute is categorical (nominal) or discrete
- **Regression**: The learned attribute is numeric/continuous

In unsupervised learning or data mining, the learning program is fed with inputs but does without the corresponding outputs. This input data is referred to as unlabeled data. The goal of machine learning in such cases is to learn or decipher the hidden label. Such problems include the following:

- Clustering
- Dimensionality reduction

Illustration using document classification

A common usage of machine learning techniques is in the area of document classification. The two main categories of machine learning can be applied to this problem—supervised and unsupervised learning.

Supervised learning

Each document in the input collection is assigned to a category; that is, a label. The learning program/algorithm uses the input collection of documents to learn how to make predictions for another set of documents with no labels. This method is known as **classification**.

Unsupervised learning

The documents in the input collection are not assigned to categories; hence, they are unlabeled. The learning program takes this as input and tries to *cluster* or discover groups of related or similar documents. This method is known as **clustering**.

How machine learning systems learn

Machine learning systems utilize what is known as a classifier to learn from data. A *classifier* is an interface that takes a matrix of what is known as *feature values* and produces an output vector, also known as the class. These feature values may be discrete or continuously valued. There are three core components of classifiers:

- **Representation**: What type of classifier is it?
- **Evaluation**: How good is the classifier?
- **Optimization**: How can you search among the alternatives?

Application of machine learning – Kaggle Titanic competition

To illustrate how we can use pandas to assist us at the start of our machine learning journey, we will apply it to a classic problem, which is hosted on the Kaggle website (`http://www.kaggle.com`). **Kaggle** is a competition platform for machine learning problems. The idea behind Kaggle is to enable companies that are interested in solving predictive analytics problems with their data to post their data on Kaggle and invite data scientists to come up with proposed solutions to their problems. A competition can be ongoing over a period of time, and the rankings of the competitors are posted on a leaderboard. At the close of the competition, the top-ranked competitors receive cash prizes.

The classic problem that we will study to illustrate the use of pandas for machine learning with `scikit-learn` is the *Titanic: Machine Learning from Disaster* problem hosted on Kaggle as their classic introductory machine learning problem. The dataset involved in the problem is a raw dataset. Hence, pandas is very useful in the preprocessing and cleansing of the data before it is submitted as input to the machine learning algorithm implemented in `scikit-learn`.

The Titanic: Machine Learning from Disaster problem

The dataset for the Titanic consists of the passenger manifest for the doomed trip, along with various features and an indicator variable telling whether the passenger survived the sinking of the ship or not. The essence of the problem is to be able to predict, given a passenger and his/her associated features, whether this passenger survived the sinking of the Titanic or not. The features are as follows.

The data consists of two datasets: one training dataset and one test dataset. The training dataset consists of 891 passenger cases, and the test dataset consists of 491 passenger cases.

The training dataset also consists of 11 variables, of which 10 are features and 1 dependent/indicator variable, Survived, which indicated whether the passenger survived the disaster or not.

The feature variables are as follows:

- PassengerID
- Cabin
- Sex
- Pclass (passenger class)
- Fare
- Parch (number of parents and children)
- Age
- Sibsp (number of siblings)
- Embarked

We can make use of pandas to help us to preprocess data in the following ways:

- Data cleaning and the categorization of some variables
- The exclusion of unnecessary features that obviously have no bearing on the survivability of the passenger; for example, name
- Handling missing data

There are various algorithms that we can use to tackle this problem. They are as follows:

- Decision trees
- Neural networks
- Random forests
- Support vector machines

The problem of overfitting

Overfitting is a well-known problem in machine learning, whereby the program memorizes the specific data that it is fed as input, leading to perfect results on the training data and abysmal results on the test data.

To prevent overfitting, the tenfold cross-validation technique can be used to introduce variability in the data during the training phase.

Data analysis and preprocessing using pandas

In this section, we will utilize pandas to do some analysis and preprocessing of the data before submitting it as input to `scikit-learn`.

Examining the data

To start our preprocessing of the data, let's read in the training dataset and examine what it looks like.

Here, we read the training dataset into a pandas DataFrame and display the first rows:

```
In [2]: import pandas as pd
        import numpy as np
# For .read_csv, always use header=0 when you know row 0 is the header row
        train_df = pd.read_csv('csv/train.csv', header=0)
In [3]: train_df.head(3)
```

The output is as follows:

```
In [3]:   from matplotlib import pyplot as plt
          import matplotlib.pyplot as plt
          import pandas as pd
          import numpy as np
          import patsy as pt
```

```
In [4]:   # For .read_csv, always use header=0 when you know row 0 is the header row
          train_df = pd.read_csv('csv/train.csv', header=0)
          test_df = pd.read_csv('csv/test.csv', header=0)
```

```
In [5]:   train_df.head(3)
```

Out[5]:

	PassengerId	Survived	Pclass	Name	Sex	Age	SibSp	Parch	Ticket	Fare	Cabin	Embarked
0	1	0	3	Braund, Mr. Owen Harris	male	22	1	0	A/5 21171	7.2500	NaN	S
1	2	1	1	Cumings, Mrs. John Bradley (Florence Briggs Th...	female	38	1	0	PC 17599	71.2833	C85	C
2	3	1	3	Heikkinen, Miss. Laina	female	26	0	0	STON/O2. 3101282	7.9250	NaN	S

Hence, we can see the various features: **PassengerId**, **Survived**, **PClass**, **Name**, **Sex**, **Age**, **Sibsp**, **Parch**, **Ticket**, **Fare**, **Cabin**, and **Embarked**. One question that springs to mind immediately is this: which of the features are likely to influence whether a passenger survived or not?

It should seem obvious that **PassengerID**, **Ticket Code**, and **Name** should not be influencers on survivability since they're *identifier* variables. We will skip these in our analysis.

Handling missing values

One issue that we have to deal with in datasets for machine learning is how to handle missing values in the training set.

Let's visually identify where we have missing values in our feature set.

For that, we can make use of an equivalent of the `missmap` function in R, written by Tom Augspurger. The next screenshot shows how much data is missing for the various features in an intuitively appealing manner:

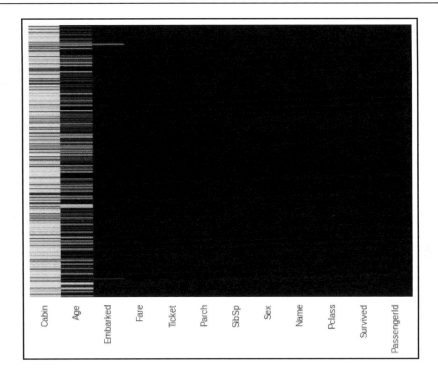

For more information and the code used to generate this data, see the following:
http://tomaugspurger.github.io/blog/2014/02/22/Visualizing%20Missing%20Data/.

We can also calculate how much data is missing for each of the features:

```
In [83]: missing_perc=train_df.apply(lambda x: 100*(1-
x.count().sum()/(1.0*len(x))))
In [85]: sorted_missing_perc=missing_perc.order(ascending=False)
         sorted_missing_perc
Out[85]: Cabin          77.104377
         Age            19.865320
         Embarked        0.224467
         Fare            0.000000
         Ticket          0.000000
         Parch           0.000000
         SibSp           0.000000
         Sex             0.000000
         Name            0.000000
         Pclass          0.000000
         Survived        0.000000
         PassengerId     0.000000
         dtype: float64
```

Hence, we can see that most of the `Cabin` data is missing (77%), while around 20% of the `Age` data is missing. We then decide to drop the `Cabin` data from our learning feature set as the data is too sparse to be of much use.

Let's do a further breakdown of the various features that we would like to examine. In the case of categorical/discrete features, we use bar plots; for continuous valued features, we use histograms. The code to generate the charts is as shown:

```
In [137]:  import random
                   bar_width=0.1
                   categories_map={'Pclass':{'First':1,'Second':2,
'Third':3},
                       'Sex':{'Female':'female','Male':'male'},
                       'Survived':{'Perished':0,'Survived':1},

'Embarked':{'Cherbourg':'C','Queenstown':'Q','Southampton':'S'},
                       'SibSp': { str(x):x for x in [0,1,2,3,4,5,8]},
                       'Parch': {str(x):x for x in range(7)}
                       }
                   colors=['red','green','blue','yellow','magenta','orange']
                   subplots=[111,211,311,411,511,611,711,811]
                   cIdx=0
                   fig,ax=plt.subplots(len(subplots),figsize=(10,12))
                   keyorder =
['Survived','Sex','Pclass','Embarked','SibSp','Parch']
      for category_key,category_items in sorted(categories_map.iteritems(),
                                            key=lambda
i:keyorder.index(i[0])):
          num_bars=len(category_items)
          index=np.arange(num_bars)
          idx=0
          for cat_name,cat_val in sorted(category_items.iteritems()):

ax[cIdx].bar(idx,len(train_df[train_df[category_key]==cat_val]),
label=cat_name,
                       color=np.random.rand(3,1))
              idx+=1
          ax[cIdx].set_title('%s Breakdown' % category_key)
          xlabels=sorted(category_items.keys())
          ax[cIdx].set_xticks(index+bar_width)
          ax[cIdx].set_xticklabels(xlabels)
          ax[cIdx].set_ylabel('Count')
          cIdx +=1
      fig.subplots_adjust(hspace=0.8)
      for hcat in ['Age','Fare']:
          ax[cIdx].hist(train_df[hcat].dropna(),color=np.random.rand(3,1))
          ax[cIdx].set_title('%s Breakdown' % hcat)
```

```
    #ax[cIdx].set_xlabel(hcat)
    ax[cIdx].set_ylabel('Frequency')
    cIdx +=1
fig.subplots_adjust(hspace=0.8)
plt.show()
```

Take a look at the following output:

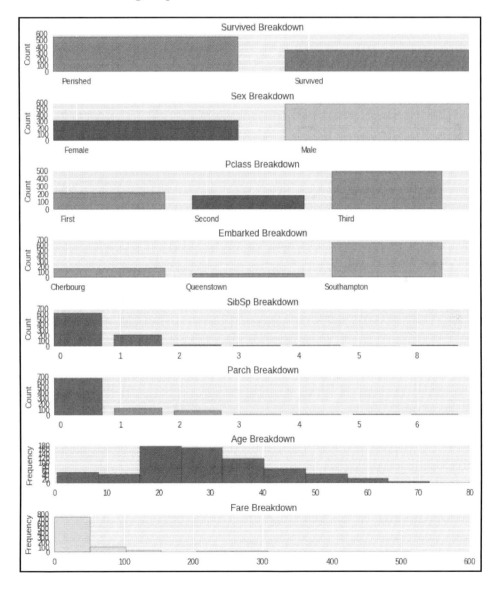

From the data and illustration in the preceding screenshot, we can observe the following:

- About twice as many passengers perished than survived (62% versus 38%).
- There were about twice as many male passengers as female passengers (65% versus 35%).
- There were about 20% more passengers in the third class versus the first and second together (55% versus 45%).
- Most passengers were solo; that is, had no children, parents, siblings, or spouse on board.

These observations might lead us to dig deeper and investigate whether there is some correlation between the chances of survival and gender and fare class, particularly if we take into account the fact that the Titanic had a women-and-children-first policy and the fact that the Titanic was carrying fewer lifeboats (20) than it was designed to (32).

In light of this, let's further examine the relationships between survival and some of these features. We'll start with gender:

```
In [85]: from collections import OrderedDict
         num_passengers=len(train_df)
         num_men=len(train_df[train_df['Sex']=='male'])
         men_survived=train_df[(train_df['Survived']==1 ) &
(train_df['Sex']=='male')]
         num_men_survived=len(men_survived)
         num_men_perished=num_men-num_men_survived
         num_women=num_passengers-num_men
         women_survived=train_df[(train_df['Survived']==1) &
(train_df['Sex']=='female')]
         num_women_survived=len(women_survived)
         num_women_perished=num_women-num_women_survived
         gender_survival_dict=OrderedDict()

gender_survival_dict['Survived']={'Men':num_men_survived, 'Women':num_women_
survived}

gender_survival_dict['Perished']={'Men':num_men_perished, 'Women':num_women_
perished}
         gender_survival_dict['Survival Rate']= {'Men' :
         round(100.0*num_men_survived/num_men,2),
         'Women':round(100.0*num_women_survived/num_women,2)}
     pd.DataFrame(gender_survival_dict)
     Out[85]:
```

Take a look at the following table:

Gender	Survived	Perished	Survival Rate
Men	109	468	18.89
Women	233	81	74.2

We'll now illustrate this data in a bar chart:

```
In [76]: #code to display survival by gender
         fig = plt.figure()
         ax = fig.add_subplot(111)
         perished_data=[num_men_perished, num_women_perished]
         survived_data=[num_men_survived, num_women_survived]
         N=2
         ind = np.arange(N)      # the x locations for the groups
         width = 0.35
         survived_rects = ax.barh(ind, survived_data,
width,color='green')
         perished_rects = ax.barh(ind+width, perished_data,
width,color='red')
         ax.set_xlabel('Count')
         ax.set_title('Count of Survival by Gender')
         yTickMarks = ['Men','Women']
         ax.set_yticks(ind+width)
         ytickNames = ax.set_yticklabels(yTickMarks)
         plt.setp(ytickNames, rotation=45, fontsize=10)
         ## add a legend
         ax.legend((survived_rects[0], perished_rects[0]), ('Survived',
'Perished') )
         plt.show()
```

The preceding code produces the following bar graph diagram:

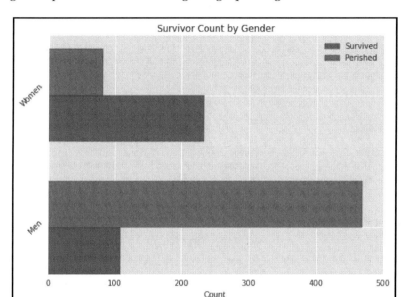

From the preceding diagram, we can see that the majority of the women survived (74%), while most of the men perished (only 19% survived).

This leads us to the conclusion that the gender of the passenger may be a contributing factor to whether a passenger survived or not.

Next, let's look at passenger class. First, we generate the survived and perished data for each of the three passenger classes, as well as survival rates:

```
In [86]:
from collections import OrderedDict
num_passengers=len(train_df)
num_class1=len(train_df[train_df['Pclass']==1])
class1_survived=train_df[(train_df['Survived']==1 ) &
(train_df['Pclass']==1)]
num_class1_survived=len(class1_survived)
num_class1_perished=num_class1-num_class1_survived
num_class2=len(train_df[train_df['Pclass']==2])
class2_survived=train_df[(train_df['Survived']==1) &
(train_df['Pclass']==2)]
num_class2_survived=len(class2_survived)
num_class2_perished=num_class2-num_class2_survived
num_class3=num_passengers-num_class1-num_class2
class3_survived=train_df[(train_df['Survived']==1 ) &
```

```
(train_df['Pclass']==3)]
    num_class3_survived=len(class3_survived)
    num_class3_perished=num_class3-num_class3_survived
    pclass_survival_dict=OrderedDict()
    pclass_survival_dict['Survived']={'1st Class':num_class1_survived,
                                      '2nd Class':num_class2_survived,
                                      '3rd Class':num_class3_survived}
    pclass_survival_dict['Perished']={'1st Class':num_class1_perished,
                                      '2nd Class':num_class2_perished,
                                      '3rd Class':num_class3_perished}
    pclass_survival_dict['Survival Rate']= {'1st Class' :
round(100.0*num_class1_survived/num_class1,2),
                    '2nd
Class':round(100.0*num_class2_survived/num_class2,2),
                    '3rd
Class':round(100.0*num_class3_survived/num_class3,2),}
    pd.DataFrame(pclass_survival_dict)
    Out[86]:
```

Then, we show them in a table:

Class	Survived	Perished	Survival Rate
First Class	136	80	62.96
Second Class	87	97	47.28
Third Class	119	372	24.24

We can then plot the data by using `matplotlib` in a similar manner to that for the survivor count by gender described earlier:

```
In [186]:
fig = plt.figure()
ax = fig.add_subplot(111)
perished_data=[num_class1_perished, num_class2_perished,
num_class3_perished]
survived_data=[num_class1_survived, num_class2_survived,
num_class3_survived]
N=3
ind = np.arange(N)                  # the x locations for the groups
width = 0.35
survived_rects = ax.barh(ind, survived_data, width,color='blue')
perished_rects = ax.barh(ind+width, perished_data, width,color='red')
ax.set_xlabel('Count')
ax.set_title('Survivor Count by Passenger class')
yTickMarks = ['1st Class','2nd Class', '3rd Class']
ax.set_yticks(ind+width)
ytickNames = ax.set_yticklabels(yTickMarks)
```

```
    plt.setp(ytickNames, rotation=45, fontsize=10)
    ## add a legend
    ax.legend( (survived_rects[0], perished_rects[0]), ('Survived',
'Perished'),
            loc=10 )
    plt.show()
```

This produces the following bar plot diagram:

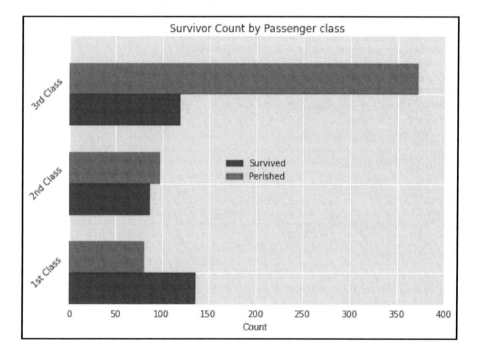

It seems clear from the preceding data and diagram that the higher the passenger fare class, the greater the passenger's chances of survival.

Given that both gender and fare class seem to influence the chances of a passenger's survival, let's see what happens when we combine these two features and plot a combination of both. For this, we will use the crosstab function in pandas:

```
In [173]:
survival_counts=pd.crosstab([train_df.Pclass,train_df.Sex],train_df.Survive
d.astype(bool))
survival_counts
Out[173]:      Survived False   True
               Pclass        Sex
               1             female    3      91
                             male     77      45
```

2	female	6	70
	male	91	17
3	female	72	72
	male	300	47

Let's now display this data using `matplotlib`. First, let's do some re-labeling for display purposes:

```
In [183]: survival_counts.index=survival_counts.index.set_levels([['1st',
'2nd', '3rd'], ['Women', 'Men']])
In [184]: survival_counts.columns=['Perished','Survived']
```

Now, we plot the passenger data by using the `plot` function of a pandas `DataFrame`:

```
In [185]: fig = plt.figure()
          ax = fig.add_subplot(111)
          ax.set_xlabel('Count')
          ax.set_title('Survivor Count by Passenger class, Gender')
          survival_counts.plot(kind='barh',ax=ax,width=0.75,
                               color=['red','black'], xlim=(0,400))
Out[185]: <matplotlib.axes._subplots.AxesSubplot at 0x7f714b187e90>
```

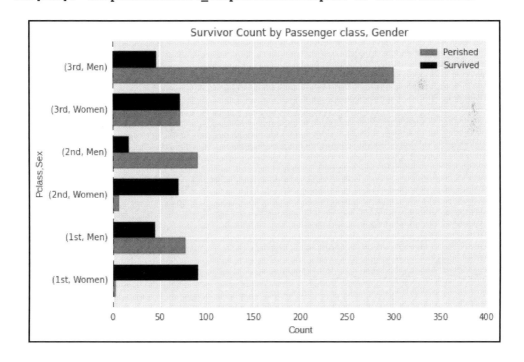

A naive approach to the Titanic problem

Our first attempt at classifying the Titanic data is to use a naive, yet very intuitive, approach. This approach involves the following steps:

1. Select a set of features, *S*, that influence whether a person survived or not.
2. For each possible combination of features, use the training data to indicate whether the majority of cases survived or not. This can be evaluated in what is known as a survival matrix.
3. For each test example that we wish to predict survival, look up the combination of features that corresponds to the values of its features and assign its predicted value to the survival value in the survival table. This approach is a naive K-nearest neighbor approach.

Based on what we have seen earlier in our analysis, three features seem to have the most influence on the survival rate:

- Passenger class
- Gender
- Passenger fare (bucketed)

We include passenger fare as it is related to passenger class.

The survival table looks something similar to the following:

	NumberOfPeople	Pclass	PriceBucket	Sex	Survived
0	0	1	0	female	0
1	1	1	0	male	0
2	0	1	1	female	0
3	0	1	1	male	0
4	7	1	2	female	1
5	34	1	2	male	0
6	1	1	3	female	1
7	19	1	3	male	0
8	0	2	0	female	0
9	0	2	0	male	0
10	35	2	1	female	1
11	63	2	1	male	0
12	31	2	2	female	1
13	25	2	2	male	0
14	4	2	3	female	1
15	6	2	3	male	0
16	64	3	0	female	1
17	256	3	0	male	0
18	43	3	1	female	1

19	38	3	1	male	0
20	21	3	2	female	0
21	24	3	2	male	0
22	10	3	3	female	0
23	5	3	3	male	0

To see how we use this table, let's take a look at a snippet of our test data:

```
In [192]: test_df.head(3)[['PassengerId','Pclass','Sex','Fare']]
Out[192]: PassengerId  Pclass  Sex       Fare
          0            892     3     male     7.8292
          1            893     3     female   7.0000
          2            894     2     male     9.6875
```

For passenger 892, we see that he is male, his ticket price was 7.8292, and he traveled in the third class. Hence, the key for the survival table lookup for this passenger is *{Sex='male', Pclass=3, PriceBucket=0 (since 7.8292 falls in bucket 0)}*. If we look up the survival value corresponding to this key in our survival table (row 17), we see that the value is 0, that is, perished; this is the value that we will predict.

Similarly, for passenger 893, we have *key={Sex='female', Pclass=3, PriceBucket=0}*. This corresponds to row 16, and hence, we will predict 1, that is, survived, and her predicted survival is 1, that is, survived.

Hence, our results look like the following command:

```
> head -4 csv/surv_results.csv
PassengerId,Survived
    892,0
    893,1
    894,0
```

The source of this information is at http://www.markhneedham.com/blog/2013/10/30/kaggle-titanic-python-pandas-attempt/.

Using the survival table approach outlined earlier, we can achieve an accuracy of 0.77990 on Kaggle (http://www.kaggle.com). The survival table approach, while intuitive, is a very basic approach that represents only the tip of the iceberg of possibilities in machine learning.

In the following sections, we will take a whirlwind tour of various machine learning algorithms that will help you, the reader, to get a feel for what is available in the machine learning universe.

The scikit-learn ML/classifier interface

We'll be diving into the basic principles of machine learning and demonstrate the use of these principles via the `scikit-learn` basic API.

The `scikit-learn` library has an estimator interface. We illustrate it by using a linear regression model. For example, consider the following:

```
In [3]: from sklearn.linear_model import LinearRegression
```

The estimator interface is instantiated to create a model, which is a linear regression model in this case:

```
In [4]: model = LinearRegression(normalize=True)
In [6]: print model
    LinearRegression(copy_X=True, fit_intercept=True, normalize=True)
```

Here, we specify `normalize=True`, indicating that the *x*-values will be normalized before regression. **Hyperparameters** (estimator parameters) are passed on as arguments in the model creation. This is an example of creating a model with tunable parameters.

The estimated parameters are obtained from the data when the data is fitted with an estimator. Let's first create some sample training data that is normally distributed about `y = x/2`. We first generate our `x` and `y` values:

```
In [51]: sample_size=500
         x = []
         y = []
         for i in range(sample_size):
             newVal = random.normalvariate(100,10)
             x.append(newVal)
             y.append(newVal / 2.0 + random.normalvariate(50,5))
```

`sklearn` takes a 2D array of `num_samples` × `num_features` as input, so we convert our `x` data into a 2D array:

```
In [67]: X = np.array(x)[:,np.newaxis]
         X.shape
Out[67]: (500, 1)
```

In this case, we have 500 samples and 1 feature, x. We now train/fit the model and display the slope (coefficient) and the intercept of the regression line, which is the prediction:

```
In [71]: model.fit(X,y)
         print "coeff=%s, intercept=%s" %
(model.coef_,model.intercept_)
         coeff=[ 0.47071289], intercept=52.7456611783
```

This can be visualized as follows:

```
In [65]: plt.title("Plot of linear regression line and training data")
         plt.xlabel('x')
         plt.ylabel('y')
         plt.scatter(X,y,marker='o', color='green', label='training
data');
         plt.plot(X,model.predict(X), color='red', label='regression
line')
         plt.legend(loc=2)
Out[65]: [<matplotlib.lines.Line2D at 0x7f11b0752350]
```

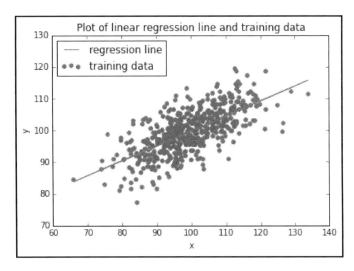

To summarize the basic use of the estimator interface, follow these steps:

1. Define your model: `LinearRegression`, `SupportVectorMachine`, `DecisionTrees`, and so on. You can specify the required hyperparameters in this step; for example, `normalize=True`, as specified earlier.

2. Once the model has been defined, you can train your model on your data by calling the `fit(..)` method on the model defined in the previous step.

3. Once we have fit the model, we can call the `predict(..)` method on test data to make predictions or estimations.

4. In the case of a supervised learning problem, the `predict(X)` method is given unlabeled observations, X, and returns predicted labels, y.

For extra information, please see the following:
`http://scikit-learn.org/stable/tutorial/statistical_inference/su`
`pervised_learning.html`

Supervised learning algorithms

We will take a brief tour of some well-known supervised learning algorithms and see how we can apply them to the Titanic survival prediction problem described earlier.

Constructing a model using Patsy for scikit-learn

Before we start our tour of the machine learning algorithms, we need to know a little bit about the `Patsy` library. We will make use of `Patsy` to design features that will be used in conjunction with `scikit-learn`. `Patsy` is a package for creating what is known as design matrices. These design matrices are transformations of the features in our input data. The transformations are specified by expressions known as formulas, which correspond to a specification of what features we wish the machine learning program to utilize in learning.

A simple example of this is as follows: suppose that we wish to linearly regress a variable, y, against some other variables—x, a, and b—and the interaction between a and b; then, we can specify the model as follows:

```
import patsy as pts
pts.dmatrices("y ~ x + a + b + a:b", data)
```

In the preceding line of code, the formula is specified by the following expression: y ~ x + a + b + a:b.

For further information, look at `http://patsy.readthedocs.org/en/`
`latest/overview.html`.

General boilerplate code explanation

In this section, we will introduce boilerplate code for the implementation of the following algorithms by using `Patsy` and `scikit-learn`. The reason for doing this is that most of the code for the following algorithms is repeatable.

In the following sections, the workings of the algorithms will be described together with the code specific to each algorithm:

1. First, let's make sure that we're in the correct folder by using the following command line. Assuming that the working directory is located at `~/devel/Titanic`, we have the following:

```
In [17]: %cd ~/devel/Titanic
         /home/youruser/devel/sandbox/Learning/Kaggle/Titanic
```

2. Here, we import the required packages and read in our training and test datasets:

```
In [18]: import matplotlib.pyplot as plt
         import pandas as pd
         import numpy as np
         import patsy as pt
In [19]: train_df = pd.read_csv('csv/train.csv', header=0)
         test_df = pd.read_csv('csv/test.csv', header=0)
```

3. Next, we specify the formulas we would like to submit to `Patsy`:

```
In [21]: formula1 = 'C(Pclass) + C(Sex) + Fare'
         formula2 = 'C(Pclass) + C(Sex)'
         formula3 = 'C(Sex)'
         formula4 = 'C(Pclass) + C(Sex) + Age + SibSp + Parch'
         formula5 = 'C(Pclass) + C(Sex) + Age + SibSp + Parch +
         C(Embarked)'
         formula6 = 'C(Pclass) + C(Sex) + Age + SibSp + C(Embarked)'
         formula7 = 'C(Pclass) + C(Sex) + SibSp + Parch + C(Embarked)'
         formula8 = 'C(Pclass) + C(Sex) + SibSp + Parch + C(Embarked)'
In [23]: formula_map = {'PClass_Sex_Fare' : formula1,
                        'PClass_Sex' : formula2,
                        'Sex' : formula3,
                        'PClass_Sex_Age_Sibsp_Parch' : formula4,
                        'PClass_Sex_Age_Sibsp_Parch_Embarked' :
                        formula5,
             'PClass_Sex_Embarked' : formula6,
             'PClass_Sex_Age_Parch_Embarked' : formula7,
             'PClass_Sex_SibSp_Parch_Embarked' : formula8
                }
```

We will define a function that helps us to handle missing values. The following function finds the cells within the DataFrame that have null values, obtains the set of similar passengers, and sets the null value to the mean value of that feature for the set of similar passengers. Similar passengers are defined as those having the same gender and passenger class as the passenger with the null feature value:

```
In [24]:
def fill_null_vals(df,col_name):
    null_passengers=df[df[col_name].isnull()]
    passenger_id_list = null_passengers['PassengerId'].tolist()
    df_filled=df.copy()
    for pass_id in passenger_id_list:
        idx=df[df['PassengerId']==pass_id].index[0]
        similar_passengers = df[(df['Sex']==
        null_passengers['Sex'][idx]) &
        (df['Pclass']==null_passengers['Pclass'][idx])]
        mean_val = np.mean(similar_passengers[col_name].dropna())
        df_filled.loc[idx,col_name]=mean_val
    return df_filled
```

Here, we create filled versions of our training and test DataFrames.

Our test DataFrame is what the fitted `scikit-learn` model will generate predictions on to produce output that will be submitted to Kaggle for evaluation:

```
In [28]: train_df_filled=fill_null_vals(train_df,'Fare')
         train_df_filled=fill_null_vals(train_df_filled,'Age')
         assert len(train_df_filled)==len(train_df)
         test_df_filled=fill_null_vals(test_df,'Fare')
         test_df_filled=fill_null_vals(test_df_filled,'Age')
         assert len(test_df_filled)==len(test_df)
```

Here is the actual implementation of the call to `scikit-learn` to learn from the training data by fitting a model and then generate predictions on the test dataset. Note that even though this is boilerplate code, for the purpose of illustration, an actual call is made to a specific algorithm—in this case, `DecisionTreeClassifier`.

The output data is written to files with descriptive names, for example, `csv/dt_PClass_Sex_Age_Sibsp_Parch_1.csv` and `csv/dt_PClass_Sex_Fare_1.csv`:

```
In [29]:
from sklearn import metrics,svm, tree
for formula_name, formula in formula_map.iteritems():
        print "name=%s formula=%s" % (formula_name,formula)
        y_train,X_train = pt.dmatrices('Survived ~ ' + formula,
```

```
train_df_filled,return_type='dataframe')
        y_train = np.ravel(y_train)
        model = tree.DecisionTreeClassifier(criterion='entropy',
                max_depth=3,min_samples_leaf=5)
        print "About to fit..."
        dt_model = model.fit(X_train, y_train)
        print "Training score:%s" % dt_model.score(X_train,y_train)
        X_test=pt.dmatrix(formula,test_df_filled)
        predicted=dt_model.predict(X_test)
        print "predicted:%s" % predicted[:5]
        assert len(predicted)==len(test_df)
        pred_results = pd.Series(predicted,name='Survived')
        dt_results = pd.concat([test_df['PassengerId'],
                pred_results],axis=1)
        dt_results.Survived = dt_results.Survived.astype(int)
        results_file = 'csv/dt_%s_1.csv' % (formula_name)
        print "output file: %s\n" % results_file
        dt_results.to_csv(results_file,index=False)
```

The preceding code follows a standard recipe, and the summary is as follows:

1. Read in the training and test datasets.
2. Fill in any missing values for the features we wish to consider in both datasets.
3. Define formulas for the various feature combinations we wish to generate machine learning models for in `Patsy`.
4. For each formula, perform the following set of steps:

> 1. Call `Patsy` to create design matrices for our training feature set and training label set (designated by `X_train` and `y_train`).
>
> 2. Instantiate the appropriate `scikit-learn` classifier. In this case, we use `DecisionTreeClassifier`.
>
> 3. Fit the model by calling the `fit(..)` method.
>
> 4. Make a call to `Patsy` to create a design matrix (`X_test`) for our predicted output via a call to `patsy.dmatrix(..)`.
>
> 5. Predict on the `X_test` design matrix, and save the results in the variable predicted.
>
> 6. Write our predictions to an output file, which will be submitted to Kaggle.

We will consider the following supervised learning algorithms:

- Logistic regression
- Support vector machine
- Random forest
- Decision trees

Logistic regression

In logistic regression, we attempt to predict the outcome of a categorical, that is, discrete-valued dependent variable based on one or more input predictor variables.

Logistic regression can be thought of as the equivalent of applying linear regression but to discrete or categorical variables. However, in the case of binary logistic regression (which applies to the Titanic problem), the function to which we're trying to fit is not a linear one as we're trying to predict an outcome that can take only two values—0 and 1. Using a linear function for our regression doesn't make sense as the output cannot take values between 0 and 1. Ideally, what we need to model for the regression of a binary valued output is some sort of step function for values 0 and 1. However, such a function is not well-defined and not differentiable, so an approximation with nicer properties was defined: the logistic function. The logistic function takes values between 0 and 1 but is skewed toward the extreme values of 0 and 1 and can be used as a good approximation for the regression of categorical variables. The formal definition of the logistic regression function is as follows:

f(x) = 1/((1+e^(-ax))

The following diagram is a good illustration as to why the logistic function is suitable for binary logistic regression:

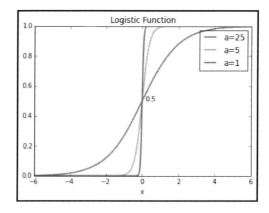

We can see that as we increase the value of our parameter, *a*, we get closer to taking on the 0 to 1 values and to the step function we wish to model. A simple application of the preceding function would be to set the output value to 0, if *f(x)* <0.5, and 1 if not.

The code for plotting the function is included in `plot_logistic.py`.

> A more detailed examination of logistic regression may be found
> at `http://en.wikipedia.org/wiki/Logit` and
> `http://logisticregressionanalysis.com/86-what-is-logistic-regres`
> `sion`.

In applying logistic regression to the Titanic problem, we wish to predict a binary outcome, that is, whether a passenger survived or not.

We adapted the boilerplate code to use the `sklearn.linear_model.LogisticRegression` class of `scikit-learn`.

Upon submitting our data to Kaggle, the following results were obtained:

Formula	Kaggle Score
C(Pclass) + C(Sex) + Fare	0.76077
C(Pclass) + C(Sex)	0.76555
C(Sex)	0.76555
C(Pclass) + C(Sex) + Age + SibSp + Parch	0.74641
C(Pclass) + C(Sex) + Age + Sibsp + Parch + C(Embarked)	0.75598

The code implementing logistic regression can be found in the `run_logistic_regression_titanic.py` file.

Support vector machine

A **Support Vector Machine (SVM)** is a powerful supervised learning algorithm used for classification and regression. It is a discriminative classifier—it draws a boundary between clusters or classifications of data, so new points can be classified based on the cluster that they fall into.

SVMs do not just find a boundary line; they also try to determine margins for the boundary on either side. The SVM algorithm tries to find the boundary with the largest possible margin around it.

Support vectors are points that define the largest margin around the boundary—remove these points, and possibly, a larger margin can be found. Hence the name, support, as they support the margin around the boundary line. The support vectors matter. This is illustrated in the following diagram:

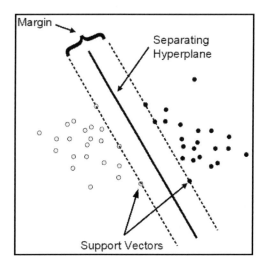

For more information on this, refer to
http://winfwiki.wi-fom.de/images/c/cf/Support_vector_2.png.

To use the SVM algorithm for classification, we specify one of the following three kernels: linear, poly, and **rbf** (also known as **radial basis functions**).

Then, we import the **Support Vector Classifier (SVC)**:

```
from sklearn import svm
```

We then instantiate an SVM classifier, fit the model, and predict the following:

```
model = svm.SVC(kernel=kernel)
svm_model = model.fit(X_train, y_train)
X_test = pt.dmatrix(formula, test_df_filled)
. . .
```

Upon submitting our data to Kaggle, the following results were obtained:

Formula	Kernel Type	Kaggle Score
C(Pclass) + C(Sex) + Fare	poly	0.71292
C(Pclass) + C(Sex)	poly	0.76555
C(Sex)	poly	0.76555
C(Pclass) + C(Sex) + Age + SibSp + Parch	poly	0.75598
C(Pclass) + C(Sex) + Age + Parch + C(Embarked)	poly	0.77512
C(Pclass) + C(Sex) + Age + Sibsp + Parch + C(embarked)	poly	0.79426
C(Pclass) + C(Sex) + Age + Sibsp + Parch + C(Embarked)	rbf	0.7512

The code can be seen in its entirety in the following file: `run_svm_titanic.py`.

Here, we see that the SVM with a kernel type of poly (polynomial) and the combination of the `Pclass`, `Sex`, `Age`, `Sibsp`, and `Parch` features produces the best results when submitted to Kaggle. Surprisingly, it seems as if the embarkation point (**Embarked**) and whether the passenger traveled alone or with family members (**Sibsp + Parch**) do have a material effect on a passenger's chances of survival.

The latter effect was probably due to the women-and-children-first policy on the Titanic.

Decision trees

The basic idea behind decision trees is to use the training dataset to create a tree of decisions to make a prediction.

It recursively splits the training dataset into subsets based on the value of a single feature. Each split corresponds to a node in the decision tree. The splitting process is continued until every subset is pure; that is, all elements belong to a single class. This always works except in cases where there are duplicate training examples that fall into different classes. In this case, the majority class wins.

The end result is a ruleset for making predictions on the test dataset.

Decision trees encode a sequence of binary choices in a process that mimics how a human might classify things, but decide which question is most useful at each step by using the information criteria.

An example of this would be if you wished to determine whether animal x is a mammal, fish, or reptile; in this case, we would ask the following questions:

```
- Does x have fur?
Yes: x is a mammal
No: Does x have feathers?
Yes: x is a bird
No: Does x have scales?
Yes: Does x have gills?
Yes: x is a fish
No: x is a reptile
No: x is an amphibian
```

This generates a decision tree that looks similar to the following:

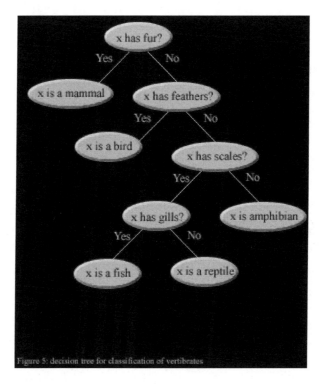

Figure 5: decision tree for classification of vertibrates

Refer to the following link for more information: https://labs.opendns.com/wp-content/uploads/2013/09/animals.gif.

The binary splitting of questions at each node is the essence of a decision tree algorithm. A major drawback of decision trees is that they can *overfit* the data. They are so flexible that, given a large depth, they can memorize the inputs, and this results in poor results when they are used to classify unseen data.

The way to fix this is to use multiple decision trees, and this is known as using an ensemble estimator. An example of an ensemble estimator is the random forest algorithm, which we will address next.

To use a decision tree in `scikit-learn`, we import the `tree` module:

```
from sklearn import tree
```

We then instantiate an SVM classifier, fit the model, and predict the following:

```
model = tree.DecisionTreeClassifier(criterion='entropy',
            max_depth=3,min_samples_leaf=5)
dt_model = model.fit(X_train, y_train)
X_test = dt.dmatrix(formula, test_df_filled)
    #. . .
```

Upon submitting our data to Kaggle, the following results are obtained:

Formula	Kaggle Score
C(Pclass) + C(Sex) + Fare	0.77033
C(Pclass) + C(Sex)	0.76555
C(Sex)	0.76555
C(Pclass) + C(Sex) + Age + SibSp + Parch	0.76555
C(Pclass) + C(Sex) + Age + Parch + C(Embarked)	0.78947
C(Pclass) + C(Sex) + Age + Sibsp + Parch + C(Embarked)	0.79426

Random forest

Random forest is an example of a non-parametric model, as are decision trees. Random forests are based on decision trees. The decision boundary is learned from the data itself. It doesn't have to be a line or a polynomial or radial basis function. The random forest model builds upon the decision tree concept by producing a large number of, or a forest of, decision trees. It takes a random sample of the data and identifies a set of features to grow each decision tree. The error rate of the model is compared across sets of decision trees to find the set of features that produce the strongest classification model.

To use a random forest in `scikit-learn`, we import the `RandomForestClassifier` module:

```
from sklearn import RandomForestClassifier
```

We then instantiate a random forest classifier, fit the model, and predict the following:

```
model = RandomForestClassifier(n_estimators=num_estimators,
                               random_state=0)
rf_model = model.fit(X_train, y_train)
X_test = dt.dmatrix(formula, test_df_filled)
    . . .
```

Upon submitting our data to Kaggle (using the formula: *C(Pclass) + C(Sex) + Age + Sibsp + Parch + C(Embarked))*, the following results are obtained:

Formula	Kaggle Score
10	0.74163
100	0.76077
1000	0.76077
10000	0.77990
100000	0.77990

Unsupervised learning algorithms

There are two tasks that we are mostly concerned with in unsupervised learning: dimensionality reduction and clustering.

Dimensionality reduction

Dimensionality reduction is used to help to visualize higher-dimensional data systematically. This is useful because the human brain can visualize only three spatial dimensions (and possibly, a temporal one), but most datasets involve much higher dimensions.

The typical technique used in dimensionality reduction is **Principal Component Analysis (PCA)**. PCA involves using linear algebra techniques to project higher-dimensional data onto a lower-dimensional space. This inevitably involves the loss of information, but often, by projecting along the correct set and number of dimensions, the information loss can be minimized. A common dimensionality reduction technique is to find the combination of variables that explain the most variance (proxy for information) in our data and project along those dimensions.

In the case of unsupervised learning problems, we do not have the set of labels (Y), and so, we only call `fit()` on the input data, X, itself, and for PCA, we call `transform()` instead of `predict()` as we're trying to transform the data into a new representation.

One of the datasets that we will be using to demonstrate USL is the iris dataset, possibly the most famous dataset in all of machine learning.

The `scikit-learn` library provides a set of pre-packaged datasets, which are available via the `sklearn.datasets` modules. The iris dataset is one of them.

The iris dataset consists of 150 samples of data from three different species of iris flowers—versicolor, setosa, and virginica—with 50 samples of each type. The dataset consists of four features/dimensions:

- Petal length
- Petal width
- Sepal length
- Sepal width

The length and width values are in centimeters. It can be loaded as follows:

```
from sklearn.datasets import load_iris
iris = load_iris()
```

In our examination of unsupervised learning, we will be focusing on how to visualize and cluster this data.

Before discussing unsupervised learning, let's examine the iris data a bit. The `load_iris()` command returns what is known as a bunch object, which is essentially a dictionary with keys in addition to the key containing the data. Hence, we have the following:

```
In [2]: iris_data.keys()
   Out[2]: ['target_names', 'data', 'target', 'DESCR', 'feature_names']
```

Further, the data itself looks similar to the following:

```
In [3]: iris_data.data.shape
    Out[3]: (150, 4)
```

This corresponds to 150 samples of four features. These four features are shown as follows:

```
In [4]: print iris_data.feature_names
    ['sepal length (cm)', 'sepal width (cm)', 'petal length (cm)', 'petal
width (cm)']
```

We can also take a peek at the actual data:

```
In [9]: print iris_data.data[:2]
    [[ 5.1  3.5  1.4  0.2]
     [ 4.9  3.   1.4  0.2]]
```

Our target names (what we're trying to predict) look similar to the following:

```
In [10]: print iris_data.target_names
            ['setosa' 'versicolor' 'virginica']
```

As noted earlier, the iris feature set corresponds to five-dimensional data and we cannot visualize this on a color plot. One thing that we can do is pick two features and plot them against each other while using color to differentiate between the species features. We do this next for all possible combinations of features, selecting two at a time for a set of six different possibilities. These combinations are as follows:

- Sepal width versus sepal length
- Sepal width versus petal width
- Sepal width versus petal length
- Sepal length versus petal width
- Sepal length versus petal length
- Petal width versus petal length

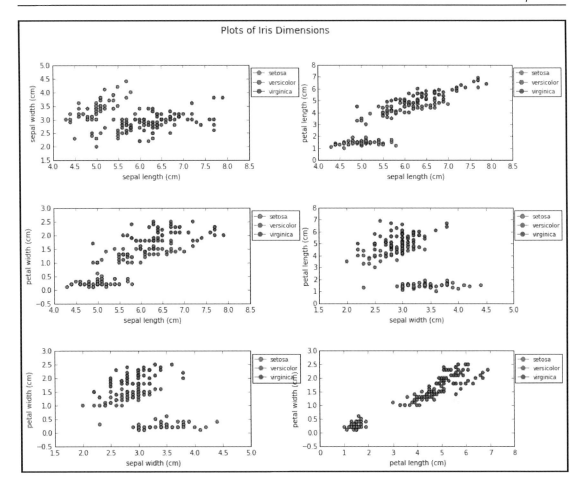

The code for this can be found in the following file: `display_iris_dimensions.py`. From the preceding plots, we can observe that the setosa points tend to be clustered by themselves, while there is a bit of overlap between the virginica and the versicolor points. This may lead us to conclude that the latter two species are more closely related to one another than to the setosa species.

These are, however, two-dimensional slices of data. What if we wanted a somewhat more holistic view of the data, with some representation of all four sepal and petal dimensions? What if there were some hitherto undiscovered connection between the dimensions that our two-dimensional plot wasn't showing? Is there a means of visualizing this? Enter dimensionality reduction. We will use dimensionality reduction to extract two combinations of sepal and petal dimensions to help to visualize it.

We can apply dimensionality reduction to do this as follows:

```
In [118]: X, y = iris_data.data, iris_data.target
          from sklearn.decomposition import PCA
          pca = PCA(n_components=2)
          pca.fit(X)
          X_red=pca.transform(X)
          print "Shape of reduced dataset:%s" % str(X_red.shape)
        Shape of reduced dataset:(150, 2)
```

Hence, we see that the reduced dataset is now in two dimensions. Let's display the data visually in two dimensions as follows:

```
In [136]: figsize(8,6)
          fig=plt.figure()
          fig.suptitle("Dimensionality reduction on iris data")
          ax=fig.add_subplot(1,1,1)
          colors=['red','yellow','magenta']
          cols=[colors[i] for i in iris_data.target]
          ax.scatter(X_red[:,0],X[:,1],c=cols)
Out[136]:
<matplotlib.collections.PathCollection at 0x7fde7fae07d0>
```

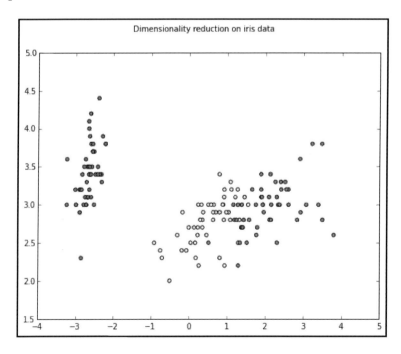

We can examine the makeup of the two PCA-reduced dimensions as follows:

```
In [57]:
print "Dimension Composition:"
idx=1
for comp in pca.components_:
    print "Dim %s" % idx
    print " + ".join("%.2f x %s" % (value, name)
                        for value, name in zip(comp,
iris_data.feature_names))
    idx += 1
Dimension Composition:
Dim 1
0.36 x sepal length (cm) + -0.08 x sepal width (cm) + 0.86 x petal
length (cm) + 0.36 x petal width (cm)
Dim 2
-0.66 x sepal length (cm) + -0.73 x sepal width (cm) + 0.18 x petal
length (cm) + 0.07 x petal width (cm)
```

Hence, we can see that the two reduced dimensions are a linear combination of all four sepal and petal dimensions.

The source of this information is at `https://github.com/jakevdp/sklearn_pycon2014`.

K-means clustering

The idea behind clustering is to group together similar points in a dataset based on a given criterion, hence finding clusters in the data.

The K-means algorithm aims to partition a set of data points into *K* clusters such that each data point belongs to the cluster with the nearest mean point or centroid.

To illustrate K-means clustering, we can apply it to the set of reduced iris data that we obtained via PCA, but in this case, we do not pass the actual labels to the `fit(..)` method as we do for supervised learning:

```
In [142]: from sklearn.cluster import KMeans
          k_means = KMeans(n_clusters=3, random_state=0)
          k_means.fit(X_red)
          y_pred = k_means.predict(X_red)
```

We now display the clustered data as follows:

```
In [145]: figsize(8,6)
          fig=plt.figure()
          fig.suptitle("K-Means clustering on PCA-reduced iris data,
          K=3")
          ax=fig.add_subplot(1,1,1)
          ax.scatter(X_red[:, 0], X_red[:, 1], c=y_pred);
```

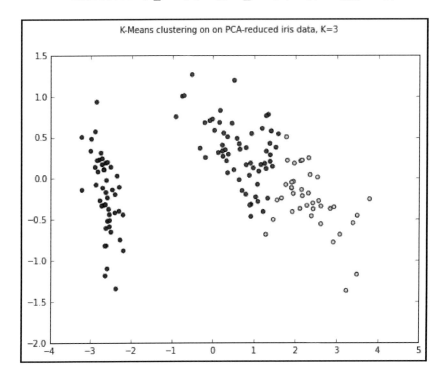

Note that our K-means algorithm clusters do not exactly correspond to the dimensions obtained via PCA. The source code is available at
`https://github.com/jakevdp/sklearn_pycon2014`.

More information on K-means clustering in `scikit-learn` and, in general can be found
at `http://scikit-learn.org/stable/auto_examples/cluster/plot_clus ter_iris.html` and
`http://en.wikipedia.org/wiki/K-means_clustering`.

XGBoost case study

XGBoost is an ensemble algorithm popular for its outstanding performance. An ensemble algorithm involves multiple models instead of just one. Ensemble algorithms are of two types:

- **Bagging**: Here, a result from the algorithm is the average of results from individual models.
- **Boosting**: Here, we start from a base learner model. Each successive model gets created with better-trained parameters. The learning of new parameters happens through optimization algorithms such as gradient descent.

Next, we will look at the application of XGBoost on a dataset to predict the testing time of a newly manufactured car.

It is a step-by-step guide and you can just follow along:

1. Import the required packages:

```
# In[1]:
    import os
    import pandas as pd
    import numpy as np
    from sklearn import preprocessing
    from sklearn.decomposition import PCA
    from sklearn.preprocessing import scale
    import matplotlib.pyplot as plt
    import xgboost
```

2. Change the working directory:

```
# In[24]:
    os.chdir('C:/')
```

3. Read the train and test data:

```
# In[19]:
    train = pd.read_csv('train.csv')
    test = pd.read_csv('test.csv')
```

4. Prepare for removing columns with zero variance:

```
# In[31]:
    #train.dtypes[train.dtypes=='float64'or train.dtypes ==
'int64']
    varcs = train.var(axis=0)
    varcs = varcs[varcs == 0]
    to_drop = list(varcs.index)
    dt = train.drop(to_drop, axis=1)
    print("The variables {} have been dropped as they have zero
variance".format(to_drop))
```

5. Input the function for removing columns with zero variance:

```
# In[20]:
# drops the variables with zero variance in a given dataset
  def drop_zerovarcs(data):
      varcs = data.var(axis=0)
      varcs = varcs[varcs == 0]
      to_drop = list(varcs.index)
      #data_new = data.drop(to_drop, axis=1, inplace=True)
      print("The variables {} have zero variance".format(to_drop))
      return to_drop
```

6. Get a list of zero variance columns in the train and test datasets:

```
# drops columns from test where variance is zero in test data as
well as the columns for which variance is zero in train data
# In[21]:
    test_drops = drop_zerovarcs(test)
    train_drops = drop_zerovarcs(train)
    test_train_drop = [x for x in train_drops if x not in
test_drops]
# train and test have different columns which have zero variance
# Hence dropping the same columns in train and test data. Dropping
the columns with zero variance in train data from test data.
test.drop(test_train_drop, axis=1,inplace=True)
```

7. Remove zero variance columns in the train data from test data:

```
# In[22]:
# drop the columns in test for which variance is zero in train data
    train.drop(train_drops, axis=1,inplace=True)
    #len(list(train.drop(train_drops,axis=1).columns))
    test.drop(train_drops,axis=1,inplace=True)
    #len(list(test.drop(train_drops,axis=1).columns))
```

8. Find `Unique,` `Total Count` and `NAs` and write it to a CSV file:

```
# In[25]:
# Find Unique, Total Count and NAs
    def uni_ct_na(data):
        unique = data.apply(lambda x: x.nunique(), axis=0)
        count = data.apply(lambda x: x.count(), axis=0)
        null = data.isnull().sum()
        na = data.isna().sum()
        summary_df = pd.DataFrame([unique, count, null,
na],index=['Unique', 'Count', 'Null', 'NA'])
        summary_df.T.to_csv('summary_df.csv')
# In[26]:
    uni_ct_na(train)
```

9. Find a list of categorical variables:

```
# In[27]:
#Finding the list of categorical variables
    obj = list(train.dtypes[train.dtypes=='object'].index)
```

10. Create dummy variables from the categorical variables:

```
# In[28]:
#Dummy variables using categorical variables
    obj_dum_train = pd.get_dummies(train[obj])
    train =
pd.concat([train,obj_dum_train],axis=1).drop(obj,axis=1)
    obj_dum_test = pd.get_dummies(test[obj])
    test = pd.concat([test,obj_dum_test],axis=1).drop(obj,axis=1)
```

11. Delete the categorical variables from `train` and `test`:

```
# In[29]:
# Keeping only numeric variables to apply PCA
    train_cols = train.columns
    train_not_obj = [x for x in train_cols if x not in obj]
    train = train[train_not_obj]
    test_cols = test.columns
    test_not_obj = [x for x in test_cols if x not in obj]
    test = test[test_not_obj]
```

12. Plot a scree plot to get the number of components that will explain the 90% variance in the data:

```
# In[30]:
# Plotting Scree plot to get the number of components which will
explain 90% variance in data
    X=train.iloc[:,1:].values
    X = scale(X)
    pca = PCA()
    pca.fit(X)
    var= pca.explained_variance_ratio_
    var1=np.cumsum(np.round(pca.explained_variance_ratio_,
decimals=4)*100)
    plt.plot(var1)
```

13. Perform PCA on the train and test data:

```
# In[31]:
# Performing PCA on train and test data
    X=train.iloc[:,1:].values
    X = scale(X)
    pca = PCA(n_components=300)
    pca.fit(X)
    train_pca = pca.transform(X)
    train_pca.shape
    X_test=train.iloc[:,1:].values
    X_test = scale(X)
    test_pca = pca.transform(X_test)
```

14. Separate the x and y variables to be passed to xgboost:

```
# In[32]:
# Separating x and y variables to be passed to xgboost
    train_y = train_pca[:,1]
    train_x = train_pca[:,2:]
    test_y = test_pca[:,1]
    test_x = test_pca[:,2:]
```

15. Define the xgboost model:

```
# In[33]:
# Fitting a xgboost model with default options
    model = xgboost.XGBRegressor()
    model.fit(train_x, train_y)
```

16. Predict from the `xgboost` model:

```
# In[34]:
# Predict from the model on test data
    pred_y = model.predict(test_x)
# In[189]:
    test_y
```

17. Calculate the root mean square error:

```
# In[35]:
# Calculating Root Mean Square Error
    rmse = np.sqrt(np.sum((pred_y-test_y)**2)/len(pred_y))
    rmse
```

Entropy

Entropy is a measure of the homogeneity (or heterogeneity) of data. The more homogeneous the data, the more entropy it has. Please keep in mind that, to make a better classification decision, heterogeneous data is better.

For example, consider a dataset where 1,000 people were surveyed about whether they smoke or not. In the first case, let's say that 500 people said yes and 500 said no. In the second case, let's assume that 800 people said yes and 200 said no. In which case would the entropy be more?

Yes, you guessed right. It is the first one because it is more homogeneous or, in other words, the decisions are equally distributed. If a person had to guess whether a survey participant answered yes or no, without knowing the actual answer, then the chances of them getting the right answer are less in the first case. Hence, we say that the data is messier in terms of classification information and hence has more entropy.

The goal of any classification problem, especially decision tree (and hence random forest and XGBoost), is to decrease this entropy and gain information. Next, let's see how we can quantify this seemingly qualitative term.

Equation for calculating entropy for the overall dataset is mathematically defined as follows:

$$initEnt = \sum_{i=1}^{n} p_i * log_2 p_i$$

Here, p_i is the proportion of the dataset with the ith class.

For example, in the first case we suggested earlier, p_{yes} would be 500/1,000 and p_{no} would be 500/1,000.

The following diagram shows the variation of entropy (the y variable) as the p_i (the x variable) changes from 0 to 1. Please notice that the p_is have been multiplied by 100 for plotting purposes:

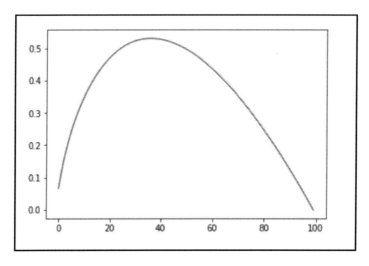

Plot of entropy versus fraction / proportion (0 to 1)

Observe the following about the graph:

- It's almost symmetric, about $p=0.5$.
- It maximizes at $p=0.5$, which makes sense as the messiness is maximal when the two classes are equally distributed.

The code used to generate this plot is as follows:

```
import matplotlib.pyplot as plt %matplotlib inline entropies = [-
(p/100)*np.log2(p/100) for p in range(1,101)] plt.plot(entropies)
```

Next, let's see how we can write a function using pandas to calculate the entropy of a dataset on its own and of a column from a dataset. For this purpose, we can first create dummy data with two columns: purchase (the y variable) and se_status (the predictor variables).

Define the unique values of the categorical variables:

```
  se_status_u = ['Rich','Poor','Affluent']
purchase_u = ['yes','no','yes']

# Creating the dataframe with 10,000 rows and 2 columns viz. purchase and
se_status
import random
import pandas as pd
se_status = []
purchase = []
for i in range(10000):
    se_status.append(random.choice(se_status_u))
    purchase.append(random.choice(purchase_u))
df = pd.DataFrame({'se_status':se_status,'purchase':purchase})
```

Next, we write a function to calculate the initial entropy of a dataset given the dataset and the name of the *y* variable:

```
# Function for calculating initial entropy of the dataframe
def int_entropy(df, ycol):
        y_u = list(df[ycol].unique())
        p = [df[df[ycol] == res].shape[0]/df.shape[0] for res in y_u]
        entropy = np.sum([-(e*np.log2(e)) for e in p])
        return entropy

df_int_entropy = int_entropy(df,'purchase')
df_int_entropy
```

Once we have the initial entropy, the next goal is to find the entropy assuming that one of the predictor variables was used for classification. To calculate entropy for such a case, we follow these steps:

1. Subset the data based on categories in the particular predictor column—one dataset for one category.

2. Calculate the entropy for each of these datasets so that you have one entropy value for each category of the variable.

3. Take a weighted average of these entropies. Weights are given by the proportion of that category in that dataset.

Mathematically, it can be represented by the following:

$$catEnt = \sum_{j=1}^{m}(f_j * (\sum_{i=1}^{n} p_{ij} * log_2 p_{ij}))$$

Equation for calculating entropy for a column

Here, f_j represents the proportion of the ith category in the dataset, and p_{ij} represents the proportion of the j_{th} category of the y variable in the dataset for the ith category of the predictor column. Let's see how a function can be written to calculate this entropy for a given dataset, the y variable, and a predictor variable:

```
# Function for calculating entropy of a particular column of the dataframe
def col_entropy(df,ycol,col):
    y_u = df[ycol].unique()
    col_u = df[col].unique()
    ent_colval = []
    final_ent_col = 0
    for colval in col_u:
        p = [(df[(df[ycol] == yval) & (df[col] ==
colval)]).shape[0]/(df[col] == colval).shape[0] for yval in y_u]
    ent_colval = np.sum([-(e*np.log2(e)) for e in p])
    final_ent_col += ent_colval* ((df[df[col] ==
colval]).shape[0]/(df.shape[0]))   return final_ent_col
```

Information gain is defined as the reduction in entropy when we move from making a classification decision based on only the y variable distribution to making this decision based on a column. This can be calculated as follows:

```
df_se_entropy = col_entropy(df,'purchase','se_status')
print(df_int_entropy)
information_gain = df_int_entropy - df_se_entropy
print(information_gain)
```

For the dataset that I have in this instance, I got an information gain of around 0.08. While making a decision tree, this information gain is calculated for every column. The column with the highest information gain is selected as the next branching node in the tree.

Summary

In this chapter, we embarked on a whirlwind tour of machine learning, examining the role of pandas in feature extraction, selection, and engineering as well as learning about key concepts in machine learning such as supervised versus unsupervised learning. We also had a brief introduction to a few key algorithms in both methods of machine learning, and we used the `scikit-learn` package to utilize these algorithms to learn and make predictions on data. This chapter was not intended to be a comprehensive treatment of machine learning, but rather to illustrate how pandas can be used to assist users in the machine learning space.

Other Books You May Enjoy

If you enjoyed this book, you may be interested in these other books by Packt:

Pandas Cookbook

Theodore Petrou

ISBN: 978-1-78439-387-8

- Master the fundamentals of pandas to quickly begin exploring any dataset
- Isolate any subset of data by properly selecting and querying the data
- Split data into independent groups before applying aggregations and transformations to each group
- Restructure data into tidy form to make data analysis and visualization easier
- Prepare real-world messy datasets for machine learning
- Combine and merge data from different sources through pandas SQL-like operations
- Utilize pandas unparalleled time series functionality
- Create beautiful and insightful visualizations through pandas direct hooks to matplotlib and seaborn

Hands-On Data Analysis with Pandas
Stefanie Molin

ISBN: 978-1-78961-532-6

- Understand how data analysts and scientists gather and analyze data
- Perform data analysis and data wrangling using Python
- Combine, group, and aggregate data from multiple sources
- Create data visualizations with pandas, matplotlib, and seaborn
- Apply machine learning (ML) algorithms to identify patterns and make predictions
- Use Python data science libraries to analyze real-world datasets
- Use pandas to solve common data representation and analysis problems
- Build Python scripts, modules, and packages for reusable analysis code

Leave a review - let other readers know what you think

Please share your thoughts on this book with others by leaving a review on the site that you bought it from. If you purchased the book from Amazon, please leave us an honest review on this book's Amazon page. This is vital so that other potential readers can see and use your unbiased opinion to make purchasing decisions, we can understand what our customers think about our products, and our authors can see your feedback on the title that they have worked with Packt to create. It will only take a few minutes of your time, but is valuable to other potential customers, our authors, and Packt. Thank you!

Index

Made in the USA
San Bernardino, CA
07 February 2020